A Cosmos of Many Mansions
varieties of science fiction

by Don Sakers

A COSMOS OF MANY MANSIONS
copyright © 2017, Don Sakers

All rights reserved

Published by
Speed-of-C Productions
811 Camp Meade Rd
Linthicum, MD 21090-3030

ISBN: 978-1-934754-20-7

Print Edition: October 2018

Dedication

To Thomas A. Easton, Stanley Schmidt, Trevor Quachri,
and Emily Hockaday

Contents

First Words..1
Behind the Scenes..5

Varieties of SF

Alien Beings...9
Alternate History...13
Animal Companions..15
Beloved Worlds..19
Biography...23
Big Books..27
Bigger Than Worlds...31
Change..35
Clarke's Law...39
Collaboration...43
Diversity in SF...49
Dying Each...53
Eagerly Awaited..55
Ebooks...59
Exploration & Discovery...65
Genetics..69
Historical Fiction & SF..73
Keeping Up..75
Literary SF..81
Mars..87
Military SF...91
Mooreeffoc..99
Movies..101
Music & SF...105
Nonfiction..109
Prisons..111
Robots...115
Series...119
SF Thrillers..125
Short Stories..129

Space Opera 135
Steampunk 139
Time Travel 143
To the Moon 147
Transhumanism 151
Tribute Anthologies 155
Varieties of Length 157
Young Adult SF 161
Additional Varieties 165
    Adventure SF 165
    Animal Companions 166
    Biological SF 167
    Cyberpunk 167
    Dystopian Futures 168
    Ecological/Environmental SF 166
    Fortress City 167
    Galactic Empires 167
    Games & Gaming 170
    Generation Ships 170
    Graphic Novels 170
    Hard SF 171
    High Frontier 171
    Humorous SF 172
    Immortals &Immortality 172
    Man &Machine 173
    Near Future SF 173
    New Wave SF 174
    Other Worlds 174
    Parallel Worlds/Other Dimensions 175
    Philosophical/Religious SF 175
    Post-Apocalyptic SF 176
    Psychological/Sociological SF 177
    Romantic SF 178
    Retro SF 178
    Satire SF 179
    Science Fantasy 179
    SF Horror 180

SF Mystery 180
Shared/Franchised Worlds 181
Space Colonization 181
Superheroes 182
Teleportation***182
TV 182
Venus 183
Visitors From Space 183

Reviews

Reviews: A 185
Reviews: B 193
Reviews: C 215
Reviews: D 233
Reviews: E 247
Reviews: F 251
Reviews: G 265
Reviews: H 275
Reviews: I 291
Reviews: J 295
Reviews: K 303
Reviews: L 315***
Reviews: M 331
Reviews: N-O 357
Reviews: P-Q 367
Reviews: R 371
Reviews: S 387
Reviews: T 413
Reviews: U-V 419
Reviews: W 425
Reviews: X-Y-Z 451
Reviews: Anthologies 453
Reviews: Nonfiction 485

First Words

Science Fiction

(Mar 2017) Science fiction—or "sf," if you'll allow me—isn't just one thing; it comes in many varieties. Some readers like their sf heavy with cutting-edge science, others prefer more of a focus on characters and their relationships. Some want action, others want introspection, still others want meaningful insights into the nature of reality. Some sf is set on today's familiar Earth, but sf can also be set on other planets, millennia in the future (or the past!), on alternate Earths where history unfolded along different paths, or in in times and spaces so unlike our own that they defy comprehension.

In short, the field of science fiction is a cosmos of many mansions, and as a reader it's easy to wind up in a neighborhood you don't enjoy. The sf universe, like the real one, continues to expand as more and more authors take advantage of more and more options for getting their work before readers.

Fortunately, there are professional and amateur guides to help sf readers find their way. I'm one of them. I'm an sf writer, retired Librarian, and book reviewer for *Analog Science Fiction and Fact* magazine.

Analog

The history of the magazine now called *Analog* is inextricable from the history of science fiction itself. While sf as a literature dates back to the Greeks at least (and some trace it further back, to the oldest known human tales), science fiction as a commercial publishing category began in April 1926 with the debut of *Amazing Stories*, the first pulp magazine exclusively focused on sf.

The magazine proved popular, and spawned many imitators. One of these, first published in January 1930, was

Astounding Stories of Super-Science. Astounding became the premier sf magazine— in the period from 1937 to 1950, under the editorship of the legendary John W. Campbell, Jr., it was the undisputed center of the science fiction universe.

After 1950, sf exploded. More authors, more magazines, the beginning of a thriving market in science fiction books. No longer was there a single center—no one magazine, editor, publisher, or even format would ever again dominate the field.

Still *Astounding* continued. In 1960 the magazine changed name, becoming *Analog Science Fiction & Fact*, universally known as *Analog*. With slight variations in title, it has continued publishing to this very day. In 2010 *Analog* celebrated its 80th anniversary, and with the June 2015 issue it reached the milestone of 1,000 continuous issues.

The Reference Library

Astounding's first book reviews didn't appear until the October 1947 issue (the book was *Spacehounds of IPC* by E. E. "Doc" Smith). Prior to this, a book review column wouldn't have worked, for the simple fact that few science fiction books were published. For the first few years book reviews were sporadic.

With the October 1951 issue, the column became a permanent department of the magazine, known as "The Reference Library." The first regular reviewer was P. Schulyer Miller, who kept the position until his death in 1975. From 1975 to 1979 Lester Del Rey and Spider Robinson shared the job. Thomas A. Easton took over in 1979 and maintained the column for a remarkable 30 years.

In 2009, I was one of several candidates who auditioned for the gig as guest reviewers. My guest column was in the March 2009 issue, and I was thrilled to get the job. June 2009 was the first of my regular columns. As I write this, I've been at it for eight years, and the job just keeps getting better.

A Cosmos of Many Mansions

After the first few issues, the column settled into the format I still use today: I generally start off with a short essay on some aspect of science fiction, then dive into reviews of specific books.

Since the magazine is *Analog Science Fiction and Fact*, I generally limit the books I review to science fiction and related nonfiction—I usually don't review the various types of fantasy, horror, paranormal romance, or weird fiction. That still gives me an enormous amount of leeway, and I've found that *Analog* readers enjoy stretching their horizons now and again.

About This Book

A Cosmos of Many Mansions is drawn from my first five years of book review columns. Rather than present the columns sequentially, I've rearranged things to make the book more useful. (Of course, if you want to ignore that and read straight through, I have no objection.)

After this introduction and a section called **Behind the Scenes**, there are two major parts.

Varieties of SF contains my essays on 39 different types of science fiction and related work—plus a catch-all section that covers varieties I haven't yet written essays about. After most of these you'll find a list of **Titles Reviewed**, which leads you to the next section.

That's **Reviews**, which presents hundreds of reviews of separate works. These are arranged alphabetically by author with two minor exceptions. Anthologies—collections of stories by many authors—are in their own section arranged by title, and Nonfiction books are grouped together by author.

This all takes a lot longer to explain than to experience. Read an essay in **Varieties of SF**; the list of titles will tell you the review is on the page number that appears in [square brackets].

Reviews, by and large, appear as they did in the magazine —if this occasionally makes things sound a little disjointed, I appreciate your forbearance.

Finally, I want to explain my holiday columns. It's my tradition to use the end-of-year column to recommend books for gift-giving. The subversive idea is to give sf books to your non-sf-reading friends, thus hooking them on the field. You'll find an occasional review that seems aimed at a specific type of reader—now you know why.

That's it for preparation; read on. Whether you're exploring the state of the field or looking for just the right sf book for you, I hope *A Cosmos of Many Mansions* is the guidebook you need. Enjoy!

-Don Sakers

Behind the Scenes

(Mar 2009 - my first column) A few words of introduction, then on to this month's books.

I'm a librarian by day and science fiction writer by night. I've had stories published in *Analog* as well as other genre magazines, and various books available hither and yon. I've been reading SF for over four decades, since I was a little tyke spending my allowance on Heinlein paperbacks and newsstand issues of this very magazine. I might be an old-timer, but I keep up with the cutting edge of the field. I hope you'll find me a reliable guide to the landscape of current books.

Pulling Back the Curtain

(Apr 2014) This column is something of an anniversary: it's my 50th "Reference Library" column. With your indulgence, I thought I would take this opportunity to pull back the curtain and talk about my approach, philosophy, and practice of reviewing.

Q: What is your background for being a reviewer, particularly for *Analog*?

A: I'm a lifelong reader and student of science fiction. I started reading SF as soon as I could read, and *Analog* when I was thirteen (in 1971). I have a B.A. in math with a minor in English literature. I've been a published SF writer since 1980; my first *Analog* story appeared in 1982. For 36 years I worked at a public library, where I frequently helped people find books they might like.

Q: Where do you get the books that you review?

A: Mostly from publishers. Lots of books arrive in the mail, but I also receive electronic copies either by email or via industry websites like *netgalley.com*. Some small-press publishers hand me books at conventions. Enterprising authors also contact me to send galleys or even manuscripts of upcoming books.

I'm not above contacting a publisher (or author) to get a review copy, if I see something that I think might be of interest to *Analog* readers. And, of course, I still buy books, especially obscure ones.

Q: Do you see everything that's published in sf?

A: Alas, no. Some publishers are scrupulous about sending me everything—sometimes including things I have no chance of reviewing, like vampire romances and epic fantasy. Others send me only selected titles, and many small press and indie publishers are completely off my radar.

If you are, or know, a publisher or author of a book that might appeal to *Analog* readers, please take a look at my review guidelines at *tinyurl.com/dsreflib*.

Q: Do you read on paper or e-books?

A: Both. After a lifetime of reading SF (and being married to a *Star Wars* collector), my house is full, so I currently have a preference for e-books. Those I read on my iPad, which can handle just about any e-book format out there. But I haven't lost my love for paper books.

Q: Where do you find time to read all those books?

A: Like many of you, I read constantly and voraciously. Even before this gig, I grew twitchy if reading material was out of my reach. If, as one of my library friends says, "it's a sickness"—then I'm beyond cure or even treatment.

Q: What do you do with the books you receive?

A: Books I like go into my personal collection. I give the rest away to various charities.

Q: How do you decide which books to review?

A: I try to pick books that will interest *Analog* readers. That doesn't (necessarily) mean books that would appear in these pages—as regular readers know, sometimes I'll throw in some distinctly non-*Analog* type books. I know that *Analog* readers are voracious readers with wide-ranging interests, who appreciate variety.

Q: Why are all your reviews positive?
A: Both life and my allotted pages are way too short to spend time on unsuitable books. My job is to bring to your attention books that you might enjoy...not to waste your time on things you won't like.

Q: Do you personally like every book you recommend?
A: My public library training and experience have taught me that there's no such thing as "good" or "bad" books—one reader's life-changing classic is another's snoozefest. The goal is to match the right book with the right reader.

To accomplish this, I try to give readers enough information to decide for themselves whether a given book sounds like something they'd enjoy. Among the considerations are subgenre, audience, and the relative mix of basic elements like plot, character, and setting. When I can, I try to identify similar authors you might have read. If I'm successful, you'll at least have a good idea of what to expect from a book.

Of course, it's neither satisfactory nor healthy to read only he same thing again and again, so I try to encourage readers to expand their range. I try to tell you what it is about an unfamiliar book or genre that fans like, so you can decide if it sounds like your cup of tea.

To get back to the original question: Between you, me, and the clock on the wall, I don't personally like every book I recommend. My personal tastes are as subjective and limited as anyone else's. But why should my personal preferences matter? Just because I don't like, say, football doesn't mean I can't recognize a well-executed forward pass.

Q: How do you research your introductory essays?
A: As a retired librarian, I have what we in the business refer to as "mad reference skillz." Science fiction fandom has been assiduous about putting reference material online. I also have multiple shelves of books about the SF field, biographies of SF authors, and critical works. In addition, I draw on friends and associates, as well as the members of the Science Fiction &

Fantasy Writers of America. And I can always count on my editors to catch any mistakes or omissions.

Thank you for your indulgence; now let me draw the curtain back into place and get on with this issue's reviews.

Why We Read SF

(May 2010) We read science fiction for a lot of reasons. SF can be inspiring, educational, exciting. Science fiction can exercise the mind, stir the spirit, tug at the heart, and stretch the imagination. Science fiction can make us laugh and bring us to tears; it c.an lead us to question our firmest beliefs or to see our familiar world from a different perspective. Science fiction can be funny, tragic, even transcendently sublime.

And besides all this, SF can be fun.

Alien Beings

(Nov 2012) Real-word science is always stealing the best disciplines from science fiction. Selenology, robotics, genetic engineering, gravitics, xenology...all taken from science fiction. And not only did they steal psychohistory from us, but they got it wrong. In twenty thousand years, Hari Seldon will be spinning in his grave!

At least there are *some* disciplines we can still call our own... although it's just a matter of time before science comes in and starts ruining them too. So let's enjoy them while we can.

The field that's on my mind today is xenopsychology—the study of how alien minds work. It's been a concern of science fiction and SF writers since the field's very beginning. Readers and writers alike are reasonably familiar with various techniques for imagining and portraying alien biology, but there's much less discussion of how writers handle alien psychology.

The most basic way is to have aliens be primarily just like Humans. Give them a different language and some unusual customs, and you've got your aliens. We might call this the "aliens as foreigners" strategy—just like the French, Chinese, and Zulus, we're all essentially the same under the skin (or feathers, scales, or whatever).

Don't pooh-pooh this technique as simplistic or unimaginative. It can produce some pretty effective science fiction. Many of the aliens in Ursula K. LeGuin's Hainish Cycle (for instance, those in 1974's Hugo winner *The Dispossessed*), fall into this category—and it's the formula behind some of the most powerful episodes of the original *Star Trek* and *The Twilight Zone*.

A step further are aliens who are psychologically Human, but even more so. They might be more moral (like the Sorns in C. S. Lewis's *Out of the Silent Planet*), intellectual (*Star Trek's* Vulcans), immortal (The Overlords in Arthur C. Clarke's *Childhood's End*), or any number of other desirable characteristics (the eponymous Doctor from *Doctor Who* deserves special mention here). Or they might be go in the other direction, being like Humans but worse—think of H. G. Wells's Morlocks (from *The Time Machine*) or the evil Mesans from David Weber's *Honor Harrington* series. *Star Trek's* Romulans and Cardassians are also examples of this type, as are Isaac Asimov's Gaians from the *Foundation* series.

The late Hal Clement, who had several excellent alien races under his belt, used to joke that when he wanted bizarre yet comprehensible aliens, he just made them behave completely rationally and logically.

Moving further in the same direction are aliens psychologically defined by a single Human characteristic. These range from fairly complex warrior races like *Star Trek's* Klingons or Larry Niven's Kzinti to simplistic, almost mindless examples such as H. R. Giger's *Aliens* and the Bugs from Robert A. Henlein's *Starship Troopers*. One of the difficulties with this kind of alien is the question of the society behind such single-purpose species. A functioning advanced society needs farmers, bankers, shopkeepers, educators, and even traffic cops. (The late Amanda Allen called this the "Klingon Meter Maid Problem," and appeared at conventions in a stunning Klingon battle-dress costume as "Ri'tah the Klingon Meter Maid.")

Another way to deal with alien psychology is to throw out all the stops and abandon comprehensibility altogether. This is a lot harder than it looks, because readers can only stand so much unexplained mystery. Arthur C. Clarke was a master: he gave us many incomprehensible aliens. The unseen race that supervised the aforementioned Overlords, the folk who constructed the monolith in his *2001* series, and the race that built Rama (*Rendezvous with Rama* and sequels) spring to mind immediately. The Caliban in C. J. Cherryh's *Forty Thousand in Gehenna* are quite successfully incomprehensible, as is the title character(?) in Stanislaw Lem's *Solaris*. An outstanding recent example is the Ariekei from China Miéville's *Embassytown*.

Surely the most interesting examples of xenopsychology, though, come from an entirely different approach. Here, the author begins with specifics of alien biology and environment, and works from there to develop and deduce psychology. Some of the most satisfying alien races in science fiction have emerged from this technique. The behavior of Larry Niven's Puppeteers derives from their biological origins as an intelligent herd creature. Ursula K. LeGuin's Gethenians (*The Left Hand of Darkness*) periodically change gender; the psychology of Anne McCaffrey's Dragons stems from both native biology and genetic engineering; Alan Dean Foster's Thranx act just the way you'd expect of intelligent insects. The aliens in Isaac Asimov's *The Gods Themselves* are a stunning example of biology determining psychology. And surely, biology and environment are perfectly reflected in the psychology of one of SF's most beloved aliens, the Horta from *Star Trek*.

Finally, there's one last category of xenopsychology, and that's aliens based on ideas from psychology itself. The earliest example is probably L. Ron Hubbard's Xenu. Vernor Vinge's Tines (*A Fire Upon the Deep*) are the ultimate in multiple personalities. Some of James White's aliens embody various psychological conditions. *Forbidden Planet* introduced a whole generation of SF fans to the concept of the id. And of course, we mustn't forget Douglas Adams's Marvin the Paranoid Android.

Titles Reviewed

- *Bowl of Heaven* by Gregory Benford and Larry Niven [198]
- *Of Wind and Sand* by Sylvie Bérard [200]
- *The Return* by Ben Bova [206]
- *A Glimpse of Splendor and Other Stories* by Dave Creek [230]
- *Guardian of Night* by Tony Daniel [233]
- *Fuzzy Ergo Sum* by Wolfgang Diehr [240]

- *Steal Across the Sky* by Nancy Kress [311]
- *InterstellarNet: Origins* by Edward M. Lerner [326]
- *Embassytown* by China Miéville [345]
- *The One-Eyed Man* by L. E. Modesitt, Jr [350]
- *Pennterra* by Judith Moffett [351]
- *Destroyer of Worlds* by Larry Niven & Edward M. Lerner [360]
- *Beyond the Doors of Death* by Robert Silverberg and Damien Broderick [400]

Alternate History

(Oct 2009) In science fiction, the alternate history story has a long and venerable...er...history. The first alternate histories developed in the 1800s from the fields of nonfiction and historical fiction. Some were downright essays, others were essays wrapped in just enough plot to disguise them as fiction. As with much else, H.G. Wells dabbled—his *Men Like Gods* tells the story of some Englishmen transported into a utopian alternate world. It's a gripping read, but ultimately is more philosophical treatise than novel.

It took the Campbell revolution, in *Astounding* and its sister magazine, *Unknown*, to bring about the birth of the alternate history as we know it: actual stories with genuine characters, set against the background of a world with a different history. Murray Leinster's "Sideways in Time" and L. Sprague de Camp's *Lest Darkness Fall* introduced the notion of coexisting divergent timelines, a concept that today we call the multiverse. Other writers, most notably Poul Anderson in his *Time Patrol* stories, explored the deliberate manipulation of alternate histories by time travelers. Currently, alternate history is more popular than ever; the steampunk craze shows how far the genre has penetrated into popular culture.

Today it is possible to distinguish between two types of alternate history stories. There's the basic alternate history tale, which is set entirely in a different timeline; and then there's the multiverse story, involving multiple timelines and travel between them (often including time travel as well). The king of the first type is Harry Turtledove, with Eric Flint as Archduke of his own territory. Most of the royalty of the multiverse story, unfortunately, have passed on to the great typewriter in the sky: Poul Anderson, Fritz Leiber, L. Sprague de Camp, André Norton, and Robert A. Heinlein were among them. But there are plenty of up-and-comers out there.

Generally, those who are passionate and knowledgeable about history are more fond of the first type; those who are looking for the adventure of science fiction are more likely to refer the multiverse story.

Titles Reviewed

- *Written in Time* by Jerry & Sharon Ahern [186]
- *Tales of the Clockwork Empire* by Ian Duerden [245]
- *This Shared Dream* by Kathleen Ann Goonan [267]
- *Watchmen* by Alan Moore and Dave Gibbons [352]
- *Blood of Tyrants* by Naomi Novik [363]
- *Coup D'Etat* by Harry Turtledove [415]
- *The War That Came Early: West and East* by Harry Turtledove [414]
- *Golden Reflections* edited by Joan Spicci Saberhagen & Robert E. Vardeman [459]
- *Other Earths* edited by Nick Gevers and Jay Lake [468]

Animal Companions

(May 2010) From Andre Norton's *Beast Master* to Alan Dean Foster's *Pip and Flinx* stories, faithful animal companions (often telepathically linked to their owners) have a long and illustrious history in science fiction. Heinlein's young adult books featured a veritable menagerie of flat cats, bouncers, and a *Star Beast* named Lummox. And there are mice, from Frederic Brown's Mitkey ("The Star Mouse," 1942) to Daniel Keyes's Algernon ("Flowers for Algernon," 1959). Marion Zimmer Bradley's *Hawkmistress* (part of her Darkover series) features a relationship between girl and hawk. Andre Norton's *Catseye* gives us a whole pet store full of unusual animals. Harlan Ellison famously explored the bond between *A Boy and His Dog*. Superman has his Krypto and *Doctor Who* his robot dog K-9. And by far the most beloved animal companions in all of SF are the dragons and fire lizards in Anne McCaffrey's *Dragonriders of Pern* books. (Oddly enough, one doesn't often see my favorite animal, hamsters, in science fiction.)

Animal companions can usually be distinguished from intelligent aliens by their relative lack of autonomy. While the animals can (and do) act independently of their human owners, it's still obvious who's in charge. Animals that evolve sapience on their own don't really fall into this category. I'm thinking here of the intelligent dogs from Clifford Simak's "City" stories, of the bears in Terry Bisson's "Bears Discover Fire," of Cordwainer Smith's animal-derived Underpeople, and (of course) of the primates in the *Planet of the Apes* universe.

Which brings us to cats.

Now, I believe in revealing my biases and prejudices right up front, so let me get this out of the way at once: I am not a cat person. I am violently allergic to cats (a state which I blame entirely on them) and cats know it. In fact, they revel in their dastardly power. However, even I can't deny that cats have a unique hold on the imaginations of science fiction writers and readers.

Maybe it's their aloofness, their independence of thought and action, the way that they stand outside the rules and strictures of society. Cats are free spirits, deciding for themselves what they like and what they don't, and so are science fiction people. Or at least that's the way we like to see ourselves.

Stories involving cats are legion. Heinlein gave us Pete in *The Door Into Summer*, Pixel in *The Cat Who Walks Through Walls*, and assorted felines in *To Sail Beyond the Sunset*. Cats pop up all the time in Andre Norton's books. Cordwainer Smith had cats defending starships ("The Game of Rat and Dragon," 1955) and even planets ("Mother Hitton's Littul Kittons," 1961). In Alan Dean Foster's *Cat-a-Lyst*, cats were the guardians of the galaxy. Tara K. Harper's excellent *Cat Scratch Fever* gave a new take on the "telepathic cat companion" story. *Star Trek's* resident android, Data, had a cat named Spot, and in *Alien* Ripley very nearly sacrificed everything for Jonesie. Schrödinger's Cat may or may not be relevant here; we'll never know until we open the box.

And I'm not even going to get into the many cat-derived alien species like Niven's Kzinti or Cherryh's Hani.

Titles Reviewed

- *Flinx Transcendant* by Alan Dean Foster [256]
- *Catalyst* by Anne McCaffrey and Elizabeth Ann Scarborough [333]
- *Dragongirl* by Todd McCaffrey [334]
- *Dragon's Time* by Anne McCaffrey & Todd McCaffrey [336]
- *Sky Dragons* by Anne McCaffrey [337]
- *A Beautiful Friendship* by David Weber [425]
- *Fire Season* by David Weber [426]
- *Implied Spaces* by Walter Jon Williams [433]
- *Dogs of War* edited by Mike McPhail [457]

Before the Golden Age

(Jan/Feb 2012) It is generally agreed the the so-called "Golden Age" of science fiction spanned the years between the late 1930s and the early 1950s. Personally, I dislike the term "Golden Age" with its built-in assumption of subsequent decline...as if post-1955 sf was uniformly awful. I prefer to refer to that period as "the Campbell Age," for it covers the the time when *Astounding* was the most important magazine in the field, and editor John W. Campbell, Jr. was sf's undisputed monarch. In the long history of commercial sf (now over 80 years), there have been many ages that might be called golden, but only one when Campbell reigned supreme.

Still, in one respect the Campbell Age *was* Golden: the science fiction of the period, overall, was a quantum leap ahead of what went before. In the period from 1929 to 1939 (which we might as well call the Gernsback Age, even though Grandaddy Hugo didn't quite dominate the field the way Campbell did), sf was merely one species of pulp adventure. (Prior to 1929 and Gernsback's establishment of the magazine *Amazing Stories*, sf was not even recognized as a distinct category.)

By today's standards, pre-Campbell sf was generally overwritten, melodramatic, and unsubtle as a boot to the head. Adverbs and exclamation points tend to crowd the text. Characters are one-dimensional and morality strictly a matter of black and white. Plots are simple, primarily based on nonstop action, and riddled with holes. To a present-day reader, the casual racism and sexism of the times borders on offensive.

All that being said...those antediluvian stories had a certain raw excitement, the fabled "sense of wonder" that drew—and still draws—so many of us to sf. In that innocent world of earthbound telescopes and optical microscopes, where there were no space probes or computers, where relativity was still new and antimatter a dream, so much lay beyond the frontiers of science. It was still possible to argue that other planets were inhabited by human-like beings, that prehistoric creatures still lived in unexplored jungles, or that a man could continue to breathe and think when shrunk to the size of an atom.

In those stories, mystery and wonder were around every corner, a single bright scientist working in his basement could create anything from a telepathic helmet to an antigravity starship, and an author could always whip up a new element with any outlandish properties desired. Compared to post-Campbell sf, there was a freedom that today's readers can only regard wistfully.

Not much sf from this age survived the Campbell revolution. Many of the older writers stopped publishing as their brand of sf fell out of fashion. A few novels and short stories became classics, but most pre-Campbell stories stayed entombed in decaying pulps. An occasional anthology reprinted some of the best: Damon Knight's *Science Fiction of the 30s*, Isaac Asimov's *Before the Golden Age*, Forrest J. Ackerman's aptly-title *Gosh! Wow! (Sense of Wonder) Science Fictio*n. Lately, as early copyrights run out, some of the earlier stories have been showing up in electronic format on sites like Project Gutenberg (*www.gutenberg.com*).

Titles Reviewed
- *Into Plutonian Depths* by Stanton A. Coblentz [221]
- *From the Pen of Paul: The Fantastic Images of Frank R. Paul* edited by Stephen D. Korshak [498]

Beloved Worlds

(Sep 2010) One of the key skills of the science fiction writer is worldbuilding: the process of constructing consistent, believable planets. Selecting and calculating a planet's physical parameters (orbital dynamics, axial tilt, mass, surface gravity, atmosphere, temperature, and so on) is only the first step in building a world. After that comes geography, climate, biology, history, sociology, and economics...to name just a few. All of these factors define and constrain characters and plot elements, giving shape to the kinds of stories the writer can tell. Then, if the writer does a good job, all of this effort becomes largely invisible to the reader, serving as the unique background of the story.

Examples of fine worldbuilding are legion in science fiction. Some of the great names of the past were masters: Poul Anderson, Hal Clement, Philip José Farmer, Robert L. Forward, Harry Harrison, E.C. Tubb, and Jack Vance instantly spring to mind. David Brin, C.J. Cherryh, and Larry Niven made their names with excellent worldbuilding. Other recent notable worldbuilders include Stephen Baxter, Kim Stanley Robinson, Dan Simmons, Sheri S. Tepper, John Varley, Joan D. Vinge, and Vernor Vinge. Really, just about any science fiction writer of tales set on another planet has engaged in worldbuilding to one degree or another.

What I want to talk about now, however, goes beyond mere worldbuilding. In some cases, a writer presents a particular fictional world that is so interesting and compelling that it moves out of the background, transcending mere setting to become almost a character in its own right. These are SF's beloved worlds, places so convincing in their artificial reality that readers feel as if they've actually been there—or even that they want to move in. These are the worlds that so fascinate readers that their creators have no choice but to keep writing books set there.

In the early days of SF, Edgar Rice Burroughs turned Mars into the world Barsoom, and for decades readers longed to visit its dead sea bottoms and ruined cities. The field has since moved on and modern readers are likely to find the Barsoom books less than accessible; if you once loved them and now feel the urge to revisit, you're well advised to approach them in a spirit of friendly nostalgia. (Nevertheless, there's a killer movie or several waiting in those books, now that special effects technology has caught up to Burroughs' imagination. Do you hear me, Hollywood?) [2017 addition: Hollywood heard me. The movie was released in 2012, and it was pretty good...but it flopped. See my review of *John Carter and the Gods of Hollywood* by Michael D. Sellers in the Nonfiction section.]

Frank Herbert's desert world Arrakis, usually quite rightly quoted as the premier example of worldbuilding, is another world that's become almost real to readers. I don't know how many of us would want to actually live there, but everyone certainly wanted more than one visit: the ever-expanding *Dune* series is the result. About the only planet that can compete with Arrakis in readers' hearts is Anne McCaffrey's Pern. Compared to Arrakis, Pern is a lovely place...and now that they've got that Thread problem licked, I don't know anyone who wouldn't want to have at least a summer house there. (And while we're at it, where are the *Dragonriders of Pern* movies? Peter Jackson, I'm looking at you.) [2017 addition: We're *still* waiting.] Incidentally, both Pern and Arrakis first saw print in the pages of *Analog*, a fact which gives an interesting perspective on the eternal question of whether Pern is SF or fantasy. (My own argument is that any books which repeatedly reference the chemical formula for nitric acid, as the Pern books do with the compound called "agenothree," clearly belong under the SF umbrella. I don't know whether it was McCaffrey or Campbell who came up with that one, but either way it's sheer genius.)

Other such beloved places in SF include Marion Zimmer Bradley's Darkover, Philip José Farmer's Riverworld, and Larry Niven's Ringworld. All of these took hold of readers' hearts and imaginations and did not let go, resulting in multiple books. Some other classic beloved worlds such as Discworld, Earthsea, Witch World, and of course Middle Earth are fantasy and thus beyond our immediate purview -- but don't let that stop you from paying a visit.

Titles Reviewed

- *Fuzzy Ergo Sum* by Wolfgang Diehr [240]
- *Dragongirl* by Todd McCaffrey [334]
- *Dragon's Time* by Anne McCaffrey & Todd McCaffrey [336]
- *Sky Dragons* by Anne McCaffrey [337]
- *Coyote Destiny* by Allen Steele [406]

Biography

(Apr 2012) If the field of science fiction had an official religion, ancestor worship would doubtless be a major component. We have always revered our elders, read and re-read their stories, passed their books on to newer generations, and...er...borrowed their ideas. An older, well-established science fiction author is honored and respected, and no matter how obscure there's always some reader with a tattered magazine or paperback to have autographed.

Once one of those elder statesmen goes on to the great typewriter in the sky, his or her stature in the field increases. After all, a deceased author can't insult anyone or participate in feuds (not that this has stopped some from trying). And this phenomenon isn't just limited to older writers; in a few unfortunate cases, an untimely death turns out to be the best career move the author ever made.

Now that the field of commercial science fiction is in its ninth decade, the ranks of our honored ancestors, alas, continue to swell. It's gotten so bad now that authors who entered the field as child prodigies are dying of old age.

Fortunately, the field remembers. Science fiction writing is a "pay it forward" game: established authors inspire and help newcomers, who in turn become established and pass the inspiration and help onward. In such a climate, its natural to honor those who came before.

Nowadays, too, it's become much easier for current readers to discover the works of those who went before. Older works remain in print—and if not, they're available for a pittance from online booksellers. E-book editions are easy to get; many of the earliest books and stories are free for the taking on Project Gutenberg (*www.gutenberg.org*). And increasingly, we're learning about the lives of our forbears through autobiographies and biographies.

The idea that science fiction writers' lives were worthy of being enshrined in biographical amber dates from 1966, when

Sam Moskowitz published *Seekers of Tomorrow* in a small press edition. The book mixed biography with literary criticism, and set the pattern for subsequent works such as Donald A. Wollheim's *The Universe Makers* (1971), Charles Platt's two volumes of *Dream Makers* (1980, 1983), and even John Clute and Peter Nicholls' *Encyclopedia of Science Fiction* (1979, revised 1993, now exclusively online at *www.sf-encyclopedia.com*).

Beginning in 1972, Doubleday published a series of collections that featured early stories of a big-name author, stitched together by the author's autobiographical musings. The first was *The Early Asimov*; later volumes included *The Early Del Rey* and *The Early Pohl*.

In 1975 Brian W. Aldiss and Harry Harrison released *Hell's Cartographers*. This seminal volume contained autobiographical essays by six writers (including Aldiss and Harrison), and proved fairly popular. In 1977 Damon Knight took a different tack on group biography with *The Futurians*, which told the story of a dozen or so big-name authors and the social groups to which they belonged.

Then, in 1978 Frederik Pohl (one of the six essayists included in *Hell's Cartographers*) released his own book-length autobiography, *The Way the Future Was*. Isaac Asimov's life story filled two huge and fascinating volumes, *In Memory Yet Green* (1979) and *In Joy Still Felt* (1980). Subsequent years have brought autobiographies from such names as Piers Anthony (*Bio of an Ogre* in 1988 and *How Precious Was That While* in 2001), Ray Bradbury (*Becoming Ray Bradbury*, 2011), Arthur C. Clarke (*Astounding Days*, 1989), Jack Vance (*This is Me, Jack Vance!*, 2009), and Jack Williamson (*Wonder's Child*, 2005). Newer writers, too, are telling parts of their life stories, such as *The Motion of Light in Water* by Samuel R. Delany (1993) and *Nested Scrolls* by Rudy Rucker (2011).

Sadly, there are even posthumous autobiographies, published after the author's death. Robert A. Heinlein's *Grumbles From the Grave* (1990) is a collection of Heinlein's letters, and Isaac Asimov's *I. Asimov* (1994) was written as a third volume of his autobiography.

We have even entered the era in which we learn about the lives of science fiction writers through third-party biographies such as Brian Herbert's *Dreamer of Dune: The Biography of Frank Herbert* (2004) and this year's *Robert A. Heinlein: in Dialogue With His Century volume 1* by William H. Patterson.

Titles Reviewed
- *In Other Worlds* by Margaret Atwood [485]
- *From the Pen of Paul* edited by Stephen D. Korshak [498]
- *Rocket Girl* by George D. Morgan [502]
- *Robert A. Heinlein: In Dialogue With His Century: Volume 1* by William H. Patterson, Jr. [506]
- *C. M. Kornbluth* by Mark Rich [510]
- *Fantasy Commentator* edited by M. Calice Becker Searles [511]
- *Murray Leinster* by Billee J. Stallings and Jo-An J. Evans [514]

Big Books

(Mar 2013) For those of us who grew up in the print world, there's a special delight to a big, thick book with lots of pages. Part of it is simply pecuniary: buy a big book, and you feel like you're getting a good deal. Another part, face it, is intellectual pride: people who read big books must be terribly smart.

The majority of the thrill, though, comes from anticipation of the sheer joy that awaits between those widely-separated covers. Experience taught us that big science fiction books meant a richer reading experience: more time to spend in an invented world, more details about that world and its people, more wonders, more complexity...more, in fact, of everything we liked about sf in the first place.

There weren't always big science fiction books. Verne and Wells wrote mostly in the range of 200-300 pages (although Wells' classic *The Time Machine* was quite short; at barely over 100 pages, it was what we now call a novella.) In the 1930s and 1940s sf novels were almost exclusively published as magazine serials, usually in two or three parts and filling roughly 150 pages. An editor could run four three-part serials in a year; longer novels would mean less variety for the readers.

When sf moved between book covers in the 1950s, it was a rare novel that exceeded 180 pages, and 200 pages was almost unheard of. Many books were reprints of novels first published as magazine serials, and even original novels kept to the same length restrictions. Conventional wisdom among publishers said that sf readers would not buy books over 200 pages.

A memory of that time still exists today, frozen in the amber of the Hugo Award rules, codified in the early 1960s. For Hugo purposes, a "novel" is defined as a story of 40,000 words or longer—about 160 printed pages. If we were setting those rules today, surely we'd raise the threshold to something more like 60,000 words (240 pages).

As far as I can tell, the first sf book to break the length barrier was Robert A. Heinlein's *Stranger in a Strange Land*, published in 1961. The original version was over 200,000 words; at the publisher's behest Heinlein cut it down to a svelte 160,083 words, which filled almost 450 pages in print. (Heinlein always joked that he wanted to type those extra 83 words on a postcard and mail them away.)

The success of *Stranger in a Strange Land* proved conventional wisdom wrong, and emboldened publishers to try occasional longer books. Thus the 1960s saw such books as Frank Herbert's *Dune* (400+ pages), Roger Zelazny's *Lord of Light* (300+ pages), and John Brunner's *Stand on Zanzibar* (nearly 600 pages).

Meanwhile, the venerable Science Fiction Book Club (SFBC) was becoming another source of big books. The first was the club's October 1963 selection, a one-volume edition of Isaac Asimov's *Foundation Trilogy* (600+ pages). Soon the club was routinely producing one-volume editions of trilogies and 500+ page collections of shorter works. It's a rare science fiction reader from the 1970s whose shelves didn't hold copies of the SFBC *Foundation Trilogy*, *The Science Fiction Hall of Fame Volume One* (550+ pages), and the two-volume *A Treasury of Great Science Fiction* (each volume over 500 pages).

With the rise in book prices of the 1970s and 1980s, there was a perception in publishing that readers wanted more for their money, and book lengths on average crept upward. An average midlist sf novel in 1960 might have been 170 pages; by 1990, 300-350 pages was more normal.

Until the early 1990s, the majority of paperbacks (including sf) were sold in grocery or drug stores rather than bookstores. In the early 90s a crash among distributors led to a collapse in that market, and bookstores like Waldenbooks and Borders were left as the major market for paperbacks. Readers who shopped in bookstores (especially sf readers) liked longer books, and the 400+ page novel became common.

By the turn of the century, publishers had about reached the limits of how big books could get and still be affordable. The economics of paper printing are such that better-selling books can have more pages than their less-selling siblings—so all else being equal, a bestselling sf author's books are likely to be a hundred pages or more longer than a relatively obscure author's. An unknown, entry-level author will probably have books around the low end, 250-350 pages; a guaranteed bestseller might average more like 500-600 pages. But there's enormous variation.

And now, of course, we have the new wrinkle of e-books. Electrons are far more flexible than paper, and stories can take whatever length is necessary. Already we're seeing a fair-sized market for novella-length e-books alongside novels that would be over 500 pages if printed. Some authors are making short fiction available in stand-alone e-book format. As the mainstream of publishing moves into the electronic realm, I expect that enormous variation in length will come to be standard.

And eventually, just as we all learned that a lot of pages promised a richer reading experience, we'll come to learn that a big byte-count will promise the same thing...and "4000 Kb" will give us the same thrill that "500 pages" does now.

Let's talk about some satisfyingly big books.

Titles Reviewed

- *The Hydrogen Sonata* by Iain M. Banks [194]
- *Ride the Star Winds* by A. Bertram Chandler [220]
- *To the Galactic Rim* by A. Bertram Chandler [219]
- *Caliban's War* by James S. A. Corey [226]
- *Geosynchron* by David Louis Edelman [248]
- *The Crucible of Empire* by Eric Flint and K. D. Wentworth [251]
- *The Evolutionary Void* by Peter F. Hamilton [275]
- *Great North Road* by Peter F. Hamilton [276]
- *Kea's Flight* by Erika Hammerschmidt and John C. Ricker [277]
- *Webdancers* by Brian Herbert [279]

- *Imperium* by Keith Laumer [317]
- *Ghost Spin* by Chris Moriarty [353]
- *Win Some, Lose Some* by Mike Resnick [374]
- *Blue Remembered Earth* by Alastair Reynolds [375]
- *2312* by Kim Stanley Robinson [377]

Bigger Than Worlds

(Oct 2011) Sometimes the really big thing is science fiction is a Really Big Thing. Here I'm talking about construction projects that make the Great Wall of China look like a Lego starter set. Never mind being visible from orbit; any halfway-decent Really Big Thing can easily perturb other objects in orbit—and most fill up their own orbits.

There's a whole subgenre of sf that deals with Really Big Things. We call this subgenre "Bigger Than Worlds," after the title of an essay by Larry Niven that appeared in the March 1974 issue of *Analog*.

Some trace Bigger Than Worlds stories to the early 1300s and Dante's *Divine Comedy*. Isaac Asimov in particular argued that Dante's elaborate Hell, Purgatory, and Heaven were constructed worlds. In standard science fiction, though, the honor of first on the scene goes to Olaf Stapledon, whose 1937 novel *Star Maker* featured artificial planets and even what we today call Dyson spheres (immense structures enclosing entire stars). In 1962, *Hothouse* by Brain Aldiss described a far-future Earth linked to the Moon by enormous spiderwebs, and Robert Silverberg explored a Dyson sphere in *Across a Billion Years* (1969).

It wasn't until 1970 that the subgenre really came into its own, with the publication of Larry Niven's *Ringworld*. This story of a literal ring around a star, with a million times the habitable surface area of the Earth, took the field by storm. It wasn't long before tales of other Really Big Things were all the fashion. Huge artificial worlds showed up in the work of Arthur C. Clarke (*Rendezvous with Rama*, 1973, and later sequels), Jack Chalker (*Midnight at the Well of Souls*, 1977, and sequels), and John Varley (*Titan*, 1979, and sequels). G. David Nordley took *Analog* readers to a big construct called Cubeworld in the serial "To Climb a Flat Mountain" (November and December 2009). And need I mention the moon-sized Death Star from *Star Wars* (1977)?

Dyson spheres featured prominently in Frederik Pohl & Jack Williamson's *Farthest Star* (1975) and *Wall Around a Star* (1983) as well as Bob Shaw's *Orbitsville* (1975) and sequels. A smaller sphere built around a black hole appeared in Tony Rothman's *The World is Round* (1978). In his *Cageworld* series (starting in 1982), Colin Kapp gave us a whole series of nested Dyson spheres. Gene Wolfe used the Dyson sphere concept as the basis for his *Book of the Long Sun* series (1993 and after). In 1992, *Star Trek: The Next Generation's* starship *Enterprise* visited an alien-built Dyson sphere.

Ringworlds also proved popular. As early as 1973 Harry Harrison used one to great effect in his satire *Star Smashers of the Galaxy Rangers*. Several Iain M. Banks novels have featured multiple ringworlds (and Dyson spheres), notably *Consider Phlebas* (1987) and *Matter* (2008). Banks invented what he calls "Orbitals," which are sort of junior ringworlds with diameters only about the size of planets. In 2001, the mega-popular video game Halo took that idea and ran with it...all the way to the bank.

Surely the grandest ring-shaped structure in sf (so far) is Stephen Baxter's *Ring* (1994), which is built of cosmic string and stretches across millions of lightyears.

Many different types of Really Big Things have appeared in science fiction. Thin structures looped around stars like spaghetti featured in Timothy Zahn's *Spinneret* (1985), *White Light* (1998) by William Barton and Michael Capobianco, and *Helix* by Eric Brown (2007). In his 1981 pre-Discworld sf novel *Strata*, Terry Pratchett used the concept of the Alderson Disk, a huge disc-shaped platter with a star nestled in a hole in the center. My own *Weaving the Web of Days* (2004) involved a semi-living network stretching between stars in the Tarantula Nebula. Karl Schroeder's *Virga* series (starting with *Sun of Suns* in 2006) presented a giant inhabited balloon the size of several planets.

Titles Reviewed

- *Bowl of Heaven* by Gregory Benford and Larry Niven [198]
- *Webdancers* by Brian Herbert [279]
- *Destroyer of Worlds* by Larry Niven & Edward M. Lerner [360]
- *The Sunless Countries* by Karl Schroeder [394]
- *Hex* by Allen Steele [408]

Change

(Oct 2012) Science fiction, at its heart, is about change. We want to read about worlds that are different, in some fundamental way, from the familiar world of today. If sf readers wanted stories set in the world as it is, we would all be reading Nora Roberts, Janet Evanovich, and John Grisham.

Just about every science fiction story is based on ringing at least one major change on the familiar world. By convention, in sf those changes ought to have at least the appearance of scientific plausibility. (Changes without the appearance of plausibility are usually classified as fantasy.) Just listen to the language we use when describing stories to one another: it's all about the idea, the change. A guy builds a time machine and travels into the future. Someone discovers an invisibility serum. Some folks build a starship and roam the galaxy. A hole between universes opens a parallel Earth populated by Neanderthals instead of us. A world on which there is no fixed gender. A mathematics that predicts the future. A buried alien artifact is uncovered on the Moon.

Science fiction, to be sure, is much more complicated than that. An interesting change doesn't make a story—there have to be characters, and a well-developed background, and a plot that exists because of the interesting change, and considerable skill in the telling of the tale. There can be more than one major change, and many minor changes, and it all has to make logical and emotional sense to the reader.

Nevertheless, for now let's speak in terms of a single key change that defines an sf story.

When authors are planning out how to present their interesting change, long before setting down a single word of story, they have available two basic approaches.

First, the interesting change could affect one person, two people, or any small finite number of people. I'll call this the Individual approach. Think of such sf classics as *Frankenstein*, *The Time Machine*, *From the Earth to the Moon*, or even the *Skylark* series—in each, only a small number of people are impacted by the major change. The rest of the world rolls on, indifferent.

A second approach is to have the interesting change affect everyone: a whole society, or a sub-population of society. We can call this the Society approach. Think *War of the Worlds, Last and First Men, When Worlds Collide,* or the *Lensman* series.

At first glance, this might seem a rather obvious point. Yet I think the distinction between Individual and Society approaches provides an interesting lens through which to examine science fiction.

Consider the history of the field. While both approaches are always present, they go through cycles of popularity. Early pulp sf, it seems to me, was primarily in the Individual mold. How many individual inventors or explorers went off on adventures, usually with a few friends in tow? The Campbell Revolution began to turn the tide toward the Society approach. Postwar sf was all about Society: I think of the work of Frederik Pohl, C.M. Kornbluth, Frank Herbert, Ursula K. LeGuin, and dozens of others.

In the New Age period, there seemed to be a swing back toward the Individual approach. (Remember that New Age sf coexisted with the more traditional stuff for much of the 1960s and 1970s.) Much of Michael Moorcock's work, for example, is more on the Individual end of the spectrum.

Modern sf, it seems to me, is fairly balanced between the two approaches. Authors move back and forth between them freely.

These two approaches allow authors to say different things, depending on their own purposes. Let's take a look at some examples.

A couple of guys go to the Moon and you get *From the Earth to the Moon* and *First Men in the Moon*. A society goes to the Moon and you get *The Moon is a Harsh Mistress*. A small group develops advanced psi abilities, and it's Theodore Sturgeon's *More Than Human*; all Earth's children do it, and it's Arthur C. Clarke's *Childhood's End*. One superior fighter goes into space and he's *Flash Gordon*; a whole interstellar society of them are Gordon R. Dickson's *Dorsai*.

One more thought on this matter: because sf is complicated, and because an sf story can involve many different changes, most stories have elements of both Individual and Society approaches. Some of the greatest stories in our field defy categorization as one or the other. It's easy enough to say "In story A only a few people are telepaths, whereas in story B just about everyone is." But what about *Stranger in a Strange Land*, or the *Foundation* series, or Nancy Kress's *Beggars in Spain*, or Connie Willis's *Oxford Historians* stories? Surely these stories are a fusion of the two approaches, showing the effect of major changes upon both individuals *and* whole societies.

Titles Reviewed

Virtually every sf title reviewed in this volume is of this variety.

Clarke's Law

(Jul/Aug 2013) Science fiction is based on science. It's right there in the name. And since one of the major concerns of science is classification, it's not surprising that sf readers concern themselves with boundaries—particularly the boundaries of the field itself.

One of the boundaries that most fascinates us is the one between sf and fantasy. Every reader and writer, it seems, places the dividing line differently...and for different reasons. For one, the concept of time travel may be too much of a fantasy element; for others, it's faster-than-light travel. Another may be more comfortable focusing on methods rather than concepts: traveling into the past by wishing is fantasy, but doing it with a machine is sf. Still another might insist that the defining quality is the writer's approach: magical spells can be part of an sf story as long as they're dealt with in the same logical, self-consistent manner as the laws of physics.

Arthur C. Clarke spoke to this boundary with his Third Law (I'll let you look up the other two): "Any sufficiently advanced technology is indistinguishable from magic." Actually, a lot of today's real-world technology might as well be magic to most of us; for example, who completely understands Google's search algorithms?

Science fiction that conforms to Clarke's Third Law is sf on the fuzzy, ever-shifting boundary of fantasy. It is often on scales that boggle the mind: very long spans of time, vast spaces, gargantuan feats of engineering, enormous amounts of energy. In these parts, we like our technological magic big.

Sometimes the "sufficiently advanced technology" belongs to aliens and impinges upon humans more or less like us. Clarke's own *Childhood's End* and *2001* series are perfect examples, as are Fritz Leiber's 1965 Hugo-winning novel *The Wanderer* and Frederik Pohl's *Gateway* series.

A minor variation, particularly popular in the Campbell Age, had humans as the technologically advanced aliens. The story of a present-day Earthman who impresses backward savages with superior technology was cliché a generation ago—it goes back at least to Mark Twain's *A Connecticut Yankee in King Arthur's Court*, and appeared in countless B movies as European explorers entranced primitive natives with flashlights and kitchen matches. Today, the concept smacks of colonialism and borders on offensive, but as late as 1971 it formed the basis of a truly fun romp, *The Flying Sorcerers* by David Gerrold and Larry Niven.

More often, though, Clarke's Third Law stories are set in the distant future, when humans themselves command magical technologies, often in concert with other sapient races. Examples abound; this is one of the most popular types of science fiction. Iain M. Banks' *Culture* series springs immediately to mind. So do Kay Kenyon's superb *The Entire and the Rose* series, Kurt Schroeder's *Virga* series, Dan Simmons' *Hyperion* novels, Vernor Vinge's *A Fire Upon the Deep* and *A Deepness in the Sky*, and much of Gene Wolfe's work. The late Roger Zelazny was a master of "sufficiently advanced" technology, especially in his classics *Creatures of Light and Darkness* and *Lord of Light*.

In these tales, there's a certain optimism to Clarke's Third Law.

A subset of this far-future type is the so-called "dying Earth" genre. Dying Earth stories are set in a real of metaphorical End of Time, a future so distant that everything is in decline. The inhabitants of these worlds, human as well as other sapients, have often lost the secrets to the high technologies of their ancestors; to them, the technologies really are magic. Arthur C. Clarke's own *The City and the Stars* falls into this category, as do Michael Moorcock's *Dancers at the End of Time* series and M. John Harrison's *Virconium* books. Mark Charan Newton's *Legends of the Red Sun* series and Elizabeth Bear's *All the Windwracked Stars* stand as more recent examples of Dying Earth books.

Why are we so enamored of this idea of fuzzing the boundary between technology and magic? I think there are three reasons.

First, there's the old-fashioned "sense of wonder." Big, magical technology is cool. We wouldn't be reading sf if we didn't enjoy the occasional moment when you just have to put the book down and say, "Wow!"

Second, reading this kind of sf helps us deal with the accelerating pace of technological change in the real world. Our technologies grow more and more opaque, hidden inside chips and software that we can't access, and operating at speeds we can't apprehend. In the face of this opacity, it's comforting to think that there's an organizing logic behind everything, that we can—at least potentially—learn the logic and understand what's going on. Clarke's Third Law sf supports that belief, telling us that no matter how improbable and mysterious the magic, it's all based on tame, controllable technology.

And finally, we like this kind of sf because messing with boundaries is just plain fun. We love breaking rules. For writer and reader, there's an undeniable thrill to taking a impossible, clearly fantastic ideas and making them work as believable technology.

Titles Reviewed
- *All the Windwracked Stars* by Elizabeth Bear [197]
- *Grail* by Elizabeth Bear [196]
- *City at the Edge of Time* by Greg Bear [197]
- *The Evolutionary Void* by Peter F. Hamilton [275]
- *Open Your Eyes* by Paul Jessup [296]
- *Echo City* by Tim Lebbon [318]
- *Empress of Eternity* by L. E. Modesitt, Jr [349]
- *Ghost Spin* by Chris Moriarty [353]
- *The Sunless Countries* by Karl Schroeder [394]

- *Implied Spaces* by Walter Jon Williams [433]
- *Count to a Trillion* by John C. Wright [446]
- *The Hermetic Millennia* by John C. Wright [448]

Collaboration

(Mar 2011) In my day job as a public librarian, I learned something interesting about science fiction and fantasy. A few years ago, I had a great idea for a display of fiction books: collaborations. So I raced around the fiction shelves in search of books with two or more authors listed on the covers.

To my surprise, the only books I could find outside the science fiction and fantasy fields were a few mystery novels by Rita Mae Brown and her cat Sneaky Pie, and a single detective novel by Swedish husband-and-wife team Maj Sjowall and Per Wahloo. In sf and fantasy, however, I found plenty of examples: Larry Niven & Jerry Pournelle, Poul Anderson & Gordon R. Dickson, Frederik Pohl & Cyril M. Kornbluth, Jack Williamson & Frederik Pohl, Arthur C. Clarke & Gentry Lee, Anne McCaffrey & Elizabeth Ann Scarborough, Margaret Weis & Tracy Hickman, Mercedes Lackey & just about everyone.

So what's going on here? Surely sf and fantasy can't be the only genres in which two or more authors collaborate?

Certainly not. There are plenty of collaborations outside sf/fantasy—but there's a cultural difference. In other genres, the usual practice is for co-authors to choose a single name as a byline. Thus, cousins Manfred B. Lee and Frederic Dannay wrote detective stories under the name Ellery Queen, and husband-and-wife team Judith Barnard and Michael Fain wrote as Judith Michael.

Now, this sort of thing went on in sf as well: Earl and Otto Binder wrote as Eando Binder, Henry Kuttner and C. L. Moore used both Lewis Padgett and Lawrence O'Donnell as pseudonyms, and Cyril M. Kornbluth and Judith Merril wrote two novels under the name Cyril Judd. It's far more common, though, for two (or more) sf/fantasy writers to use all their own names on their books.

And I'm not claiming that two-name collaborations never occur in mainstream fiction. In fact, they've been happening more often in the last decade or so, particularly in the suspense/thrillers genre.

I've yet to see a convincing explanation for this difference in genre culture. Perhaps it has something to do with the tradition of fierce individuality in sf/fantasy; perhaps the custom dates form the early years of the field when just about all the authors knew each other personally.

The fact remains that sf in particular is a highly collaborative field. And the simple matter of authors teaming up is only the tip of the iceberg. Let us examine the different ways that sf authors work together.

A variation of the simple co-author team is the senior-junior author arrangement. Here, a well-known author joins with a less familiar name. Anne McCaffrey's collaborations with various authors (Jody Lynn Nye, Margaret Ball, and Elizabeth Ann Scarborough) fit this mold. Nowadays it's almost forgotten that SF's most successful team, Larry Niven & Jerry Pournelle, started out as another senior-junior partnership; when they wrote *The Mote in God's Eye*, Pournelle was definitely the lesser-known of the two. On the covers of most senior-junior collaborations, the junior author's name appears in marginally smaller letters than the senior's.

A recent variation on the senior-junior arrangement is the author-successor partnership. Here, an aging author writes a book or books with an up-and-coming name who will, presumably, take take over when he/she goes to the great wordprocessor in the sky. Thus, Arthur C. Clarke wrote the *Time Odyssey* trilogy with Stephen Baxter, who is arguably the closest thing to a Clarke successor. Similarly, Anne McCaffrey's collaborations with her son Todd were a step along the way in turning the *Dragonriders of Pern* series over to the younger McCaffrey.

Another type of senior-junior partnership enjoyed a vogue in the 1980s and 1990s: the franchised universe. In these cases, the senior author created a background and perhaps a few scenarios, then a junior author or authors wrote the actual books. When the books are printed, the senior author's name generally appears in giant letters near the top of the cover, while the junior partner's byline is in much smaller type toward the bottom. You may remember such examples as Isaac Asimov's *Robots in Time* series, Arthur C. Clarke's *Venus Prime* series, or anthologies set in the *Man-Kzin Wars* period of Larry Niven's Known Space universe. Franchised universes have become scarce nowadays, perhaps because sales never met publishers' high expectations.

Lately, in the odder corners of the field, there have been a number of "collaborations" with long-deceased authors, especially those whose works have passed out of copyright. Jane Austen is a frequent target; currently there are two different books titled *Pride and Prejudice and Zombies* (one by Seth Grahame-Smith and the other by Steve Hockensmith, if you can't resist), and we've also been treated to *Mansfield Park and Mummies* (by Vera Nazarian) and *Sense and Sensibility and Sea Monsters* (by Ben H. Winters). The true sf reader will naturally gravitate toward Winters' joint effort with Mr. Tolstoy, *Android Karenina*.

Of course, another collaborative model that's akin to the franchised universe is the familiar media or game tie-in book. In this case, the franchised universe is itself a product of collaboration; in addition, the "universe" has an existence outside the books —the original movie, tv show, or game that inspired the whole thing.

A rather more interesting type of collaboration is what's known as the "shared world." In this type of collaboration, all the participating authors have a hand in creating the universe, the characters, and the plots. The grandaddy of all shared worlds was the fantasy series *Thieves' World*, conceived and coordinated by Robert Lynn Asprin. Well-known sf examples include Harlan Ellison's anthology *Medea: Harlan's World* and C. J. Cherry's *Merovingen Nights* series.

In the final analysis, though, the entire sf field is, in a way, a great big collaboration among all the authors out there. Isaac

Asimov reacted to stories of robots run amuck by creating the Three Laws of Robotics. Many Golden Age authors considered John W. Campbell, Jr. to be an uncredited collaborator on most of their works. Gordon R. Dickson responded to Asimov's *Foundation* series with his own *Dorsai* books, which in turn helped inspire the whole subgenre of military sf. After reading Robert A. Heinlein's *Starship Troopers*, Joe Haldeman wrote *The Forever War*. And so the collaboration continues, a worldwide multi-threaded conversation that's been going on for the better part of a century...and shows no sign of tapering off any time soon.

Titles Reviewed

- *Written in Time* by Jerry & Sharon Ahern [186]
- *The Sorceress of Karres* by Eric Flint & Dave Freer [252]
- *Stargate Atlantis: Homecoming* by Jo Graham & Melissa Scott [270]
- *Kea's Flight* by Erika Hammerschmidt & John C. Ricker [277]
- *Final Crisis: Legion of 3 Worlds* by Geoff Johns, George Pérez, Scott Koblish [298]
- *Steelhands* by Jaida Jones & Danielle Bennett [300]
- *Shades of Gray* by Jackie Kessler & Caitlin Kittredge [304]
- *The Unincorporated Man* by Dani Kollin and Eytan Kollin [307]
- *How to Defeat Your Own Clone: And Other Tips for Surviving the Biotech Revolution* by Kyle Kurpinski & Terry D. Johnson [499]
- *Ghost Ship* by Sharon Lee & Steve Miller [319]
- Dragon's Time by Anne McCaffrey & Todd McCaffrey [336]
- *Catalyst* by Anne McCaffrey and Elizabeth Ann Scarborough [333]
- *Why Beautiful People Have More Daughters* by Alan S. Miller and Satoshi Kanazawa [500]
- *Watchmen* by Alan Moore & Dave Gibbons [352]
- *Destroyer of Worlds* by Larry Niven & Edward M. Lerner [360]

- *The Business of Science Fiction: Two Insiders Discuss Writing and Publishing* by Mike Resnick and Barry N. Malzberg [509]
- *Ice City of the Gorgon* by Richard S. Shaver & Chester S. Geier [238]
- *Back to the Moon* by Travis S. Taylor & Les Johnson [413]
- *Extremis* by Steve White & Charles E. Gannon [432]

Diversity in SF

(Mar 2014) Science fiction has a very mixed record on issues of human diversity.

On one hand, much of sf celebrates diversity in a way no other literature can match. Science fiction taught us to respect intelligent life regardless of its outward form: robot or lizard-creature, microscopic entity or living planet, million-year-old vegetative consciousness or sapient rock, all deserved to be treated fairly.

On the other hand, sf was (and arguably still is) behind the curve when it came to human diversity. How could it be otherwise? Modern sf was born and came of age in the WASP-dominated world of the 1920s-50s; it was largely written and edited by and for white American males of the educated class. The few prominent women writers in the field went by initials (C. L. Moore) or used gender-ambiguous bylines (Leigh Brackett, Andre Norton), allowing squeamish male readers to convince themselves they were reading the work of other men.

When non-WASP characters appeared at all in sf stories of the period, they were treated stereotypically. Women characters, in general, conformed to the most sexist cliches—and the vanishingly few gay characters, always predatory villains, had it even worse.

These excesses were relatively few; much more frequently, non-male-WASP characters were simply invisibly absent... which was just a different level of chauvinism.

One can't fault the writers of the day; they were products of their culture. Especially in pre-war America, casual racism and sexism were pervasive in a way that's hard to believe today. *Astounding/Analog*, as the center of the sf universe at the time, was certainly complicit. Isaac Asimov, in his autobiography *In Memory Yet Green*, said of the legendary editor John W. Campbell, "He was a devout believer in the inequality of man and felt that the inequality could be detected by outer signs such as skin and hair coloring. Though he treated all men kindly and decently in his personal life...the fact is that, in theory, he felt that people of northwestern European extraction were the best human beings." Campbell was fairly typical in this.

Fortunately, time and the larger culture didn't stand still. As diversity gained traction in America, this progress was reflected in the pages of sf. With the civil rights movement, the women's movement, the counterculture message of nonconformity, and associated phenomena, science fiction became (a little) more diverse.

Occasional characters of color started to appear in sf, especially in the works of the field's leaders Arthur C. Clarke and Robert A. Heinlein—although many readers and critics missed them entirely. Strong, independent women also showed up in the pages of sf stories and novels. Gradually, character names took on more varied ethnic flavors.

Of particular note is a trilogy written by Mack Reynolds, one of the most popular sf writers of the time. The first two books, published as serials in *Analog*, are *Black Man's Burden* (December 1961 & January 1962) and *Border, Breed nor Birth* (July & August 1962). The third, *The Best Ye Breed*, was not published until 1978. This trilogy deals with a future independent, progressive North Africa and features many characters of color. To modern ears parts of the stories border on offensive, but they were revolutionary for their time.

In many ways, *Star Trek* was a fine representative of the sf of this period, with its inclusion of a black woman as an integral part of the Enterprise bridge crew. These days, it's hard to appreciate what a breakthrough Lieutenant Uhura symbolized —just as it's hard to believe that *Star Trek* was the venue for television's first interracial kiss.

The broadening popularity of the field in the wake of *Star Trek* brought a greater diversity of readers (and writers). Also, society became more accepting of diversity—in fact, society seemed almost to move more quickly than sf did. By the 1980s and 1990s, real-life space shuttle crews were more diverse than the average starship crew in sf.

So where are we are today? We have characters (and writers) of color and lesbian/gay/transgender characters (and writers) —but they're largely obligatory tokens. Women appear as fully-rounded characters, and women writers are well-represented in the field—but many women sf writers still have trouble being taken seriously, and the sf community is convulsed over issues of sexism and sexual harassment. Science fiction, by history and (arguably) by its very nature, remains a product of Western culture, imbued will all the associated values—good and bad alike.

Let me share an illustrative anecdote. In 2012, there was a sensation involving the movie *The Hunger Games*. One beloved character, Rue, was played by an actor of color. (In the book Rue is specifically and carefully described as being what we would call African-American.) A substantial number of viewers objected...vehemently. They didn't like having this very sympathetic character portrayed as black. Another substantial number of viewers spoke out against this display of racism, feeling that Rue's skin color was a vital part of the character. Two competing worldviews competing in the arena of science fiction.

All things being equal, I think science fiction is still much more comfortable with the ideas of cultural and biological diversity, than with their reality. We're much more likely to want to read about green-blooded insectoid aliens than about African Muslim women.

Yet I also believe that most of us are intellectually and emotionally honest enough to feel uncomfortable with our discomfort. When push comes to shove, we believe all that stuff about respecting all intelligent life in spite of its outward form...and so, more often than not, we choose to swallow our discomfort and expand our horizons.

Fitfully and falteringly, we move in the right direction...and bring the field along with us.

Titles Reviewed
- *Mothership* edited by Bill Campbell and Edward Austin Hall [464]

Dying Earth

(Jun 2009) As usual, it started with H.G. Wells. In *The Time Machine* he presented a far-future in which everything had worn down: the Earth, the human race, even the sun. John Campbell's "Twilight" and Arthur C. Clarke's *Against the Fall of Night* further explored these cold, cheerless eras, where advanced science became decadent magic, and science fiction was all but indistinguishable from fantasy. It fell to Jack Vance to produce the book that would give this subgenre its generally-accepted name: *The Dying Earth*.

Dying Earth novels have been out of favor in recent years. In fantasy, the subgenre devolved (what else?) into generic sword-and-sorcery; in sf, it seemed that Michael Moorcock's *Dancers at the End of Time* series had said everything there was to say.

Titles Reviewed

- *All the Windwracked Stars* by Elizabeth Bear [197]
- *City at the Edge of Time* by Greg Bear [197]
- *Nights of Villjamur* by Mark Charan Newton [358]

Eagerly Awaited

(Apr 2011) Perhaps the most overused phrase in science fiction publishing (besides "space opera") is "eagerly awaited." It's not a claim that's easily disproved—after all, every book is eagerly awaited by *someone*, if only its author. But that's not how the marketers want you to see it. They want to give the impression that hordes of rabid fans are lined up for blocks in front of bookstores, in the fashion of *Harry Potter* or *Twilight*, counting the seconds until they get the new title in their hot little hands. In this way they hope to build excitement, leading to more sales.

And we really can't blame the marketers; it's their job to sell books. But let's be honest for a moment...very few books are actually "eagerly awaited" by more than a comparative handful of readers. If that phrase is to mean anything useful, there ought to be some ground rules. Let's count the ways that science fiction can legitimately be "eagerly awaited."

First, consider the science fiction magazines. As far back as the pulp era of the 1930s, readers impatiently anticipated each new issue. Isaac Asimov told of filling school notebooks with calculations of how many seconds remained until the next issue of *Astounding* hit the stands. To judge from the message boards, modern subscribers to *Analog* know exactly how he felt. Here, then, is our first category of "eagerly awaited": magazines—or, indeed, anything that's published periodically on a more-or-less regular schedule (and now you know why librarian-types often call magazines "periodicals.") Periodic anthologies also count, like the various "best of the year" reprint volumes or well-regarded original anthologies like George Mann's *Solaris Book of New Science Fiction* or Roby James' *Warrior Wisewoman*.

A second kind of "eagerly awaited" book is one that continues a story begun in an earlier book (or books). Cliffhanger endings are particularly effective in building eagerness; if you leave your characters in jeopardy at the end of one book, you'll have readers salivating for the next one. But even without a cliffhanger, a continuing story has its own built-in appeal.

In the same vein, a book which completes a story can be awaited even more eagerly. Think of *Return of the Jedi*, E. E. "Doc" Smith's *Children of the Lens*, or Anne McCaffrey's *All the Weyrs of Pern*. This is the classic pattern of the trilogy: A popular first book is followed by an eagerly awaited sequel that continues the story; next comes the more eagerly awaited third book, which brings the story to a satisfactory ending.

With an ongoing series, where there is no natural end to the story, the "eagerly awaited" status comes less automatically. All things being equal, the eighth book of a series is less eagerly awaited than the concluding book of a series. In some cases, a lengthy series can even decrease the eagerness for each successive book—how often have you felt that an author ran out of steam about book six, and everything since then has been sub-par? And since we're being honest...how many times have you stopped reading a series after book seven or eight? Now we're into negative eagerness.

Elapsed time can help (you might think of this as the "absence makes the heart grow fonder" category). Isaac Asimov published the third *Foundation* book in 1953, and it wasn't until 28 years later that the fourth book appeared. In the interim, whole generations of readers devoured the original trilogy and begged for more. *Foundation's Edge* was certainly one of the most "eagerly awaited" sf novels ever. Even a lapse of a seven or eight years can ratchet the eagerness up to pretty high levels, as we'll see below.

A good enough writer can produce high eagerness without the help of cliffhangers, continued stories, or series at all. One classic example is Arthur C. Clarke, who wrote mostly standalone novels that certainly fell into anyone's definition of "eagerly awaited." Here, too, a hiatus can boost eagerness—how often have you seen a book advertised as "So-and-so's first novel in x years"? Alfred Bester and Theodore Sturgeon were both stellar writers who produced books so irregularly that each one was most "eagerly awaited."

Finally, there are eagerly awaited books that come out of nowhere. Sometimes the eagerness stems from the author—Carl Sagan's first sf novel, *Contact*, wasn't "eagerly awaited" because the world wanted another First Contact story. If Stephen Hawking or Neil deGrasse Tyson were to write a science fiction novel, you can bet that book would be "eagerly awaited" indeed. Sometimes a movie or tv show can generate an "eagerly awaited" book, as with Alan Dean Foster's *Splinter of the Mind's Eye*, which was marketed in 1978 as a continuation of the *Star Wars* story. And sometimes the subject of a book builds expectations all on its own, even if the author is relatively unknown in the field—again, we'll see an example below.

With all this buildup, I'm sure you're waiting to hear about some books that truly are eagerly awaited. So let's begin.

Titles Reviewed

- *Cryoburn* by Lois McMaster Bujold [211]
- *Stargate Atlantis: Homecoming* by Jo Graham & Melissa Scott [270]
- *Robert A. Heinlein: In Dialogue With His Century: Volume 1* by William H. Patterson, Jr. [506]
- *All Clear* by Connie Willis [437]

Ebooks

(Apr 2013) One of the biggest themes in science fiction is the effect of technological change upon individuals and societies. In the last decade, art and life have become entwined, as technological changes in the real world cause social and economic changes which, in turn, affect the science fiction field itself.

I'm speaking, of course, about e-books.

Science fiction has always been rather indifferent regarding the future of books and reading. To be sure, books and reading usually had their place in our future worlds. One convention of the field, stretching back at least as far as the 1930s, is that of quotes from fictional books, be it the authoritative *Encyclopedia Galactica*, the venerable *Orange Catholic Bible*, or the irreverent *Hitch-hikers Guide to the Galaxy*. Books might change their format—microfilm was popular in postwar sf, supplanted by tapes, discs, memory crystals, even hand-held devices like the Hitch-hiker's Guide. Every so often, a character emerged— usually a wise old eccentric—who preferred "old-fashioned" books printed and bound on paper.

Despite the technological trappings, most sf pictured future books as little different from traditional ones. No matter what the format or display, a "book" would be a discrete object containing written (or possibly spoken) words; so far as anyone could tell, books would be published and distributed through channels essentially unchanged since the 1930s. (Last century's audiobooks, whether cassette or CD, fell into this vision perfectly.)

Some writers (Arthur C. Clarke and Isaac Asimov spring to mind, although Murray Leinster was probably there first) went so far as to divorce divorce bytes and atoms, and picture a future in which a reader could call up any desired title on a single display screen—but the implication was that those books were still published by traditional means.

In *2001: A Space Odyssey* (1968), Arthur C. Clarke wrote of the "newspad," essentially a modern tablet combining newspapers, magazines, and television news in one package. Ben Bova's *Cyberbooks* (1989) was a masterful satire on the publishing industry; the cyberbook of the title was a fairly good approximation of Amazon's Kindle twenty years early—but the novel was primarily an action-filled story that didn't explore the cyberbook's impact beyond the publishing industry.

So now that the e-book revolution is here, how is it affecting sf?

First, there's the simple matter of availability. In the past, most books had a short shelf life. An average sf book would be on sale at general bookstores for a few months, a year at most, before it went out of print. If you'd just discovered an author and wanted to read all of their previous books, you'd be haunting used book stores.

E-books, however, never go out of print. Only discover an author after her twelfth book? No problem—just go online and buy the previous eleven. Nearly 90 years worth of sf books have been published; authors and their agents are working furiously to put much of that into e-book format.

Then there's the matter of length. In the discussion of Big Books I talked about the forces that have led sf novels to grow in length over the years—but e-books are independent of length. A short story can be made just as available as a gargantuan 800-page novel. History has shown that sf writers will produce whatever lengths the market wants: in the future we'll certainly see a greater range of lengths.

Another consequence of e-books is removing traditional publishers as gatekeepers of content. This has both good and bad implications for sf. On the positive side, much more good sf will be published. The age of the mass market is fading; in a sense, we're entering the age of the niche. To be sure, some niches are larger than others. There will always be big-name authors—but now, we'll also have medium-size names, small names, tiny names, microscopic and nano-scale names, all equally available to readers.

The bad news is that the same expansion will result in enormously more bad sf. No one reader has the time to wade through thousands of unsuitable books in search of the one or two that are suitable.

Perhaps the solution to the unsuitable books problem lies with another change that has come with e-books: smart recommendation algorithms. Today's "Other books you might enjoy..." will surely become tomorrow's "Here are four new titles you're guaranteed to love."

Like all good science fiction technology, the e-book revolution is sure to bring additional, totally unpredictable changes. All we know for sure is that the entire publishing world is in flux, sf included, and in ten more years the face of the field will look completely different.

What a great time to be reading sf!

Ebook Prices

((Nov 2012) (And while this is hardly the place or time to start a discussion about high prices of e-books—perhaps in a future column—I just can't pass up the chance to wag my finger at Tor. Fifteen dollars for an e-book? Really? As I write this, readers can pre-order the hardcover from Amazon for just a dollar and a quarter more. With a great product like *Energized*, you'd think they'd want to...I don't know...sell some of them? Talk about incomprehensible alien psychology....)

(Readers, please don't take it out on Lerner. He doesn't set prices. If you can't stomach paying that much for an e-book, bite the bullet and buy the hardcover. The man is one of us.)

(Dec 2013) That's three titles form Baen Books in a row; before I leave them for this issue, I have a bit of scolding to do. The once-dependable Baen Ebooks price of $6.00 has been creeping upwards lately, and here we have two ebooks priced higher than mass market editions of the same books. Readers aren't fooled; they know that paper costs way more than electrons. What's going on over there, folks?

E-Readers

((Dec 2012) I'd like to make a general recommendation for any voracious readers you know: if they don't already have an e-reader, it's time to get them one. The e-book revolution is in full swing, and enormous tectonic shifts are happening throughout the geology of the publishing world. As you've probably noticed in this column, most new books are available as e-books, usually from multiple vendors and in multiple formats. Small presses and individual authors are scrambling to make older, out of print works available as e-books. Increasingly, low-price e-books are the place to try out new and unfamiliar authors without risking your money on paperbacks that are quickly approaching $10. Such are the economics of e-publishing that it's not uncommon for authors to have at least some of their work unavailable in print at all. Over the next decade, I wouldn't be surprised to see mass market paperbacks start to disappear, replaced by e-books.

The publishing business aside, there are plenty of other reasons to have an e-reader. While e-book prices are still too high, at least from the big publishers, you can almost always get them cheaper than their print counterparts. For voracious readers, the experience of having dozens (or hundreds) of books at one's fingertips is heady...as is the instant gratification of being able to read a book seconds after discovering its existence. More and more public libraries are making e-books available to their patrons, despite opposition from many publishers.

I'm not going to tell you which e-reader to get. There are a variety of manufacturers, styles, and prices; judge by your own means and needs. I've used most of the major competitors—iPad, Kindle, Nook, Sony—and have friends who use just about everything. Any of them are fine for reading, especially fiction and popular nonfiction. Don't worry about picking the "perfect" device, this isn't a lifelong commitment.

Exploration & Discovery

(Jan/Feb 2013) As long as people have been around, we've told tales of exploration and discovery. One imagines a group of Homo habilis gathered around the fire spinning yarns about bold adventurers daring to climb the hills and venture into adjacent valleys, and the wonders they found there. From Pharaoh Necho's Phoenician sailors to Saint Brendan and Marco Polo, real and imaginary journeys of discovery have long had a hold on humanity's imagination.

Science fiction is no exception. If there's one type of story that's most characteristic of sf, it's the exploration tale. Even before sf was thought of as a distinct genre, Verne and Wells took readers flying to the Moon, voyaging under the sea, hitching rides on comets, and riding off to the distant future. In those days maps of the world still had huge blank spots, and readers were devoured stories of mysterious islands, lost worlds, and the hidden cities of deepest Africa. In fact, I believe that this shared spirit of exploration and discovery explains why an earlier generation of sf readers were almost as enamored of Tarzan as of John Carter, and enjoyed Quartermain's adventures almost as much as Professor Challenger's.

In the fullness of time, as Earthly frontiers closed and Hugo Gernsback worked his magic, science fiction established its identity. The writers of this new genre worked their will on the "exploration and discovery" story, giving it a particularly science-fictional twist.

This twist was simple: in science fiction, we don't just care what happens to voyagers on their journey—we also care how they get there. Taking a cue from Verne and Wells, a science fiction journey of discovery attempts to create a plausible technology for getting to new, exciting destinations.

Thus came about the familiar sf concept of the "space drive"—a specific technology that could propel and maneuver vessels into and through space. More often than not, these technologies were based on the best science of the day.

For journeys to the Moon and elsewhere within the Solar System, rockets were the most popular method. In fact, between the late 1920s and the 1960s, there was a burgeoning subgenre of "first trip to the Moon" stories, almost all of them based on real-world and theoretical advances in rocketry. Before Apollo, just about every sf writer of any prominence at all penned at least one "trip to the Moon" tale.

There were, of course, other ways to get into space and explore the Solar System. Refinements of rocketry, such as ion, plasma, or fusion drives and laser-assisted launch systems, were just the tip of the iceberg. Peruse the pages of *Astounding/Analog* and you'll find light sails, mass drivers, catapults, gravitational assist, space elevators, steam power, propulsion by black hole...Poul Anderson even propelled a spaceship with beer!

Expanding beyond the Solar System, unless you want to travel by generation ship, more exotic methods are necessary. Antigravity and E. E. "Doc" Smith's reactionless drive are handy, but sf voyagers have also used Bussard ramjets, antimatter propulsion, cosmic wormholes, and transmission via radio waves. Then of course, there are nearly infinite varieties of faster-than-light gimmicks, ranging from various warp drives to hyperspace shortcuts to technologically-produced stargates. Some really advanced species can move their minds through space without the need for technology at all.

(Want a fun parlor game? Try to name at least six stories that use each one of the gimmicks above.)

Even when space drives have little (if any) justification in current science, rigorous science fiction demands that they operate in a believably rational fashion, according to self-consistent rules that the author imposes. We don't have to know how to build Captain Presto Whizbang's magneto-gravitic stardrive, but we do need to know that it behaves like technology, with consistent limitations and abilities. We need to be confident that when Whizbang's ship is surrounded by space pirates in Chapter 16, he won't get away by pressing the previously-unmentioned magical "Teleport To Earth" button.

Of course, all this focus on the technology behind the journey doesn't make a story. SF writers still have to provide all the age-old elements of an exploration tale: wonder, excitement, adventure, suspense, character, meaning. It's just that science fiction, as with so many things, adds a special extra dimension to the story.

Titles Reviewed

- *Through Struggle, The Stars* by John J. Lumpkin [328]
- *Hex* by Allen Steele [408]
- *Back to the Moon* by Travis S. Taylor and Les Johnson [413]
- *Going Interstellar* edited by Les Johnson and Jack McDevitt [458]
- *Starship Century* edited by James Benford and Gregory Benford [474]

Genetics

(Sep 2012) Even before the word "genetics" existed, science fiction writers were speculating and writing stories about the subject. Although Gregor Mendel's work was first published in the 1860s, his ideas didn't penetrate the scientific mainstream until William Bateson rediscovered his results in 1905 (and coined the word "genetics") and publicized them. Meanwhile, in 1896 H. G. Wells published *The Island of Doctor Moreau*, arguably the first important novel of genetic engineering. (To be sure, Wells calls Dr. Moreau's techniques "vivisection," but the results look an awful lot like genetic engineering.)

Before actual genetic engineering emerged, science fiction interpreted the concept through several different lenses. The primary method was good old selective breeding, sometimes called "eugenics." Biological change came to the human race across many generations, usually according to some master plan.

Thus, in Olaf Stapeldon's *Last and First Men* (1930), we follow the development of eighteen successive species of humanity into a far-distant future. E. E. "Doc" Smith's *Lensman* series (beginning in *Astounding* with *Galactic Patrol* in 1937-38) involves millennia-long bloodlines, both human and alien, controlled by the benevolent Arisians. In Robert A. Heinlein's Howard Families series (starting with *Methuselah's Children* in *Astounding*, 1941), the Howards are bred for their longevity, becoming a race of near-immortals. Heinlein's *Beyond This Horizon* (*Astounding*, 1942) told of a world in which selective breeding had created a near-utopia. Frank Herbert's *Dune* series (serialized in *Analog* starting in 1963) gives us the ten-thousand-year bloodlines supervised by the Bene Gesserit Sisterhood.

Selective breeding involves large populations and long time-frames. Another way to view genetic engineering was more focused on small populations or individuals, using a variety of unspecified chemical and biological methods to alter germ plasm and create new forms of life. We're all familiar with the various biological castes depicted by Aldous Huxley in *Brave New World* (1932). The first great sf practitioner of this method, James Blish, gave it the name "pantropy." Several of his pantropy stories (including "Sunken Universe," 1942, and the classic "Surface Tension," 1952) were published in one volume as *The Seedling Stars* (1956). In C.L. Moore's "Promised Land" (*Astounding*, 1950), pantropy is used to adapt colonists to life on Ganymede. "Between the Dark and the Daylight" by Algis Budrys (1958) settlers on a hostile planet develop adaptations such as claws and armored hides, and eventually overrun the unmodified humans. Pantropy allows humans to live underwater and even in space in A. E. van Vogt's *The Silkie* (1964).

A third take on genetic engineering follows in the steps of Doctor Moreau by breeding or mutating animals to give them more human-like aspects. Robert A. Heinlein's "Jerry Is a Man" (1947) was a prescient early example of this approach, in which an intelligent ape stands trial to determine his humanity. In Cordwainer Smith's *Instrumentality of Mankind* series (notably "Alpha Ralpha Boulevard," 1961, "The Ballad of Lost C'Mell," 1962, "Under Old Earth," 1966, and *Norstrilia*, 1975), a host of half-animal Underpeople are the true heirs of humanity. Curt Siodmak's *Hauser's Memory* (1969) explores using genetics to transfer human memories and even personalities to animals. More recently, David Brin has used a variation on the theme of selective breeding in his Uplift stories (commencing with *Startide Rising*, serialized in *Analog* starting in 1981), in which sapient patron races "uplift" non-sapient animals to intelligence.

Once science discovered DNA, it was able to catch up to sf and give us the language and techniques of true genetic engineering. Starting about the 1970s, genetic engineering became a common theme in science fiction. In *Time Enough For Love* (1973), Robert A. Heinlein picked up the Howard Families series and took genetic engineering far beyond simple controlled breeding. Kate Wilhelm's *Where Late the Sweet Birds Sang* (1976) gives us a world in which cloning replaces sexual reproduction. Cloning and genetic engineering also figure heavily in Arthur C. Clarke's *Imperial Earth* (1976).

Geoff Ryman's *The Child Garden* (1989) presents a world in which genetic engineering results in living beings that serve as houses, vehicles, and machines. Nancy Kress has made a name for herself with genetic engineering stories like the *Sleepers* series (starting with *Beggars in Spain*, 1993)—in which a new breed of immortals result from attempts to engineer away the need for sleep—and this year's collection *Future Perfect: Six Stories of Genetic Engineering*.

Many sf movies and television shows include elements of genetic engineering (usually laughable ones), but one standout is the excellent 1997 movie *Gattaca*.

Titles Reviewed

- *Little Brother's World* by T. Jackson King [306]
- *Exogene* by T. C. McCarthy [338]

Historical Fiction & SF

(Jul/Aug 2010) When you look at it, there is considerable overlap between science fiction and, of all things, historical fiction. That shouldn't really come as a surprise; in many important ways, readers come to both fields looking for the same sorts of elements.

Both sf and historical fiction take the reader to places fundamentally different from the present-day world. In sf it's either the altered world of the future, or literally another world (or universe) altogether; in historical fiction, the different landscapes of the past. Both fields delight in presenting other cultures and unfamiliar societies. Both are often concerned with people involved in far-reaching societal changes. And in both fields, readers respect authors who do their research and provide accuracy.

Is it any wonder, then, that many readers like both sf and historical fiction? And what could make those readers happier, than when the two come together in the same book?

In general, there are three basic ways that sf and historical fiction fuse. First there's the so-called "future historical," a book that reads like a historical novel even though it's set firmly in the future. Isaac Asimov's *Foundation* stories were consciously written as future historicals, and when Frank Herbert's *Dune* was first published, it was often compared to a historical novel.

A second fusion of sf and historical is the alternate history story, and if you haven't noticed, alternate histories are all the rage nowadays. Harry Turtledove alone keeps the genre in business, and there are many other fine practitioners.

That leaves a third way for sf and historical fiction to come together, and that's the venerable time-travel novel. Just about any time-travel story worth its salt has some kind of historical element, unless it's strictly about travel into the future. But some authors have raised the time-travel/historical blend to the level of fine art. Which brings us, happily, to Connie Willis.

Titles Reviewed

Alternate History

• See "Alternate History" section

Time Travel Historical

• *This Shared Dream* by Kathleen Ann Goonan [267]
• *Time Travelers Never Die* by Jack McDevitt [339]
• *Blackout* by Connie Willis [435]
• *All Clear* by Connie Willis [437]

Keeping Up

(Part 1)

(Sep 2013) Once upon a time, a prospective science fiction writer had only one road to success. From 1926 well to the early 1950s, virtually the entire sf field consisted of short stories and occasional longer works published in print magazines. All the big name authors we associate with the so-called Golden Age—from Poul Anderson to Jack Williamson and everyone in between—got their start in the pulps, or fanzines that imitated them.

From a reader's standpoint, the age was indeed Golden. A reader could keep up with the field by following at most a dozen or so magazines (assuming, of course, that one had the money to buy them—or failing that, friends from whom to beg, borrow, or steal).

In the 1950s, things began to change. Science fiction gained a new respectability in society, and the field expanded into print books, movies, even radio.

For readers in this period, it wasn't enough just to read the magazines. The center of the sf world moved between the covers of books, first hardcovers and then (in the 1960s), original paperbacks.

Many authors still started their careers in the magazines — names like Samuel R. Delany, Frank Herbert, Anne McCaffrey, and Robert Silverberg—before moving into the more lucrative field of novels. Others emerged primarily as novelists, and only appeared in the magazines later: think John Brunner, Tanith Lee, or Jerry Pournelle. Books continued to be a major outlet for science fiction up to the present day, and the roster of writers who made their names with sf books is enormous and varied.

The 1960s also brought popular science fiction television shows such as *Doctor Who*, Rod Serling's *Twilight Zone*, and Gene Roddenberry's *Star Trek*. New sf authors emerged in the wake of these successful series, authors like Harlan Ellison, David Gerrold, Richard Matheson, Terry Nation, and Jerry Sohl.

Science fiction was also becoming big in film, and although many of the efforts were laughable even to contemporary sf readers, the work of some fine sf writers gained exposure from movies, people like Jerome Bixby and Jack Finney.

The sf films of the 1970s and 1980s brought more authors (although I suppose we ought to call them "creators") into the fold, people like James Cameron, George Lucas, Steven Spielberg, J. Michael Straczynski, and Robert Zemeckis. At the same time, we saw big names emerge from a new direction, what we used to call "novelizations" and we now call "tie-ins"—not just superstars Kevin J. Anderson and Alan Dean Foster, but others like Diane Carey, Brian Daley, Peter David, Keith R. A. DeCandido, and Michael Jan Friedman.

Around the same time, one beloved author got his start in the world of radio, a man named Douglas Adams. (To be fair, the aforementioned J. Michael Straczynski also did some of his early work in radio.)

Science fiction has been an influence in comics since the days of *Buck Rogers* and *Superman*. Beginning in the 1980s and 1990s, many top-notch comics writers crossed over into books, including sf-themed graphic novels. A few of the most prominent were Chris Claremont, Neil Gaiman, Geoff Johns, Jim Starlin, and Mark Waid. (Peter David and Straczynski have also done well-regarded work in comics.)

As big name authors grew older, some turned to a kind of apprenticeship, working with younger, less-known names (and sadly, in the fullness of time, being replaced by them.) Thus we had teams like Anne McCaffrey and Elizabeth Ann Scarborough, or her son and literary heir Todd McCaffrey, or Kevin J. Anderson and Brian Herbert continuing Frank Herbert's *Dune* series.

The coming of the World Wide Web and print-on-demand technology brought new and expanded outlets for science fiction authors. Small presses, which had for decades produced mainly reprints and niche titles, benefited from lower production costs and increased availability—and became yet another venue for emerging sf authors such as Mike McPhail, Vera Nazarian, and Steven H. Wilson. (Wilson, like Adams and Straczynski, also works in audio—not radio but podcasts. I'm sure there are others.)

The Web also brought new life to short fiction in the form of webzines such as *Lightspeed*, *Penumbra*, and *Strange Horizons*. Recent novice authors appearing in webzines include Saladin Ahmed, Lauren Beukes, and Tony Pi (all nominees for the John W. Campbell Award for the best new sf writer).

The revitalization of small press lowered the cost of publication; the e-book revolution of the past decade quantum-jumped costs to the lowest level yet. We're still in the midst of this revolution, but one result is clear: increased availability of more sf writers than ever before.

New technology has also brought the gaming field (both video and role playing games), a sector which is larger than Hollywood -- and which is rife with science fiction themes and content. Game tie-in novels are everywhere nowadays.

For the sf reader of today who wants to keep up with the field and spot emerging talents, reading the print magazines and prowling bookstore sf racks is nowhere near enough. (Hey, remember bookstores?) You need to keep an eye on television and movies, but also radio and podcasts, comics, webzines, small presses, e-books, and games. Oh, and it doesn't hurt to keep part of your attention alert for the next new venue, which will probably be along in a few months.

(Part 2)

(Oct 2013) Last issue I talked about the vast expansion of places to find good science fiction. Reading the print magazines and prowling bookstores used to be enough, but now quality sf also appears in television and movies, radio and podcasts, comics, webzines, small presses, e-books, and games. New venues spring up without warning.

How is an sf reader to keep up?

First, don't overlook the obvious: review columns in sf magazines (to paraphrase an old commercial, you're soaking in one right now). There's Peter Heck at our sibling publication, *Isaac Asimov's Science Fiction Magazine*, and a whole stable of book and film reviewers at *The Magazine of Fantasy and Science Fiction*. *Interzone* from the U.K. has a large array of reviewers (*ttapress.com/interzone/*). Many online sf zines also have review columns, *Strange Horizons* in particular (*www.strangehorizons.com*).

Then there are zines devoted to news and reviews of sf publishing. The grandaddy of them all is *Locus* (P.O. Box 13305, Oakland, CA 94661); the online version (*www.locusmag.com*) is a distinct yet related entity. The annual Locus Awards are well worth following. *Romantic Times* also reviews new sf of interest to romance readers, available online at *www.rtbookreviews.com/genre/science-fiction*. The *New York Review of Science Fiction* (*www.nyrsf.com*) is a good source for reviews of literary sf.

You'll want to watch sf reviews in some of the publishing industry's standard sources: *Publishers Weekly* (*www.publishersweekly.com*), *Library Journal* (*lj.libraryjournal.com*), and *Kirkus* (*www.kirkusreviews.com*). These sources, aimed at bookstores and libraries, review scads of sf books in each issue.

It helps to pay attention to the websites of your favorite publishers and authors, which you can find with a simple online search. A caution about author websites, though—many of them are not as frequently updated as one would wish, so take them with a grain of salt. (Authors: update your websites! The readers who come there are generally already fans—just the people you *want* to inform about your newest titles. Sheesh!)

There are a number of specialty sites that have lists and recommendations of sf books. First are the booksellers:

Amazon.com, *BN.com*, iBooks, etc. You should also be aware of online communities of readers, such as Goodreads (*www.goodreads.com*) and Library Thing (*www.librarything.com*). One interesting site is BookLamp (*booklamp.org*), which uses computer text-analysis to analyze books and offer recommendations. [2017 addition: BookLamp has since been bought by Amazon.]

A great place to find quality sf is in the various "best of the year" anthologies. At the moment, four are regularly published: *The Best Science Fiction and Fantasy of the Year* (edited by Jonathan Strahan), *The Year's Best Science Fiction* (edited by Gardner Dozois), T*he Year's Best Science Fiction and Fantasy* (edited by Richard Horton), and *Nebula Awards Showcase* (with a different editor each year).

If your eyes aren't glazed over yet, you'll want to check out some sf news sites. Some that lean more in the direction of books are Fantastic Reviews (*www.fantasticreviews.com*), Science Fiction World (*sciencefictionworld.com*), SFRevu (*sfrevu.com*), SF Signal (*www.sfsignal.com*), SF Site (*www.sfsite.com*), SFF World (*www.sffworld.com*), and Worlds in Ink (*worldsinink.blogspot.com*).

Sites that lean more toward visual and audio sf include Slice of SciFi (*www.sliceofscifi.com*), SciFi News (*www.scifinews.net*), SciFi Stream (*www.scifistream.com*), SFcrowsnest (*sfcrowsnest.co.uk*), and SFX (*www.sfx.co.uk*).

The Anime News Network (*www.animenewsnetwork.com*) does a great job of following developments in the anime world, with an emphasis on science fiction. The Geek's Guide to the Galaxy (*geeksguideshow.com*) is a podcast that covers the whole continuum of science fiction in all formats.

Finally, *Analog* readers in particular need to pay attention to io9 (*io9.com*), which bills itself as "a daily publication that covers science, science fiction, and the future." Think of it as the electronic equivalent of *Analog* without the fiction.

I know keeping up with all these sources sounds like an awful lot of work, but most of them offer RSS feeds so you can arrange to get the majority of your sf news in one place. Making the time to keep up with it, I leave to you.

Literary SF

I

(Jul/Aug 2009) When I was a mere slip of a lad in my first year of college, I naturally signed up for the one and only class in science fiction and fantasy. I liked the professor so much that I took the next class she offered, and the next, and so on...which is how I wound up with a minor in English literature to go with my major in math (thank you, Sue Abromaitis).

In one of the early classes, probably Eighteenth Century Novels, our first assignment was Swift's *Gulliver's Travels*. I plunged into it expecting a dull, turgid classic; instead, I found tiny people, giants, alien races and societies, and an aerial city populated by advanced scientists and held aloft by antigravity.

I raced off to the professor's office, determined that she was alone, and said, "I just finished *Gulliver's Travels*. Does the rest of the class know that we're reading science fiction?"

She smiled and held a finger to her lips. "Don't tell them, otherwise they'll decide they have to hate it."

The point of this whole dreary story is to illustrate the uneasy tension that exists between the universe of Science Fiction and the world of Literature.

When the Earth was young and there was no such thing as genre, what passed for SF was just another part of Literature. The *Epic of Gilgamesh* was the first post-apocalyptic story on record, and Daedalus the first scientist-hero. Lucian of Samosata wrote space opera in the second century, Dante meticulously built worlds according to the best medieval science, Shakespeare penned the preliminary screenplay for *Forbidden Planet*, and Cyrano de Bergerac talked about sending rockets into space in the 1600s...all well before Dean Swift sent Gulliver off on his adventures. Mary Shelley's speculations about the uses of electricity paved the way for the careers of Great-Grandpappys Verne and Wells. And every one of those authors is undeniably a part of Literature, published in respectable Penguin Classics editions available at the nearest college bookstore.

Then Grandaddy Hugo came along and gave Science Fiction its own separate playground, and Father-of-Us-All John Campbell refined it into a thriving genre. And so it happened that Science Fiction waved goodbye to Literature, and the two went their separate ways.

Ever since then, stuffy old Literature has turned up its nose at its younger sibling...while upstart Science Fiction, for its part, has often delighted in tweaking the nose of its big brother. But underneath, each has always envied the other, if only a little bit.

Every once in a while, Literature takes ahold of the conventions of Science Fiction, and produces a minor masterpiece. Huxley's *Brave New World* and Orwell's *1984* are well-known examples. In later years, ultra-Literary authors such as Margaret Atwood, Caleb Carr, P. D. James, Doris Lessing, and even John Updike tried their hands at SF-type books, with varied degrees of success. Recently, even Philip Roth ventured into SF territory, with an alternate history novel called *The Plot Against America*. (Although poor Mr. Roth, in a poignant author's note, begs his reader's indulgence for this queer notion of a story in which history went off in a different direction—a notion that he seems to think he invented himself. As Professor Abromaitis might say, don't tell him that Murray Leinster was there seventy years before.)

To be sure, when Literature plays with Science Fiction's toys, it doesn't dig too deeply into the toybox. You're not likely to see Barbara Kingsolver exploring post-Singularity AIs, Ann Tyler writing the definitive First Contact novel, or Iain Pears writing of murder on a generation ship.

No, what's popular in Literature these days is a touch of environmentalism (like T. C. Boyle's *A Friend of the Earth*) or good old dystopian futures. In fact, since Cormac McCarthy's *The Road* was published in 2006, Literary dystopias (also known as "post-apocalyptics") have been all the rage.

But let's not forget that for every bit as long as Literature's been messing around in Science Fiction's playground, SF has been sneaking into the house and putting its feet up on Literature's furniture.

There have always been the Brits. In England, the split between Literature and SF was never as serious as in the States. John Wyndham, Brian Aldiss, John Brunner, J. G. Ballard...all were more-or-less accepted as at least literary-with-a-small-l. Even among the Campbell stable there was Arthur C. Clarke—I am far from the only one to have noticed that some passages in Sir Arthur's work are sheer poetry.

The whole New Wave Movement of the 1960s, a British import to begin with, was largely an attempt to move SF closer to the Literature side of the yard (and further away from the disreputable neighbors like Westerns and other pulp fiction).

But still, even pulpy American SF had its Literary lights...and still has them today. True, some of the usual names have lately been having out-of-genre experiences: Ursula K. LeGuin in ancient Italy *(Lavinia)*; Norman Spinrad exploring the halls of Montezuma *(Mexica)*; and Samuel R. Delany experimenting in alternative autobiography *(Dark Reflections)*. But that still leaves a few SF writers to proudly carry the banner into Literary territory.

II

(Mar 2012) Within the cosmos of science fiction, there is an alternate universe—one whose biggest names include the likes of Margaret Atwood, Jorge Luis Borges, Mary Doria Russell, and Kurt Vonnegut. More traditional sf names like Samuel R. Delany, William Gibson, and Ursula K LeGuin are part of this universe—but Poul Anderson, Isaac Asimov, and Robert A. Heinlein are not. It is a universe in which pulp magazines might as well not have existed, and the Campbell revolution is largely irrelevant.

In this parallel universe, you won't catch readers perusing the pages of *Analog* or *Asimov's* (although they might occasionally glance at an issue of *Fantasy and Science Fiction*), and they usually walk right by the sf/fantasy section of their local bookstore. Yet here, sf is thriving; sales are good and much exciting work is being published.

I'm speaking, of course, about the universe of Literary Science Fiction.

LitSF (if I may be a bit familiar) traces its roots back to the same place as our familiar, non-Lit variety: at least to Mary Shelley's Frankenstein, and from there through Jules Verne and H.G. Wells. But whereas regular sf evolved in the direction of Gernsback and the pulp magazines of the 1920s, LitSF took a different path, a path that led through Franz Kafka, Aldous Huxley, B.F. Skinner, George Orwell, and C. S. Lewis. Ray Bradbury somehow managed to straddle the two paths.

LitSF had its next milestone when Michael Moorcock launched the so-called "New Wave" in the pages of *New Worlds* magazine in 1964. Moorcock's writers—the likes of Brian Aldiss, J. G. Ballard, M. John Harrison, Charles Platt, John Sladek, and Norman Spinrad—were more consciously literary than previous writers. As Robert Silverberg said in *Musings and Meditiations*, their work "...had overtones of Joseph Conrad and Graham Greene, not Robert Heinlein or A. E. van Vogt."

In the States, editors such as Terry Carr, Avram Davidson, Damon Knight, Judith Merrill, and Frederik Pohl provided both markets and publicity for LitSF "New Wave" authors. Some of these authors are considered minor names in traditional sf, but well-known to LitSF readers—authors like David R. Bunch, Tom Disch, Carol Emshwiller, R. A. Lafferty, and Joanna Russ. Others managed to keep a foot in both universes, and are household names no matter what kind of sf one reads: John Brunner, Samuel R. Delany, Philip K. Dick, Harlan Ellison, Philip José Farmer, Roger Zelazny, and Michael Moorcock himself.

As time went on the "New Wave" phenomenon faded. To an extent, the evolution of LitSF and traditional sf converged for a time. New writers of the period were respected by readers in both universes—writers like Gardner Dozois, Ursula K. LeGuin, Barry Malzberg, James Tiptree, Jr., John Varley, and Gene Wolfe.

To this day there are still writers who appeal to both universes: Octavia Butler, William Gibson, Dan Simmons, Bruce Sterling, Sheri S. Tepper, and Connie Willis are among them. But a funny thing happened in the 1980s: the two universes began to separate once again.

Doris Lessing, later a Nobel laureate in literature, was a major light in the literary world when she embarked on a series of novels of what she called "space fiction." Suddenly, writers of LitSF didn't have to come up through the ranks of traditional sf (as did, say, Kurt Vonnegut, who spent most of his life denying that he was an sf writer).

With the doors opened, other big names in literature turned to work that could only be described as science fiction. Marge Piercy used time travel in *Woman on the Edge of Time*. Margaret Atwood gave us a dystopian future in *The Handmaid's Tale*. Cormac McCarthy's much-imitated *The Road* was a post-apocalyptic dystopia. Audrey Niffenegger revisited time travel in *The Time Traveler's Wife*. Michael Chabon (*The Yiddish Policeman's Union*) and even Philip Roth (*The Plot Against America*) joined in with alternate history stories.

To the average *Analog* reader, modern LitSF seems rather lightweight, not "real" science fiction at all. But we should be charitable to our literary sibling. Despite the nasty things their critics occasionally say about traditional sf (Brian Aldiss calls it "power-fantasy and escapism," and you should hear him badmouth Asimov's work), LitSF readers are still reading science fiction; it's just a different *kind* of science fiction. There's still considerable cross-pollination between our universes; they learn from us and we learn from them. And to judge from their various apologias, the writers get a lot of grief from their literary cronies. It behooves us to be generous and welcome them to the fold.

Titles Reviewed
- *In Other Worlds* by Margaret Atwood [485]
- *We'll Always Have Paris* by Ray Bradbury [207]
- *Veracity* by Laura Bynum [213]
- *The Pesthouse* by Jim Crace [229]
- *The Passage* by Justin Cronin [232]
- *Railsea* by China Miéville [347]
- *Watchmen* by Alan Moore and Dave Gibbons [352]
- *Jamestown* by Matthew Sharpe [396]
- *The Best of Gene Wolfe* by Gene Wolfe [443]
- *The Best Science Fiction & Fantasy of the Year* edited by Jonathan Strahan [454]
- *Like Water For Quarks* edited by Elton Elliott & Bruce Taylor [462]
- *Mothership* edited by Bill Campbell and Edward Austin Hall [464]
- *The Year's Best Science Fiction: Thirtieth Annual Collection* edited by Gardner Dozois [482]
- *The Year's Best Science Fiction: Twenty-Ninth Annual Collection* edited by Gardner Dozois [481]

Mars

(Jan/Feb 2014) Mars has been a favorite subject of science fiction since before there was science fiction.

As early as the 16th century, scientist-philosophers such as Johannes Kepler and Emanuel Swedenborg wrote about journeys to Mars. It wasn't until Schiaparelli's observations, during the so-called "Great Opposition" of 1877, that awareness of Mars began to spread in popular fiction. Percy Greg's *Across the Zodiac* (1880), perhaps the first modern space-travel novel, tells of a trip to the Red Planet and an encounter with its small inhabitants (who refuse to believe that their visitor is from Earth, since life on other worlds is patently impossible). *Journey to Mars* by Gustavus W. Pope (1894) seems to be a precursor of things to come: a shipwrecked Navy man is kidnapped and taken to a Mars populated by three races of humanoids who live in a feudal society that nevertheless is technologically advanced. Pope's hero Frederick Hamilton falls in love with Princess Suhlamia and strives to save the Martians from destruction. In the end, he returns to Earth with his Martian bride. In the next book the happy couple goes to Venus.

We're all familiar with H.G. Wells's *War of the Worlds* (1898), but perhaps less so with its immediate (unauthorized) sequel by Garrett P. Serviss, *Edison's Conquest of Mars* (1898), in which Edison led an expedition to wipe out the Martians.

Gullivar of Mars (Edwin L. Arnold, 1905) was another romantic story of a single Earthman on Mars. In 1909 French author Gustave Le Rouge brought us a novel whose theme would be right at home on today's bookshelves: *Le prisonnier de la planète Mars* (*Vampires of Mars*). And of course there was *A Princess of Mars* (1912) and its many sequels by Edgar Rice Burroughs, which brought the "planetary romance" fashion to science fiction.

The legendary Stanley G. Weinbaum wrote "A Martian Odyssey" (*Wonder Stories*, July 1934), arguably the first story to feature a truly alien being. Over on then literary side, C.S. Lewis's *Out of the Silent Planet* (1938) was a philosophical answer to H.G. Wells and showed peaceful Martians of several species living in harmony with one another.

Ray Bradbury addressed a similar theme in *The Martian Chronicles* (1950), turning Wells on his head by showing Martians corrupted and destroyed by the arrival of humans from Earth.

The colonization of Mars took hold of science fiction's imagination in the 1930s, and never really let go. Until the era of space probes, we continued to read of noble Martians haunting the ruins of ancient cities on the banks of drying canals. Just about every sf writer of the time wrote about Mars. Notable examples included *Red Planet* by Robert A. Heinlein (1949), "Omnilingual" by H. Beam Piper (*Astounding*, February 1957), *The Sands of Mars* by Arthur C. Clarke (1951), *Lost Race of Mars* by Robert Silverberg (1960), and "A Rose for Ecclesiastes" by Roger Zelazny (*F&SF*, November 1963).

Beginning in 1965, the Mariner probes returned spectacular results that changed our perception of Mars, with huge impact on science fiction. It soon became clear that there were no canals, no ancient cities, no intelligent inhabitants at all—and that the environment of Mars was more hostile than we thought.

Martian colonization was still the name of the game, but the technological challenges were greater. Mars stories, by and large, moved into the nuts-and-bolts realm of hard sf. The notion of terraforming Mars was in the air, and several authors riffed on that theme.

Major appearances of Mars in science fiction included Frederick Pohl's *Man Plus* (1976); Gordon R. Dickson's *The Far Call* (1978); Kim Stanley Robinson's *Red Mars* (1993), *Green Mars* (1994), and *Blue Mars* (1996); Ben Bova's Mars books (beginning in 1992); William K. Hartman's *Mars Underground* (1997); *White Mars* by Brian Aldiss and Roger Penrose (1999);

Geoffrey A. Landis's *Mars Crossing* (2000); and John Barnes's *The Sky So Big and Black* (2002).

Mars has always been popular in film; Thomas Edison actually produced a 1910 silent film called *A Trip to Mars*. Other notable Mars films include *Robinson Crusoe on Mars* (1964), the awful yet ever-popular *Santa Claus Conquers the Martians* (also 1964), *Mars Needs Women* (1967), *The Martian Chronicles* tv miniseries (1980), *Total Recall* (1990), and a trio of unrelated Mars movies in 2000/2001: *Mission to Mars*, *Red Planet*, and *Ghosts of Mars*.

On television, Mars was visited frequently by *Doctor Who*, appeared on *Twilight Zone*, and played major roles in *Babylon 5* and *Futurama*. Of the dozens of Martians who have appeared on tv, special mention must be made of Ray Walston's *My Favorite Martian* (1963-66) and Bugs Bunny's nemesis Marvin the Martian.

Titles Reviewed
- *Mars, Inc.* By Ben Bova [203]
- *Mars Life* by Ben Bova [205]
- *Ares Express* by Ian McDonald [341]
- *If By Reason of Strength* by Jamie Todd Rubin [380]
- *Red Planet Blues* by Robert J. Sawyer [388]
- *Old Mars* edited by George R. R. Martin and Gardner Dozois [467]

Military SF

I

(Jun 2011) Military science fiction is one of the most dynamic and commercially successful areas of the field. There's nothing odd about that: fiction is usually based on conflict, and war is the ultimate form of conflict. War stories are instantly accessible; there are usually bad guys and good guys for the reader to identify with, the world of the military is a familiar one, and there's plenty of occasion for action.

In addition, no matter how little we may want to admit this, trends in science fiction parallel those in the wider culture. In our current era—unlike, say, the late 1960s or 1970s—war is a popular topic. (And even in the most pacifist age, war is a concern of fiction. The most ardently antiwar novel is still a novel about war.)

In the beginning there was no separate genre of military sf; as with other themes that later grew into their own genres, war and military personnel were just occasional parts of sf stories. Jules Verne's Captain Nemo carried on his own war to end war. John Carter was a former military man who moved to Mars and achieved the rank of Warlord. H. G. Wells's Martians came to Earth for—guess what?—a *War of the Worlds*. E. E. "Doc" Smith's Lensmen were players in a millennia-old war between implacable enemies.

In the wake of World War II—and subsequent anxiety about possible imminent nuclear armageddon—sf writers frequently addressed war and military matters. Some of the direct precursors of modern military sf included Robert A. Heinlein's *Space Cadet* and *Starship Troopers*, Gordon R. Dickson's *Dorsai* books, Fred Saberhagen's *Berserker* stories, and Poul Anderson's tales of Sir Dominic Flandry and his standalone novel *The High Crusade*. The Vietnam War brought a different sensibility and works like Joe Haldeman's *The Forever War* (a direct response to *Starship Troopers*), Gregory Benford's *Deeper*

Than the Darkness, and David Drake's *Hammer's Slammers* series.

Experts point to the 1975 reprint anthology *Combat SF*, edited by Gordon R. Dickson, as helping to establish the concept of military sf as a separate genre. This remarkable volume included a *Berserker* story, an early *Hammer's Slammers* tale, one of Keith Laumer's *Bolo* stories, a *Forever War* story, Poul Anderson's "The Man Who Came Early" (an early story of a military man who brings modern war technology into the past), and other tales by Harry Harrison, Jerry Pournelle, and Dickson himself.

If Robert A. Heinlein and Gordon R. Dickson are the grandfathers of military sf, then David Drake certainly deserves to be credited as the genre's father. In the mid-1980s, his *Hammer's Slammers* series paved the way for the resurgence of military sf that has lasted to this day. While these books are firmly in the tradition of modern military sf, Drake (a Vietnam vet) has stated that one of his motivations was to educate nonmilitary readers about the horror and inadequacy of war. In this way, he bridges the gap between Vietnam-era antiwar feelings and today's more pro-military attitudes.)

Military sf exploded (no pun intended) in the late 1980s and early 1990s with the arrival of Chris Bunch & Allan Cole's *Sten* series, David Weber's *Honor Harrington* series, Larry Niven's *Man-Kzin Wars* anthologies, and the ascendancy of Baen Books (then and now a chief publisher of military sf). The next two decades brought more superstar names like Dan Cragg, John Dalmas, William C. Dietz, David Feintuch, Eric Flint, John Hemry (aka Jack Campbell), Elizabeth Moon, John Ringo, John Scalzi, and David Sherman.

Before diving into this month's books, I'd like to mention a few sf genres that are related to (and often confused with) military sf.

First is the venerable Space Opera, which I've defined as "grand, melodramatic sf stories with great scenery, anguish, death, and an occasional fat lady." Space Opera often includes war and military elements, but it is properly a distinct type of sf. Readers who like one may not necessarily like the other—although publishers have a tendency to call any sf with military elements "Space Opera."

Similarly, stories of Galactic Empires often involve wars and the military, but are not necessarily military sf. (Poul Anderson's Dominic Flandry novels are a great example.) Far Future and Hard SF stories might feature battles and wars, but aren't technically military sf. Many stories of aliens, either in space or visiting Earth, are cast as war books—and many military sf stories involve wars against aliens. While it's possible for a book to be both, a good rule of thumb is to look at the main focus of the story. Is it more concerned with the biology and culture of the aliens, or with the technology and tactics of the war?

Finally, there are stories of independent agents such as spies (Harry Harrison's *Stainless Steel Rat*), diplomats (Keith Laumer's *Retief*), couriers (Robert A. Heinlein's *Friday*) , and the like. These operatives may move through a landscape of war and deal with the military, but they are not necessarily examples of true military sf.

So what is this stuff called "military sf" that we've been talking about? I'd like to spend the rest of this column talking about some recent examples that demonstrate the variety of the genre.

II

(Jul/Aug 2012) Military science fiction continues to be one of the most popular niche markets in the field. To those who aren't aficionados, it's sometimes hard to understand the appeal of the genre. I've even heard science fiction readers dismissively ask, as they would of romances or westerns, "If you've read one military sf book, haven't you read them all?"

The answer, of course, is a resounding, "No, of course not."

We live in a consumer culture that values consistent, repeatable experiences. Every McDonald's burger or Taco Bell burrito tastes exactly like every other. Advertising to the contrary, a gallon of regular unleaded gasoline delivers identical performance whether you purchase it from Shell or Exxon. Most mass-produced consumer products, from lightbulbs to underwear to staples, are bought on the assumption that all units in the same category (size, style, capacity) will be essentially identical.

Intellectual property—books, magazines, comics, songs, poems, movies, plays, etc.—isn't like that.

I'm not talking here about formatting standards. Yes, all printed books are alike in format: made of paper, bound in folio fashion, with covers and pages, margins and page numbers, ISBN and UPC codes, etc. Music is (almost always) based on the same scale of notes, and distributed in standard formats (compact disc, MP3, etc.) These are simply infrastructure—the important part, the essence, is the specific arrangement of words, pictures, music, voice, video, action.

Still, in a lot of mass culture, near-identical performance is a goal. Let's take television sitcoms for an example. In each successive episode of the average sitcom, the specifics of the plot may differ—but enormous effort is given to ensure that the viewer's emotional response will remain roughly the same. If everyone does their jobs right, you should feel the same at the end of the twelfth episode as you did at the end of the first. (At least, that's what the marketers and advertisers are hoping.)

To be sure, there are certain genres of books that have similar goals. The category romances, thrillers, and westerns— your Harlequins and Silhouettes, your Mack Bolans and Executioners, your Longarms and Slocums—strive to produce books that will give the reader a consistent emotional experience with each and every volume. SF has not been immune to these marketing goals in its history: long-running series such as Perry Rhodan and Dray Prescott explicitly produced cookie-cutter books one after another.

However, in most intellectual property, there's a constant creative tension between predictability and variety. For a perfect example, look no further than the magazine you're reading. *Analog* would quickly lose readers if every story in every issue were exactly like every other story in every other issue. At the same time, there's a necessary consistency, a synergy between writers and editor and readers. Even though it may be impossible to define and may change with time, it's the quality ensuring that if you like one issue of *Analog*, you'll probably like other issues.

Different writers and different genres place this line, between predictability and variety, in different places. Robert J. Sawyer's books are all different, but they all share the same qualities (of tone, character, subject) that make them Sawyer books. Time travel stories, on the other hand, have even less in common with one another, sharing only the fundamental concept (moving about in time) and the same literary ancestors.

At the extreme end is the genre of science fiction itself; it's so hard to determine what all sf books have in common that we've been at it for nine decades and still haven't come up with a good definition.

Back to military sf. To some degree, all military sf stories are more like one another than all time travel stories are. Yet they're certainly more different from one another than are, say, Robert J. Sawyer books. If you are passionate about, say, David Weber's military sf, that doesn't mean that you are assured of also liking Eric Flint's.

At this point, channeling my early math training, I'm tempted to start drawing Venn diagrams and talking about sets and intersections of sets, in an attempt to formulate a Grand Theory of Military SF.

But then I take a deep breath and realize that there's something fractal about this whole thing. As with any other field, the more you know, the more you can make distinctions. If you only read an occasional military sf book every few years, then of course you'll perceive that all of them are pretty much the same. On the other hand, if you read just about everything that comes out, you'll know David Drake from David Weber, and you'll see immense differences between two given books.

In fractal terms, if you get close enough, you'll find that two random military sf books differ to precisely the same degree that two random sf books do. It's all a matter of perspective.

III

(Nov 2013) Military sf is a particularly tricky genre, both for writers and readers. This is in large part because there's not just one audience for military sf: there are at least four. And while it goes without saying that all of these audiences want good science fiction, each of them is looking for something a little different.

The first audience is made up of current and ex-military sf readers. These folks want to see sf stories that speak to their own military experience; they want military sf that rings true for them.

The second audience consists of military history buffs. These are the kind of readers who pay attention to strategy and tactics, and are intimately familiar with the battles and personalities of the Civil War, World War II, Ancient Greece, the Napoleonic Wars, or obscure campaigns from the Middle Ages.

The third audience are the techno-enthusiasts who come to military sf for the technology. For these readers, it's important that the tech—real or imagined—be well-described and internally consistent.

Finally, the last audience is the folks who are in it for the adventure; they want good characters, lots of action, and enough plot to hold it all together.

It's a rare author who can forge all these different desires and expectations together into a single work that satisfies all four audiences.

Titles Reviewed
- *Written in Time* by Jerry & Sharon Ahern [186]
- *Prometheus II* by S. J. Byrne [215]
- *The Lost Fleet: Relentless* by Jack Campbell [215]
- *Ride the Star Winds* by A. Bertram Chandler [220]
- *To the Galactic Rim* by A. Bertram Chandler [219]
- *Monster Hunter Legion* by Larry Correia [227]
- *Guardian of Night* by Tony Daniel [233]
- *The Road of Danger* by David Drake [243]
- *The Crucible of Empire* by Eric Flint and K. D. Wentworth [251]
- *Fire With Fire* by Charles E. Gannon [265]
- *Star Wars: Fate of the Jedi: Omen* by Christie Golden [266]
- *Death's Head: Day of the Damned* by David Gunn [271]
- *A Few Good Men* by Sarah A. Hoyt [289]
- *Mass Effect: Retribution* by Drew Karpyshyn [303]
- *Through Struggle, The Stars* by John J. Lumpkin [328]
- *Exogene* by T. C. McCarthy [338]
- *Blood of Tyrants* by Naomi Novik [363]
- *The Battle for Commitment Planet* by Graham Sharp Paul [367]
- *Citadel* by John Ringo [376]
- *Children No More* by Mark L. Van Name [420]
- *Ragnarok* by Patrick A. Vanner [421]
- *Transgalactic* by A. E. Van Vogt [422]
- *House of Steel* by David Weber and BuNine [427]
- *A Rising Thunder* by David Weber [428]
- *Wolf Among the Stars* by Steve White [431]
- *Extremis* by Steve White and Charles E. Gannon [432]
- *Unfriendly Persuasion* by Steven H. Wilson [442]
- *Beginnings* by David Weber et al [453]
- *By Other Means* edited by Mike McPhail [455]
- *Dogs of War* edited by Mike McPhail [457]

- *In Fire Forged* edited by David Weber [461]
- *Man-Kzin Wars XIII* created by Larry Niven [463]
- *War World: Discovery* edited by John F. Carr [475]

Mooreeffoc

(Jan/Feb 2010) People read science fiction for many different reasons, reasons that vary from reader to reader; even the same reader can be looking for different things at different times or in different moods.

One big reason people read sf (and fantasy, but that's another matter) is to experience places, people, and things beyond the everyday world: exotic planets, fascinating futures, alien beings and cultures, superhuman achievers. In lit-crit circles this is called "otherness"—the depiction and appreciation of that which is unlike oneself. It's this focus on otherness that leads many mundanes to dismiss sf as "escape literature." Science fiction readers, they imagine, must seek to experience otherness in order to escape the real world which dissatisfies us.

As we all know, that's only part of the story. Sure, some of it is a desire to escape, at least temporarily, the real world around us. The rest, though, is the marvelous way that otherness allows us to experience everyday reality from different perspectives. It's often said that you never really know your own native language until you learn another; similarly, we don't truly know our own reality until we spend some time in another.

It was Maestro Tolkien, quoting G.K. Chesterton's riff on Dickens, who gave us a wondrous term for this phenomenon: mooreeffoc. All of those fine English gentlemen, you see, spent many hours in Britain's ubiquitous Coffee-rooms (here-and-now we call them Starbucks). From the outside, these establishments are totally ordinary and familiar, with their plate glass windows bearing the letters "Coffee-Room." But from inside, ah, the letters spell out something exotic, enticing, glamorous: "mooreeffoc."

This is the perspective that the otherness of sf can offer: a new way of looking at the ordinary, a way to see magic in the everyday. Escape literature? Yes: because sometimes you can only see aspects of reality by escaping it and looking back.

Titles Reviewed

- *Of Wind and Sand* by Sylvie Bérard [200]
- *The Sunless Countries* by Karl Schroeder [394]
- *The Highest Frontier* by Joan Slonczewski [401]

Movies

(May 2013) From the very beginning, science fiction and the movies have been partners in a love-hate relationship. One one hand, the pairing is a natural one: both sf readers and movie viewers are looking for the proverbial "sense of wonder," and written sf abounds in unusual visions and grand spectacles that just cry out for realization on the big screen. Yet on the other hand, written sf can be a very cerebral pursuit, uniquely suited to presentation in words rather than pictures—almost the opposite of what makes a good film. In this relationship, tension is inevitable.

This hasn't stopped a constant cross-fertilization between the worlds of print and film. It started almost as soon as movies did: the first science fiction film came out in 1902. (This was *Le Voyage dans la lune* aka *A Trip to the Moon* by Georges and Gaston Méliès -- notable for its iconic image of the Man in the Moon with a rocket ship protruding from one eye, which has become a part of popular culture.) Nowadays, of course, sf movies are hugely popular, and most action/adventure films include sf-inspired elements.

From the perspective of the sf reader (I trust we all know one or two of those, eh?), cross-fertilization generally flows in one direction or the other, from written sf to film or vice versa. The reality is a bit more complex. Let's look at some cases.

Sometimes an existing sf book is made into a movie, with varying degrees of fidelity to the original book. Some of the classics of sf cinema have been produced this way: think of Disney's *Twenty Thousand Leagues Under the Sea* (1954), George Pal's *The Time Machine* (1960), Nathan Juran's *The First Men in the Moon* (1964), Franklin J. Schaffner's *Planet of the Apes* (1968), or Richard Fleischer's *Soylent Green* (1973, based on Harry Harrison's novel *Make Room! Make Room!*). There are many contemporary examples, although many of the best sf books remain unfilmed.

When judging the success of these movies-from-books, readers must be conscious of (at least) two dimensions. The question of whether the movie is a faithful adaptation of a book should be distinct from the question of whether it stands as a good movie. SF movies fall everywhere along both axes. The Holy Grail, a great movie that's utterly faithful to the book, is seldom achieved.

Sometimes a movie is an original conception, based on no single book. *Le Voyage dans la lune* fell into this category; it was loosely based on work by Jules Verne and H.G. Wells. Fred M. Wilcox's 1956 masterpiece *Forbidden Planet* is a prime example; the story certainly owes a debt to Shakespeare's *The Tempest*, but was largely the original work of screenplay writer Cyril Hume. Many popular sf films are such original productions, including some of the top grossing films of all time. Franchises such as *Star Wars*, *Star Trek*, and *The Matrix* were originals, as were standalone blockbusters like *Avatar*, *Inception*, and *ET: the Extraterrestrial*. (Yes, yes, yes, all of these were highly derivative from the corpus of sf literature—but the point is, they didn't stem from a single identifiable book.)

In almost all cases, the producers of an original movie commission the writing of a book version of the movie. Sometimes these "novelizations" are written by big-name writers. The novelization of *Forbidden Planet*, released under the pseudonym W.J. Stuart, was penned by bestselling mystery writer Philip MacDonald. Isaac Asimov wrote the novelization of *Fantastic Voyage* (1966). Some writers are well-known for their skill at producing novelizations: Alan Dean Foster and Kevin J. Anderson spring instantly to mind.

In most cases, novelizations are written based on a movie's original screenplay, so they can be in print by the film's release date. Since it's not uncommon for a screenplay to go through many versions during the filming process. sometimes events in the novelization diverge from those in the final film. In general, though, a novelization remains fairly faithful to its movie.

From a reader's perspective, a novelization can usually be judged solely on the quality of the book as a book.

Sometimes things are more complicated. The book and movie versions of Arthur C. Clarke and Stanley Kubrick's *2001: A Space Odyssey* (1968) were produced simultaneously with constant feedback between writer and producer. Still, there were some major differences between book and movie. (To complicate matters still more, the project was loosely based on Clarke's 1948 short story "The Sentinel.")

That's not the end. Clarke's 1982 sequel novel, *2010*, was consciously written as a sequel to the movie, not the book. The 1984 Peter Hyams film was firmly based on the book, but took liberties of its own.

An extreme example of cross-fertilization is the case of Paul Verhoeven's 1990 film *Total Recall*. The movie was based on Philip K. Dick's 1966 story "We Can Remember it For You Wholesale." That film was novelized by Piers Anthony as *Total Recall*.

Titles Reviewed
- *Transformers: Dark of the Moon* by Peter David [237]
- *Star Wars: Fate of the Jedi: Omen* by Christie Golden [266]
- *Transformers: Exodus* by Alex Irvine [293]
- *Star Wars: Scoundrels* by Timothy Zahn [451]
- *Claws & Saucers* by David Elroy Goldweber [492]
- *Jar Jar Binks Must Die* by Daniel M. Kimmel [497]
- *John Carter and the Gods of Hollywood* by Michael D. Sellers [513]

Music & SF

(May 2012) Almost as long as science fiction has been around, music has been there as well. There's nothing mysterious about this. Music is an important element of the human experience, and there isn't a part of human culture that science fiction hasn't addressed, one way or another.

In some sf, music is a bit of stage-dressing, one of many details that writers include to flesh out their imagined worlds. Thus, in E.E. "Doc" Smith's *Skylark* series, the Earth heroes amaze and amuse alien races with old-fashioned singalongs. Communal concerts add color to Arthur C. Clarke's *Songs of Distant Earth*, and in Frank Herbert's *Dune* series minstrel Gurney Halleck was always strumming his baliset. Music comes up often in Zenna Henderson's stories of *The People*. This sort of thing works far better in movie and tv sf, where viewers can actually see and hear the alien or futuristic music. In the *Star Wars* films we have the Mos Eisley cantina band and performers in Jabba the Hutt's palace. *Star Trek* gave us Spock's Vulcan harp and Uhura's haunting vocals. Movies as diverse as *Forbidden Planet* and *The Fifth Element* have featured musical performances by aliens, as have TV shows from *Alien Nation* to *Stargate: Atlantis*. And let's not forget poor HAL singing "Daisy, Daisy..." in *2001: A Space Odyssey*.

By far the most extensive use of music for verisimilitude was in Ursula K. LeGuin's tour de force *Always Coming Home*, in which indigenous music is one of many well-wrought anthropological details that define her post-apocalyptic society; when the book first came out, it came accompanied with a cassette tape of "native" music.

Frequently, sf uses traditional songs as a way to present important background information as well. Robert A. Heinlein and Poul Anderson were big users of this technique, but the true master has to be Cordwainer Smith, whose uniquely lyrical prose was itself almost a form of music.

In other sf, music is an actual important plot element. In Isaac Asimov's *Foundation and Empire*, the villainous Mule uses a musical instrument called a Visi-Sonor to control emotions (an instrument to which the tv show *Futurama* paid marvelous homage in several episodes). Robert A. Heinlein's "The Green Hills of Earth" is all about a song. *Space Opera* by Jack Vance concerns a spacefaring opera troupe who use music for diplomatic purposes. *Songmaster* by Orson Scott Card (an expansion of his short story "Mikal's Songbird" in the May 1978 issue of *Analog*) is all about music and its importance. Kathleen Ann Goonan's *Nanotech Quartet* (*Queen City Jazz* and sequels) uses jazz extensively, and music figures prominently in Mary Doria Russell's *The Sparrow* and its sequels.

During the 1960's and 70's, the rebellious spirit of rock music infused a lot of New Age sf, especially the work of Michael Moorcock (who was part of the band Hawkwind), Samuel R. Delany, and Thomas M. Disch. The theme of music as rebellion also featured in many of the works of the cyberpunk movement. In John Shirley's *Eclipse* trilogy, musician Rick Rickenharp became the central figure in worldwide revolution, and the punk music aesthetic figured heavily in Paul Di Filippo's *Ciphers*, William Gibson's *Idoru*, and Bruce Sterling's *Zeitgeist*, among many others.

Some science fiction trades on the concept of music as the universal language to portray music as a way to communicate with alien beings. I'm sure we all remember the five-tone motif from *Close Encounters of the Third Kind*, and the scene of a musical scientist jamming with the mothership. In Spider and Jeanne Robinson's *Stardance* trilogy, music and dance were the only way to communicate with the aliens; *Blood Music* by Greg Bear had a completely different take on music and alien intelligence. In my own *The Leaves of October*, arboreal aliens use mental music to stitch together a multi-species galaxy.

And then there's the queen of musical sf, the late Anne McCaffrey. Music informs just about all of her work. In her *Dragonriders of Pern* series, music is local color, provides background information, provides at least one major plot point, and is central to one sub-series, the Harper Hall trilogy. One of the saga's most important and beloved characters, the Masterharper Robinton, is a musician.

In McCaffrey's *Crystal Singer* series, music is essential for interstellar travel, and the series revolves around the challenges and triumphs of the musician.

Recently, the field has seen a number of anthologies based on the intersection of music with sf. *Stars*, edited by Janis Ian and Mike Resnick, featured stories inspired by Ian's music. Last year's *Music for Another World*, edited by Mike Harding, was made up of sf stories on the theme of music in general. Among the most interesting examples is *Eighty-Nine*, edited by Jodi Cleghorn: this one is a collection of speculative fiction stories (including some sf) based on a playlist of 26 specific songs from 1989.

And then there's the music itself. Themes and styles from sf movies and tv have taken their place in popular culture. Think of the electronic music of *Forbidden Planet*, or the iconic themes from 2001, *Doctor Who*, *Star Trek*, and *Star Wars*.

Titles Reviewed

- *Aurora in Four Voices* by Catherine Asaro [190]
- *Carnelians* by Catherine Asaro [190]
- *In the Lion's Mouth* by Michael Flynn [254]
- *This Shared Dream* by Kathleen Ann Goonan [267]
- *Year Zero* by Rob Reid [372]
- *Sine Fiction* [401]

Nonfiction

(Jan 2017) The magazine I write for is currently titled *Analog Science Fiction and Fact*. Through the decades the exact title has varied, but it's always included "Fact" as well as "Fiction."

Analog readers are interested in a vast variety of subjects: Science, technology, history, space exploration...and, of course, the field of science fiction itself. That's why I try to include a nonfiction book or two in just about every column.

Every once in a while I learn of something that doesn't exactly fit an established category—a website, say, or a collection of comic strips. Those items also land in the Nonfiction section.

One last word. Biographies of SF professionals are so popular that I've placed them in their own distinct category, Biography.

Titles Reviewed

- *Starship Century* edited by James Benford and Gregory Benford [474]
- *Wookiee-Ookkies* by Kevin Bolk [487]
- *Ensign Sue Must Die* by Kevin Bolk and Clare Moseley [487]
- *The Lives of Stars* by Ken Crowell [488]
- *Galaxiki* [489]
- *The Science of Fear* by Daniel Gardner [490]
- *Claws & Saucers* by David Elroy Goldweber [492]
- *Physics of the Impossible* by Michio Kaku [493]
- *What Technology Wants* by Kevin Kelly [495]
- *Jar Jar Binks Must Die* by Daniel M. Kimmel [497]
- *From the Pen of Paul* edited by Stephen D. Korshak [498]
- *How to Defeat Your Own Clone* by Kyle Kurpinski and Terry D. Johnson [499]
- *Why Beautiful People Have More Daughters* by Alan S. Miller and Satoshi Kanazawa [500]

- *Rocket Girl* by George D. Morgan [502]
- *Time Travel* by Paul J. Nahin [503]
- *The Science of Doctor Who* by Paul Parsons [503]
- *Scatter, Adapt, and Remember* by Annalee Newitz [504]
- *Death From the Skies!* By Philip Plait, Ph.D. [507]
- *Hank Reinhardt's Book of Knives* by Hank Reinhardt [508]
- *The Business of Science Fiction* by Mike Resnick and Barry N. Malzberg [509]
- *John Carter and the Gods of Hollywood* by Michael D. Sellers [513]
- *A New American Space Plan* by Travis S. Taylor with Stephanie Osborn [515]
- *The Medea Hypothesis* by Peter Ward [516]
- *The Great Heinlein Mystery* by Edward M. Wysocki, Jr. [518]

Prisons

(Apr 2010) Prisons have been an element in science fiction ever since the evil goddess Issus tossed Dejah Thoris into that revolving jail cell at the end of *The Gods of Mars* (Edgar Rice Burroughs, 1918). More often than not, prison is a plot device, another obstacle that the protagonist must overcome on the way to the happy ending. The Good Guys are thrown in prison, where they must band together with other inmates and find a way to escape (no, this isn't why science fiction is called "escape literature.") Escape from prison played a major role in Alfred Bester's *The Stars My Destination*. In the movie *Escape From New York* and similar tales, getting out of prison is the whole story.

In other stories, prison is part of the background, a deliberate element in the author's worldbuilding, with a specific impact on the shape of the story. This is often where we find the fine old concept of the "prison planet"—a sort of Australia in space, where criminals and dissidents transported for life make a society, usually one that's superior in some fashion or another. In Heinlein's *The Moon is a Harsh Mistress*, the Moon is a prison planet that breaks away from Earth in a parallel to the American Revolution. In Frank Herbert's *Dune* universe, the Empire's harsh prison planet Salusa Secundus is a breeding ground for the Emperor's personal guard, the most vicious and feared fighters in the Galaxy. *Alien 3* and *THX 1138* are both movies in which prisons, one way or another, are part of the background. The classic TV show *The Prisoner* was set almost entirely in one of the most bizarre prison communities ever conceived (and no, I didn't understand the ending either).

Then there are those rare sf stories that deal with prison as a concept, usually in the larger context of the moral nature of crime and punishment. In Anthony Burgess' *A Clockwork Orange*, for example, juvenile delinquent Alex accepts psychological conditioning as an alternative to prison time as punishment for his crimes. In "Coventry," Robert Heinlein had antisocial citizens given a choice between psychological adjustment or exile to an anarchist region separated from the rest of the country by an impenetrable force field. Robert Silverberg's story "To See the Invisible Man" (the basis for a 1986 *Twilight Zone* episode) substitutes psychological imprisonment for physical, having convicts treated as if they were invisible to others; similarly, in Melissa Scott's *The Kindly Ones* those who transgress the law are declared "dead" and become socially-invisible "ghosts."

Science fiction has come up with a number of other innovative ways to handle prisoners. Instead of a prison planet, one can play tricks with time: exile prisoners to the distant past, accelerate their personal time so that a sentence of many subjective years lasts only minutes or days objectively, or do the reverse and suspend their personal time by freezing or other form of hibernation (this last has been practiced everywhere from *Star Trek* to *Lost in Space*). Prisoners can serve their sentences in virtual worlds, robot or android bodies, or some high-tech variation of solitary confinement. In the *Red Dwarf* episode "Justice," convicts suffer whatever harm they did to their victims.

Interestingly enough, the inmates in science fiction prisons are usually not the habitual criminals and incorrigible psychopaths that we imagine occupy present-day prisons. Oh, there are exceptions, truly bad people who usually get their just deserts by the end of the story—but most characters one encounters in sf prisons don't really belong there. If they aren't innocents herded into concentration camps, they are prisoners of war, political prisoners, or just plain malcontents jailed by an establishment that wants them out of the way. If they were actual criminals, they have usually reformed during their time in the slammer. On a prison planet or other prison colony, those who survive are deemed to have proven their moral worth by virtue of that survival. The hapless hero unfairly thrown into prison can always count on finding other unjustly-imprisoned individuals as friends and allies. In fact, frequently the hero manages to organize these noble souls into a mass escape or rebellion against the powers that be. The heroic interstellar rebels of *Blake's 7* met on board a transport to the evil Federation's prison planet.

Why don't we see more hardened criminals in sf prisons, or stories dealing with prison-as-punishment-for-crime? For one thing, many science fiction stories implicitly accept the convention of advanced societies in which criminal behavior is regarded as a symptom of mental illness, which is treated or cured. This idea is made explicit in the classic *Star Trek* episodes "Whom Gods Destroy" and "Dagger of the Mind," in which two prison planets hold the mere handful of criminally insane inmates who have not yet responded to rehabilitation treatment. Contrariwise, a repressive or totalitarian establishment can usually just execute hardened criminals or wipe their brains and set them to work in the mines (any respectable dictator always has a few mines around). Once you cure (or otherwise eliminate) all the true criminals, what you have left as prisoners are people who, one way or another, don't fit into your enlightened (or repressive) society.

Viewed in this light, the whole matter of prisons and prisoners can be seen as another expression of one of the overarching themes of science fiction (and, for that matter, much of American mundane literature): the individual's place in society, and the tension between the two. Here the prisoner (like the alien, the psionic superman, the gifted genius, and the time traveler) is yet another manifestation of the Outsider. Unfairly separated from a society that doesn't accept or want him, the Outsider can flee that society altogether (escape from prison), integrate into the society (work for rehabilitation), attempt to overthrow the society (lead a revolution), or craft a version of society more to his liking (seek independence for the prison planet).

This month I have for you two books that deal specifically with prison, another that features themes of imprisonment, and a graphic novel that includes a prison planet.

Titles Reviewed

- *The Prisoner* by Carlos J. Cortes [226]
- *The Eternal Prison* by Jeff Somers [404]

Robots

(Nov 2011) In Matt Groening's *Futurama*, delivery boy Philip J. Fry is asked, "You really want a robot for a friend?" His enthusiastic reply: "Yeah! Ever since I was six." This one exchange perfectly illustrates the fascination of sf readers with robots. And later the series sums up our ambivalent feelings toward them, as Fry's robot friend Bender repeats his mantra "Kill all humans." Love them or fear them, robots are an integral part of science fiction.

By now the literary antecedents of robots are so well known that I'm sure you can recite them along with me. The *Iliad* refers to gold mechanical servants constructed by Hephaestus; both Norse and Jewish mythology include humanlike clay creatures (giants and golems, respectively); Talus the "iron man" in Edmund Spenser's 1590 epic poem *The Faerie Queene*; the monster in Mary Shelley's *Frankenstein*; Carlo Collodi's *Pinocchio*; and of course Tik-Tok from the *Oz* books.

The word "robot" (derived from Czech words for "worker") comes from Karel Capek's 1921 play R.U.R. (which stands for Rossum's Universal Robots).

Pre-Golden Age sf was filled with robots: notable examples include Edmond Hamilton's *The Metal Giants* (1926), David H. Keller's "The Threat of the Robot" (1929), and Harl Vincent's "Rex" (1934). (I'd love to put in a plug for Neil R. Jones's 1930s-era "Professor Jameson" stories, but their lovable main characters were cyborgs—biological brains in mechanical bodies—and not true robots. Another column, perhaps.)

In the Golden Age robots were further refined by such authors as Eando Binder (whose Adam Link stories were published in book form as *I, Robot* in 1938), Lester Del Rey ("Helen O'Loy," 1938), Jack Williamson (the *Humanoids* series, beginning in 1947); and of course, Isaac Asimov (Positronic Robots series, beginning in 1940).

Robot stories continued in the sf of later eras. Of particular note are Fred Saberhagen's *Berserker* stories (1963); Philip K.

Dick's *Do Androids Dream of Electric Sheep?* (1968); Ira Levin's *The Stepford Wives* (1972); John Sladek's *Roderick* (1980); Tanith Lee's *The Silver Metal Lover* (1982); and Charles Stross's *Saturn's Children* (2008).

Movies have featured a long string of robots: Futura (aka Maria) in *Metropolis* (1927); Gort in *The Day the Earth Stood Still* (1951); Robby (*Forbidden Planet*, 1956, and numerous other appearances); drones Huey, Dewey, and Louie from *Silent Running* (1972); the murderous robots of *Westworld* (1973); the droids of *Star Wars* (1977) and sequels; the androids Ash (*Alien*, 1979) and Bishop (*Aliens* 1986); Dot Matrix (*Spaceballs*, 1987); *The Terminator* (1984 and sequels); *WALL-E* (2008); the list goes on and on.

Television has also had its share of robots, probably because it requires minimal makeup and special effects for a human actor to portray a robot. Robby had a fruitful career as a guest star in many TV shows. *The Jetsons* (1962) brought us Rosie the robot maid; *Doctor Who* (1963) featured so many robots that it's easy to lose track; *Astro Boy* debuted in 1963. Those who wasted too much of their childhoods on bad TV (like me) will surely remember *Tobor The 8th Man* (1965), the Robby-inspired Robot from *Lost in Space* (1965), and Hymie the Robot from *Get Smart* (1964). Of particular note are the robot Questor in 1974's *The Questor Tapes* and the Cylons from *Battlestar Galactica* (both the 1978 original and the 2004 remake).

In more recent times the number of TV robots has exploded, and it's impossible to list even the most notable. Still, one must acknowledge *The Transformers* (1984), Data (*Star Trek: The Next Generation*, 1987), the wacky robots of *Mystery Science Theatre 3000* (1988), and the aforementioned Bender (*Futurama*, 1999).

And what discussion of famous sf robots could be complete without mentioning Marvin the Paranoid Android from Douglas Adams's *Hitchhiker's Guide to the Galaxy*?

Writers of sf have approached robots from three different (but not necessarily exclusive) directions. We might call these Robot-as-Menace, Sympathetic-Robot, and Robot-as-Tool.

Robot-as-Menace is the old Frankenstein formula: robots out to destroy us. Either they invade, or they rebel, or they serve us so well that we lose our initiative and die off. One way or another, robots replace us.

In the Sympathetic-Robot approach, the robot is a full-fledged character in the story, usually with a kind heart (mechanical though it may be). In extreme examples we get the Pinocchio story of the robot who ultimately wants to be human.

With Robot-as-Tool, robots are generally there to do a job—usually a job that humans can't or won't do. (When robots take jobs away from humans, the story shades over into Robot-as-Menace.)

Often (as in Asimov's Positronic Robot stories or *Futurama*) all three elements appear. Some robots are tools, some are menaces, and others are sympathetic characters.

One related theme that I haven't explored is Artificial Intelligence. While robots can be A.I.s, the A.I. story is essentially a different beast...one that we'll take up at another time.

Titles Reviewed

- *Transformers: Dark of the Moon* by Peter David [237]
- *Transformers: Exodus* by Alex Irvine [293]
- *Robopocalypse* by Daniel H. Wilson [441]

Series

(Jun 2010) Series. Love them or hate them, there's no denying that series are everywhere in science fiction. Sequels, trilogies, longer series both finite and open-ended have been with us since the time of Jules Verne at least (although Homer was known to dabble—*The Odyssey* is a sequel to *The Iliad*, after all—and Dante's *Divine Comedy* is arguably the first science fiction trilogy on record.)

In one sense, it's not unusual that science fiction should so frequently spill beyond the covers of a single volume. An important part of any well-wrought SF tale is a consistent, detailed background compellingly different from readers' present-day world. Even a long novel is hardly roomy enough to explore an entire world, much less a planetary system or galactic empire. Even when the story is over and the characters have all met their deserved ends, readers may want to see more of the universe—and the writer may not have explored all the nooks and crannies. (Besides, developing a good universe is hard work...who can blame a writer who wants to conserve time and brainpower by reusing a good background?)

This is why some critics have suggested that the natural form for book-length science fiction is the trilogy, as opposed to the single novel. (In the short fiction realm, you'll see similar arguments that the novelette or novella is the natural length for sf.)

Science fiction is not the only genre where series proliferate, by the way. Our sister field, fantasy, has long had a much higher series count. In mystery fiction, Arthur Conan Doyle showed the way and Dame Agatha Christie blazed a trail that has since become a twelve-lane superhighway. Ever since the MacDonald/McBain Act of 1964, it has been illegal for any author to write a mystery novel that is not part of a series. (Okay, I made that up...but it sure seems like the truth, doesn't it?) Westerns, romances, Christian fiction, and military fiction of the Tom Clancy/W.E.B. Griffin stripe are all dominated by series books. Series are still fairly rare but increasing in the thriller, historical fiction, and horror genres. Even literary fiction authors occasionally yield to the series urge.

From a publisher's standpoint, series are particularly desirable. Publishing is a business, and business thrives on consistency and predictable sales. The sequel to a popular book, or the second or third volume of a trilogy, represent a much surer sale than an original title. A well-selling ongoing series is money in the bank for publisher and author alike.

Here's the rub. In science fiction and fantasy, "series" isn't the simple matter it is in other genres. In mundane fiction, a series almost always involves continuing characters: a specific detective or cowboy, or (in romances) a particular family. In SF and fantasy, the word "series" has as many meanings as "snow" does to the proverbial Eskimo.

Some critics have made stabs at creating terms for various kinds of series, differentiating (for example) "serials" from "milieus" and "narrative arcs" from "sagas." And there's always the fallback "in the same universe." However, there is no generally accepted terminology, and I'm certainly not going to foist such a baroque system on long-suffering *Analog* readers. But what do we mean when we say that books are "in a series"?

The simplest form of series is a continuing narrative that's published in more than one volume. The book may be too big (like *Lord of the Rings*) or it may take a while to write, or there may be other legitimate reasons the publisher issues separate chunks over time (Robert Sawyer's *Neanderthal Parallax* series is a good recent example). The key here is that the whole narrative is planned as a unit, regardless of how many physical volumes wind up in the bookstore. There is continuity of characters and storyline across the series.

Another simple form of series is the humble sequel or succession of sequels. Here, the first book usually stands alone, but is successful enough that the author decides (for whatever reasons, generally including money) to revisit the characters, story, or background. Edgar Rice Burroughs was a master of successive sequels. Fred Pohl wrote *The Merchant's War* as a sequel to *The Space Merchants*, Hal Clement gave us *Star Light* and *Through the Eye of a Needle* as sequels to *Mission of Gravity* and *Needle*. After many years Arthur Clarke wrote several sequels to *2001: A Space Odyssey*, and Isaac Asimov was persuaded to continue both the *Foundation* and *Positronic Robot* series. And I will go to my grave believing that when he made *Star Wars*, George Lucas was not planning to make any more movies in that universe.

A series of sequels often has some continuity of characters or storyline, but the most defining attribute is continuity of background.

Things get a little more complex when books in a series break out of chronological order. Easiest is a single prequel: a story set earlier in time than the main series, but having some strong relationship to the first book(s). Think of Episodes 1-3 of *Star Wars*, or Asimov's *Prelude to Foundation* and *Forward the Foundation*, or Lois McMaster Bujold's *Vorkosigan* series. Here there may still be some overlap in characters and storyline, but the continuity of background is much more important.

It gets more complicated when an author remains in the same universe but bids farewell to the characters and storyline of the first books. Anne McCaffrey's *Moreta* and *Nerilka's Story* take place centuries before the preceding Pern books, and have little direct relationship to those titles—and *Dragonsdawn* goes back two millennia to the initial colonization of the planet. Later books have featured different eras of Pernese history.

In these cases, continuity of background is everything. In fact, one of the joys of reading this sort of book is discovering the roots (or later fates) of elements and people from the first books.

One fairly rare permutation is the shared-background series of seemingly-unconnected books that form a larger pattern greater than the sum of its parts, like a mosaic. Gordon

Dickson's *Childe Cycle* is an example, as is my own *Scattered Worlds* series.

A special case of sequels is the "rewrite." Here, an author is dissatisfied with a book and writes a new title as a revision. The most famous case in science fiction is Arthur Clarke's 1948 novella *Against the Sea of Stars*, which he rewrote as *The City and the Stars* (1956). In 1970 Gregory Benford rewrote *Deeper Than the Darkness* as *The Stars in Shroud* (1979). (To complicate matters, Benford also wrote *Beyond the Fall of Night*, a sequel to Clarke's later-rewritten *Against the Fall of Night*.)

Most abstract of all, a series can be a set of books that share a continuity of theme or idea. Asimov revisited *Fantastic Voyage* (1966) in 1987 and produced *Fantastic Voyage II: Destination Brain*, which was a completely different story, with different characters, and set in a different universe, but based on the same notion. Still later, Kevin J. Anderson wrote *Fantastic Voyage: Microcosm* (2001), which was still another take on the idea of shrinking a submarine of scientists to explore a body.

And now we've come full circle back to Jules Verne, for both *Twenty Thousand Leagues Under the Sea* (1870) and its direct sequel, *The Mysterious Island* (1874), were published as part of a thematic series of novels and nonfiction books called "The Extraordinary Voyages." Other titles in the series included *Journey to the Center of the Earth* (1864), *From the Earth to the Moon* (1865), its own sequel *Around the Moon* (1870), and *Around the World in Eighty Days* (1873).

As I've mentioned in earlier columns, there seems to be a new vogue for authors combining previously-distinct series into multiversal meta-series which can grow to encompass every book the author has ever written (as well as, in some cases, series by other authors as well).

A particularly successful and beloved series becomes that holy grail of publishers and marketers alike, the Franchise. Modern Franchises include Frank Herbert's *Dune*, Anne McCaffrey's *Dragonriders of Pern*, Marion Zimmer Bradley's *Darkover*, and just about every movie or TV series that produces spinoff novels. A Franchise may even continue after the original author's death, with new authors commissioned to write further books.

As with all categorical schemes, these groups are inexact and often overlap. Real-life series are messy things, part one thing and part another.

Take one of the most successful series in science fiction, first published in *Analog's* predecessor, *Astounding Stories*: Doc Smith's Lensman series. The four middle books—*Galactic Patrol* (193), *Gray Lensman* (1940), *Second Stage Lensman* (1942), and *Children of the Lens* (1948)—form a continuing narrative, and Smith considered them one long story in four volumes. The first book (chronologically), *Triplanetary*, appeared in *Amazing Stories* in 1934, but in 1948 Smith rewrote it (under the same title) to better fit the series. Book number two, *First Lensman*, was published in 1950 to bridge #1 and #3. Sometimes listed as book number seven is *Masters of the Vortex* (1968), a slight rewrite of two 1942 stories set in the same universe, but otherwise unconnected to the series.

Now it gets complex. The Lensman series achieved Franchise status. William B. Ellern wrote an authorized continuation of the series, *New Lensman* (1975)—a portion of which appeared in the April 1966 *Analog* as "Moon Prospector." And in the early 1980s Smith's friend David Kyle published three authorized Lensman novels that fit chronologically between books five and six.

It doesn't stop there. Asimov's now-combined *Foundation* and *Positronic Robot* series have histories just as convoluted, Heinlein's shared-background *Future History* series expanded to become the all-encompassing *World as Myth* meta-series, and don't even get me started on Michael Moorcock's *Eternal Champion* multiverse, which reduces even hardened bibliographers to tears. James Patterson fans think they have it bad trying to figure out which book is part of which series: they should try our side of the fence sometime.

Where there are series, there are numbers—for every reader wants to know the proper order of the books in a series. A simple narrative or open-ended series is easy: start and the beginning and work forward. When books jump around in time, it's more difficult: should one read the books in chronological order, in order of publication, or in some other arrangement? The answer, of course, depends on the series. Sometimes the author has a preference; sometimes fan sites can give hints. In the want of any further information, I usually recommend reading series books in order of publication.

SF Thrillers

(Jun 2012) In the extended family of current genre fiction, science fiction has a tough and scrappy sibling. This genre is more gregarious and considerably more popular, but also somewhat less intelligent. The two often hang out together and play with each other's toys, and unsophisticated friends frequently have trouble telling one from another. I'm speaking, of course, of the genre known as the Thriller.

Like sf, thriller fiction is easy to identify but hard to define. For a story to be sf, it must contain some essential element of science or technology; for a thriller, the essential element is suspense. That doesn't mean that every story with suspense is a thriller; just as the scientific idea is central to an sf story, the suspense is central to a thriller.

Thrillers are big. As I write this, more than half the novels on the New York Times Bestseller List are thrillers; the names of thriller authors such as David Baldacci, Mary Higgins Clark, Robin Cook, Clive Cussler, Dean Koontz, and John Sandford are household names both in publishing and in Hollywood. (And of course one mustn't forget the mega-superstar behind the James Patterson Book-of-the-Month Club.)

There's an entire subgenre of thrillers based on scientific (or pseudo-scientific) concepts; the late Michael Crichton was the absolute king of this type of thriller, borrowing sf ideas from alien invasion (*The Andromeda Strain*) and cyborgs (*The Terminal Man*) to time travel (*Timeline*) and nanotechnology (*Micro*). Lately, Douglas Preston and Lincoln Childs, separately and in collaboration, have become very popular with science-based thrillers.

From the perspective of a science fiction reader, these books seem rather weak; if you're going to read about time travel or nanotech, why not just read some real sf and be done with it? Aren't there science fiction stories that have enough suspense?

That's precisely what I want to talk about in this column. When sf borrows the techniques and tropes of the thriller, the result can be very powerful indeed.

Edgar Allan Poe, master of the suspense story, was also arguably an sf writer, and H. G. Wells gave us an inarguable sf thriller in *The Invisible Man*. The preeminent example, though, was John W. Campbell, Jr.'s classic novella "Who Goes There?" (*Astounding*, 1938) -- filmed as *The Thing From Another World* in 1951 and *The Thing* in 1982. (In this column I usually refer to Campbell in his editorial position; it's well worth remembering that prior to taking the reins at *Astounding*, he was a popular and influential sf author.)

Lester del Rey's 1942 novelette "Nerves" (expanded into a 1956 novel of the same title) is a model thriller set in a nuclear power plant. *The Puppet Masters* by Robert A. Heinlein (1951) perfectly blends the thriller and the alien invasion story, while Alfred Bester did the same with teleportation (*The Stars My Destination*, 1953) and telepathy (*The Demolished Man*, 1956).

The Cold War period spawned a lot of sf thrillers; among the best of them was a book nearly forgotten today, *Who?* by Algis Budrys (1958). In this near-future espionage thriller, a scientist returns from behind the Iron Curtain with his face and half his body replaced by cybernetic prostheses—but is this man the original scientist, or a double agent? The book revolves around the question of his identity, and although its politics and history are long outdated, it's still as thrilling a read as the day it was published.

One can't discuss sf thrillers without mentioning the late Philip K. Dick, much of whose work involved secrets, deceptions, conspiracies, paranoia, chases, and other tropes of thrillerdom. For a long time Dick was our own little secret, but the mundane world discovered him and has been turning his sf thrillers into blockbuster movies ever since. Don't let yourself be satisfied by the films: the books and stories are, if anything, even more suspenseful and thrilling.

In the realm of movies and TV, sf thrillers are far from rare. The Cold War gave us the excellent *Invasion of the Body Snatchers* (1956) and dozens of others, most not so excellent. *Alien* (1979) was a triple-threat combining the genres of sf, thriller, and horror in one movie. *Bladerunner* (1982) owes a debt to Dick (it was based on his novel *Do Androids Dream of Electric Sheep?*) but is certainly its own distinct work.

Most sf television series have episodes that qualify as thrillers: *Doctor Who*, *Firefly*, and *Star Trek* spring immediately to mind. Two series deserve mention as maintaining major thriller aspects throughout: *The Invaders* (1967-68) and *U.F.O.* (1970-71); both were stories of alien invasion. And finally, no discussion of sf thrillers on TV could be complete without bringing up *The Outer Limits* and *Twilight Zone*, both of which have had various incarnations through the years.

Titles Reviewed

- *After America* by John Birmingham [201]
- *The Death Cure* by James Dashner [235]
- *Energized* by Edward M. Lerner [324]
- *Fade to Black* by Josh Pryor [369]
- *Anniversary Day* by Kristin Kathryn Rusch [383]
- *Snipers* by Kristin Kathryn Rusch [384]
- *Amped* by Daniel H. Wilson [440]

Short Stories

(Jul/Aug 2011) Ah, short stories! Who doesn't love a good sf one? I know I'm preaching to the choir here; *Analog* readers obviously appreciate short stories. But what is it about the form that we like so much?

For one thing, a short story is quick to read. When you enter the world of a novel, you know that you're going to be in and out, like a tourist in a fancy parking garage. Like it or not, you have to put the book down now and again to deal with with the real world and its distractions. Not so with a short story; one can often finish in a single setting, so the outside world never has to intrude.

Another appeal of the short story is its focus. Novels have room to spread out all over the place: multiple interesting locations, complex multilayered plots, many intriguing ideas, and the proverbial cast of thousands. A short story, on the other hand, is all about minimalism: one idea, one plot, one major setting, at most a handful of characters. If the best novels are a full-course gourmet meal, the best short stories are a perfect, exquisite, hand-picked strawberry.

This quality of focus allows a short story to pack an enormous punch in a way that longer forms simply can't. Think of some of the classic short stories of the field, and how they left you reeling the first time you read them: Arthur C. Clarke's "The Star," Harlan Ellison's "I Have No Mouth and I Must Scream," or Damon Knight's "To Serve Man."

In terms of focus and punch, you can't beat the "short-short story" of under 1,000 words—the length featured in *Analog's* Probability Zero department. A good short-short is a whiff of ammonia, a shot of smooth whiskey, a bite-size confection that lingers for hours on the taste buds.

Finally, short stories—like tapas or smorgasbord—allow one to sample unfamiliar things. The investment of time isn't huge; if you don't like the story, you haven't lost much. Readers can try out new authors, different genres, exotic voices. Writers can experiment with techniques, viewpoints, modes of expression. And short stories are a great way to introduce sf to those who don't ordinarily read it.

For a long time the sf field was composed almost exclusively of short stories. This period lasted form the foundation of the pulp sf magazines in the 1920s until after World War II, and covered the entire era usually called "The Golden Age of Science Fiction." In those days, the field's most talented writers worked in short stories, and the magazines were the only source of the full variety of SF. However, finding older stories required enormous effort, haunting used book stores and digging through endless bins of moldering pulps.

That changed in 1946, with the publication of perhaps the most important sf anthology ever published. *Adventures in Time and Space*, edited by Raymond J. Healy and J. Francis McComas, collected 33 of the best stories (and 2 essays) from the prewar pulps (most of them originally published in *Astounding*). The list of contributors is a "Who's Who" of Golden Age sf. The commercial success of this anthology demonstrated that there was a market for science fiction in book form; it's entirely fair to call it, as Frederik Pohl did, "the book that started the science-fiction publishing industry."

When the sf community began giving the annual Hugo Awards in 1955, it was only natural to include short stories as one of the main categories. In 1966 the Science Fiction and Fantasy Writers of America (SFWA) followed suit with their own Nebula Award.

While magazines (and now, webzines) have remained an important source of short stories, anthologies and collections are an important way to preserve and spread good stories. (A collection is usually made up of stories by one author, while an anthology consists of many different authors.) *Adventures in Space and Time*, sadly out of print, remains a good source of Golden Age stories. *The Science Fiction Hall of Fame*, edited by Robert Silverberg based on a vote by the membership of SFWA, contains 26 of the best short stories published before 1965.

Over the years, many editors have put together annual "Best of the Year" collections of short stories; currently *The Year's Best Science Fiction* edited by Gardner Dozois is into its 27th year, and editor Rich Horton's *The Year's Best Science Fiction and Fantasy* is on its third annual volume.

Not all anthologies contain reprints. In 1953 Frederik Pohl published *Star Science Fiction*, the first of a series of anthologies of previously-unpublished stories (such an anthology is termed an "original anthology.") Star was essentially a magazine in book form, and that pattern continues today in such anthologies as *The Solaris Book of New Science Fiction* edited by George Mann.

But there's another type of original anthology, and that's the "theme" anthology—a book where all the short stories flow from the same inspiration. These can be as sublime as Bruce Sterling's *Mirrorshades* or Nick Gevers's *Steampunk* (both of which encapsulated entire literary movements: cyberpunk and steampunk respectively) or as ridiculous as my own *Carmen Miranda's Ghost is Haunting Space Station Three*. The heyday of theme anthologies was the mid 1970s, when literally hundreds of them flooded the market—as much as 25% of them produced by a single editor (the infamous Roger Elwood).

Titles Reviewed

Single-Author Collections

- *A Legacy of Stars* by Danielle Ackley-McPhail [186]
- *Aurora in Four Voices* by Catherine Asaro [190]
- *We'll Always Have Paris* by Ray Bradbury [207]
- *A Glimpse of Splendor and Other Stories* by Dave Creek [230]
- *Decimated* by Jack Dann and George Zebrowski [234]
- *Maine Quartet* by Thomas A. Easton [247]
- *Worlds* by Eric Flint [253]

- *A Liaden Universe Constellation: Volume 1* by Sharon Lee and Steve Miller [322]
- *Frontiers of Space, Time, and Thought* by Edward M. Lerner [325]
- *After the Sundial* by Vera Nazarian [357]
- *Stars and Gods* by Larry Niven [359]
- *Near + Far* by Cat Rambo [371]
- *Win Some, Lose Some* by Mike Resnick [374]
- *Dream of Venus* by Pamela Sargent [234]
- *Sex and Violence in Zero-G* by Allen Steele [410]
- *The Best of Connie Willis* by Connie Willis [438]
- *The Best of Gene Wolfe* by Gene Wolfe [443]

Original Anthologies

- *Beginnings* by David Weber et al [453]
- *By Other Means* edited by Mike McPhail [455]
- *Dark Futures* edited by Jason Sizemore [456]
- *Dogs of War* edited by Mike McPhail [457]
- *Going Interstellar* edited by Les Johnson and Jack McDevitt [458]
- *Golden Reflections* edited by Joan Spicci Saberhagen and Robert E. Vardeman [459]
- *Impossible Futures* edited by Judith K. Dial and Thomas Easton [460]
- *In Fire Forged* edited by David Weber [461]
- *Like Water For Quarks* edited by Elton Elliott & Bruce Taylor [462]
- *Mothership* edited by Bill Campbell and Edward Austin Hall [464]
- *Old Mars* edited by George R. R. Martin and Gardner Dozois [467]
- *Other Earths* edited by Nick Gevers and Jay Lake [468]
- *Shadows of the New Sun* edited by J. E. Mooney and Bill Fawcett [471]

- *The Solaris Book of New Science Fiction Volume Two* edited by George Mann [472]
- *The Solaris Book of New Science Fiction Volume Three* edited by George Mann [473]
- *Starship Century* edited by James Benford and Gregory Benford [474]
- *War World: Discovery* edited by John F. Carr [475]
- *Warrior Wisewoman 2* edited by Roby James [476]
- *Warrior Wisewoman 3* edited by Roby James [478]
- *Welcome to the Greenhouse* edited by Gordon van Gelder [479]
- *Worlds of Edgar Rice Burroughs* edited by Mike Resnick and Robert T. Garcia [480]

Reprint Anthologies

- *The Best Science Fiction & Fantasy of the Year* edited by Jonathan Strahan [454]
- *Like Water For Quarks* edited by Elton Elliott & Bruce Taylor [462]
- *Nebula Awards Showcase 2011* edited by Kevin J. Anderson [465]
- *Nebula Awards Showcase 2013* edited by Catherine Asaro [466]
- *War World: Discovery* edited by John F. Carr [475]
- *The Year's Best Science Fiction, Thirtieth Annual Collection* edited by Gardner Dozois [482]
- *The Year's Best Science Fiction: Twenty-Ninth Annual Collection* edited by Gardner Dozois [481]

Space Opera

(Nov 2010) Space opera isn't what it used to be. And that's a good thing.

When Wilson Tucker coined the phrase in 1941, "space opera" was a term of derision. It was analogous to the earlier term "horse opera," a pejorative label for Western films. Tucker used the expression to refer to "the hacky, grinding, stinking, outworn space-ship yarn." He decidedly did not mean the stuff John Campbell was publishing in *Astounding*; Tucker was thinking of innumerable hack stories appearing in pulp magazines such as *Amazing, Future Fiction, Planet Stories,* and *Comet Stories*. These tales, most of them long forgotten, were also described as "westerns in space"—stories that read as if the author had taken a familiar cowboy story and changed horses to spaceships, six-shooters to blasters, and wide-open prairies to trackless interstellar space.

As sf matured over the next decades, the old-fashioned "western in space" story became scarcer than water in the desert. But "space opera" was too good a phrase to give up. For a while "space opera" meant any adventure story involving space travel, other planets, and/or aliens. Eventually, however, "space opera" came to mean what used to be called "super-science stories" of the sort written in the late 1920s and 1930s by Edmond Hamilton, Jack WIlliamson, and the master of super-science, E. E. "Doc" Smith. By this time, the "super-science story" had fallen out of fashion, and no one was publishing them any more. "Space opera" became a term of affection, heavily flavored by the nostalgia of older fans for the stirring stories of their youth. In this period, space opera was a sort of guilty pleasure among readers.

By now the marketing divisions of publishers, sensing the good feelings that the words "space opera" evoked, started using the term to sell books. Before long, anything and everything was being marketed as space opera—including the likes of *I, Robot* and *Stranger in a Strange Land* (two titles that would top my list of "Books Not At All Resembling Space Opera.") To a degree, this tendency continues today, so be careful when reading publishers's blurbs and other advertising material.

In 1977, a tiny little art film called *Star Wars* brought pure-quill space opera to a larger audience. (If you haven't seen the movie, you'd probably enjoy it.) In the me-too world of film, space opera enjoyed a brief renaissance (although no one called it that outside the sf field).

Notice the delicious anachronistic irony here: those books and stories now falling under the category of space opera were not called that when they appeared. Historians of sf, wrangling over which stories are space opera, are in somewhat the same predicament as modern mundane historians trying to determine what, if any, abnormal psychology applied to Lincoln, Nero, or Akhenaten. Take the works of Olaf Stapledon as a prime example. Stapledon's books *Last and First Men* and *Star Maker* are both star-spanning epics in true space opera fashion, but they certainly aren't "Doc" Smith style super-science stories. If you want a long, pointless argument, ask some old-time sf readers if they are space opera or not.

In the late 1980s a small number of British writers began to consciously reinvent literary space opera in the "Doc" Smith style. These included M. John Harrison, Iain M. Banks, and Paul J. McAuley. (At the same time, Brit Harry Harrison started his *Bill, the Galactic Hero* series, which was a hilarious satire of space opera.) These "new space opera" books were of higher literary quality, featuring non-cardboard characters and more elegant prose, and also included speculations based on cutting-edge science. In time, this new space opera became very popular—as it remains to this day.

But why did the space opera renaissance spring from Britain, not the States? I've seen a number of analyses, but nothing authoritative. My own theory is that American publishers in the 1980s were reluctant to publish space opera, considering it either old-fashioned or like *Star Wars*—and in those pre-Timothy-Zahn days, there was no market for *Star Wars*-like books. It took the Brits to convince American publishers that space opera would sell...at least, space opera written by British writers.

Today's big names in space opera include the fellows mentioned above, and also Steven Baxter, Alastair Reynolds, Ken MacLeod, and Peter F. Hamilton.

Two subgenres often related to space opera are hard sf and military sf. There's a lot of overlap around the edges; it's impossible to draw hard-and-fast dividing lines. Similarly, the subset of sf that deals with Galactic Empires often bleeds into space opera. Are the *Foundation* books space opera? Almost certainly not. The *Dune* books? That one's a little harder.

So what is space opera? The term defies exact description, but lately I've been calling it "grand, melodramatic science fiction productions without the music, but with lots of great scenery, anguish, death, and an occasional fat lady." It's as good a definition as any.

If you want to know more about space opera, look for David G. Hartwell and Kathryn Cramer's comprehensive 2006 anthology *The Space Opera Renaissance*.

Titles Reviewed

- *The High Crusade* by Poul Anderson [187]
- *Young Flandry* by Poul Anderson [188]
- *The Hydrogen Sonata* by Iain M. Banks [194]
- *Caliban's War* by James S. A. Corey [226]
- *In the Lion's Mouth* by Michael Flynn [254]
- *On the Razor's Edge* by Michael Flynn [255]
- *Stargate Atlantis: Homecoming* by Jo Graham and Melissa Scott [270]
- *The Evolutionary Void* by Peter F. Hamilton [275]
- *Great North Road* by Peter F. Hamilton [276]
- *Webdancers* by Brian Herbert [279]

- *Transformers: Exodus* by Alex Irvine [293]
- *Open Your Eyes* by Paul Jessup [296]
- *Dragon Ship* by Sharon Lee and Steve Miller [321]
- *Ghost Ship* by Sharon Lee and Steve Miller [319]
- *A Liaden Universe Constellation: Volume 1* by Sharon Lee and Steve Miller [322]
- *Necessity's Child* by Sharon Lee and Steve Miller [323]
- *Blue Remembered Earth* by Alastair Reynolds [375]
- *Skirmishes* by Kristin Kathryn Rusch [385]
- *Saga* by Brian K. Vaughan and Fiona Staples [423]
- *Count to a Trillion* by John C. Wright [446]
- *The Hermetic Millennia* by John C. Wright [448]
- *Star Wars: Scoundrels* by Timothy Zahn [451]

Steampunk

(Oct 2010) Science fiction, like most areas of human endeavor, has its fashions. Across the history of the field, individual fashions go through a fairly consistent progression. First, someone writes a groundbreaking new story that becomes hugely popular. Then other writers jump on the bandwagon, at first mostly producing imitative and derivative stories to fill the demand created by the seminal work. This goes on for a while. Then, more and more writers explore the new territory, blazing their own trails and taking the original story in different directions. What was a bestseller-and-followups becomes a full-fledged movement. For a time, it seems that everything published is part of the movement.

Eventually the new movement attenuates, like the shell of gas around a nova. Other types of sf reappear, the field returns to its pre-movement diversity...but the movement's influences remain. The movement has become a fashion. Then, slowly, the fashion fades as other things take its place—although its impact remains and the field is stronger for it. After a decade or so, everyone wonders what all the fuss was about.

Take, for instance, one of sf's first fashions: the "super-science" stories of E. E. "Doc" Smith, of which *The Skylark of Space* (1928) was the seminal work. It didn't take long for other writers to join the fun. Before he became editor of *Astounding/Analog*, John W. Campbell, Jr. made his name with his Arcot, Wade, and Morley stories, which were firmly in the Smith style. Edmond Hamilton was another major writer of Smith-like super-science epics.

After a while super-science stories morphed into what we now call "space opera," and a movement came into being. Many of the big names of the field wrote space opera: Ray Cummings, Raymond Z. Gallun, P. Schuyler Miller, and Jack Williamson were particular favorites.

Then, as space opera became a full-fledged fashion, its elements spread through the field, as all manner of writers took them up in stories that went far afield. Galactic Empires, universe-spanning wars, powerful technologies, multitudes of aliens, swashbuckling adventure—all elements that continue to appear in sf to this day.

The most recent fashion in science fiction...and well on its way to being a fashion in larger society as well...is steampunk.

As with most fashions, there's no authoritative definition of exactly what constitutes steampunk. That's entirely fitting, as steampunk is in a period of flux, on the brink of the stage when it will begin to disperse itself across the whole field. But as commonly understood, steampunk involves stories set against an anachronistic quasi-Victorian or -Edwardian background. Steampunk stories may take place in the past, present, or future —but it's an alternate universe in which the primary technology is steam power. It's a world in which Jules Verne and H. G. Wells would be entirely at home.

The first steampunk books, in the early-to-mid 1980s, were published as fantasy rather than science fiction: novels by James Blaylock, K. W. Jeter, and Tim Powers. In fact, it was K. W. Jeter who gave the movement its name, in a tongue-in-cheek letter in 1987.

Steampunk, however, straddles the already-indistinct line between fantasy and science fiction. Since steampunk stories are alternate-universe fiction, a case can be made for considering them to be sf unless they include overt magic or other supernatural elements (some do). Perhaps the best answer is to categorize steampunk as science-fantasy. Or to simply say that if they read like science fiction, then they *are* science fiction.

The first steampunk novel acknowledged as sf was *The Difference Engine* by William Gibson and Bruce Sterling (1990), set in an alternate history in which Charles Babbage's steam-powered analytical engine brought about the computer revolution a hundred years early.

By now, as I said, steampunk has passed beyond the boundaries of sf, fantasy, and even literature itself. Steampunk has become an artform, a musical genre, even a distinct culture. There are steampunk conventions, steampunk dances, and steampunk stores selling all sorts of steampunk merchandise: costumes, goggles, clocks, and assorted objets d'art.

In reality, of course, the aesthetic that we call steampunk has been around since...well, since the Victorian Age itself. Verne and Wells were writing steampunk a century before steampunk existed. Harry Harrison, Keith Laumer, and Michael Moorcock all wrote stories that would definitely be considered steampunk if they were published today. (*Analog* did its part: Harrison's 1973 pre-steampunk novel *A Transatlantic Tunnel, Hurrah!* was serialized starting in the April 1972 issue.)

In media, George Pal's 1960 film *The Time Machine* had a definite steampunk look-and-feel. The TV show *The Wild, Wild West* had a steampunk aesthetic; even *Doctor Who* had its steampunk-ish moments.

So in one sense, steampunk is the newest fashion in sf; in another sense, it's been part of sf since the beginning.

Titles Reviewed

- *Railroad Spine* by Geonn Cannon [217]
- *Tales of the Clockwork Empire* by Ian Duerden [245]
- *Wrath of the Lemming Men* by Toby Frost [362]
- *Steelhands* by Jaida Jones and Danielle Bennett [300]
- *Pinion* by Jay Lake [316]
- *Ghosts of Manhattan* by George Mann [331]
- *Ares Express* by Ian McDonald [341]
- *The Black Lung Captain* by Chris Wooding [445]

Time Travel

(Mar 2010) Time travel has been around at least since the eighteenth century, but it took Charles Dickens (in *A Christmas Carol*, first published in 1843) to introduce the concept into general consciousness. Even then, time travel was always accomplished by supernatural means: angels, demons, spirits of one kind or another.

It wasn't until 1881 that an author came up with a method of time travel linked to a machine: that was Edward Page Mitchell in *The Clock That Went Backward*. H.G. Wells deserves credit for being the first author (in English, at least) to use a true "time machine"—and it's not in the story you're thinking of. Wells' short story "The Chronic Argonauts" appeared in 1888, and tells the story of an inventor named Dr. Moses Nebogipfel and his invention, a machine that travels in time. In the end, Dr. Nebogipfel departs, searching for an era more suited to his abilities (and admit it, haven't we all wanted to do the same, at one point or another?) Wells revisited the concept of mechanical time travel in 1895, with the much more successful short novel *The Time Machine*.

Science fiction in the Gernsback age (before 1939) did not concern itself much with time travel. But in the Campbell "Golden Age" and later, authors such as Heinlein, Asimov, and Poul Anderson took up the theme and wrote some of the seminal works of temporal journeying—many of them in *Analog's* predecessor, *Astounding*.

With a background like that, it may seem heretical to raise the question of whether time travel is truly science fiction at all.

One quick-and-dirty distinction between science fiction and fantasy is this: sf deals with things that are possible, while fantasy is the realm of the impossible. And despite a few promising loopholes in quantum physics, time travel is very probably not possible, at least in the universe as we currently understand it.

Yes, but: loopholes aside, time travel is one of those concepts that has been, as they say, grandfathered in. Sure, the laws of physics make it most unlikely that a real time machine could ever exist—but the same can be said for faster-than-light travel, miniaturization, psionics, and other staples of science fiction. In truth, this is one of those questions which prove that science fiction and fantasy are more a continuum, rather than mutually exclusive categories.

There's a fairly pragmatic rule of thumb that helps draw the line in most time travel stories, and it's based on the exact method used for moving through time. If the temporal displacement is carried out by supernatural forces, magical spells, or sheer force of will, then the story is presumed to be fantasy. If the time travel takes place using a machine, vehicle, gadget, or some other technological-sounding method, then you're most likely dealing with science fiction.

There are many very fine time travel fantasy tales (as well as a great many more dreadful ones, especially since Diana Gabaldon's excellent *Outlander* series established the field of "time travel romances"). Among them are Twain's *A Connecticut Yankee in King Arthur's Court*, Jack Finney's *Time and Again*, Richard Matheson's *Bid Time Return* (filmed as *Somewhere in Time*), and even Audrey Niffeneggar's recent *The Time Traveler's Wife*. But we're here to talk about science fiction, not fantasy.

In sf, there are two basic ways to approach time travel, and both of them revolve around what's called the Grandfather Paradox. For those who aren't familiar with this situation, here's how it goes: A time traveler goes back into the past and kills her own grandfather in the cradle. But if Grandpa dies before he gets together with Grandma, then the time traveler will never be born...so she won't be able to go back and kill Gramps. But if Gramps lives, then his granddaughter will be born after all, will grow up to become the time traveler, and will go back to kill him.

One way out of the Grandfather Paradox is to assume a multiverse of many different parallel and divergent universes. (I talk about the multiverse and alternate universes in the Alternate History section). Our hero kills Grandpa and instantly an alternate timeline branches off: one that contains both dead infant Gramps and the adult time traveler. Unless she can cross universes, the traveler is marooned in a world in which she will never exist. Sometimes there is only one timestream, with previous alternate histories erased.

Various authors have played with this basic notion, perhaps the most definitive being David Gerrold in *The Man Who Folded Himself*.

This approach leads naturally to a much grander concept, that of a corps of time travelers on a mission to police the multiverse and steer the timeline(s) in the direction that seems best to them. Among the classic examples are Jack Williamson's *Legion of Time*, Poul Anderson's *Time Corps* series, Isaac Asimov's *The End of Eternity*, Kage Baker's *Company* series, Heinlein's later "World as Myth" novels, and the Time Lords of *Doctor Who*.

Back to the Grandfather Paradox. There's another answer, and that's to assume that the timestream is absolutely invariant. Everything that has happened, will always have happened. No matter how hard our intrepid hero tries, she will never succeed in killing the infant Grandpa. Her gun will jam, her garrote cord will break, the stresses of time travel will have rendered her poison harmless. Even if she does kill Gramps, it will turn out that Grandma was having an affair with someone else, who (surprise) was her real Grandfather. Anything that seems to be a paradox will inevitably have a logical explanation. In this sort of tale, people are always becoming their own ancestors or descendants (or both), or taking the place of some actual historical figure whom they've accidentally removed from history.

As near as I can tell, the first person to explore this idea was Heinlein, in the story "By His Bootstraps" (in the October 1941 issue of *Astounding*). He later refined the notion in a shorter and tighter story called "—All You Zombies—" in which a whole raft of seeming paradoxes turn out to be nothing more than a matter of perspective. In *The Door Into Summer*, Heinlein explored the question once again; his hero traveled both forward and backward in time and tied up every loose end. Quite a while later, Michael Moorcock's powerful *Behold the Man* showed a time traveler who went back to first-century Jerusalem in search of the historic Jesus, with shattering consequences.

In recent years, the multiverse theory of time travel has become almost the default in science fiction. Part of this, I'm sure, is due to the physicists prattling on about parallel universes and alternate timelines as if they invented them, once again stealing our best ideas and transforming them into banal-but-respectable talk about strings and branes and itty-bitty particles doing bizarre things to one another in the odd corners of spacetime. When Anderson and Heinlein and *Doctor Who* were exploring the multiverse, it was "just science fiction"—but let a few cosmologists get into a drunken gabfest on a train, and suddenly the idea is respectable, thank you very much.

Titles Reviewed

- *This Shared Dream* by Kathleen Ann Goonan [267]
- *Exogene* by T. C. McCarthy [338]
- *Snipers* by Kristin Kathryn Rusch [384]
- *Pirates of the Timestream* by Steve White [430]
- *All Clear* by Connie Willis [437]
- *Blackout* by Connie Willis [435]
- *Golden Reflections* edited by Joan Spicci Saberhagen and Robert E. Vardeman [459]

To the Moon

(May 2011) If there is a story that is quintessentially science fiction, it is the trip to the Moon.

Earth's Moon—huge in proportion to its primary—makes Earth relatively unusual among planets. Scientists have long speculated about the role the Moon played in the development of life on our world, some suggesting that without Luna we would never have seen life at all, the migration of life onto land, Human culture, or the idea of space travel. It can similarly be argued that without the Moon—a nearby world hanging visibly in the sky—science fiction itself would have developed in a far different fashion, if at all.

Writers have been telling stories of trips to the Moon since at least the first century, when Antonius Diogenes had explorers walk there in a book called *Of Wonderful Things Beyond Thule*. Lucius of Samosata's *True Story* (c. 180 C.E.)—a parody of travelers' tales that is arguably the world's first science fiction novel—delivered protagonists to the Moon via waterspout; they found themselves in the thick of interplanetary war.

The real flowering of Moon-trip stories began in the 1630s with astronomer Johannes Kepler's *Somnium*, in which a demon takes the hero to the Moon. Other 17th century Lunar explorers included Bishop Francis Godwin (*The Man in the Moon*, 1638) and Cyrano de Bergerac (*The Other World: The Societies and Governments of the Moon*, 1656). Daniel Defoe took readers moonward in *The Consolidator*, 1705. (The title vessel, *The Consolidator*, is perhaps the first named spaceship in fiction.) Baron Munchhausen went to the Moon in 1786, Washington Irving published *The Conquest of the Moon* in 1809, and even Edgar Allan Poe had a fling with Moon travel in his 1835 story "The Unparalleled Adventure of One Hans Pfaall."

Jules Verne's *From the Earth to the Moon* (1865) and sequel *Around the Moon* (1870) set the stage for hard sf moon voyages and anticipated Apollo in a number of startling ways—his three-man space capsule, for instance, is launched from Florida and splashes down in the Pacific. Verne's astronauts merely circled the Moon (in today's terms, they did a fly-by); in 1901's *The First Men in The Moon* H. G. Wells had his crew set foot on the Lunar surface. Of course, they had the help of that marvelous antigravity compound Cavorite—unfortunately, the secret of its composition never made it back home.

Raised on such dreams of moon landings, the science fiction writers of the pulp age were well-primed to tell tales of Lunar landings and exploration...and tell they did. It's hard to find a pulp-era sf writer of consequence who didn't write about the Moon. Edgar Rice Burroughs turned his attention to the Moon in 1926's *The Moon Men/The Moon Maid* (variously published under both titles). C. L. Moore's hero Northwest Smith adventured on the Moon in *Lost Paradise* (1936). Isaac Asimov's first sale to *Astounding* was a short story called "Trends" (1939), and he revisited the Moon in his 1972 Hugo and Nebula winning novel *The Gods Themselves*. Arthur C. Clarke, an early member of the British Interplanetary Society, made his career with Moon-exploration novels and stories: *Prelude to Space* (1951), "The Sentinel" (1951), *Earthlight* (1955), *Venture to the Moon* (1956), *A Fall of Moondust* (1963)...not to mention his involvement in an obscure film called *2001: A Space Odyssey*.

The preeminent Lunar tourguide in this period was Robert A. Heinlein. In stories such as "Requiem" (1940), "The Black Pits of Luna" (1948), "The Man Who Sold the Moon" (1951), and "The Menace From Earth" (1957) he created a consistent future history of Lunar exploration and colonization. His first children's book, *Rocket Ship Galileo* (1947) sent three teenage boys on the first moon flight. Lunar prison colonies featured in the Hugo-winning *The Moon is a Harsh Mistress* (1966) and *The Cat Who Walks Through Walls* (1985). To legions of readers, the archetypal Moon experience is Kip and Peewee's trek across the Lunar landscape in *Have Space Suit—Will Travel* (1958). Heinlein was also deeply involved in the influential 1950 film *Destination Moon*.

A Cosmos of Many Mansions

You might expect that the Apollo Moon landings would have ruined Lunar science fiction (technological progress is always ruining sf's best notions—see "Mars, Canals of" and "Venus, Oceans of"), but you'd be wrong. Writers of Moon stories since Apollo include Kevin J. Anderson and Doug Beason (*Assemblers of Infinity*, 1993), Ben Bova (*Moonrise*, 1996 and *Moonwar*, 1998), Jack McDevitt (*Moonfall*, 1998), and Allen Steele (*Lunar Descent*, 1991).

Titles Reviewed

- *Back to the Moon* by Travis S. Taylor and Les Johnson [413]

Transhumanism

(Sep 2011) One of the biggest current buzzwords in sf is "transhumanism." Transhumanism is a set of ideas which began in science fiction and were then appropriated by the futurist community; like steampunk, transhumanism has also become something of a pop culture movement.

The concept is a familiar one to science fiction readers. Technological advances, particularly in nanotechnology and genetics, will soon make it possible for us to remake our bodies and minds, enhance our abilities, and conquer death—leading to a radical redefinition of what it means to be human. Modern transhumanism is tied up with Vernor Vinge's notion of the technological singularity, a period when the pace of technological advance becomes so fast that it overwhelms human society and psychology, representing a quantum leap into a future that's literally incomprehensible.

Of course, the idea of a new and improved human race was around in science fiction long before the transhumanism movement came along.

This is the point at which I usually go back to the ancient Greeks, or at least the 1600s, to trace the development of a notion in sf. But transhumanism is something different; the concept doesn't seem to have existed prior to the mid-1800s, and science fiction is arguably the only route through which it could be explored in popular culture.

Here's the story.

Throughout the history of literature, there had always been races superior to humanity: gods, angels, all manner of supernatural entities. But humanity was humanity, and the notion that it could evolve into something better was nonexistent. To be sure, individuals could, through heroic feats, achieve apotheosis and join the ranks of the advanced beings— think of Imhotep, Hercules, Elijah, or the Hindu hero-king Yudhisthira. That was fine for the occasional hero; as for the race as a whole, if there was any change at all, it was a devolution from the Golden Age of the distant past.

Before Darwin spread the idea that species (including humans) could evolve, there was no intellectual framework for imagining that the future of humanity would be any different from its past. And it wasn't until the end of the nineteenth century that philosopher Friedrich Wilhelm Nietzsche introduced his idea of the *übermensch*, a new breed of superior humans.

Nietzsche's ideas would probably have languished in the realms of philosophy and racist politics (where the evolution idea got dropped and various groups proclaimed themselves as the *übermensch*), had it not been for the science fiction writers.

About the same time, *The Time Machine* by H.G. Wells at last depicted a far future in which the human race became something different in the future—although Wells' Morlocks and Eloi were bother clearly devolutions. In 1930 Olaf Stapledon published *Last and First Men*, a brilliant work that chronicled the development (positive and negative) of the human race into the far future.

Then, out of biology there came a new metaphor for the advancement of humanity: the mutant. Olaf Stapledon's *Odd John* (1935) set the fashion: a mutant or group of mutants with superior abilities (usually mental in nature), persecuted and hunted by the society of normal humans. It was a theme that resonated with the sf readers of the period, and with the coming of the Campbell age, stories of mental and psionic supermen were everywhere. A.E. van Vogt's *Slan* (1940) and Theodore Sturgeon's *More Than Human* (1953) were among the best and most influential of these.

A slightly different strain of sf, exemplified by E.E. "Doc" Smith's *Children of the Lens* (1947) and Arthur C. Clarke's *Childhood's End* (1953), portrayed the arrival of mental superfolk as a natural step toward the next stage in human evolution.

As all this mental evolution was going on, another strain of sf grew up investigating the possibilities of physical enhancements to the human form. Frederik Pohl's *Man Plus* (1976) and Martin Caidin's *Cyborg* (1972; the basis of the popular TV show *The Six Million Dollar Man*) dealt with bionic enhancements, and soon cyborgs were all the rage.

Recently, with the growth of nanotechnology, neurology, and genetics, speculation about transhumanism moved in those directions, led by Marc Stiegler's classic short story "The Gentle Seduction" (*Analog*, April 1989). Other authors who've explored this territory include Greg Egan, Linda Nagata, Rudy Rucker, Bruce Sterling, Charles Stross, and David Zindell. A 2008 anthology (*Transhuman*, edited by Mark L. Van Name & T.K.F. Weisskopf) simultaneously demonstrated and capitalized on transhumanism's growing popularity.

Titles Reviewed

- *The Hydrogen Sonata* by Iain M. Banks {194]
- *Grail* by Elizabeth Bear [196]
- *Pink Noise* by Leonid Korogodski [309]
- *Ghost Spin* by Chris Moriarty [353]
- *Blue Remembered Earth* by Alastair Reynolds [375]
- *Hylozoic* by Rudy Rucker [381]
- *The Sunless Countries* by Karl Schroeder [394]
- *Implied Spaces* by Walter Jon Williams [433]
- *Count to a Trillion* by John C. Wright [446]
- *The Hermetic Millennia* by John C. Wright [448]

Tribute Anthologies

(Apr 2012) Another type of ancestor veneration is the tribute anthology, which gathers stories (and sometimes essays) by many different writers, all in honor of a big name author. The first sf tribute anthology I can find was Harry Harrison's 1973 anthology *Astounding!*, which was published as a posthumous tribute to John W. Campbell, Jr. While most tribute anthologies, unfortunately, are occasioned by the death of the honoree, there have been a few published while the author was still alive. Notable among these are *Foundation's Friends* (edited by Martin H. Greenberg in 1989 in honor of Isaac Asimov) and *Gateways* (edited by Elizabeth Anne Hull and published in 2011 in honor of Frederik Pohl's 90th birthday).

Titles Reviewed

- *Golden Reflections* edited by Joan Spicci Saberhagen and Robert E. Vardeman [459]
- *Sentinels in Honor of Arthur C. Clarke* edited by Gregory Benford and George Zebrowski [469]
- *Shadows of the New Sun* edited by J. E. Mooney and Bill Fawcett [471]

Varieties of Length

(Jan/Feb 2011) Science fiction is unusual among the genres because it routinely appears in all different lengths. This isn't quite the case with other types of fiction. It's rare to see romance stories shorter than novella-length; historical fiction and thrillers almost exclusively appear in novel length or longer. Fantasy and mystery short stories do appear, but the dominant form in both genres is the series of novels. Only in science fiction do readers regularly find works of all lengths from the short-short all the way up to the novel series, and everything in between.

I should pause here for some definitions. Most sf readers are accustomed to a division of short fiction by word counts, as codified in the rules for the Hugo and Nebula Awards. A short story is anything up to 7,500 words; 7,500 to 17,500 is a novelette; 17,500 to 40,000 is a novella; and anything over 40,000 words is a novel. This system, while useful and necessary for the fair administration of awards, leaves something to be desired from a literary criticism standpoint.

In lit-crit circles, a primary distinction is made between the short story and the novel. A novel generally features many characters and multiple subplots, has a broad range in time and space, and explores the world (or worlds) and culture(s). A short story, by contrast, focuses on a small number of characters (generally three at most) and has at most one subplot, is sharply limited in time and space, and illuminates one aspect of a world or culture.

A novelette is essentially a long short story, with the same focus and economy; a novella is a short novel, sharing the novel's broad range only in fewer words.

This whole scheme is complicated by the economics of publishing. Prior to the mid-1970s, it was uneconomical to publish science fiction books of much over 200 pages (about 60,000 to 70,000 words). Nowadays, the average novel runs between 300 and 400 pages (about 100,000 to 150,000 words) and 500+ pages is not unusual. In today's terms, most of the classic works of the past—most of books of Poul Anderson, Isaac Asimov, Arthur C. Clarke, Gordon R. Dickson, Robert Heinlein, Ursula LeGuin, Anne McCaffrey, and a hundred others—would be considered novellas. At the time they were published, though, they were full-grown novels one and all.

I need to make special mention of some length categories that aren't covered above. If a short story is focused, then a "short-short" is a laser beam, usually clocking in at under 1,000 words and concentrating on one single event or idea: *Analog's* "Probability Zero" stories are short-shorts. And the series is definitely a literary form in its own right—I cover the various kinds of series in the Series section.

In the beginning, there were only novels. The first recognized short story writers were Edgar Allan Poe and Nathaniel Hawthorne in the 1840s, but short stories didn't become commercially widespread until the arrival of the pulp magazines in the early 1900s. The ascendancy of Street & Smith Publications in the 1910s brought about the era of genre pulps: magazines dedicated to romance, mysteries, adventure, sports, westerns...and, of course, science fiction. (*Analog* is perhaps the last remaining vestige of that era, having started its life as the pulp *Astounding Stories* in 1930.) Even in those days, science fiction magazines regularly published novel-length works in serial form.

World War II paper shortages damaged the pulps—competition from comic books, paperbacks, and television destroyed them. Writers in most other genres moved almost exclusively to novels—but science fiction magazines thrived, and writers continued producing short fiction. Books of short stories appeared, whether single-author collections or multi-author anthologies. Although the magazines faced difficulties (and still do), short fiction remained a perfectly viable length for science fiction...as it does even today.

At the other end of the scale, science fiction novels expanded. The 1960s brought Heinlein's *Stranger in a Strange*

Land and Herbert's *Dune*, both considered exceptionally long novels for the time. Trilogies and longer series proliferated. Science fiction settled into its current range across all lengths of fiction.

The obvious question is why? What is it about science fiction that allows it to thrive at all lengths? One is tempted to credit tradition, the historical accident of the sf magazines' survival and their continued outlet for short fiction—but that merely begs the question. Why did sf magazines survive, of all other genres?

I believe that the true answer lies in the unique nature of science fiction. All fiction is entertainment, but sf aspires also to stimulate the intellect and provoke thought. In the postwar world, comics and television could supply entertainment, but not intelligent thought. Science fiction is, and always has been, primarily a literary form.

Ideas come in all sizes, short and long, simple and complex, focused and broad. Concerned as it is with ideas, science fiction likewise fits a variety of lengths. That, I believe, is why you'll find sf in every length from short-short to twenty-volume series.

Young Adult SF

(Jun 2013) Much of the excitement in today's publishing world is happening in the field of young adult fiction, also known as teen fiction or simply YA. We have J. K. Rowling to thank for this; the enormous success of the *Harry Potter* books showed publishers that YA represented a vast untapped market, especially for fantasy and science fiction.

Of course, science fiction for younger readers is nothing new. The *Tom Swift* series, published by the Stratemeyer Syndicate beginning in 1910, were arguably the first science fiction books aimed at younger readers. (In those days, there was no real consciousness of "teenager" as a separate developmental phase; in general society, people were either children or adults. According to most sources, it wasn't until after World War II that we began to think of teens as different than children.)

In the prewar period, outside sf fandom, all of science fiction was considered literature for the young. Fans and writers who were adults in that period often spoke of being belittled for reading "that crazy Buck Rogers stuff." The Campbell revolution was the real beginning of science fiction for adults, and it was nearly another two decades before book publishers took sf seriously as an adult market.

Throughout the late 1940s and into the early 1960s, many well-known sf authors wrote what we now recognize as young adult sf (although at the time they were called "juveniles.") The best known and most beloved are Robert A. Heinlein and Andre Norton, but there were numerous other examples. By then the distinction between YA and adult sf was well-established, and longtime readers have endless fun arguing whether *Podkayne of Mars* or *Witch World* fit into one category or the other. (Not to keep you in suspense, the answer is "both.")

During the 1980s and most of the 1990s, YA fiction was essentially undifferentiated by genre; instead, it was dominated by temporary fads. There would be a bestseller about, say, wilderness survival or death in the family, and for a year or so every other book would be similar...until the readers lost interest and moved on to the next fad.

That changed in 1997 with the arrival of Harry Potter. At first, Harry looked like just another fad—the cry among booksellers and librarians alike was "more books like Harry Potter." Yet soon, the realization dawned that what many teens really wanted was imaginative, speculative novels: fantasy and science fiction.

So what makes a novel a YA book? As a publishing category, YA books are aimed at an audience roughly 12-18 years old. However, recent surveys estimate that more than half the YA books published are read by older (sometimes much older) readers.

It doesn't have to do with sex or violence, either. YA literature deals with all sorts of topics once considered taboo.

YA books most often have protagonists under 21—but so do a lot of unquestionably adult books. No one considers Alexei Panshin's *Rite of Passage* to be a YA book, for example, even though its protagonist is under 15.

Putting on my librarian hat here, true YA literature embodies the concerns of teenagers. That covers everything from bedwetting and complexion problems to questions of life, death, and the meaning of the universe. Yet it also leaves out a lot. You're unlikely to see a YA book focusing on career anxiety, for instance.

In the typical YA novel, adult characters tend to be ineffectual, villains, or missing altogether. If there were competent adults around, how could the teenage protagonists have an active role in solving major problems? If the staff of Hogwarts were fully responsible adults, Harry and his young friends would never be confronting the dangers they do—not without the adults going on trial for criminal negligence.

Nowadays, though, there are two categories of YA books being published. First are traditional YA books with all the characteristics listed above. Second are books that would have been published as adult titles ten years ago, but with a few tweaks can be marketed as YA. In the field of science fiction, where the adult market is perceived to be in the doldrums, publishing as YA can make a significant difference in sales. In essence, these are adult books masquerading as YA.

As with all classification schemes, these aren't hard-and-fast categories but rather a continuum. My favorite example is the *Hunger Games* books. These are sophisticated sf books; if the protagonists were in their 20s rather than their teens, the books would almost surely be considered adult fiction. (As it is, parents of younger teens will want to think seriously about how to expose their young readers to the books.)

Sure, adults can read both types of YA. But if a steady diet of books addressing the concerns of teenagers make you feel a bit limited, don't write off YA books altogether. Just look for the adult books that are wearing disguises.

Titles Reviewed

- *The Hunger Games* by Suzanne Collins [223]
- *Catching Fire* by Suzanne Collins [224]
- *Mockingjay* by Suzanne Collins [225]
- *The Death Cure* by James Dashner [235]
- *Little Brother* by Cory Doctorow [224]
- *The Star Beast* by Robert A. Heinlein [278]
- *Rootless* by Chris Howard [287]
- *Unwind* by Neil Shusterman [399]
- *A Beautiful Friendship* by David Weber [425]
- *Fire Season* by David Weber [426]

Additional Varieties

(Jan 2017) Science fiction comes in many more varieties than the ones I've written about in these columns. I'll probably be doing essays on some of these in future columns. For convenience, here are short descriptions and title lists for some of these varieties.

Adventure SF

Science fiction stories in which the focus is grand adventure, close escapes, and derring-do.

Titles Reviewed

- *The Return* by Ben Bova [206]
- *Captain Vorpatril's Alliance* by Lois McMaster Bujold [212]
- *Cryoburn* by Lois McMaster Bujold [211]
- *Prometheus II* by S. J. Byrne [215]
- *Railroad Spine* by Geonn Cannon [217]
- *Ride the Star Winds* by A. Bertram Chandler [220]
- *To the Galactic Rim* by A. Bertram Chandler [219]
- *Into Plutonian Depths* by Stanton A. Coblentz [221]
- *Monster Hunter Legion* by Larry Correia [227]
- *The Prisoner* by Carlos J. Cortes [226]
- *When the World Tottered* by Lester Del Rey [238]
- *The Sorceress of Karres* by Eric Flint and Dave Freer [252]
- *Body, Inc.* By Alan Dean Foster [260]
- *The Human Blend* by Alan Dean Foster [258]
- *The Sum of Her Parts* by Alan Dean Foster [261]
- *Impulse* by Steven Gould [268]
- *The Darwin Elevator* by Jason M. Hough [282]
- *The Exodus Towers* by Jason M. Hough [284]
- *The Plague Forge* by Jason M. Hough [285]
- *Darkship Renegades* by Sarah A. Hoyt [288]

- *A Few Good Men* by Sarah A. Hoyt [289]
- *Little Brother's World* by T. Jackson King [306]
- *Channel 37* by Paul Lagasse and Gary Lester [315]
- *Imperium* by Keith Laumer [317]
- *Tuf Voyaging* by George R. R. Martin [332]
- *Catalyst* by Anne McCaffrey and Elizabeth Ann Scarborough [333]
- *The Walls of the Universe* by Paul Melko [342]
- *The Broken Universe* by Paul Melko [344]
- *The Forerunner Factor* by Andre Norton [362]
- *Gaia's Web* by Steve Proskauer [368]
- *The Shaver Mystery Book One* by Richard S. Shaver [396]
- *The Shaver Mystery Book Two* by Richard S. Shaver [396]
- *Ice City of the Gorgon* by Richard S. Shaver and Chester S. Geier [238]
- *The Eternal Prison* by Jeff Somers [404]
- *Deus Ex; Icarus Effect* by James Swallow [411]
- *Transgalactic* by A. E. Van Vogt [422]
- *Saga* by Brian K. Vaughan and Fiona Staples [423]
- *A Beautiful Friendship* by David Weber [425]
- *Pirates of the Timestream* by Steve White [430]
- *Home Fires* by Gene Wolfe [444]
- *Man-Kzin Wars XIII* created by Larry Niven [463]

Animal Companions

Science fiction where the science element is drawn from biology, genetics, or medicine.

Titles Reviewed

- *The Return* by Ben Bova [206]

Biological SF

Science fiction where the science element is drawn from biology, genetics, or medicine.

Titles Reviewed

- *The Return* by Ben Bova [206]
- *Cryoburn* by Lois McMaster Bujold [211]
- *Body, Inc.* By Alan Dean Foster [260]
- *The Human Blend* by Alan Dean Foster [258]
- *The Sum of Her Parts* by Alan Dean Foster [261]
- *New Under the Sun* by Nancy Kress and Therese Pieczynski [310]
- *The Games* by Ted Mosmatka [355]
- *Fade to Black* by Josh Pryor [369]
- *If By Reason of Strength* by Jamie Todd Rubin [380]
- *The Highest Frontier* by Joan Slonczewski [401]
- *Uglies: Shay's Story* by Scott Westerfeld [429]
- *Amped* by Daniel H. Wilson [440]

Cyberpunk

Gritty, hard-hitting stories of human beings and their relationship with the worldwide computer net.

Titles Reviewed

- *Noise* by Darin Bradley [209]
- *The Gravity Pilot* by M. M. Buckner [210]
- *Little Brother* by Cory Doctorow [242]

- *Geosynchron* by David Louis Edelman [248]
- *Brain Thief* by Alexander Jablokov [295]
- *The Eternal Prison* by Jeff Somers [404]
- *Deus Ex; Icarus Effect* by James Swallow [411]

Dystopian Futures

Stories set in the near future, when conditions are worse than today.

Titles Reviewed

- *Noise* by Darin Bradley [209]
- *The Gravity Pilot* by M. M. Buckner [210]
- *Veracity* by Laura Bynum [213]
- *Jamestown* by Matthew Sharpe [396]
- *King Freedom* by Uncle River [419]
- *Dark Futures* edited by Jason Sizemore [456]

Ecological/Environmental SF

Science fiction concerned with ecology and the environment, especially with threats thereto.

Titles Reviewed

- *The Gravity Pilot* by M. M. Buckner [210]
- *Rootless* by Chris Howard [287]
- *Tuf Voyaging* by George R. R. Martin [332]
- *The One-Eyed Man* by L. E. Modesitt, Jr [350]
- *Pennterra* by Judith Moffett [351]

- *Gaia's Web* by Steve Proskauer [368]
- *Welcome to the Greenhouse* edited by Gordon van Gelder [479]

Fortress City

Science fiction stories involving isolated cities separated from the hostile lands that surround them.

Titles Reviewed

- *Echo City* by Tim Lebbon [318]

Galactic Empires

Science fiction stories of interstellar republics, empires, kingdoms, federations, and political/economic unions of all types.

Titles Reviewed

- *Young Flandry* by Poul Anderson [188]
- *Flinx Transcendent* by Alan Dean Foster [256]

Games & Gaming

Science fiction stories based on specific games, or stories about games and gaming.

Titles Reviewed

- *Mass Effect: Retribution* by Drew Karpyshyn [303]
- *Deus Ex; Icarus Effect* by James Swallow [411]

Generation Ships

A generation ship is a large vessel that is a self-contained world carrying the descendants of an original crew across interstellar gulfs at sublight speed.

Titles Reviewed

- *Grail* by Elizabeth Bear [196]

Graphic Novels

Science fiction stories told in comics format.

Titles Reviewed

- *Tales from the Clockwork Empire* by Ian Duerden [245]
- *Final Crisis: Legion of 3 Worlds* by Geoff Johns, George Pérez, and Scott Koblish [298]
- *Watchmen* by Alan Moore and Dave Gibbons [352]
- *Gantz* by Hiroya Oku [364]

- *Saga* by Brian K. Vaughan and Fiona Staples [423]
- *Uglies: Shay's Story* by Scott Westerfeld [429]

Hard SF

Science fiction stories based on rigorous extrapolation of hard sciences (physics, chemistry, astronomy, etc.)

Titles Reviewed

- *Bowl of Heaven* by Gregory Benford and Larry Niven [198]
- *Farside* by Ben Bova [202]
- *Energized* by Edward M. Lerner [324]
- *Blue Remembered Earth* by Alastair Reynolds [375]

High Frontier

Science fiction stories of the industrialization of space, space settlements, lunar colonies, etc.

Titles Reviewed

- *Farside* by Ben Bova [202]
- *Mars Life* by Ben Bova [205]

Humorous SF

The lighter side of science fiction.

Titles Reviewed

- *And Another Thing...* by Eoin Colfer [222]
- *Total Oblivion, More of Less* by Alan DeNiro [239]
- *The Sorceress of Karres* by Eric Flint and Dave Freer [252]
- *Wrath of the Lemming Men* by Toby Frost [362]
- *Shh! It's a Secret* by Daniel M. Kimmel [305]
- *Year Zero* by Rob Reid [372]
- *Unfriendly Persuasion* by Steven H. Wilson [442]
- *Wookiee-Ookkies* by Kevin Bolk [487]
- *Ensign Sue Must Die* by Kevin Bolk and Clare Moseley [487]

Immortals & Immortality

Stories about immortality and those who achieve it.

Titles Reviewed

- *Implied Spaces* by Walter Jon Williams [433]

Man & Machine

Science fiction stories of humanity's relationship with our non-robot tools and machine intelligence. (See also Robots)

Titles Reviewed

- *Zendegi* by Greg Egan [E]
- *Body, Inc.* By Alan Dean Foster [260]
- *The Human Blend* by Alan Dean Foster [258]
- *The Sum of Her Parts* by Alan Dean Foster [261]
- *Gaia's Web* by Steve Proskauer [368]
- *WWW: Wake* by Robert J. Sawyer [390]
- *WWW: Watch* by Robert J. Sawyer [392]
- *WWW: Wonder* by Robert J. Sawyer [393]
- *The Highest Frontier* by Joan Slonczewski [401]

Near Future SF

Science fiction stories set in the next hundred years or so.

Titles Reviewed

- *Mars Life* by Ben Bova [205]
- *Zendegi* by Greg Egan [249]
- *Buyout* by Alexander C. Irvine [291]
- *Energized* by Edward M. Lerner [324]
- *The Games* by Ted Mosmatka [355]
- *Back to the Moon* by Travis S. Taylor and Les Johnson [413]

New Wave SF

The "New Wave" was a movement in the science fiction field during the 1960s and 1970s. New Wave stories are characterized by a focus on more literary and experimental styles, emphasis on soft sciences, and countercultural sensibilities.

Titles Reviewed

- *Decimated* by Jack Dann and George Zebrowski [234]

Other Worlds

Science fiction stories that focus on depicting an alien world or another society, often in such detail that the reader feels as if he/she has lived there.

Titles Reviewed

- *Of Wind and Sand* by Sylvie Bérard [200]
- *A Glimpse of Splendor and Other Stories* by Dave Creek [230]
- *Little Brother's World* by T. Jackson King [306]
- *Steal Across the Sky* by Nancy Kress [311]
- *Embassytown* by China Miéville [345]
- *Railsea* by China Miéville [347]
- *The One-Eyed Man* by L. E. Modesitt, Jr [350]
- *2312* by Kim Stanley Robinson [377]
- *Coyote Destiny* by Allen Steele [406]

Parallel Worlds/Other Dimensions

Science fiction adventures involving places and spaces beyond our spacetime universe. Other Dimensions are any spaces not our own. Parallel Worlds are generally alternate versions of our own; Alternate History is a subset of those worlds which share out history up to a specific point of departure.

Titles Reviewed

- *This Shared Dream* by Kathleen Ann Goonan [267]
- *Imperium* by Keith Laumer [317]
- *Final Crisis: Legion of 3 Worlds* by Geoff Johns, George Pérez, and Scott Koblish [298]
- *The Walls of the Universe* by Paul Melko [342]
- *The Broken Universe* by Paul Melko [344]
- *Hylozoic* by Rudy Rucker [381]
- *On the Train* by Harry Turtledove [416]
- *Golden Reflections* edited by Joan Spicci Saberhagen and Robert E. Vardeman [459]

Philosophical/Religious SF

Science fiction stories concerned with the great questions of human existence, including SF that deals specifically with religion.

Titles Reviewed

- *Transcendental* by James Gunn [273]
- *Steal Across the Sky* by Nancy Kress [311]
- *Pennterra* by Judith Moffett [351]
- *WWW: Wake* by Robert J. Sawyer [390]

- *WWW: Watch* by Robert J. Sawyer [392]
- *WWW: Wonder* by Robert J. Sawyer [393]
- *Vixen* by Bud Sparhawk [405]

Post-Apocalyptic SF

Stories set in a world changed by a widespread disaster in the (sometimes distant) past.

Titles Reviewed

- *After America* by John Birmingham [201]
- *The Hunger Games* by Suzanne Collins [223]
- *Catching Fire* by Suzanne Collins [224]
- *Mockingjay* by Suzanne Collins [225]
- *The Pesthouse* by Jim Crace [229]
- *The Passage* by Justin Cronin [232]
- *The Death Cure* by James Dashner [235]
- *Total Oblivion, More of Less* by Alan DeNiro [239]
- *The Darwin Elevator* by Jason M. Hough [282]
- *The Exodus Towers* by Jason M. Hough [284]
- *The Plague Forge* by Jason M. Hough [285]
- *Rootless* by Chris Howard [287]
- *Transgalactic* by A. E. Van Vogt [422]

Psychological/Sociological SF

Science fiction stories based on extrapolation in the "soft" sciences of the mind and society.

Titles Reviewed

- *Railroad Spine* by Geonn Cannon [217]
- *The Prisoner* by Carlos J. Cortes [226]
- *Zendegi* by Greg Egan [249]
- *Transcendental* by James Gunn [273]
- *Kea's Flight* by Etrika Hammerschmidt and John C. Ricker [277]
- *Buyout* by Alexander C. Irvine [291]
- *The Unincorporated Man* by Dani Kollin and Eytan Kollin [307]
- *New Under the Sun* by Nancy Kress and Therese Pieczynski [310]
- *Steal Across the Sky* by Nancy Kress [311]
- *The Best of All Possible Words* by Karen Lord [327]
- *Exogene* by T. C. McCarthy [338]
- *Pennterra* by Judith Moffett [351]
- *2312* by Kim Stanley Robinson [377]
- *WWW: Wake* by Robert J. Sawyer [390]
- *WWW: Watch* by Robert J. Sawyer [392]
- *WWW: Wonder* by Robert J. Sawyer [393]
- *Unwind* by Neil Shusterman [399]
- *Beyond the Doors of Death* by Robert Silverberg and Damien Broderick [400]

Romantic SF

Science fiction stories that involve the tropes and concerns of the romance genre.

Titles Reviewed

- *Blood Law* by Jeannie Holmes [281]
- *Dragon Ship* by Sharon Lee and Steve Miller [321]
- *Ghost Ship* by Sharon Lee and Steve Miller [319]
- *A Liaden Universe Constellation: Volume 1* by Sharon Lee and Steve Miller [322]
- *Necessity's Child* by Sharon Lee and Steve Miller [323]
- *The Best of All Possible Words* by Karen Lord [327]

Retro SF

Modern science fiction that invokes the ideas, characters, settings, and/or themes of classic works, but with modern style and sensibilities.

Titles Reviewed

- *Impossible Futures* edited by Judith K. Dial and Thomas Easton [460]
- *Old Mars* edited by George R. R. Martin and Gardner Dozois [467]
- *Worlds of Edgar Rice Burroughs* edited by Mike Resnick and Robert T. Garcia [480]

Satire SF

Science fiction that satirizes current society by exaggerating trends and setting the story in the future or on another world.

Titles Reviewed

- *Shh! It's a Secret* by Daniel M. Kimmel [305]

Science Fantasy

The flavor of science fiction combined with the impossible elements of fantasy, often takes place on worlds that once were possible but now could never be.

Titles Reviewed

- *All the Windwracked Stars* by Elizabeth Bear [197]
- *City at the Edge of Time* by Greg Bear [197]
- *Pinion* by Jay Lake [316]
- *Echo City* by Tim Lebbon [318]
- *Saga* by Brian K. Vaughan and Fiona Staples [423]
- *Implied Spaces* by Walter Jon Williams [433]
- *Impossible Futures* edited by Judith K. Dial and Thomas Easton [460]
- *Old Mars* edited by George R. R. Martin and Gardner Dozois [467]
- *Worlds of Edgar Rice Burroughs* edited by Mike Resnick and Robert T. Garcia [480]

SF Horror

Science fiction stories that involve the tropes and concerns of the horror genre.

Titles Reviewed

- *Open Your Eyes* by Paul Jessup [296]
- *Echo City* by Tim Lebbon [318]
- *The Games* by Ted Mosmatka [355]
- *The Ocean Dark* by Jack Rogan [378]

SF Mystery

Science fiction stories that involve the tropes and concerns of the mystery genre.

Titles Reviewed

- *Brain Thief* by Alexander Jablokov [295]
- *Red Planet Blues* by Robert J. Sawyer [388]

Shared/Franchised Worlds

Science fiction stories in which authors share a world, or in which an established author sublets his/her own world.

Titles Reviewed

- *Beginnings* by David Weber et al [453]
- *Golden Reflections* edited by Joan Spicci Saberhagen and Robert E. Vardeman [459]
- *In Fire Forged* edited by David Weber [461]
- *Man-Kzin Wars XIII* created by Larry Niven [463]
- *War World: Discovery* edited by John F. Carr [475]

Space Colonization

Science fiction involving the settlement of other worlds.

Titles Reviewed

- *Mars Life* by Ben Bova [205]

Superheroes

Stories of crimefighting heroes with extraordinary or superhuman abilities.

Titles Reviewed

- *Final Crisis: Legion of 3 Worlds* by Geoff Johns, George Pérez, and Scott Koblish [298]
- *Shades of Gray* by Jackie Kessler and Caitlin Kittredge [304]
- *Ghosts of Manhattan* by George Mann [331]
- *Watchmen* by Alan Moore and Dave Gibbons [352]

Teleportation

Science fiction that deals with the mechanical or paranormal ability to move from one point to another without crossing the intervening space.

Titles Reviewed

- *Impulse* by Steven Gould [268]

TV

Science fiction set in the universe of specific television shows.

Titles Reviewed

- *Stargate Atlantis: Homecoming* by Jo Graham and Melissa Scott [270]

Venus

Science fiction set on or involving the planet Venus.

Titles Reviewed

- *Dream of Venus and Other Stories* by Pamela Sargent [234]

Visitors From Space

The aliens come, either to visit or to move in.

Titles Reviewed

- *The Darwin Elevator* by Jason M. Hough [282]
- *The Exodus Towers* by Jason M. Hough [284]
- *The Plague Forge* by Jason M. Hough [285]
- *Pirates of the Timestream* by Steve White [430]

Reviews: A

(alphabetical by author)

A Legacy of Stars
Danielle Ackley-McPhail
DTF Publications, 230 pages, $14.95 (trade paperback)
Kindle, Nook: $2.99 (e-book)
ISBN: 978-1-937051-95-2
Genre: Short Stories

Danielle Ackley-McPhail is one of the up-and-coming storytellers and editors in sf/fantasy. She's best known for her series of humorous fantasy anthologies, the *Bad-Ass Faeries*. Here she serves up a baker's dozen science fiction short stories, ranging from military sf to sf horror to one of the cleverest first contact stories to come along in a long time. Each story is introduced by an editor or sf writer, and there are five of Ackley-McPhail's poems as well.

If you're in the mood for a smorgasbord of enjoyable tales from a fresh new voice, at an e-book price that won't break the bank, give *A Legacy of Stars* a try.

Written in Time
Jerry & Sharon Ahern
Baen, 644 pages, $7.99 (paperback)
Baen Webscriptions: $6.00 (ebook)
ISBN: 978-1-4391-3399-6
Genre: Alternate History, Military SF, Time Travel

For an sf writer, the idea is irresistible: take a military force armed with modern weapons and throw them back in time. As mentioned above, Poul Anderson pulled the trick in "The Man Who Came Early," and other writers have been doing it ever since. Among the notable examples are Leo Frankowski's

Cross-Time Engineer series, John Birmingham's *Axis of Time* series, and the 1980 movie *The Final Countdown*. By far the biggest name in this area, however, is Eric Flint, whose *Ring of Fire* series tells of the contemporary town of Grantville, West Virginia, which is somehow thrown back to Germany in the 1630s. *The Ring of Fire* series has spawned a vast number of followup books by Flint and various other writers.

Add Jerry & Sharon Ahern to the list.

In *Written in Time*, a present-day Nevada family is transplanted back to 1904 by unknown hostiles. But they come prepared with modern weapons, and battle rages between the Naile family and a time-traveling army intent on conquering the world. Things look bad, but the Nailes have some unexpected allies: the Seventh United States Cavalry and Teddy Roosevelt.

Part alternate history, part military sf, *Written in Time* is all fun.

The High Crusade: 50th Anniversary Edition
Poul Anderson
Baen, 262 pages, $7.99 (mass market paperback)
Baen WEbooks: $6.00 (ebook)
ISBN: 978-1-4516-3832-5
Genre: Space Opera

Do you know a history buff, or someone who reads historical fiction? Introduce them to this classic sf tale by a master of sf and history.

The High Crusade appeared as a serial in *Analog* in 1960, and stayed in print for decades as a standalone novel. Now this story of medieval knights in combat against an alien interstellar empire is back in print along with a sequel short story and appreciations from various sf luminaries.

The story is as audacious as it is entertaining. In England in 1345, Sir Roger Baron de Tourneville is training his knights to join in the war against France. Suddenly, a huge spaceship lands in the quiet Lincolnshire village. Out come the alien Wersgorix, bent on invasion and conquest. The Wersgorix rule a vast galactic empire, and they're very good an conquering planets. Or so they think.

Unfortunately, all the weaponry and tactics are based on high tech, and they've long forgotten the techniques of hand-to-hand combat. Frankly, the aliens don't stand a chance against Sir Roger's knights.

Eager to deliver the captured spaceship to the battlefields of France, Sir Roger brings the entire population of the town aboard with all their belongings. They take off successfully, but miss the mark and wind up on a Wersgorix outpost world instead of France.

What with one thing and another, it isn't long before the knights control the outpost world, and Sir Roger leads them on a new Crusade to defeat the Empire and free all its slave races.

The characters are compelling, the adventure thrilling, and the history spot on correct. Seeing interstellar technology through the eyes of 14th century knights is one of the delights of the tale. Your history buff reader will love this book as generations before have.

By the way, *The High Crusade* would make a killer film. There was a 1994 movie version, but by all accounts it was dreadful...it's high time for a good one. Besides, I have the perfect tagline for the action-packed trailer, filled with shots of knights battling hideous aliens: "Resistance is feudal!"

Ahem.

Young Flandry
Poul Anderson
Baen, 736 pages, $7.99 (mass market paperback)
Baen Webscriptions: $6.00 (e-book)
ISBN: 978-1-4391-3465-8
Series: Technic Civilization/Flandry of Terra
Genre: Galactic Empires, Space Opera

Longtime *Analog* readers need no introduction to Poul Anderson. Across a career that stretched from the Golden Age to the 21st century, Anderson wrote over a hundred books of science fiction and fantasy. He won the Hugo Award seven times, the Nebula thrice, and SFWA's Grand Master Award—as well as just about every other award in the field. He was a master of short stories as well as novels, and his worldbuilding skills were legendary.

Anderson died in 2001, leaving a legacy of generations of satisfied readers.

Among Poul Anderson's greatest work was the multivolume future history chronicling the rise and fall of what he called the *Technic Civilization*. The stories and books of this series, many first published in *Astounding/Analog*, include pure idea-based problem stories, sophisticated tales of alien societies, ripping adventure yarns, military sf stories, and riveting mysteries. Lately, we've become used to writers who specialize in one type of sf or another—Poul Anderson did it all, sometimes melding several different types in the same story.

With the state of sf publishing today, it's often getting harder and harder to find affordable new editions of classics by the great writers of the past. But the field can't survive on old used books: they aren't attractive to new readers, they can be hard to get ahold of, and a dog-eared 30-year-old copy of *The Rebel Worlds* just doesn't make an acceptable gift.

Luckily, Baen Books has taken on the mission of re-issuing Anderson's *Technic Civilization* books. These are omnibus editions, which means each one contains several books at once. They're attractive paperbacks, either trade or mass market size, and they're priced pretty reasonably. If you've joined the digital bandwagon and want e-book editions, you can generally get them from Baen for six bucks apiece.

The history of the Technic Civilization breaks into two eras, each typified by one main character. The first era, of exploration and settlement, featured master trader Nicholas van Rijn. The second era, dominated by the decline and fall of the Terran Empire, is told through the eyes of Dominic Flandry.

Flandry, in true military tradition dating back to Horatio Hornblower, starts out as an Ensign in the Imperial Navy, and works his way up to a position as personal agent of the Emperor. All the time, the Empire is decaying and dissolving, and throughout his adventures across eight volumes we watch Flandry's ultimately doomed struggle to preserve the good and eliminate the bad.

Young Flandry, as you might expect from the title, is set at the beginning of Flandry's long career. The book includes the first three Flandry novels in chronological order: *Ensign Flandry* (originally published in 1966), *A Circus of Hells* (1970), and *The Rebel Worlds* (1969).

Here Flandry is young, ambitious, and resourceful as he confronts the Empire's enemies, both internal and external. The focus in these books is mostly on adventure and exotic locales (and nobody does those better than Anderson). If you've never read these books, you have quite a treat in store. And if you dimly remember them as fairly old-fashioned sf, you owe it to yourself to rediscover Anderson's inventive imagination. I promise you, these books are fresher than you remember them.

Aurora in Four Voices
Catherine Asaro
ISFiC Press, 274 pages, $30.00 (hardcover)
ISBN: 978-0-9759156-9-1
Series: Skolian Empire (some stories)
Genre: Music, Short Fiction Collection

Last issue, you may recall, I talked about Catherine Asaro's long-running space opera series, the *Skolian Empire* series. As long-time *Analog* readers know, Asaro also writes some mean short fiction, some of it set in the same universe. *Aurora in Four Voices* collects six of her finest pieces in a handsome volume that any Asaro fan will want.

There are four *Skolian Empire* tales, all of them different. The title story (first published in *Analog* December 1998) deliciously blends music and mathematics. "Light and Shadow" (*Analog*, April 1994) is a story of men and machines pushed to their limits. "Ave de Paso," published elsewhere in 2001, is strictly fantasy rather than sf, and it's interesting to see the connection to the Skolian Empire. And "City of Cries" (also published elsewhere, in 2005) is an sf noir detective story.

"The Spacetime Pool" (*Analog*, March 2008) won the Nebula Award and is another math story, not at all connected with the Skolian Empire.

After all this math, Asaro includes a nonfiction article on Riemann surfaces, titled "A Poetry of Angles and Dreams." In it she manages to convey to the reader some of the sublime beauty that pure mathematics can engender. (All right, I admit it, I majored in math in college. But any intelligent sf reader will have no trouble with the concepts here.)

Asaro introduces each of the stories, and an afterword by Aly Parsons completes the package.

Carnelians
Catherine Asaro
Baen, 373 pages, $25.00 (hardcover)
Baen Webscriptions: $6.00 (e-book)
ISBN: 978-1-4516-3748-9
Series: Skolian Empire
Genre: Music, Space Opera

Catherine Asaro is the latest author to fuse music and science fiction in a big way.

Longtime *Analog* readers are already familiar with Asaro's *Skolian Empire* series; several stories in the series have appeared in these pages in the past. The series, consisting of over a dozen books and various pieces of short fiction, is set in a galaxy divided between three powers. The Skolian Empire, the good guys, is a deliciously intricate empire with lots of advanced nanotechnology, ruled by the (sometimes) noble Ruby Dynasty. The bad guys, the Eubian Traders, are a slave-holding society of genetically-engineered drones. The third group, known as the Allieds (which includes Earth), struggle to remain neutral parties in the eternal conflict between Skolians and Eubians.

The politics of the two empires are marvelously convoluted and labyrinthine, reminiscent of the Borgias or Byzantine courts. There's also a strong element of romance in the books.

Carnelians is a continuation (of a sort) of a story begun in *Diamond Star* (2010). In that book we met Del Valdoria, youngest son of the current Skolian ruler. Poor Del had no interest in politics; all he wanted was sing holo-rock. So he was shuffled off to Earth to hide under an assumed identity, where he wouldn't embarrass the royals.

Except Del turned out to be a superstar, and became hugely popular. And suddenly he was in danger from assassins, kidnappers, and nefarious agents who knew his true identity and weren't above using him and his music to heat up the Skolian/Eubian war.

Now in *Carnelians*, there's uneasy peace between the Skolian Empire and the Eubian Traders. Asaro broadens the focus, taking us into the ruling houses of both empires, where well-meaning leaders are trying to keep the fragile peace despite opposition from many forces, in both empires, who are happy with the war and want it to continue.

Eubian Emperor Jaibriol and Skolian Imperator Kelric mirror one another as they face rebellious advisors, ambitious opponents, and the ever-present threat of assassination while struggling to complete an effective treaty. There are double-agents, hidden agendas, intrigues aplenty, treachery and betrayal...everything that makes imperial politics so much fun to read about.

To complicate matters, holo-rock star Del emerges with a new hit, "Carnelians Finale," an inflammatory song about some Eubian atrocities during the war. Opposition forces on both sides take up the anthem as a rallying cry, and it begins to look like they might just succeed in plunging the galaxy back into war.

If you're a fan of the Skolian Empire and of *Diamond Star/Carnelians* in particular, you'll want to know about a companion musical album (also titled *Diamond Star*) from Starflight Music. Alternative rock band Point Valid, helped out by Asaro herself, presents a soundtrack for the book, featuring Del's song and including "Carnelians Finale." The album is readily available in both compact disc and electronic form; if nothing else, you can order it online from *www.starflight-music.com*.

Reviews: B

(alphabetical by author)

The Hydrogen Sonata
Iain M. Banks
Orbit, 517 pages, $25.99 (hardcover)
iBooks, Kindle, Nook: $12.99 (e-book)
ISBN: 978-0-31621237-3
Series: The Culture
Genre: Big Bools, Space Opera, Transhumanism

The drawback to a truly big book is that it can seem imposing. One doesn't read a big book casually over the course of a few lunch breaks; a good big book requires a certain commitment of time and attention. This drawback is amplified with a series of big books -- and *The Hydrogen Sonata* is tenth in a series of very good, very big books.

So it's quite understandable if you are not familiar with Iain R. Banks' *Culture* books. Let me set your mind a little at ease: the Culture is a universe, not a sequential narrative. Each book stands alone, and readers can start exploring the Culture anywhere they wish.

The Culture is a galactic-scale society with at least eleven millennia of history. It was the product of a number of sapient humanoid species and equally-sapient AIs achieved transhuman status and formed a stable union. Earth was contacted by the Culture about 2100 CE, roughly halfway through Culture history.

The Culture is a rich society, so rich that its inhabitants can literally have anything they wish. Hunger, disease, poverty, even the concept of possession no longer exist. There is no money and very little that we would recognize as an economy. Super-powerful AIs (called Minds) administer the society, delegating all drudge work to nonsapient machines.

In the Culture, people do whatever they want. Uncontrolled aggression and pathological behavior have been bred out of the population; crime and antisocial behavior are virtually nonexistent. To be sure, there are still a few crimes of passion—but generally, someone who's unhappy can always move somewhere else.

The galaxy is extensively settled, with most members of the Culture living in huge artificial constructs: ships dozens of kilometers in size, ring-shaped Orbitals the size of planets, and even larger habitats.

The Culture is an egalitarian society with few laws (social customs regulate behavior instead). Personal liberty and the pursuit of happiness are the main aims of life, and the biggest sin is to compel intelligent entities to act against their wills.

One might think that stories of such a utopia would be dull. However, the Culture is not alone in the galaxy: there are hundreds or thousands of other societies at all levels of moral and technological development. Most of the action in the Culture books takes place at the boundaries where these societies meet the Culture.

A Culture group called Contact, working through a network of spies called Special Circumstances, frequently intervenes to guide (and in some cases, defend against) other societies not as advanced. And against the background of Contact and Special Circumstances, there is intrigue and adventure enough to satisfy any reader.

In *The Hydrogen Sonata*, the Culture has been around for ten thousand years. The Gzilt, an ancient race that has never joined the Culture, is preparing for Sublimation—a process by which they will transcend physical existence and move on to a higher plane. In the course of these preparations, violence breaks out between the Gzilt and another ancient race. Culture agents are dispatched to handle the trouble—and soon find themselves on quest to track down the oldest person in the galaxy, a man who was there at the beginning of the Culture and who seems to be the key to getting the Gzilt to a safe and happy Sublimation.

This book is big in many ways beyond its 500+ pages. The scope is tremendous, the plot and characters of mythic dimensions, and like all Culture novels the questions of morality, individuality, and the meaning of life are immense. If you need a place to start with the Culture, this is a good one.

Grail
Elizabeth Bear
Spectra, 352 pages, $7.99 (paperback)
iBooks, Kindle, Nook: $7.99 (ebook)
ISBN: 978-0-553-59109-5
Series: Jacob's Ladder 3
Genre: Clarke's Law, Generation Ships, Transhumanism

Take a generation ship, a large vessel that is a self-contained world carrying the descendants of an original crew across interstellar gulfs at sublight speed. Stir in transhumanism, seasoned with intelligent but slightly mad artificial intelligences and a big dollop of nanotechnology. Add a generous helping of Arthurian mythology and more than a dash of Roger Zelazny. Let cook for several generations. Strain the result through Elizabeth Bear's fertile imagination and consummate writing skill.

The result is the *Jacob's Ladder* trilogy, of which *Grail* is the concluding volume (the two previous books were *Dust* and *Chill*). The generation ship Jacob's Ladder left a devastated Earth, and during its voyage the inhabitants have made the leap to transhuman status—they've spent the last two books becoming demigods in response to a variety of threats.

Now the ship's long journey is over: these transhumans are approaching their destination, a planet they call Grail. There's just one problem: Grail is already inhabited. Worse, it was settled by regular humans, who call the planet Fortune and aren't exactly in the mood to share it with a shipful of newcomers who might as well be aliens.

Like the first two books, *Grail* is a mythic story full of wonder and detailed worldbuilding, told through the eyes of sympathetic characters. If you want to spend some time in not one, but two fully-realized worlds, this is the book for you.

City at the Edge of Time
Greg Bear
Del Rey, 476 pages, $27.00 (hardcover)
ISBN: 978-0-345-44839-2

All the Windwracked Stars
Elizabeth Bear
Tor, 368 pages, $24.95 (hardcover)
Genres: Dying Earth, Far Future/Clarke's Law, Science Fantasy

As usual, it started with H.G. Wells. In *The Time Machine* he presented a far-future in which everything had worn down: the Earth, the human race, even the sun. John Campbell's "Twilight" and Arthur C. Clarke's *Against the Fall of Night* further explored these cold, cheerless eras, where advanced science became decadent magic, and science fiction was all but indistinguishable from fantasy. It fell to Jack Vance to produce the book that would give this subgenre its generally-accepted name: *The Dying Earth*.

Dying Earth novels have been out of favor in recent years. In fantasy, the subgenre devolved (what else?) into generic sword-and-sorcery; in sf, it seemed that Michael Moorcock's *Dancers at the End of Time* series had said everything there was to say.

Now, two writers named Bear have blazed trails into this long-unexplored territory, and they've come back with some pretty compelling visions.

Greg Bear's *City at the End of Time* begins in the present day with three dreamers: Daniel, Ginny, and Jack. Each, in his or her own way, is cast adrift in time; each, in his or her own way, is linked with the a city in the unimaginably distant future. This city, the Kalpa, is the last crumbling refuge against the final night. And before the end comes, all three dreamers have their parts to play.

Elizabeth Bear's *All the Windwracked Stars* starts with the desolate aftermath of a battle, the defeat of the Children of Light on the Norse-flavored world of Valdyrgard. Two survivors of that battle find each other: Muire, the last Valkyrie, and Kasimir, a winged steed.

Curtain falls, rising 2300 years later. Human civilization on Valdyrgard, once risen to tremendous heights, has fallen; one decrepit domed city remains, ruled by the despotic Technomancer. Muire walks the city in search of something she never expected: another surviving Child of Light.

These are two very different books, but they share some of the same sensibilities: grand expanses of time, epic events, technology so advanced that it's magic, powerful heroes and implacable villains, and the constant presence of entropy and despair so palpable that they might as well be characters in the story. This is science fiction taken to the level of mythology. If that sort of thing appeals to you, this is one Bear market you don't want to miss.

Bowl of Heaven
Gregory Benford and Larry Niven
Tor, 412 pages, $25.99 (hardcover)
iBooks, Kindle, Nook: $12.99 (e-book)
ISBN: 978-0-7653-2841-0
Series: Bowl of Heaven #1
Genre: Alien Beings, Bigger Than Worlds, Hard SF

Gregory Benford and Larry Niven are surely familiar names to *Analog* readers. Both have a reputation for the kind of hard sf that frequently appears in these pages. Both are bestselling, multiple award winning authors. And both have written before of Really Big Things—Benford in his *Eon* series and Niven in his *Ringworld* books.

In *Bowl of Heaven*, the first of two books, interstellar colony ship *SunSeeker* encounters a Really Big Thing—in this case, a solid hemispherical shell around a red dwarf star. This Bowl, also called *Shipstar*, dashes through relativistic space by magnetically manipulating the star's plasma into a powerful jet.

Well, of course *SunSeeker* is in trouble, and of course they change course to intercept and explore the Bowl. (I mean, who wouldn't?) A landing party encounters the Folk, the Bowl's enormous, birdlike dominant race. Half the Humans escape, while the other half is taken into captivity. The rest of the crew orbits the star in *SunSeeker*, trying vainly to help.

The Bowl is well-thought-out, and watching the escaped Humans explore it is part of the fun...but the real meat of this book is the Folk. They're a fascinating race with an unusual life cycle. They're born male, and aren't considered fully complete until a midlife change to female. The key to their psychology is that they have full awareness of the operation of their unconscious minds (which they call underminds). This gives them tremendous psychological stability, as well as enormous cognitive abilities.

The Bowl has been underway for millions of years (you'd think they'd have reached cruising speed and been able to shut off the plasma jet by now, but never mind that). In the course of this journey, the Folk have met, and integrated, countless other species both sapient and not. But in all their travels, they've never met creatures like Humans, disconnected from our own underminds.

If you like hard sf with mind-stretching ideas—both physical and psychological^then you definitely want to read this book. Be warned, this is the first part of the story. *Bowl of Heaven* raises a lot of questions that will (one hopes) be answered in the second book, *Shipstar*. My advice: Buy this volume and put it in your reading queue. Then when the next one comes out, sit down and savor both of them together.

Trouble is, you'll have to wait to read a Benford/Niven collaboration. If you can do that, your willpower is much stronger than mine.

Of Wind and Sand
Sylvie Bérard
Edge, 307 pages, $19.95 (trade paperback)
ISBN: 978-1-894063-19-7
Genres: Alien Beings, Mooreeffoc, Other Worlds

Sylvie Bérard is a French-Canadian academic, but don't let that scare you: she's a real science fiction writer who can do alien beings with the best of them. *Of Wind and Sand* is an English translation of *Terre des Autre*, which won the 2005 Québécois Grand Prix for science fiction (as well as several lesser awards). Translator Sheryl Curtis has produced an eminently readable text; it's easy to completely forget that the book you're reading was in French just a few years ago.

A human colonization mission goes off course and makes an emergency landing on a world that they name Mars II. It's a hot desert planet; humans have difficulty surviving even in the polar latitudes.

Enter the natives, reptilian creatures called darztls. Perfectly adapted to their world, the darztls contact the humans and offer their aid. Darztl help means the difference between survival and extinction for the humans.

Of course, the darztls are alien in the purest sense: their thought patterns and culture are decidedly nonhuman. Misunderstanding between the species is inevitable...and leads to disaster.

Of Wind and Sand tells the century-long story of human-darztl interaction through the eyes of Chloé Guilimpert, born on Mars II and raised by humans and darztls alike. Chloé sees the world from the darztl perspective as she leads us through violence, captivity, and slavery to the ultimate conclusion.

This is a tale of the clash of cultures and of various forms of imperialism and colonialism (on both sides). There are villains aplenty among both humans and darztls, and lots of blame to spread around.

Of Wind and Sand isn't just an example of otherness: it's also a meditation on how we react to otherness. Some characters on Mars II embrace it, others fear it, quite a few die because of it. In the end, those who can best regard themselves from the perspective of the other are the best hope. Definitely a book to be reckoned with.

After America
John Birmingham
Del Rey, 480 pages, $26.00 (hardcover)
ISBN: 978-0-345-50291-9
Series: Without Warnoing #2
Genres: Post-Apocalyptic, SF Thriller

Another post-apocalyptic, this one aimed at the techno-thriller crowd who made Tom Clancy and Dale Brown household names. Birmingham has fused sf and techno-thrillers before, in his *Axis of Time* series (in which a U.S. Navy ship from 2021 time-travels back to 1942 and settles that whole World War II unpleasantness with great dispatch), so he's no stranger to this territory.

In the first book, *Without Warning*, a mysterious energy wave devastates nearly the entire continental United States in March 2003, on the eve of the invasion of Iraq. The rest of the book is a rather fun romp through a world in which the U.S. no longer exists as a superpower, the resettlement of America, and the rise of engineer James Kipper to the post of U.S. President.

After America continues the fun. President Kipper has his plate full with pirates, carpetbaggers, an incomprehensible military, and a Texas despot who has gone and seceded from the Union. Meanwhile, a cast of characters across the world deals with rogue agents, international criminals, and other lowlifes.

Neither *Without Warning* or *After America* are too heavy on the techno-military acronym-speak that occurs in most techno-thrillers (although an occasional M249 SAW gunner or MPAT round does sneak in), so they're pretty accessible. Birmingham is Australian, and there's enough wry Aussie tongue-in-cheek to keep any reader amused, even if the politics of post-apocalyptic survival aren't quite enough.

Farside
Ben Bova
Tor, 400 pages, $24.99 (hardcover)
iBooks, Kindle, Nook: $11.99 (e-book)
ISBN: 978-0-7653-2387-3
Series: Grand Tour
Genres: Hard SF, High Frontier

The Robert A. Heinlein and Andre Norton "juveniles" of the 1950s and 1960s played a big part in inspiring an entire generation of young people to enter the fields of science and engineering. You don't have to ask very many astrophysicists or astronauts to uncover someone's happy memories of *Have Space Suit, Will Travel* or *Starman's Son*.

Currently, the inspirational torch is carried by Ben Bova. Most of Bova's books aren't actually YA, either in intent or in marketing —but they're easily accessible to bright teenagers, and they've opened the wonder of science and engineering to many a young mind.

A typical Bova book is set anywhere from twenty to two hundred years from the present, involves the exploration and industrialization of some piece of real estate in the solar system, has a varied multicultural cast, and is built around an exciting thriller plot. The book's informed by accurate science and rigorous extrapolation, and imparts the joy of learning. Scientists, technologists, and explorers are the heroes of most Bova books, rational and intelligent people all.

Farside, Bova's latest, is no exception. It's set against the background of constructing the first large observatory on the Moon's farside, where Luna's bulk shields the instruments from the electromagnetic and political interference of Earth.

Trudy Yost, astronomer, travels to the Lunar nation of Selene to become assistant to Professor Jason Uhlrich. Uhlrich is the driving force behind Farside Observatory, and a leading expert in the observatory's target: the Earth-size planet Sirius C. The planet shows hopeful signs, but critical data is tantalizingly out of reach until Farside's delicate instruments are online. But first, they have to build those instruments.

It's an unforgiving environment for construction work. Airless, bathed in hard radiation, subject to micrometeorite bombardment, everything covered in the irritating Lunar dust. Construction crews rely on robots and nanomachines for much of the work. Accidents are frequent, some of them fatal.

And some of the fatal ones aren't accidents at all. Slowly, Trudy learns that there's a saboteur at work—one, perhaps, with a good reason to want the project stopped.

In the midst of all this, Uhlrich's spectroanalysis of Sirius C finds traces of oxygen and water vapor, sure signs of life. And suddenly, the stakes are much higher....

Bova is a master storyteller, and *Farside* is a delightful read.

Mars, Inc.: The Billionaire's Club
Ben Bova
Baen, 240 pages, $25.00 (hardcover)
ISBN: 978-1-4516-3934-6
Genre: Mars

Before the Apollo Project, science fiction generally assumed that space travel would be accomplished by business and industry, not government. Government played a support role.

Only when there were enough people in space to govern, did government step in—usually in the role of police or military.

Robert A. Heinlein's 1950 novelette "The Man Who Sold the Moon" epitomized this view with the story of billionaire Delos D. Harriman and his efforts to finance and launch the first expedition to the Moon.

Now Ben Bova—who has been writing about Mars longer than just about any other living sf writer—pays homage to Heinlein's story with a twenty-first century tale of a billionaire determined to launch the first trip to Mars.

Art Thrasher, billionaire CEO of Thrasher Digital, is a man with a dream: to see humans on Mars. Angered and disgusted by continuing budget cuts to NASA, he conceives of a different way to fund the effort: a billionaire's club. Members would pledge a billion dollars a year to the Mars mission, as long as it takes to get boots on Martian ground. He figures that a group of about twenty could make the project a success.

Of course, convincing twenty billionaires (as well as their assorted Boards of Directors) to commit to his plan isn't going to be easy. It will take very ounce of charm, persuasiveness, guile, and sex appeal Thrasher possesses.

And signing up the backers is just the first step: there are all the complications of the Mars mission itself—finding and hiring the best personnel, overcoming legal and social barriers, building infrastructure...and of course there's opposition. From bureaucrats to politicians to oil barons, a lot of people have reasons to stand in Thrasher's way. Some of them are even capable of murder....

Mars, Inc. is one of those curious books that stands on the boundary between sf and mundane fiction. The technology is pretty much all off-the-shelf, primarily virtual reality and nuclear propulsion. While perfectly enjoyable as an sf book (could Bova write anything that wasn't enjoyable?), *Mars, Inc.* has that torn-from-the-headlines vibe that's obviously intended for a larger audience. As I write this, real-life billionaire Elon Musk is busy advocating his plan for a Martian colony. It's very tempting to read *Mars, Inc.* as an inspirational tale for all involved in such private-sector endeavors.

One of the fun games to play with this book is to identify some of the public figures who appear in disguise: the Koch brothers and certain Wal-Mart heirs leap off the page, but there are many others.

So what's (excuse the term) the bottom line? *Mars, Inc.* has inspiration, excitement, thrills, romance, a dash of satire—and it's a good, fun read solidly in the Analog tradition.

Mars Life
Ben Bova
Tor, 448 pages, $24.95 (hardcover)
ISBN: 978-0-7653-1787-2
Series: Grand Tour, Jamie Waterman #3
Genres: High Frontier, Mars, Near Future, Space Colonization

Ben Bova, a former editor of *Analog*, has been chronicling the exploration and settlement of the Solar System since 1992, and he's a master. The Grand Tour series is a consistent future history based on our most current scientific understanding of the planets.

In *Mars Life* Bova returns to one of his most popular characters, half-Navajo Martian explorer Jamie Waterman from *Mars* and *Return to Mars*. Twenty years ago, Waterman discovered cliff dwellings on Mars, evidence of intelligent life that existed 65 million years ago. Now Jamie is back on Earth, struggling to preserve the beleaguered Mars program.

The religious right, whose political power is ever-growing, feel their beliefs threatened by the concept of intelligent life on Mars—especially intelligent life that predates the Garden of Eden by millions of years. Government support dries up, universities are scared off, private donors stop giving...and if Jamie can't find a source of funding, the Mars program will be canceled and all its personnel recalled.

Meanwhile on Mars, anthropologist Carter Carleton is supervising an archeological dig of an ancient village. When he finds the fossilized remains of one of the Martians, the stakes are suddenly much higher. Forces of science and religion are in conflict for the fate of two worlds, with Jamie Waterman at ground zero.

As the tension mounts, interpersonal problems sprout among the scientists on Mars, and Jamie and his wife head off to the red planet to see what they can do on the scene.

No mater when or where a story takes place—past or future, on Earth or distant wolds, sf always deals with the concerns of today's world. The tension between religion and science is one of the defining conflicts of our age; with Ben Bova as author, it's not hard to guess which side ultimately prevails in *Mars Life*. Bova makes the journey exciting, and keeps the suspense going until the last page. Highly recommended.

The Return
Ben Bova
Tor, 432 pages, $25.95
ISBN: 978-0-7653-0925-9
Series: Voyagers 4, Grand Tour Universe
Genres: Adventure, Alien Beings

There seems to be a tendency, in some venerable science fiction writers, to unify their various works into one great multiverse. Poul Anderson was perhaps the first, linking the *Polesotechnic League* of Nicholas van Rijn with Dominic Flandry's Terran Empire in one future history. Asimov did it when he brought the *Foundation* and *Positronic Robot* series together; Heinlein's later books pulled together everything he'd ever written and threw in the *Oz*, *Barsoom*, and *Lensman* universes for good measure.

Now Ben Bova is apparently feeling the urge, bringing characters from his *Voyagers* series into the universe of his *Grand Tour*.

The *Voyagers* books (*Voyagers*, *The Alien Within*, and *Star Brothers*) tell the story of astronaut Keith Stoner, first explorer of a strange alien starship that entered the Solar System. Stoner acquired the abilities and memories of the long-dead alien pilot, and eventually built his own starship. With his wife and children, he fled to the stars.

Now, a century alter, Stoner and his family return to Earth. But it's not the Earth they left; somehow, they have crossed over into the *Grand Tour* universe. And Stoner's not happy about it.

In the *Grand Tour* series (as we most recently saw in *Mars Life*), Earth is no longer an attractive place. The anti-science and anti-technology kooks are winning the day, and ecological disaster looms.

If anyone's going to save humanity, it's got to be Keith Stoner. And the rest is pure Bova: careful scientific and cultural extrapolation, well-drawn characters, and interesting philosophical underpinnings. While I'm still not convinced that bringing these two universes together was the best idea ever, Bova certainly makes it work.

It'll be interesting to see where he goes next.

We'll Always Have Paris
Ray Bradbury
William Morrow, 224 pages, $24.95 (hardcover)
ISBN: 978-0-06-171977-6
Genres: Short Story Collections, Literary SF

Ray Bradbury can hold his head up high in any Literary circles...indeed, in any circles. *We'll Always Have Paris* is a collection of previously-unpublished Bradbury stories. That alone should be enough to convince you to rush out and snag a copy. But perhaps you're unconvinced.

Let me make a confession here: I didn't always like Bradbury. In my salad days, even before Professor Abromaitis and Jonathan Swift, I didn't consider Bradbury to be a real science fiction writer. He wasn't rigorous about his science. Just look at *The Martian Chronicles* (especially when compared to *Red Planet* or *The Sands of Mars*): you just know that Bradbury never calculated the intensity of solar radiation on Mars, or the heat of fusion of ice in the thin Martian atmosphere—heck, he had people walking around on Mars without breathing gear. Fantasy, yes; horror, even—but not science fiction.

It wasn't until much later, when I'd been exposed to a lot more different types of fiction and a lot more experience of life, that I came to realize that Bradbury was his own thing, independent of narrow genre definitions. And I came to understand that if Bradbury were willing to allow Science Fiction to claim him as part of the family, then Science Fiction would be smart to accept the honor. Especially in an era in which Certain Writers made it a rite of passage to loudly and conspicuously reject Science Fiction.

So I'm not going to tell you that some of the stories in *We'll Always Have Paris* are mainstream, others are fantasy, still others science fiction, and one is a poem. I'm not even going to tell you that one story, "Fly Away Home," is a Martian Chronicle. No, I'm just going to tell you that they are all Bradbury, and that should be enough. There are 22 tales in this volume, so if you read one a day and take weekends off, you can stretch it out for a whole month. Except you won't, nobody could. So it will be over all that much sooner, and you'll be out of brand-new Bradbury, and you'll have only yourself to blame.

Needless to say, this book would also be a nice present for anyone who likes good stories, SF or not.

Noise
Darin Bradley
Spectra, 222 pages, $15.00 (trade paperback)
Ebook: $9.99 (Kindle) $10.12 (Nook)
ISBN: 978-0-553-38622-6
Genre: Cyberpunk, Dystopian Futures

Since this month's theme is stories of different lengths, I am tempted to call Noise "short and sweet"—except "sweet" just doesn't apply, in so many ways. Let me simply note that in the past, this would have been classed as a standard-sized novel; nowadays it is perhaps a long novella. Which shows you exactly how artificial such length divisions ultimately are.

Set in the very near future, *Noise* is a story of economic and social collapse, and those who live through it.

Hiram and Levi are hackers and *Dungeons & Dragons* players when the collapse comes. Fortunately, they are prepared with The Book, which tells them everything they need to know. They compiled The Book from the pirate broadcasts of an anarchic group known as Salvage, broadcasts that went out on the unused airwaves after the switch to digital TV was complete. Amid static and noise, Salvage has been warning of the coming collapse, and giving advice on how to survive in the chaos of a fallen world.

So Hiram and Levi set forth, prepared for the newly-violent world around them, in search of a place of safety called Amaranth, where they can begin to build the world anew. Along the way they gather a band of hackers, malcontents, and misfits.

But in the real world, things aren't as cut-and-dried as The Book makes them seem, and cold-blooded decisions aren't as easy to make as the boys thought they would be. In the final analysis, Hiram and Levi are left with choices to make...and their choices will affect the sort of society that finally emerges from the collapse.

Edgy and disturbing, *Noise* is a worthy successor to all those post-holocaust books of yesteryear.

The Gravity Pilot
M. M. Buckner
Tor, 329 pages, $25.99 (hardcover)
Kindle, Nook: $12.99 (ebook)
ISBN: 978-0-7653-2286-9
Genre: Cyberpunk, Dystopian Futures, Ecological/Environmental SF

It's good to know, in this age of genetically-enhanced and nano-reconstructed transhumans, that there's still a place in sf for a character who excels by sheer physical ability. Orr Sitka is just such a character. In a dystopian near-future world, Orr has found happiness in two ways: his lover (named Dyce), and skydiving over the Alaska wilderness. One day, quite by accident, Orr makes (and survives) a jump from a record altitude—and his happy life is never the same. Suddenly he's a media darling, with ever-more-daring jumps turned into virtual reality simulations to feed the entertainment appetites of a jaded population.

The media attention is too much for Dyce; she leaves Orr to become a librarian working in the bowels of a decadent Seattle. While the media are ruining Orr, Dyce becomes addicted to seamy virtual reality. Separately but in parallel, the two of them descend into their own private hells.

Then Orr learns of Dyce's fate, and sets off to rescue her.

The book is billed as a retelling of the Orpheus myth (Orrpheus trying to rescue Euri-Dyce from Hell, get it?), but don't let that put you off. It's a rollicking good cyberpunk adventure as well as a nice love story, with a fine overlay of psychological and social commentary.

M. M. Buckner won the 2005 Philip K. Dick Award for best original paperback in sf, and she's been making a name for herself with well-crafted sf adventures. *The Gravity Pilot* is her fifth book; she's definitely a name to watch in the future.

Cryoburn
Lois McMaster Bujold
Baen, 345 pages, $25.00 (hardcover)
Baen Webscriptions: $15.00 (ebook)
ISBN: 978-1-4391-3394-1
Series: Miles Vorkosigan #16
Genre: Adventure SF, Biological SF

This may be the most eagerly awaited book here. Lois McMaster Bujold's last Miles Vorkosigan book came out in 2002, and with each passing year readers have been more and more eager for the next. In eight years, more and more new readers have discovered the series, read all the books, and wanted more. They can't help it, it's a law of nature: to read a Bujold book is to want more.

If you haven't had the pleasure of meeting Miles Vorkosigan, you might wonder what all the fuss is about. I know *I* did, for I came to the series late, after friends had been after me for years to give it a try. First, there is Miles himself: A man born small, weak, and fragile due to congenital deformities, but with quick wits, unconquerable will, and an ability to get himself into and out of trouble by taking the least direct routes. The son of a nobleman, Miles triumphs over adversity and obstacles and makes his own way in the universe.

Then there's Bujold's writing, which is like a refreshing drink from a cold, clear mountain spring. Her words sparkle and delight with ingenuity and cleverness; you'll drive everyone around you crazy by reading the better passages aloud (and there are lots of them). She is a mesmerizing storyteller. And she's funny to boot.

In the seven years since we last saw Miles, he's become a father and had various adventures, but he still holds the post of Auditor for the three-planet Barrayaran Empire. He and his armsman Roic have come to a non-Imperial world, Kiboudaini, to investigate strange goings-on. Kibou-daini is dominated by the Cryocombs, where millions of citizens are frozen awaiting immortality. Huge companies—cryocorps— maintain the sleepers and, incidentally, hold their proxies for voting in planetary elections. One of these cryocorps wants to start operations in the Barrayaran Empire, which is what brought Miles to Kibou-daini.

Except things go wrong, as they do when Miles is around, and he finds himself in the company of a boy who loves animals and a group of off-the-grid rebels operating their own cryo-facility. In no time at all Miles is up to his neck in the complex and deadly politics of this strange world. Once again it's Miles against the universe...and the universe is fearfully outmatched.

Read this book. If you've read Bujold before, you don't need me to tell you that. If you haven't, this is as good a place as any to jump on...you'll soon be reading all the others as well.

The first edition comes with a CD that contains ebook versions of most of the other Vorkosigan novels, which makes it quite a bargain if you're an ebook person.

Captain Vorpatril's Alliance
Lois McMaster Bujold
Baen, 432 pages, $25.00 (hardcover)
Baen Ebooks: $6.00 (e-book)
ISBN: 978-1-4516-3845-5
Series: Vorkosigan Saga
Genre: Adventure SF

Throughout the Vorkosigan saga, poor Ivan Vorpatril has essentially been cast in the role of lovable comic sidekick to his more famous and successful cousin, Miles Vorkosigan. We've seen Ivan bumble along, full of good intentions and displaying an uncanny talent for making things worse.

Now Ivan gets to be the hero of his own story, and it's a fun tale from beginning to end.

As the book opens, Captain Ivan Vorpatril is minding his own business at his duty station on the planet Komarr, when his calm is shattered by the late-night arrival of Imperial Security agent Byerly Vorrutyer. Before Ivan knows it, he's committed to spying on a mysterious and beautiful woman.

The woman, Tej, is accompanied by an equally mysterious companion named Rish. Soon Ivan's hiding Tej and Rish in his apartment, then smuggling them offplanet. He slowly learns that they are refugees of great importance to the interstellar balance of power, pursued by all sorts of nefarious characters.

Thrust into a very sticky situation through no fault of his own, Ivan manages to rise to the occasion, becoming (in his own way) a hero and a credit to his family.

Lois McMaster Bujold is at the top of her game here, producing a high-energy, action-filled comedy of errors filled with language that sparkles and fizzes. This book is a pure delight to read.

Veracity
Laura Bynum
Pocket, 376 pages, $25.00 (hardcover)
ISBN: 0-978-1-4391-2334-8
Genre: Dystopian Futures, Literary SF

Veracity is one of those books that's just as at home in literary circles as among science fiction readers. It's a novel of a dystopian future, and before you start groaning that you've seen this before, take a moment to look. There's a lot here that's fresh.

In 2012, terrorists unleashed a virus that killed half the world's population. The result was a new oppressive government called The Confederation of the Willing, which exists to maintain security and order at all costs. The main instrument of the Confederation is the "slate," a device implanted in the neck of every citizen. Using slates, the Confederation controls behavior by controlling speech itself. Certain words are forbidden: to utter them results in immediate physical pain—and to continue uttering them quickly brings a visit from the brutal police force known as the Blue Coats.

Most people live with the restrictions of the Confederation, grateful for the security it gives. Harper Adams is one of those people; a child during the terrorist attacks, Harper is now a grown woman with a daughter of her own, and she's as law-abiding as they come.

Until her daughter is taken from her. Until her daughter's very name, Veracity, becomes a forbidden word.

Then Harper runs, goes off the grid, destroys her own slate, and starts a search for the fabled resistance. But unlike the other rebels, Harper isn't just fighting for freedom, for liberty, or for the defeat of tyranny. No, Harper is fighting for Veracity…and for truth itself.

Not just another *Brave New World* or *Handmaid's Tale* wannabe, *Veracity* is a unique book with powerful characters and a fully realized future society. It reminds one of some of the best work of Frederik Pohl, with perhaps healthy quantities of Edgar Pangborn and Suzy McKee Charnas thrown in. This is Laura Bynum's first book; if the literary establishment doesn't seduce her away from us, she's definitely a name to watch in the future.

Prometheus II
S. J. Byrne
Armchair Fiction, 198 pages, $12.95 (trade paperback)
ISBN: 978-1-61287-124-0
Genre: Adventure SF, Military SF

Finally, let me leave you with a sample of what military sf looked like in 1948. Thanks to the fine people at Armchair Fiction, this magazine serial from *Amazing Stories* is available in an attractive trade paperback edition.

Prometheus II is actually a pretty good read, as long as you remember that it's a period piece. Nicholas I, absolute ruler of Russia, is bent on world domination. His scientists have located an underground civilization of degenerate creatures called the Deros, and Nicholas has the great idea to release them and use them in his nefarious plans.

It's up to Stephen Germain and Major "Slim" Kent to find a way to counter the Russian threat, and there's much swashbuckling adventure as they attempt to do so. But the best hope comes from far beyond Earth, with an alien race that might have the power to save humanity...if they have the will to act.

Prometheus II is a fairly painless way to relive the excitement of a previous generation of sf readers. Read it along with Van Vogt's *Trangalactic,* and you'll come away with an appreciation of the roots of modern military sf.

Reviews: C

(alphabetical by author)

The Lost Fleet: Relentless
Jack Campbell
Ace, 320 pages, $7.99 (Mass Market Paperback)
ISBN: 978-0-441-01708-9
Series: Lost Fleet #5
Genre: Military SF

I'm not one of those who believes that every sf book has to be stunningly original and deeply meaningful. Sometimes you're just in the mood for something familiar, something dependable: comfort food. In the old days, you could count on Mack Reynolds, Gordon Dickson, or Poul Anderson for a basic good, entertaining story. Nowadays there are many options; one of them is a nice military sf series.

It just figures. Military sf usually has a familiar plot, good guys vs. bad guys. The social trappings are familiar—military rank, command structure, character motivations. A multi-book series generally implies that you're going to be following the same characters through a succession of adventures. And if the series is by a familiar author whose work you know, so much the better.

Jack Campbell's *Lost Fleet* series meets all the criteria for good, solid comfort food.

To begin with, Jack Campbell is a name that all *Analog* readers should be familiar with—although you have to look on the copyright page to learn this. "Jack Campbell" is a pseudonym for none other than *Analog* regular John Hemry, and you *know* he can tell a good story.

Here's the basic set-up for the series. The Alliance and the Syndicate Worlds have been at war for a long time. Captain John ("Black Jack") Geary, commander of the Alliance heavy cruiser *Merlon*, is the last to enter an escape pod when his ship his defeated and destroyed. The pod automatically puts him into suspended animation until he reaches rescue.

A century later, Geary's pod is found by an Alliance fleet, and he's reanimated. The fleet is deep in enemy space, reeling from defeats and desperate to get home. And here's the legendary hero Black Jack Geary, back to lead them to safety. Before he knows it, Geary is in command of the Lost Fleet, and the adventure has begun.

Except that Geary knows he is only a man, not an all-powerful hero. The ships of the Fleet (there are hundreds of them) include various squabbling captains, an officious politician, an underground resistance, and an unknown number of enemy agents. Geary struggles with his own doubts and demons, uncertain that he can ever succeed in bringing the Fleet safely to Alliance space.

Geary's doubts and weaknesses only make him all the more interesting and sympathetic, which is a good thing in a series protagonist: if you've going to spend multiple volumes with a guy, you want him to be someone you like.

Through four previous books Geary and the Fleet have struggled on through nonstop pursuits, battles, food shortages, and betrayals, limping from one star system to another with barely time to nurse their wounds.

The four previous books are *Dauntless* (#1), *Fearless* (#2), *Courageous* (#3), and *Valiant* (#4). And if I may digress for a moment, here's where sf series writers and publishers could take a lesson from mystery writers such as Sue Grafton (*A is for Alibi, B is for Burglar*, etc.) and Janet Evanovich (*One for the Money, Two for the Dough*, and so forth). Would it be so hard to give the hapless reader a break and make the titles go in alphabetical order, or include numbers?

Ahem. Back to the Lost Fleet. In *Relentless*, Geary takes them to the Heradoo system to rescue Alliance prisoners of war. Of course, Heradoo is also the location of a great number of enemy vessels. Meanwhile, there's the question of what happens when the Fleet gets home—turns out that a sizable contingent wants Geary to overthrow the corrupt Alliance government. Oh, and there are these saboteurs loose in the Fleet....

The Lost Fleet isn't just mindless action. As you'd expect, Hemry/Campbell writes space battles that conform to the laws of physics; no right-angle turns or shields down by x% in these books. Unsurprisingly, his military officers also ring true; you aren't going to see third-year cadets inexplicably put in command of any flagships here.

Does the Fleet eventually get home? Does Black Jack lead a revolt against the evil politicians? Are there going to be more books in the series? I'm not going to spoil the fun by telling.

With a ragtag fleet fleeing implacable enemies, it's hard not to be reminded of *Battlestar Galactica* (whichever version you prefer). Don't be fooled; this is no warmed-over television show. *The Lost Fleet* books are real science fiction, as filling and nutritious as a meal of your favorite comfort foods.

Railroad Spine
Geonn Cannon
Supposed Crimes LLC, 435 K
Kindle, Nook, Smashwords: $5.99 (e-book)
ISBN: 9781938108044
Genre: Adventure SF, Psychological/Sociological SF, Steampunk

Dice Bodger is one of the Commonwealth's most successful Airskips, commander of the trading airship *Tamerlane*. She's good at her job, fair to her crew, and a lusty lover to both men and women. The *Tamerlane's* travels take her from one end of the continent to the other, from Potomac to Seattle and from Acadia to the Great Lakes. In short, Dice has a perfect life.

Then Levi Barton comes aboard as *Tamerlane's* new engineer. Dice and Levi fall in love, and he begins teaching her things that she should not know. First, the workings of the great engines...then more, mathematics and philosophy and chemistry and all sorts of forbidden knowledge.

In this future world, knowledge is a tightly-controlled commodity. One learns only what one needs for one's job; all else is forbidden, criminal.

At first Dice is shocked by Levi's knowledge. Soon enough, though, she finds that she enjoys learning new things. She and Levi keep their illicit activities secret, knowing they would both be in trouble if their lawbreaking was discovered.

Soon enough, Dice is pulled from *Tamerlane* for medical reasons: pregnancy, to be exact. She goes into seclusion, under the care of a midwife, until her baby boy is born. It's only then that she learns Levi has been apprehended and condemned as a traitor to society. Her child is taken from her, sent to be raised anonymously by a foster family.

Then Dice herself is brought in for questioning. Although she denies that Levi taught her anything, the authorities torture her, leaving her scarred and despondent.

Only after she returns to *Tamerlane* does Dice learn of a secret cabal devoted to freedom of knowledge. With Nikola Tesla as their patron saint, the members of this cabal preserve forbidden books and other sources, and work for the downfall of the authorities. They want Dice to join their ranks. Now all her hurt and anger focus on two goals: to topple the system that controls the population through ignorance...and to find her lost child.

While this story wears the trappings of steampunk, it's no mere adventure tale. Like *Impulse*, there's a lot more going on under the surface: questions of freedom and rebellion, and a fundamental belief in the power of knowledge. The story is well-told and the characters are compelling. Join Dice Bodger on her journey of discovery; you won't regret it.

To the Galactic Rim
A. Bertram Chandler
Baen, 553 pages, $12.00 (trade paperback)
Baen Webscriptions: $6.00 (ebook)
ISBN: 978-1-4391-3421-4
Series: John Grimes #1-4
Genre: Adventure SF, Big Books, Military SF

Before Honor Harrington, Daniel Leary, or even Miles Vorkosigan, there was John Grimes. Long out of print, now the Federation Survey officer is back. And there is great rejoicing.

The name of A. Bertram Chandler is a familiar one to longtime readers of this magazine. During the *Astounding* years he was a frequent contributor of short fiction, but first he moved into novels and then in 1984 he passed away, so those who have been reading Analog for less than 25 years might not have heard of him.

Grimes isn't, technically, a military man. Rather, he's an explorer—although like Poul Anderson's Nicholas Van Rijn and David Falkayn or Keith Laumer's Retief, he's really a problem-solver on a grand scale. Across 22 books in from the late 1960s until Chandler's death, Grimes works his way around the Galaxy. In the typical Grimes novel, Grimes and his crew encounter a new planet, realize that there's a problem, and succeed in solving it. The planets are exotic and full of wonders; the problems are extremely unusual; and Grimes' solutions are brilliantly outrageous.

Chandler was another of those Aussies who pop up in sf every once in a while, bringing their own unique viewpoint to the field. The Grimes books are filled with humor and some fine detail about the experience of space exploration.

This volume collects the first four Grimes books in chronological order: *The Road to the Rim*, *To Prime the Pump*, *The Hard Way Up*, and *The Broken Cycle*. It begins with Grimes' graduation from the Academy and takes him through a series of adventures with a planetful of frustrated women, an alien god, and various other dubious situations. In either print or ebook, this volume is a bargain not to be missed.

Ride the Star Winds
A. Bertram Chandler
Baen, 869 pages, $12.00 (trade paperback)
Baen E-Books: $6.00 (e-book)
ISBN: 978-1-4516-3812-7
Series: John Grimes #13-16
Genre: Adventure SF, Big Books, Military SF

One way to get a big book is to publish a bunch of little books in one volume. For the last few years, Baen Books has been bringing together A. Bertram Chandler's fine John Grimes books, originally published in the 1960s through 1980s.

Grimes is an explorer, an adventurer who is part diplomat, part soldier of fortune, part pirate, and part troubleshooter. He and his crew travel from world to world getting into and out of the most amusing troubles. The books are set against the common background of the Rim Worlds, which are a somewhat seedy frontier backwater of the civilized galaxy. There's plenty of humor and loads of fun—and if some of the concepts seem a bit dated, that's part of the charm.

In this volume, Grimes serves a term as governor of a planet where politicians customarily advance by the art of assassination; gets caught in the middle of a feminist revolution on a formerly all-male planet; accused of witchcraft while on a visit to Earth; and lost in time and space on an experimental sailing ship. A few Rim Worlds short stories are thrown in for good measure.

If you haven't had the chance to make the acquaintance of Commodore John Grimes, you owe it to yourself to do so. Print or e-book, it's a nice big book.

Into Plutonian Depths
Stanton A. Coblentz
Armchair, 199 pages, $12.95 (trade paperback)
ISBN: 978-1-61287-014-4
Genre: Adventure SF, Before the Golden Age

Originally published in *Wonder Stories Quarterly* in Spring 1931, *Into Plutonian Depths* appeared in a 1950 paperback from Avon. The book tells the story of inventor Andrew Stark and his friend Dan, who travel to Pluto and find themselves confronting a society of three genders: male, female, and neuter. By the way, they also have fourteen fingers and lamps in their heads, which comes in handy in the underground world of Pluto.

On Pluto, people are born male and female, and aspire to become neuter. the visiting Earthmen are shocked, especially when they meet the beautiful woman Zandaye (with whom Stark promptly falls in love). There are, as you would expect, threatening politicians, evil scientists, wild chases, stirring battles, and daring escapes. The whole thing is fun and excitement from cover to cover.

The 1950 Avon paperback edition had unexpected high sales, and there's an interesting historical story behind those sales. The cover (reproduced on the current edition) refers to "a world with three sexes." Zandaye, who features prominently, looks like a high-quality drag queen...and she's holding hands with ruggedly good-looking Andrew Stark. When you remember that "the third sex" was a 1950s euphemism for gay men, and add the gender-bending theme, it's easy to see why Into Plutonian Depths became notorious in America's underground gay community.

And Another Thing...
Eoin Colfer
Hyperion, 273 pages, $25.99 (hardcover)
ISBN: 978-1-4013-2358-5
Series: Hitchhiker's Guide to the Galaxy #6
Genre: Humorous SF

Writers are mortal, but franchises can live forever. When the author of a bestselling series goes to the great keyboard in the sky, heirs are left with the chore of searching for a successor. Sometimes a family member can step in, with or without a collaborator: Frank Herbert's son Brian and co-writer Kevin J. Anderson have successfully picked up the *Dune* series, and Anne McCaffrey is leaving the *Dragonriders of Pern* in the capable hands of her son Todd. But when no capable family member exists, the search must go further afield.

To take up the reins of Douglas Adams' *Hitchhiker's Guide to the Galaxy* series, his heirs chose Eoin Colfer, author of the bestselling *Artemis Fowl* teen fantasy series. Colfer's first book for adults is *And Another Thing...*, which is billed as "part six of three" of the *Hitchhiker's Guide* series.

Everyone is surely familiar with the *Hitchhiker's Guide* series, the premier example of humorous SF. Douglas Adams is a hard act to follow, but Colfer does an acceptable job. All the old familiar characters are here: whining Earthman Arthur Dent, galactic hitchhiker Ford Prefect, the slimy bureaucratic Vogons, and everybody's favorite two-headed President, Zaphod Beeblebrox.

After a slightly bumpy settling-in period, Colfer does a good job of capturing the spirit of zany absurdity that characterized the Hitchhiker's Guide books. There's easily enough plot to sustain the madness, and enough stream-of-consciouness comic digressions to satisfy the discriminating fan.

My spouse, who is an enormous HHGTTG fanatic—with an encyclopedic knowledge of the corpus that astonished Adams himself—pronounced himself satisfied with *And Another Thing...* Ordinary casual readers, like me, will have no cause for disappointment. It's a fun romp indeed.

The Hunger Games
Suzanne Collins
Scholastic Press, 374 pages, $17.99
ISBN: 978-0-439-02348-1
Series: Hunger Games #1
Genres: Post-Apocalyptic, Teen SF

Katniss Everdeen, 17, lives a hard life in the Seam, an impoverished village in District 12, one of the poorest of the 12 Districts that make up the nation of Panem. Ever since her father died in a mining accident, Katniss has been the primary breadwinner for her ineffectual mother and her frail younger sister. Along with her male friend Gale, Katniss spends most of her time hunting and gathering in the forbidden forest, then trading with other villagers for the necessities of life. It's subsistence living at best.

Once a year, by law, comes the Reaping. All children between 12 and 18 are entered in a lottery, and each District draws two Tributes: one boy and one girl. The Tributes are sent to the Capitol to compete in the Hunger Games: a reality show gone mad, a no-holds-barred fight to the death where only one child survives.

To Katniss's horror, this year's winner is her little sister. Without thinking, Katniss steps forward to take her sister's place in the Games.

The rest of the book tells the story of Katniss's participation in the Games, her struggle to survive and overcome the other 23 contestants, and her ultimate fate.

This gripping story is also sophisticated science fiction, as rewarding to adults as to the teens who are the main audience. Besides the survival plot, there is a larger political plot going on here. The Capitol uses the Games as but one weapon for subjugating the Districts; Katniss is as much freedom fighter as she is reality show contestant.

Along the way, Katniss learns quite a bit about her fellow Humans...and more than a bit about herself.

The Hunger Games, while a complete story, is Book One of a series. There's certainly more to be told of Katniss and the richly-detailed world she inhabits. I look forward to Book Two.

Catching Fire
Suzanne Collins
Scholastic, 391 pages, $17.99 (hardcover)
ISBN: 978-0-439-02349-8
Series: Hunger Games #2
Genres: Post-Apocalyptic, Teen SF

Last year, *The Hunger Games* took both the SF and teen fiction worlds by storm. *Catching Fire* continues the story of Katniss Everdeen, a teenage poor girl from impoverished District 12 who was taken to the Capital to fight for her life in the Hunger Games. Katniss triumphed over her opponents and struck a very public blow of defiance against the tyranny of the Capital.

Now Katniss is back home, but things are not well. The leaders of the Capital know that she is becoming a symbol of defiance in all the Districts—and they inform Katniss that she must use her status as champion to renounce her defiance and help quell rebellion. Her family and friends are hostage to her obedience.

On a victory tour of the Districts, Katniss tries to do as she is told...but as she learns more of the Capital's cruel oppression, there also comes the dawning realization that she has become an inspiration to rebels everywhere.

Then the unthinkable happens: the Capital decrees that Katniss and her fellow champion Peeta must compete once again in a bigger, more deadly round of Hunger Games.

But Katniss has secret friends in the most unusual places, and just like the ever-more-restive populace, she too is catching fire....

Catching Fire is a page-turner, and it's also brimming with questions of honor, freedom, and personal responsibility. Like the best teen books, this one is equally enjoyable to adults of all ages. If you haven't read book #1, *The Hunger Games*, you'll want to start there (which just means double the pleasure.)

Mockingjay
Suzanne Collins
Scholastic, 398 pages, $17.99 (hardcover)
Kindle, Nook: $7.58 (ebook)
ISBN: 978-0-439-02351-1
Series: Hunger Games #3
Genre: Post-Apocalyptic, Teen SF

Mockingjay is the concluding book of the enormously popular *Hunger Games* series, awaited eagerly by teens and adults alike. In the previous two books (*The Hunger Games* and *Catching Fire*) Katniss Everdeen has twice survived the Hunger Games, in which teens from the Twelve Districts of the country Panem (post-apocalypse North America) fight to the death in the Arena. In the process, Katniss became the living symbol of revolt against the despotic Capital.

Now Katniss and her family are safe in the secret District Thirteen, long thought destroyed and the base of the rebels. All of Panem is in open revolt. Katniss' home District, Twelve, has been firebombed and its inhabitants killed. The rebels, seeing possible victory for the first time in centuries, want Katniss—in her victorious and inspirational persona of the Mockingjay—for their propaganda efforts. They tell her that she can turn the tide of battle so the Capital can be defeated once and for all. Can she trust them any more than she can trust the Capital?

Everyone wants to use the Mockingjay for their own purposes. But Katniss is her own person, and if the rebels try to control their Mockingjay, they just might be sorry.

This book brings the story to an end, and shows us the final fate of Panem and the Mockingjay. It's as exciting and compelling as the previous two books. Don't blame me if you find yourself staying up late to finish it.

Caliban's War
James S. A. Corey
Orbit, 833 pages, $15.99 (trade paperback)
iBooks, Kindle, Nook: $9.99 (e-book)
ISBN: 978-0-316-12906-0
Series: The Expanse #2
Genre: Big Books, Space Opera

In the first book of The Expanse, *Leviathan Wakes*, we were introduced to a future in which Humanity has spread throughout the solar system. The stars are still out of reach, so through mega-engineering and genetic alterations Humans have settled on Mars, Luna, the asteroids, and the outer moons of the giant planets. The rivalry between Earth and Mars is the main conflict of the system, with the Outer Planets Alliance struggling to remain neutral.

We also met James Holden, ice miner become military leader, and we learned of an alien protomolecule of great destructive power, which subsequently infects Venus but is kept quarantined.

Caliban's War continues the story. A station on Ganymede, breadbasket of the Outer Planets, is attacked...not by Earth or Mars, but by some monstrous third party. The incident nonetheless sparks war between the two planets, a war in which Ganymede is ruined. In the scramble to evacuate, a botanist named Prax loses track of his daughter, Mei. It soon develops that Mei isn't the only missing child—there are 15 of them.

Enter Captain Holden and his crew of Outer Planets peacekeepers. Prax appeals for help, and Holden grants it. As the search for the missing kids proceeds, Holden is horrified to find traces of the alien protomolecule. And as war between the various Human factions becomes more heated, Holden begins to suspect that this is all a distraction from the real enemy....

James S. A. Corey is the pen name of Daniel Abraham and Ty Franck. In the *Expanse* series they've given us a huge, sprawling saga set in a fascinating future. Despite the title (and the warship on the cover), *Caliban's War* isn't primarily military sf. There are no detailed descriptions of space battles as choreographed by Admiral Nelson, no loving portrayals of weapons technology. The conflicts are as much political and emotional as military, and there's a strong flavor of Victorian horror about the whole series. Characters grow and develop as time passes. No, this is space opera—and particularly good space opera at that. Definitely recommended.

Monster Hunter Legion
Larry Correia
Baen, 521 pages, $7.99 (mass market paperback)
iBooks, Kindle, Nook: $9.99 (e-book)
ISBN: 978-1-4516-3906-3
Series: Monster Hunter International #4
Genre: Adventure SF, Military SF

Perhaps you're giving someone a game system, or some popular sf shoot-em-up games or movies involving heroes who fight nasty creatures with lots of high-tech firepower. That person will appreciate a *Monster Hunter International* book; the latest title is *Monster Hunter Legion*.

The world is full of monsters—virtually every bad thing from myth or folklore exists out there, largely unknown and forgotten by a modern society that has better things to worry about. Yet there are a few people who know the truth, and who stand on the front lines of humanity's defense, keeping the monsters at bay.

Owen Zastava Pitt is one of the best. He works for Monster Hunter International, the foremost monster-hunting company in the world. In three previous books Pitt and his compatriots have conquered an assortment of nasties with skill, derring-do, and more than their share of luck.

This current book takes place in Las Vegas, where monster hunters from all over the world have gathered for a trade conference. In no time at all, someone's reanimated a World War II era scientific experiment, a creature that's going berserk in the desert. Someone has to stop it—and for once, Monster Hunter International has rivals. There's a wager with some high stakes indeed, as competing companies set out to bag the monster.

Except, of course, there are some unfortunate complications: the awakened monster falls under the control of something very old and very powerful and very, very unpleasant. If Pitt and his crew can't stop this one, what happens in Vegas will not stay in Vegas, but will take over the whole planet....

Definitely a lot of fun, much of it tongue-in-cheek. Any shoot-em-up gamer should be delighted.

The Prisoner
Carlos J. Cortes
Bantam Spectra, 416 pages, $7.99 (paperback)
ISBN: 978-0-553-59163-7
Genre: Adventure SF, Prisons, Psychological/Sociological SF

This near-future thriller plays with the concept of suspended animation in prisons. By 2060, the prison system is contracted out to Hypnos, Inc., a company that markets safe and virtually flawless cryonic hibernation. Inmates are frozen and stacked in Hypnos detention centers known as "sugar cubes," to be reanimated when their sentences are completed.

As far as Congress and the public know, that's all there is to it. But Laurel Cole learns that there's more to the picture: undocumented prisoners who don't appear in any records, and who have no release date. Prisoners who have come to Hypnos without trial, political dissidents whose only crime is challenging the status quo. When Laurel finds that one of these inmates is reporter Eliot Russo, missing for eight years, she also learns that Russo has information that could expose both Hypnos and their secret government partners.

Aided by an oddball assortment of co-conspirators, Laurel enters the Washington, DC sugar cube as an inmate. Her first mission is to locate Russo and break him out.

But escaping from a maximum-security installation is only the first of Laurel's challenges. Once she has Russo, the race is on to bring down Hypnos its partners, and to do so before Laurel and her team find themselves permanently on ice.

As conventional as it sounds, *The Prisoner* is a gripping near-future adventure story, and the science behind it is well-researched and nicely presented. The pages fly by quickly, the characters are compelling, and the ending is quite satisfactory.

The Pesthouse
Jim Crace
Vintage, 272 pages, $13.95 (paperback)
ISBN: 978-0-307-27895-1
Genre: Literary SF, Post-Apocalyptic

The medieval post-apocalyptic America of *The Pesthouse* will be familiar to anyone familiar with SF of the 1960s and 1970s. Technology has regressed to the level of subsistence farming, transportation is by foot or horseback, and the sword and bow-and-arrow are the height of weaponry. No one remembers the exact nature of the long-ago catastrophe that left the world so changed.

When disaster destroys his village, farmboy Franklin heads off for the East, where rumor tells of ships bound for Europe, the land of milk and honey. Along the way, Franklin hooks up with Margaret, who is recovering from "the flux," a feared disease that has left her shunned and outcast.

On their journey, Franklin and Margaret fall in love and acquire a child. There are adventures: slave-traders kidnap Franklin, and Margaret spends some time with the obligatory anti-technology religious sect. Eventually they come to the East Coast to find disappointment...but also hope.

Crace does a good job of portraying various aspects of this future, and the characters are compelling. Margaret and Franklin are worth spending time with. And in the end, if the whole thing is just a little over-familiar to SF readers, it's still a rewarding journey.

A Glimpse of Splendor and Other Stories
Dave Creek
Yard Dog Press, 233 pages, $16.00 (trade paperback)
ISBN: 978-1-893687-97-4
Genres: Alien Beings, Other Worlds, Short Story Collections

One of the best ways to get a fix of otherness is with expertly-conceived and well-depicted aliens. Here we're not talking about creatures who look different but are basically human beings inside funny skins (*Star Trek* was famous for "aliens" who were humans with prosthetic foreheads). No, the pure quill is creatures who are utterly unlike human beings in significant ways. Intelligent beings whose thoughts and behavior are profoundly different.

For really satisfying aliens, an author can't just throw out a cool-sounding idea, no matter how intriguing and unusual (even Douglas Adams' Hooloovoo, who were "a superintelligent shade of the color blue"). Mere difference is not enough; great aliens have to be believably consistent, from biochemistry and evolutionary history to emotional states and cultural norms. Everything they do and say has to make sense...on their own terms, at least. Constructing and depicting truly satisfying aliens is a lot harder than you would think. As someone who has written about million-year-old sapient trees, I know a little whereof I speak. That's why it's such a joy to find an author who can do it well.

Dave Creek is one of those authors.

If the name rings a bell, there's a good reason: Creek is no stranger to *Analog's* pages. In fact, many of the stories in *A Glimpse of Splendor* first appeared here, and the book carries an introduction by some chap named Stanley Schmidt (who is himself no slouch in the alien department, as evidenced by *Sins of the Fathers*, *Lifeboat Earth*, and a little guy named *Tweedlioop*.)

But don't fear that you're getting nothing but recycled stories: there's a major tale here that has previously only appeared online at Fictionwise. Besides, it's been a decade since the first Splendor story came out; it's worth the price of admission to have them all together in one volume.

For those who don't remember or haven't read Creek's stories, here's a brief outline. The planet Splendor is home to two separate alien species who occupy completely different ecological niches...and yet who are completely interdependent. To Splendor comes Earthman Mike Christopher, an explorer with some bad news: Splendor's sun is going to explode.

Earth is perfectly willing and able to move Splendor's inhabitants to other, safer worlds...but the two races would need to be separated. And that would destroy their culture.

In between the four tales that tell the story of Splendor's dilemma, we get to follow Mike Christopher on three adventures elsewhere in Creek's rich galaxy. Just to show that Splendor wasn't a fluke, Creek invents other aliens and exotic locales; there's more than enough otherness here to satisfy any sf reader.

The Passage
Justin Cronin
Ballantine, 786 pages, $27.00 (hardcover)
ISBN: 978-0-345-50496-84
Genres: Post-Apocalyptic, Literary

If you have a friend or family member who is of a literary bent, do I have a book for you!

In literary circles, the hot buzzword is "post-apocalyptic." Post-Apocalyptic literary fiction traces its lineage back to George Stewart's 1949 book *Earth Abides*, but only became respectable and popular when Cormac McCarthy won the 2007 Pulitzer Prize for *The Road*. (What's that? You say science fiction was there decades before, that we had pretty much mined out the post-apocalyptic story by the mid-1980s? Yeah, but those books and stories weren't Serious, you see. Literary fiction is Serious and Meaningful, don'tcha know?)

The Passage is Serious and Meaningful enough to please any literary fiction reader, yet a good enough story for even *Analog's* more-experienced readers to get a kick out of. The book is set in the standard Century After the Disaster, in this case a vampire-creating plague created by scientists working in a secret government lab (oh when will they ever learn?) All that's left of normal humanity is a small walled colony off in the woods.

Then, walking out of the woods as if nothing is wrong, comes a teenage girl. Does she bring salvation, or the end of everything?

Okay, it's fun to have a good laugh at the literary folks getting excited over stories that were old news in sf last century, but the fact is that *The Passage* is a good story, well-written and filled with believable characters and plenty of well-imagined detail (over 750 pages of it!) Give it to your literary friends, and maybe in the ensuing dialogue you can slip in the fact that Theodore Sturgeon was already there 60 (gasp) years ago.

Reviews: D

(alphabetical by author)

Guardian of Night
Tony Daniel
Baen Books, 334 pages, $13.00 (trade paperback)
Baen Ebooks: $6.00 (e-book)
ISBN: 978-1-4516-3802-8
Genre: Alien Beings, Military SF

Speaking of tyrannical alien empires, meet the Administration. In the middle of the 21st century, their space fleet attacked and almost destroyed Earth. Since then the U.S. Space Fleet has bravely fought to defend the planet and prevent its annexation. The Fleet's abilities have increased under the constant pressure of decades of war, and various courageous heroes have arisen—such as plucky Captain Jim Coalbridge and linguist Lieutenant Commander Griff Leher. Still, Administration forces have superior weapons and numbers, and Earth's eventual defeat is a foregone conclusion.

Except for Administration Commander Arid Ricimer. Ricimer is everything a military commander should be: brave, bold, a brilliant tactician, and a man of unimpeachable honor. This man of honor, convinced that the Administration is on the wrong path, chooses to defect to Earth—along with his battleship, *Guardian of Night*. With Ricimer's expertise and *Guardian's* super-weapons, Earth has the opportunity to defeat the Administration and, ultimately, bring freedom to the galaxy.

But can Earth trust Ricimer? Is he the honorable defector he claims, or a double agent who will bring destruction?

This book is unusual among military sf for its well-developed alien culture and biology; Tony Daniel has done his homework, as evidenced by a dozen pages of glossary and notes at the end. Ricimer and his culture give additional dimensions to what could otherwise have been a rather ordinary military defector story in the manner of *Hunt for Red October*.

Decimated: Ten Science Fiction Stories
Jack Dann and George Zebrowski
Dream of Venus and Other Science Fiction Stories
Pamela Sargent
Wildside, 276 pages, $15.99 (trade paperback)
Kindle: $3.99, Nook: $3.79 (e-book)
ISBN: 978-1-4344-4501-8
Genres: SF Short Fiction

Wildside Press is the latest small press publisher to re-create the old Ace Doubles format of two books published back-to-back, upside down with respect to one another. (The technical term for this arrangement, by the way, is *tête-bêche*, from the French for "head-to-toe.")

Pamela Sargent's Venus series (*Venus of Dreams*, 1986, V*enus of Shadows*, 1988, and *Child of Venus*, 2001) was a family saga set against a background of the terraforming of Venus. Despite a very checkered publication history, the books captured the attention of readers and are fondly remembered. (They're also available in e-book editions.)

Really good books have a way of taking hold of an author even after she thinks she's finished with them—in Sargent's case, this meant four short stories set in the same universe as the Venus series. Three concern the impact of the terraforming effort on various characters, some of whom appeared in the books and some who didn't. As if that's not good enough, the final story, "Utmost Bones," is set in the far future and tells the story of some residents of Venus who seek to return to an Earth whose civilization is gradually fading.

Sargent balances scientific extrapolation and human interest beautifully. If you're a fan of the Venus books, you need this volume; if you've never read them, treat *Dream of Venus* as an introduction to a marvelous series.

Jack Dann and George Zebrowski are veteran sf authors who probably don't need much introduction in these pages. Both are equally at home in mainstream sf and literary sf.

Decimated brings together ten stories that Dann and Zebrowski wrote together in the early 1970s. They're interesting as period pieces—examples of the changes that the New Wave movement was ringing on the field—and they have a madcap vitality that leave readers feeling as if they've just unexpectedly downed a shot of mid-priced whiskey. To round out the ten, the authors include one previously-unpublished tale from the same period, "The Standard Crisis Scenario."

Both titles include general introductions and notes on each story from the authors.

The Death Cure
James Dashner
Delacorte, 336 pages, $17.99 (hardcover)
iBooks, Kindle, Nook: $10.99 (e-book)
ISBN: 978-0-385-73877-4
Series: Maze Runner #3
Genres: Post-Apocalyptic, SF Thriller, Young Adult SF

Meanwhile, over in the young adult arena, James Dashner has been writing an sf thriller trilogy that is just as suited to adults as to teens. If you like suspense and thrills, you'll totally enjoy reading these books—and you can impress your teenaged relatives and friends with your knowledge of them.

It's a century or three in the future, and solar flares have scorched most of the Earth's surface. The remaining population is ravaged by a virus called "the Flare," which leaves its victims as violent cannibals preying on the healthy.

Yeah, yeah, post-apocalyptic future with roving zombies. Yawn. What else ya got for us, Dashner?

In the first book, *The Maze Runner*, a young man named Thomas awakes without his memory in "the Glade," a huge enclosed bucolic paradise. Other boys, also amnesiac, have made a working society (some have been there as long as two years, although a new boy arrives roughly every month). The Glade is surrounded by an enormous labyrinth teeming with hostiles.

Then a telepathic girl arrives, and she and Thomas team up to lead the others out of the maze at last.

In the second volume, *The Scorch Trials*, Thomas and his friends discover that the surviving governments of the world have formed an organization they call WICKED, and WICKED is in control. The escaped Gladers are told that they are the key to the world's survival, and the maze was the first of several trials they must undergo before they meet their destiny. The second trial requires them to survive a trek across a hundred miles of scorched wilderness beset by cannibal zombies...all while they're infected with the Flare. At the end, it is promised, they will be cured.

Now, in *The Death Cure*, all the trials are over. It's time for Thomas and his friends to receive their memories back, to find out what WICKED is up to, and complete a final cure for the Flare.

But Thomas knows one thing for sure: WICKED can't be trusted. Are they telling the truth, or is this yet another trial?

All three books are page-turners, brimming with suspense. There's a fair amount of violence, especially with the zombies —although it serves the plot, so I can't really call it excessive. If this were a movie, it would be R-rated. Fair warning: *The Death Cure* is supposed to be the last book of the series, but there are enough loose ends left over that I'm sure we haven't seen the last of this world.

Transformers: Dark of the Moon
Peter David
Del Rey, 393 pages, $7.99 (paperback)
iBooks, Kindle, Nook: $7.99 (ebook)
ISBN: 978-0-345-52915-2
Genre: Robots, Movies

Another movie novelization, another *Transformers* story. But this one is by Peter David, who writes both comics and science fiction, and is an old hand at this stuff. His novelizations always add to the source material, and this book is no exception.

As I said when reviewing *Transformers: Exodus* in last November's issue, we have to start with a few words about the names. Decepticons, Megatron, the planet Cybertron—the authors are stuck with them. Just take a deep breath and try to get over it.

This one is a lot of fun. It starts with the truth about the Apollo program: despite what the world believes, Armstrong and Aldrin had a secret mission on the Moon. They were sent there to explore an alien starship that crashed in 1961. They brought back some of the alien tech that they found there.

Curtain up in the present day. Sam Witwicky, human friend of the Autobots, meets British scientist Carly Spencer and immediately falls in love. But there's more than love on the agenda: for the ship that crashed on the Moon was a Transformer vessel, the evil Decepticons have learned of its cargo, and they want it.

Fortunately, the ship also carried the long-lost Autobot leader Sentinel Prime. If anyone can help Sam and Carly defeat the Decpticons, it's Sentinel.

What follows is a wild series of adventures, enlivened by Peter David's ever-present sense of humor. David has the voices of his characters down pat and he never belittles or ridicules the source material. If you're in the mood for a rollicking good tale of battling giant robots, this is the book for you.

When the World Tottered
Lester Del Rey
Ice City of the Gorgon
Rochard S. Shaver & Chester S. Geier
Armchair, 215 pages, $12.95 (trade paperback)
ISBN: 978-1-61287-019-9
Genre: Adventure SF

Inspect the bookshelves of any serious sf reader, and you're sure to find some Ace Doubles. Between 1952 and 1973, Ace Books published volumes in which two short novellas (often by different authors0 were bound together, each upside-down with respect to the other. Essentially, the back cover of one novella was the front cover of the other. The distinctive spines were at first half red and half blue; later volumes used a white-and-blue color scheme. In the currency of nostalgia, Ace Doubles are hundred-dollar bills—the sight of one, along with the aroma of decaying paper, is guaranteed to touch the heart of the most unemotional reader.

Armchair Fiction has done its best to bring back the Ace Double format, complete with red-and-blue spines and the heading "two complete novels." To be sure, the constituent novellas are both face-up, appearing sequentially; the back cover illustrates the second novella, but it is unmistakably the back. Still, the effect is uncanny; Armchair Doubles definitely conjure the spirit of an earlier day.

The first novella, *Ice City of the Gorgon*, is rather late Shaver —it originally appeared in the June 1948 edition of *Amazing Stories*. Chester S. Geier was a regular in *Amazing* and its sister magazine *Fantastic Adventures*; perhaps because of his experience, *Ice City of the Gorgon* reads fairly easily. It's a typical adventure story set in a lost city in Antarctica; if you didn't look closely, you wouldn't realize it was Shaver at all.

Lester Del Rey's *When the World Tottered* appeared in *Fantastic Adventures* in 1950, and it's a ripping good yarn that would have been perfectly at home in the pages of *Unknown*. Leif Svenson is a regular guy who gets transported to the Asgard of the Norse myths—complete with Thor, Odin, Loki, and all the rest. It seems that the prophesied end of the world is finally here: Asgard is under siege by the Frost Giants, eternal opponents of the gods.

But Leif, with his knowledge of modern technology and weapons (including atom bombs), is the ace in the hole that the gods need to beat prophecy and finally defeat their old enemies. It's all great fun, and Del Rey is a good storyteller.

If this all sounds familiar, you might be remembering Del Rey's 1959 novel *Day of the Giants*, published in paperback in the 1960s and 1970s and sadly out of print today. *Day of the Giants* is a rewritten and expanded version of *When the World Tottered*. Used paperbacks seem to be available in the two-to-five dollar range. Comparing the two versions is an instructive and rewarding process for those interested in how writers work.

Total Oblivion, More of Less
Alan DeNiro
Spectra, 320 pages, $15.00 (trade paperback)
ISBN: 978-0-553-59254-2
Genre: humorous SF, Post-Apocalyptic

Post-Apocalyptic novels can be profound, meaningful, terrifying, depressing, awesome, even inspiring...but they are seldom fun. Two that spring to mind are Edgar Pangborn's *Davy* and David R. Palmer's *Emergence*, and even those weren't strolls through the park.

Get ready for *Total Oblivion, More or Less*.

Sixteen-year-old Macy had a normal life in suburban St. Paul, a dysfunctional family that drove her crazy, and the usual concerns of a midwestern teenager. Then her cell phone stopped working, the cable TV failed, and the Scythian horsemen rode into town to murder and pillage.

The Scythians are just the beginning. Various barbarian tribes from ancient history turn up all across North America, and half the country is ruled by "the Empire." Cities are ravaged, populations murdered, plagues spread. With time gone wacky and the world gone insane around them, Macy and her family find themselves in a refugee camp. They decide to board the good ship *Prairie Chicken* on its pilgrimage down the Mississippi in search of safety and sanity.

There follows a surreal journey through an ever-more-bizarre landscape as Macy's family dissolves around her. Over the next year, Macy's coming-of-age leaves her stronger, wiser, and a lot more accepting of her new world.

As a particularly fun post-apocalyptic story, *Total Oblivion, More or Less* is a success. As a parable of ordinary people confronted with changes beyond their understanding, it is superb. Reading this book will give you an insight into the experience of all your non-SF-reading friends and neighbors as they confront the onrushing future.

Fuzzy Ergo Sum
Wolfgang Diehr
Pequod Press, 299 pages, $38.00 (hardcover)
Kindle: $7.99 (ebook)
Series: Fuzzies #6
ISBN: 978-0-937912-11-9
Genre: Alien Beings, Beloved Worlds

Lately there's been something of a vogue for posthumous sequels to classic sf works. (This sort of thing happens every few decades, often when the economy turns sour and publishers are looking for "sure things" that don't require massive payments to living big-name authors.)

H. Beam Piper's original 1962 novel *Little Fuzzy* is one of the most beloved books in the field. And since Piper and his heirs weren't careful about the arcane copyright registration procedures of the time, the book is now in the public domain (i.e. anyone can write a sequel without owing Piper's heirs one red cent).

This isn't the first *Little Fuzzy* sequel; the history of the series is convoluted at best. Piper himself wrote one direct sequel, *Fuzzy Sapiens* (1964). Much later, Ace Books continued the series with *Fuzzy Bones* by William Tuning (1981). *Golden Dream: A Fuzzy Odyssey* by Ardath Mayhar (1982) retells the original story from the viewpoint of the alien Fuzzies.

Subsequently, a lost manuscript for a third Fuzzy novel was discovered among Piper's papers; it was published in 1984 as *Fuzzies and Other People*. The events of this book contradicted those in *Fuzzy Bones* (of course), so the latter book is considered as part of an alternate universe.

To make matters even more confusing, by the time you read this Tor will have published *Fuzzy Nation* by John Scalzi, which is supposed to "reboot" the whole Little Fuzzy universe and start over from the beginning.

And where does *Fuzzy Ergo Sum* fit in? It picks up where *Fuzzies and Other People* left off, continuing the story of explorer Jack Halloway (who discovered the Fuzzies), CEO Victor Grego, and Little Fuzzy himself. It's been a quiet few years on the peaceful planet Zarathustra, but now a new bureaucrat touches down on an unexplained mission. Then Zarathustra's worst criminal escapes from jail, the Chief Prosecutor is kidnapped, and the Fuzzies and the human friends have more than enough problems to deal with.

Of all the commissioned sequels, Wolfgang Diehr's most captures the voice of H. Beam Piper. One gets the feeling that he is a fan of Piper, and he's also a good enough writer to pull off the right mix of homage and originality.

At $38.00 the hardcover is pretty steep, but the ebook is well worth the asking price.

Little Brother
Cory Doctorow
Tor, 382 pages, $17.95 (hardcover)
ISBN: 978-0-7653-1985-2
Genre: Cyberpunk, Young Adult SF

It's been said that most books for teenagers are based on the literary form called Rite of Passage, a ritual in which a young person learns to assert his or her independence while becoming part of the larger society. Combine the Rite of Passage with science fiction, and the result can be very powerful. That's certainly true of many of the great classic "juveniles" by the likes of Andre Norton and Robert A. Heinlein. *Little Brother* is the first of pair of recent teen sf novels that would make great gifts for the teenagers in your life.

Marcus Yallow is a High School Senior in San Francisco, and he's a whiz at computers and the Internet. Moreover, he knows it; he is smarter than any of the adults around him, and he's not shy at expressing his contempt for them.

Now before you go disliking Marcus, you have to understand that this sort of thing is part and parcel with books for teens. If one is going to have teenage protagonists getting into various troubles and getting themselves out, then one has to de-emphasize the adult characters. It is an unspoken assumption of children's and teen fiction that most adults are stupid, ineffectual, or both. (Just look at what idiots the adults are in the *Harry Potter* books.) Adult villains can be a little more canny than friendly adults, but ultimately the kid has to outsmart them in the end.

It's no use protesting—the books aren't written for us adults, anyway. And the kids who read them don't notice.

Back to Marcus. He and his friends, deep into a live-action role-playing game, ditch school and go in search of clues. But they are in the wrong place at the wrong time when a major terrorist attack hits San Francisco, killing thousands.

Suddenly Marcus and his friends are detained by the Department of Homeland Security. With their encrypted computer files, mad hacking skills, and ability to evade school surveillance technology, they look an awful lot like terrorists.

Imprisoned and psychologically tortured, Marcus gives up his passwords and files, and after a few days he's released. One of his other friends is also set free; the third remains missing and (presumably) still in custody. But that's only the beginning of the story.

Over the next weeks, Homeland Security turns San Francisco into a police state bristling with security measures. And Marcus realizes he has a mission in life: to use his knowledge and his networks (both computer and personal) to bring down Homeland Security.

Although a little preachy in spots, the story is exciting and Marcus winds up being a fairly sympathetic character (even for old people like me). The story of one boy's opposition of authority is bound to please most teens.

The Road of Danger
David Drake
Baen Books, 368 pages, $25.00 (hardcover)
Baen Ebooks: $6.00 (e-book)
ISBN: 978-1-4516-3815-8
Series: RCN (aka Lt. Leary) #9
Genre: Military SF

David Drake's RCN (Republic of Cinnabar Navy) series draws from the same elements as Weber's *Honor Harrington* series—military historical fiction and real military history—but in a completely different manner.

The historical fiction inspiration, in this case, is Patrick O'Brian's seafaring tales of Jack Aubrey and Stephen Maturin (which were, themselves, inspired by *Hornblower*). The pairing here is RCN officer Daniel Leary and librarian/cyber-spy Adele Mundy. Leary is the son of a a high-ranking government official; Mundy's family was executed (by Leary's father) for treason. Despite this, the two have become fast friends and make a remarkable team as they travel the stars foiling threats against the Republic.

The real-world history comes from the classical world; Drake finds inspiration in the work of Greek and Roman historians. The Republic of Cinnabar and its major enemy, the Alliance of Free Stars, aren't sf versions of England and Napoleonic France; the military and political situations are much more complex.

Readers familiar with the gritty, boots-on-the-ground tone of Drake's *Hammer's Slammers* series shouldn't expect more of the same. No one would use the word "genteel" is to describe the RCN series, but "friendlier" certainly applies. If you've avoided Drake because you didn't care for the unsparing starkness, give RCN a try.

This time around Leary and Mundy find themselves in a lawless space sector of corporations gone wild, where money is king, corruption is endemic, and armed battles are standard negotiating technique.

Of course, there's a rogue spy and a sadistic thug plotting war, and once again it's up to Leary and Mundy to untangle the whole mess and defeat the growing threat. All great fun, with some nice plot twists to keep the reader paying attention (just in case the gunfights aren't sufficient).

Tales from the Clockwork Empire
Ian Duerden
Markosia Enterprises, 128 pages, $17.99 (graphic novel)
iBooks, Kindle: $5.99 Nook: 3 volumes, $0.99 each (e-book)
ISBN: 978-1-905692-67-5
Genre: Alternate History, Graphic Novels, Steampunk

Chances are good that you know someone who likes steampunk, graphic novels, or both. If so, I have a treat to tell you about.

Ian Duerden's *Tales from the Clockwork Empire* isn't, technically, steampunk at all. The story takes place in an alternate history in which the advent of steam power was delayed, and the previous clockwork technology of springs and gears continued to advance. The flavor of steampunk is here—charmingly anachronistic mechanisms, baroque designs, plenty of brass and wood—but there's nary a puff of steam.

It's 1803 and Napoleon has set his sights on England. Admiral Nelson's fleet stands ready to protect Britain..but beneath the English Channel, intricate clockwork submersibles attack with spring-powered torpedoes. Investigative reporter Calamus Quill, with the aid of the beautiful Lady Isabella Hastings, is on the trail of the genius behind submersibles and torpedoes—the dastardly turncoat inventor Lord Percy Dashwood. Their quest takes Quill and Lady Isabella to the bottom of the Channel and beyond, to an Imperial Russia besieged by flying clockwork AirKites.

Meanwhile, in a framing sequence set millennia in the future, we witness the legacy of the Clockwork Empires, a strange world in which automatons have replaced human beings. The book ends with a setup for the sequel: beneath the sands of Egypt, long-stilled clockworks are reactivated, and a 3,000-year-old Empire begins to awaken....

In graphic novels art is as important as writing, and *Tales from the Clockwork Empire* doesn't disappoint. The visuals are stunning, the technology intricate and beautiful. The pages are painted, not drawn, an effect which adds to the sumptuous air of luxury. Throughout the book Duerden constantly plays at muddying the distinction between clockworks and real life. He renders human forms and faces in a frozen, digitally-generated aspect that makes his characters seem almost like sophisticated automatons themselves.

You might have to work a little bit to get ahold of this book, but the effort is well worth it. Markosia Enterprises is a British company; their titles can be found in large comic shops, and you can always visit their website (*www.markosia.com*). For that person who likes steampunk or graphic novels, this is a special gift that won't be forgotten.

Reviews: E

(alphabetical by author)

Maine Quartet
Thomas A. Easton
SRM, 62 pages, $10.00 (chapbook)
ISBN: 978-1-935224-01-3
www.srmpublisher.com
Genre: Short Story Collections

For an incredible thirty years, Tom Easton was the voice of "The Reference Library" in *Analog*. By my count, only two people have appeared in more issues of the magazine: the legendary John W. Campbell, and that Schmidt fellow I mentioned a while back.

Last year Tom Easton took a well-deserved retirement from *Analog* and moved on to other pastures. Now SRM Publishers has given us this slim, delicious chapbook containing four tales that showcase Tom's considerable talent as a storyteller. All four stories have a connection to Tom's home, Maine.

All four of these stories amply demonstrate the quality of otherness. "Blue Bottle Fly" which appeared in *Analog* in 1981, is an alien story with a twist. The other three tales were published outside *Analog*. "Wallflower" is a fantasy of painful choices and eternal love. "A Love Story" involves a widower who gains a different perspective, and "The Bung-Hole Caper" tells what happens when flying saucers land in a small Maine town.

I can't imagine an *Analog* reader who wouldn't be interested in this delightful collection.

Geosynchron
David Louis Edelman
Pyr, 520 pages, $16.00 (trade paperback)
ISBN: 978-1-59102-792-8
Series: Jump 225 #3
Genre: Big Books, Cyberpunk

Now let's talk about a place you wouldn't want to visit in person: the future of David Louis Edelman's *Jump 225* trilogy. It's a crazy, dangerous world filled with crazy, dangerous people—and boy is it fun to read about!

If you've read the previous two books (*Infoquake* and *MultiReal*), please skip ahead while I attempt the impossible: describing Edelman's madcap future in a nutshell.

Take one part Silicon Valley, one part Wall Street, one part Libertarian philosophy, and several large parts of neurobiological nanotechnology. Stir together, add a few Machiavellian schemes and assorted psychopaths, connect the whole thing to a couple high-voltage lines, and allow to simmer for a few centuries. What you wind up with is a world of corporate power gone mad and software become the basis of reality. After the Autonomous Revolt of AIs devastated the world centuries ago, the tyrannical Defense and Wellness Council took control. Thousands of corporations (fiefcorps) market nanotech-based programs that run not on computers, but on, in, and around the human body itself. The road to success is to work for a fiefcorp that can become powerful enough to dominate.

Into this world is born Natch, a gifted programmer and total sociopath—which means he has just the skills he needs to succeed. Natch gets involved in a civil war between two of the world's richest and most powerful people: Margaret Surina and Len Borda. Along the way, Natch gains access to a new technology called MultiReal, which allows the creation and manipulation of multiple realities. By the end of MultiReal, though, Natch is infected with Black Code, a mysterious virus that render him blind and helpless, and his side seems doomed to defeat. Meanwhile, violent rebellion against the Council has sprung up worldwide.

In *Geosynchron*, the concluding volume, Natch awakens and moves from peril to peril while the world falls apart around him. No, literally: MultiReal and similar technologies have become weapons in the civil war, weapons that threaten reality itself.

Natch might just be the only person who can save the world, but there are two huge obstacles to overcome. First, he has to save himself. And second, he has to be convinced that this world he ultimately despises is worth saving.

This is the kind of book that jumps you in a dark alley, steals your wallet, and races away daring you to keep up. It's an adrenalin rush from beginning to end, and if it takes a few chapters to get your bearings, you don't really mind. Don't worry if you haven't read the first two books: *Geosynchron* contains a helpful synopsis to get you up to speed.

Zendegi
Greg Egan
Night Shade, 279 pages, $24.95 (hardcover)
ISBN: 978-1-59780-174-4
Genre: Man & Machine, Near Future, Psychological/ Sociological SF

Another hard SF writer of note is Greg Egan, and in *Zendegi* he's given us a fascinating and exciting near-future thriller set in a real but exotic locale.

As the book opens, Australian journalist Martin Seymour is stationed in Iran, covering the 2012 parliamentary elections. It turns out that the elections are anticlimactic; all the opposition candidates are disqualified so the current theocrats stay in power. Only a few weeks later, however, a sex scandal among government officials leads to widespread unrest that eventually topples the government.

Meanwhile, in the U. S., an Iranian exile scientist named Nasim works on the Human Connectome Project: an attempt to map the wiring of the Human brain. When funding vanishes and the project is cancelled, Nasim heads back to her homeland to be part of the new revolution.

Fifteen years later, in 2027, Nasim heads a company that provides access to a virtual world called Zendegi. Zendegi is a source of entertainment and a place of business for millions of people...but the competition is advancing, and Zendegi is in trouble.

Nasim uses the knowledge and skills she gained from the Human Connectome Project to engineer something new for Zendegi: avatars (called proxies) that are so lifelike that some believe they are actual living beings. For a time proxies put Zendegi far ahead of the competition. Controversy rages over whether proxies deserve human rights and whether Nasim and her company are enslaving living beings.

Into this mess comes Martin, who's been living in Iran with his wife and young son Javeed. It seems that Martin may very likely die soon, and he is troubled at the thought of abandoning his son. He asks Nasim to create a proxy, based on himself, that could carry on after his death. But will Zendegi itself survive long enough to fulfill Martin's wishes?

The story is gripping, the details of Iranian society and politics are fascinating, and the characters are well-drawn and captivating. As if that's not enough, the philosophical questions of identity and humanity, which stay with the reader long after the story is done, are most rewarding. Definitely not to be missed.

Reviews: F

(alphabetical by author)

The Crucible of Empire
Eric Flint and K. D. Wentworth
Baen Books, 593 pages, $7.99 (mass market)
Baen Ebooks: $6.00 (e-book)
ISBN: 978-1-4516-3804-2
Series: Jao Empire #2
Genre: Big Books, Military SF

Here's another tyrannical alien empire with a difference. In the first book, *The Course of Empire*, the alien Jao conquered Earth fairly easily...but as conquerors and conquered got to know one another, they developed mutual respect and eventually became allies against the Ekhat, a still more powerful and more psychotically tyrannical alien race who have the Jao Empire in their sights.

In this sequel, a joint Human/Jao starship, the *Lexington*, sets forth on a dangerous mission to track down the Lleix, a legendary race that has a bad history with the Jao...but also seems to have the power to resist the Ekhat.

These are thick, meaty books with splendid worldbuilding, fascinating alien cultures, and deliciously Byzantine politics. There are echoes of David Brin's *Uplift* series. The characters are multi-dimensional and compelling. Even readers who don't care for military sf would find plenty of rewarding reading here.

The Sorceress of Karres
Eric Flint & Dave Freer
Baen, 410 pages, $7.99 (paperback)
Baen Webscriptions: $6.00 (e-book)
ISBN: 978-1-4391-3446-7
Series: Witches of Karres #3
Genre: Adventure SF, Humorous SF

James H. Schmitz's 1966 novel *The Witches of Karres* has a special place in the heart of every science fiction reader of a certain age. An expansion of a 1949 novelette (published in *Astounding*, of course), the book was a nominee for the 1967 Hugo Award, and is universally acknowledged as an sf classic. It tells the story of space Captain Pausert and his adventures with a trio of children who are psi-powered sisters from the prohibited world Karres. The book is adventurous, funny, and tender all at once. Perhaps because the original cover featured the three girls, the book often wound up in the children's section of the public library, or even in the school library—where many of us found it and fell in love with it.

James H. Schmitz died in 1981, at the age of 69. In 2004 Baen Books published a sequel, *The Wizard of Karres* by Mercedes Lackey, Eric Flint, and Dave Freer. Now Flint and Freer continue the story. The three girls—Goth, Maleen, and the Leewit—are older, but still have their propensity for getting into trouble. When two of them are taken as slaves, the noble Captain Pausert springs into action to rescue them. From then on it's space pirates, psi-powered witchcraft, and time travel—and more than a bit of romance, as it slowly dawns on Pausert that Goth is no longer a little girl....

Flint and Freer do a great job of matching Schmitz's combination of adventure, whimsy, and plain absurdity. No one can replace Schmitz, but for those who want one more visit with the Witches of Karres, this book will do.

Worlds
Eric Flint
Baen, 780 pages, $7.99 (mass market paperback)
Baen Webscriptions: $6.00 (e-book)
ISBN: 978-1-4516-3751-9
Genre: Short Stories

There are many milestones in a writer's career. Among them are first publication, first hardcover or paperback book, various awards and honors, first collaboration, first imitators...one of these is the Retrospective Collection. Once a writer is well-known enough, someone will put out a whopping huge collection of that author's best known or most popular or highest quality stories.

Worlds is an excellent example of this type of collection. Eric Flint is one of Baen's biggest names: He's the creator of the wildly popular *Ring of Fire* alternate history franchise, he's written and edited dozens of books in the military sf genre, and he's been instrumental in bringing back into print many classics of the field.

Worlds is nearly 800 pages of Eric Flint at his best. Some of these are fantasy, some are alternate history, some are military sf, some are just plain adventure sf. Between these covers you'll find reprinted some stories and a novella in the *Ring of Fire* series; a novella from Flint and David Drake's *Belisarius* series; a novella set in David Weber's *Honor Harrington* universe; a story from the *Rats, Bats, and Vats* series that Flint co-authored with Dave Freer; and a few others. Each story has an informative introduction by Flint in which he pulls aside the curtain and shows the mind of the writer at work.

If you're an Eric Flint fan, you definitely want this book. If you haven't ever read Flint, this volume serves as a nice introduction to his work. The e-book is Baen's standard $6.00; even the print version, at a fraction more than a penny a page, is a bargain.

In the Lion's Mouth
Michael Flynn
Tor, 304 pages, $25.00 (hardcover)
iBooks, Kindle, Nook: $12.99 (e-book)
ISBN: 978-0-7653-2285-2
Series: January Dancer #3
Genre: Music, Space Opera

Music plays a part in Michael Flynn's latest, a continuation of the story begun in *The January Dancer* and *Up Jim River*.

After a thousand years colonizing the galaxy, humanity is split into hundreds of subcultures loosely organized into two opposing polities: the United League of the Periphery and the Confederacy of Central Worlds. If you thought Catherine Asaro's Skolian Empire was impossibly baroque and filled with too much intrigue, then stay away from this universe: the League and Confederacy are *War and Peace* compared to the Skolian Empire's *Cliff Notes*.

In this future, League and Confederacy are opponents in the Long Game, a sort of cold war primarily fought by agents called Hounds (on the League side) and Shadows (on the Confederacy side). The two previous books introduced us to Bridget ban, a Hound, and Donovan buigh, a former Shadow—and their daughter, the harper Mearana. After rescuing Bridget and returning her safely, Donovan has gone missing, and Bridget agrees to attempt to find him.

Enter Ravn Olafsdottr, a powerful Shadow who has intelligence about Donovan. It seems that there's a civil war going on within the Confederacy bureau that oversees the Shadows (a bureau known as The Lion's Mouth). At stake is control of the Confederacy.

And Donovan, former Shadow who was driven insane by the Lion's Mouth, is a key player in the increasingly deadly civil war. Bridget forms an uneasy alliance with Ravn to find Donovan before the wrong faction gets to him....

To call this series Space Opera is to do it a disservice. Underneath the story of politics and espionage, sabotage and assassination, there is a firm foundation of detailed extrapolation and worldbuilding. Flynn plays delightful games with language, using names and commonplace words to reveal the intricate history of his societies, leaving to the reader the thrill of discovering things about this elaborate future. His characters are complex and interesting, the science and technology are simultaneously well-thought-out and wonderful.

In the Lion's Mouth, like the previous books, is not an easy, mindless read. It demands a reader who pays attention and pulls together disparate threads. If that's your kind of book, look no further.

On the Razor's Edge
Michael Flynn
Tor, 352 pages, $25.99 (hardcover)
iBooks, Nook: $12.99; Kindle: $11.04 (e-book)
ISBN: 978-0-7653-3480-0
Series: January Dancer #4
Genre: Space Opera

Speaking of total immersion in strange and wonderful universes....

The January Dancer (2008) introduced Michael Flynn's League/Confederacy universe—millennia in the future, the United League of the Periphery and the rival Confederacy of Central Worlds have for lifetimes been locked in an interstellar cold war called the Long Game. The agents of the two—Hounds and Shadows—contend with each other across a starscape of shifting alliances, proxy wars, espionage, double and triple agents, sabotage, betrayal, and assassination.

In a story that continued through the next two books—*Up Jim River* (2010) and *In the Lion's Mouth* (2012)—readers have followed the course of Hound Bridget ban, ex-Shadow

Donovan buigh, and their harper daughter Mearana as they struggled to navigate both the Long Game and a deadly civil war within the Shadow organization.

Now it's all come down to this: Donovan buigh, captive of rebels, is taken to Old Terra, to the Secret City where the Shadows rule. Donovan has information that will allow the rebels to take the City, and the rebels are perfectly willing to use torture to get it out of him.

Meanwhile, Mearana has been kidnapped by the treacherous Shadow Ravn Olafsdattr. Bridget buigh puts together a pack of Hounds for a rescue mission—while knowing that this is exactly what Ravn wants her to do.

All the pieces are on the board, all the players are in the game, the long struggle is at last coming to an end...and the stakes are very personal. But one thing is sure in this universe: nothing is what it seems.

If you've read and enjoyed the previous books, you'll certainly enjoy this one. If not, and if you're the kind of reader who enjoys espionage and baroque politics, you'll probably want to go back and start with *The January Dancer*.

Flinx Transcendent
Alan Dean Foster
Del Rey, 398 pages, $26.00 (hardcover)
ISBN: 978-0-345-49607-2
Series: Humanx Commonwealth, Pip & Flinx #15
Genres: Animal Companions, Galactic Empires

Alan Dean Foster made his name by writing movie novelizations. There was a time when just about every sf or fantasy movie that hit the big screen was accompanied by an Alan Dean Foster novelization. (One of my all-time favorite cartoons appeared in 1984, when the unlamented DeLaurentiis version of *Dune* was released and Frank Herbert was still very much alive. The cartoon shows a Hollywood producer on the phone, *Dune* posters on the wall behind him, and he's saying, "But Frank, baby, Alan Dean Foster writes *all* our novelizations." But I digress.)

Anyone who uses those novelizations to dismiss Foster is making a big mistake. There's a reason he was the go-to guy for novelizations: he's a great storyteller. And nowhere is his storytelling ability better demonstrated than in his decades-long saga of Pip and Flinx.

Flinx (Philip Lynx) is a redheaded, green-eyed human with psi abilities; his companion Pip is a miniature telepathic flying dragon. Across fourteen previous books Pip and Flinx have had various adventures throughout Foster's larger universe, a multi-species hegemony known as the Humanx Commonwealth.

This time around, Flinx is on his biggest mission, working to prevent a threat called the Great Evil from destroying...well, everything. To foil the Great Evil, Flinx and Pip will have to travel across the Commonwealth and even beyond the universe, revisit elements from their past, and convince disparate and hostile species to work together. Along the way there are plenty of wonderful sights to see and action enough for any summer movie blockbuster.

In a well-constructed series, any particular book can be read out of sequence. That's certainly true of the Pip and Flinx books. If you've never had the pleasure, or if you've missed some volumes along the way, don't be afraid to dive into Flinx Transcendent. Foster gives you everything you need to follow the story.

For the reader who's followed Pip and Flinx all along the way, this book is even more of a delight. All the strands of Flinx's life come together (he even revisits the *Tar-Aiym Krang* from the very first book) delightfully.

The Humanx Commonwealth, and the Flinx series in particular, is a great example of the multi-culture, multi-species galactic society that *Star Trek* thought it was portraying. Fascinating aliens, diverse planets, exotic cultures—they're all here. In fact, in this book Flinx himself states what could very well be the overarching theme of the whole Humanx Commonwealth universe. Another character speaks wistfully of a time "when people were confined to one world and believed it constituted the whole universe...[t]hey never had to worry about the survival of a civilization composed of dozens of star systems and species." Flinx disagrees: "...they also worried that shape, or smell, or language differences or belief systems were important. They didn't know that all that matters is sentience and sensibility."

Flinx Transcendent is billed as Flinx's last adventure, and it does wrap up things in a satisfactory package. If it truly is the last Flinx book, readers who have come to know and love the duo will be disappointed. But I wouldn't worry: if there are two things you can count on in science fiction, they are the fact that no one ever really dies, and no popular series ever really ends while its author is alive. And sometimes, not even after.

The Human Blend
Alan Dean Foster
Del Rey, 240 pages, $26.00 (hardcover)
Kindle: $9.10 Nook: $14.30 (ebook)
ISBN: 978-0-345-51197-3
Series: Tipping Point #1
Genre: Adventure SF, Biological SF, Man & Machine

When I was coming up, if I wanted a well-written sf book that was a surefire good read, with a solid helping of adventure, an interesting society, and some interesting scientific speculation, I would pick up a Gordon R. Dickson novel. Now, with Dickson gone nearly a decade, I turn to Alan Dean Foster. *The Human Blend*, the first book in a projected trilogy, does not disappoint.

In this near future of genetic engineering, nanotechnology, and extreme body modification, criminals are punished by having their bodies transformed...and those who can afford it, enhance their abilities beyond those of unaltered humans.

Whispr is a petty thief and the kind of sympathetic rogue that you can't help rooting for. He gets his name from his punishment: surgery and implants that make him exceptionally thin. His partner, Jiminy Cricket, has prosthetic legs and enhanced muscles that allow him to jump great distances.

Whispr and Jiminy knock over a tourist in order to steal his advanced prosthetic hand. But the victim also carries a mysterious silvery thread that appears to be a data-storage medium. Whispr and Jiminy take the thread and flee...but quickly find themselves pursued by the police. Whispr is injured, and Jiminy is taken.

With the police searching for him, Whispr wants nothing more than to get rid of the thread. He turns up at the office of Dr. Ingrid Seastrom, a natural unmodified human physician. She repairs his injuries, and he offers to fence the thread and split the profits with her. But first, of course, Dr. Ingrid examines the thread...and finds out that it's much more than it appears.

Whispr and Ingrid go on the run, bearing a secret that's easily valuable enough to kill for...and more.

Foster is a consummate storyteller, transporting the reader into a world both familiar and strange, both wonderful and dangerous. Read five pages and you'll finish the book...finish the book, and you'll long for the next one.

Body, Inc.
Alan Dean Foster
Del Rey, 290 pages, $13.00 (trade paperback)
iBooks, Kindle, Nook: $9.99 (e-book)
ISBN: 978-0-345-51199-7
Series: Tipping Point #2
Genre: Adventure SF, Biological SF, Man & Machine

Centuries from now, with the world an environmental ruin, personal genetic enhancement and nanotech implants are everywhere. In *The Human Blend* we met wraith-thin lovable rogue Whispr and his friend, Dr. Ingrid Seastrom. Whispr accidentally acquired a silver data-thread that bears information about a powerful new technology, and Ingrid became his protector when dastardly forces pursued them.

Now Whispr and Ingrid are in Africa, in the territory of the South African Economic Combine (known officially as SAEC and colloquially as SICK). SICK, apparently the source of the data-thread, is the kind of evil corporate empire that we all love to hate. Whispr and Ingrid feel that they are close to the answers they seek.

Unfortunately, SICK's ultra-enhanced sadistic assassin, Napul Molé, is on their trail. By escaping him in the last book, Whispr and Ingrid showed Molé up, and now he's determined not just to catch them, but also to make them suffer.

It's all great adventure, with sympathetic characters and solid speculative science.

The Sum of Her Parts
Alan Dean Foster
Del Rey, 278 pages, $15.00 (trade paperback)
iBooks, Kindle, Nook: $9.99 (e-book)
ISBN: 978-0-345-51202-4
Series: Tipping Point 3
Genre: Adventure SF, Biological SF, Man & Machine

After all this heavy reading, perhaps you want something light and quick. Never fear, Alan Dean Foster's here.

You might remember Dr. Ingrid Seastrom, brilliant biologist, and her companion Whispr, rogue rendered a living shadow by genetic engineers, from the first two books in this series, *The Human Blend* and *Body, Inc*. In this brave new world of genetic manipulation and nanotech augmentation, Ingrid and Whispr are on the run. They possess a data thread that bears information important enough for powerful multinational biotech corporations to be after their lives.

In particular, they're hunted by a brute called Molé, an enhanced killer who's determined to get to them first. In the course of the first two books Ingrid and Whispr have managed to escape Molé and stay a step ahead of the forces tailing them. Now they've come to the end of the line: South Africa's Namib desert, and a highly-secure research facility that holds the answers they seek.

First, they have to survive the bio-engineered dangers of the desert. Then it's a simple matter of getting past the guards, taking over the lab, and figuring out what it all means—before a frustrated Molé catches up with them and starts dealing mayhem.

Jolly fun adventure. Ingrid and Whispr make a great pair, resourceful and totally sympathetic—you'll be rooting for them to survive their great adventure. And the payoff is definitely worth it.

Wrath of the Lemming Men
Toby Frost
Myrmidon Books, 320 pages, $12.95 (trade paperback)
ISBN: 978-1-905802-35-7
Series: Chronicles of Isambard Smith #3
Genre: Humorous SF, Steampunk

Captain Isambard Smith, of the British Space Empire, is a steely-thewed hero in the model of Horatio Hornblower or Honor Harrington...at least, if you believe his press releases. He is the commander of the good ship HMSC *John Pym*, the fastest ship in the fleet. His retinue includes his best friend, alien warrior Suruk the Slayer; android Polly Carveth, a former pleasurebot and the only entity who can pilot the John Pym; Rhianna Mitchell, a hippie-like free spirit who is a constant thorn in Captain Smith's side (not least because of his mad, unrequited love for her); and Gerald the hamster.

In two previous books, *Space Captain Smith* and *God Emperor of Didcot*, Isambard defended the Empire against dire threats, but now he faces his biggest challenge: the lemming-men of Yull. On the orders of their insane war god, these ruthless warriors attack the Empire, meeting Imperial forces on the planet Varanor. The Imperial army, consisting of humans and Suruk the Slayer's fellow warriors, handily defeat the lemmings.

Into the breach come Captain Smith and his valiant crew. Their assignment: to civilize the brutal lemming people and end their assault on the Empire. Isambard has no doubt that he'll succeed, but he isn't counting on the defeated lemming commander, who has sworn vengeance against Suruk and all who travel with him.

Oh, and there's the Empire's primary foes, the merciless Ghasts, who are close on Isambard's trail. And Leighton-Wakazashi, an evil robotics company that just might be in league with the Ghasts. Yet Isambard has an ace up his sleeve:

an age-old society of Morris dancers who hold the key to universal peace....

Wrath of the Lemming Men is a hilarious read, filled with references to science fiction and other pop culture. It more than lives up to the publisher's tag line: "An epic tale of war, honour, and suicidal rodents!"

Reviews: G

(alphabetical by author)

Fire With Fire
Charles E. Gannon
Baen, 475 pages, $14.00 (trade paperback)
Baen ebooks: $8.99 (e-book)
ISBN: 978-1-4516-3883-7
Genre: Military SF

And here's Charles E. Gannon with his own book set in a universe decidedly different than the Honorverse.

Twelve years ago Caine Riordan, 22nd century spy, was on the Moon—on the verge of uncovering the last pieces in a conspiracy he'd followed to the highest levels of the military. Next thing he knows, he's waking from cryosleep aboard a starship bound for a distant planet, in a universe changed beyond recognition.

While he slept, humanity discovered interstellar travel through a network of natural shift points between nearby stars, and everyone's busy settling habitable planets. Riordan's been conscripted and sent to the Delta Pavonis system to investigate a lost civilization.

Putting scattered pieces together, Riordan discovers that Humans aren't alone—in fact, there are plenty of alien societies out in the stars, all competing for control of habitable worlds and the shift point network that allows access to them. Worse, the Solar system occupies a key position in the network. Sooner or later, some very hostile aliens are going to want to move on Earth and eliminate the competition.

Now all Riordan has to do is survive assassins, saboteurs, and enemy spies so he can get to Earth...and then convince the very conspirators who put him in cryosleep that war is coming, and Earth needs to be prepared.

This is definitely one to appeal to the adventure fans. Riordan is a smart hero, up against enormous obstacles and surrounded by enemies. Author Gannon does a good job of managing action and tension to keep the story moving, and the details of the worlds Riordan visits are interesting in their own right.

Be warned, though: although the immediate story comes to a satisfactory conclusion, there's plenty of room for a sequel or two. I don't think we've seen the end of Caine Riordan or his universe.

Star Wars: Fate of the Jedi: Omen
Christie Golden
Del Rey, 250 pages, $27.00 (hardcover)
ISBN: 978-0-345-50912-3
Series: Fate of the Jedi #2
Genre: Military SF, Movies

Sometimes you don't want a big meal; you're more in the mood for something less substantial...maybe some kind of fruit-gelatin salad with those little marshmallows, or something involving things dipped in chocolate. In this mood, you might want to try a *Star Wars* novel. The background and characters are familiar enough, and you can't beat ultimate good vs absolute evil.

It's 40+ years after the original *Star Wars*, and there's been a lot of water under the bridge in the meantime. Don't worry about catching up; Christie Golden is an old hand at this sort of thing and she rapidly fills in the blanks for any reader who's missed the dozens of novels that have come before. In particular, you won't miss much if you haven't read *Fate of the Jedi: Outcast*, the volume that immediately precedes this one.

In the wake of a galactic civil war, the Jedi Knights are facing multiple problems. For one, a mysterious disease is turning responsible Jedi into raving lunatics. For another, the head of the Galactic Alliance has turned against the Jedi and is trying to reduce their influence in the government. Finally, über-Jedi Luke Skywalker is trying to find out what turned his late nephew, Jacen Solo, to the Dark Side. Meanwhile, mad Jedi threaten Jacen's parents, better known as Han Solo and Princess Leia.

As if all this isn't enough, a long-lost tribe of the evil Sith have surfaced, using their Dark Side powers in a bid to subjugate the whole Galaxy.

It's all great fun. Fair warning, though, *Omen* is the middle book of a trilogy, so although it comes to a satisfactory ending, don't expect every loose thread to be wrapped up.

This Shared Dream
Kathleen Ann Goonan
Tor, 400 pages, $25.99 (hardcover)
Kindle: $17.15 (ebook)
ISBN: 978-0-7653-1354-6
Series: Dance Family #2
Genre: Alternate History, Music, Parallel Worlds/Other Dimensions, Time Travel

What do you do after you've created utopia?

In her Campbell Award winning novel *In War Times* (2007), Kathleen Ann Goonan introduced Sam and Bette Dance, a couple of time travelers who went back to World War II in an attempt to make our present world a better one. They succeeded, and a long period of peace replaced the Cold War.

This Shared Dream takes up the story of the present-day children that Sam and Bette left behind. Jill, Brian, and Megan Dance are all bothered by shadowy memories of the world as it was, as well as the mystery of their parents' disappearance. Jill even seems to remember that her mother departed to prevent the assassination of John F. Kennedy...an event that never occurred in the current timeline.

As they grow, the Dance children develop strong desires, almost compulsions, to improve the world. At first their means are politics, music, and science. Then comes the fly in the ointment: in creating this new alternate world, the Dance parents caused the erasure from history of a good many powerful and malicious people. But it turns out that previous timelines don't cease to exist; instead, there's a multiverse of alternate histories.

And what Sam and Bette did once, others can un-do. Soon enough, the Dance kids find their utopian timeline threatened with destruction. All they have is their own abilities, their drive for improvement...and the power of jazz music.

Goonan's previous work (*The Nanotech Quartet*) was more cyberpunk in nature; in the *Dance Family* books, there's nary a nanobot to be seen. She masterfully relates this story mainly from the separate viewpoints of the three Dance children, and it works beautifully. The details of her alternate world are fascinating and fun to uncover; the personality of this utopian timeline is almost a fourth main character in the book.

A great adventure story, an engaging alternate history, characters the reader can really care about, and jazz. What more can you ask?

Impulse
Steven Gould
Tor, 368 pages, $25.99 (hardcover)
iBooks, Kindle, Nook: $12.99 (e-book)
ISBN: 978-0-7653-2757-4
Series: Jumper 4
Genres: Adventure SF, Teleportation

Steven Gould's *Jumper* series is a convoluted example of the porous boundary between print and film. The first book, *Jumper*, was published in 1992 to near-universal acclaim. In 2004, Gould followed up with the superb *Reflex*, a direct sequel to *Jumper*.

Then in 2008 a movie based on *Jumper* appeared. The film diverged from the novel in some very significant ways. Along with the movie, Gould released *Jumper: Griffin's Story*—a prequel to the movie, very clearly set in the universe of the film rather than that of the books.

Well, now it's 2013 and *Impulse* returns to print continuity. It is, in fact, a direct sequel to *Reflex*. Those who weren't fond of the movie (and there were many) can easily pretend that it, along with *Griffin's Story*, never existed.

In *Jumper* we met Davy Rice, an otherwise-ordinary teen who discovered that he had the ability to teleport. In *Reflex* Davy, now a young adult, married his sweetheart Millie, and worked part-time for the National Security Agency. He ran afoul of a group of international criminals who captured and tormented him for his abilities—in the course of his resistance and escape, Millie also developed the teleportation power. At the end of the book, they went off to live happily ever after.

Impulse joins the family fifteen years later. The main character is Cent, Davy and Millie's 15-year-old daughter. The three of them live in seclusion in an isolated cabin in the Yukon. To Cent's parents, anywhere in the world is just a step away; they've taken her everywhere…but Cent herself is unable to teleport. Like any teenager, she chafes at her confinement and longs to have a more normal life with school and friends.

Until Cent sneaks out to go snowboarding, gets caught in an avalanche, and teleports to the safety of home.

Now that her power has manifest itself, Cent argues that she can go to a real school and live a real life. Soon she has friends and is involved in the social swirl of her school. But even the most careful teenager can't keep teleportation a secret forever, and while Cent can escape any danger, her friends are not so fortunate.

Like the two previous books, *Impulse* is a multilayered book. It's a great adventure story. On another level, it's an idea story, exploring the implications and consequences of teleportation.

On yet another level, it raises questions of good and evil, personal responsibility, interdependence, and the nature of freedom. And it does all this in a cracking good yarn.
Definitely recommended.

Stargate Atlantis: Homecoming
Jo Graham & Melissa Scott
Fandemonium, 320 pages, $7.99 (paperback)
ISBN: 978-1-90558650-9
Series: Legacy #1
Genre: Space Opera, TV

In the "eagerly awaited" competition, this one has two things going for it. First, it's a continuation of a one of the best sf television shows in a long while. Second, it's Melissa Scott's first book since 2001. Let me handle these in reverse order.

Melissa Scott is best known for her *Roads of Heaven* trilogy (*Five-Twelfths of Heaven*, *Silence in Solitude*, and *Empress of Earth*) and intelligent cyberpunk novels like *Trouble and Her Friends* and *The Jazz*. Scott is one of the most inventive and intelligent authors in sf; I would easily stack her up against Samuel R. Delany and Robert Sawyer. That she hasn't had a new book out in ten years is a pity. (He co-author, Jo Graham, is an up-and-coming author of marvelous historical fantasies; it's great to see her playing on the sf side of the fence.)

Stargate Atlantis was a spinoff of its older brother, *Stargate SG-1*. Unlike the current spawn of the franchise, *Stargate Universe*, *Atlantis* and *SG-1* were both intelligent science fiction presented with true sense of wonder, the most authentic-sounding technobabble anywhere, and more than a dollop of good humor. *Atlantis* was cancelled after its fifth season; what Scott and Graham have done is to plot out the unaired sixth season, and they'll be presenting it in a series of books of which *Homecoming* is the first.

It was worth the wait.

At the end of the series, the flying city Atlantis had returned to Earth from the Pegasus Galaxy. In this book, set a few months later, the scattered crew come together (along with some new faces) to take the city back to Pegasus. There they will continue the fight against the vampiric Wraith who threaten the human populations of that Galaxy.

Make no mistake, this is real science fiction. Sure, the authors capture the voices and personalities of the various characters very well, and they stay faithful to the background established in the two shows—but they go beyond all that, adding new depth as only the printed word can.

Fan of *Stargate* or not, if you like good, intelligent space opera, you'll like this book.

Death's Head: Day of the Damned
David Gunn
Del Rey, 346 pages, $26.00 (hardcover)
ISBN: 978-0-345-48404-8
Series: Death's Head #3
Genre: Military SF

In the mainstream Suspense/Thriller genre, there is a very popular subset of books written by former military men (and, sometimes, women): rough-talking, hard-living men who sling authentic lingo about weapons and warfare, men who, given the slightest provocation, are two-fisted death. Some of these authors use pseudonyms; one gets the idea that hostile foreign mercenaries are close on their trail. In extreme cases, author bios hint that the writer spends most of his time on covert missions in the Middle East, Central Asia, or the jungles of Latin America...presumably dashing off books by flickering torchlight during lulls in the fighting.

All of this is meant in the spirit of fun; after all, who wants to read a military adventure written by an accountant from Connecticut?

Now SF has its own mysterious military man: David Gunn. According to his bio, Mr. Gunn (we all believe that's his real name, right?) "has undertaken assignments in Central America, the Middle East, and Russia (among numerous other places). Coming from a service family, he is happiest when on the move and tends not to stay in one town or city for very long."

Death's Head: Day of the Damned continues the story of Sven Tveskoeg, a Lieutenant in the Death's Head, the elite fighting force of the Octovian Empire sometime in the distant future. Sven is a genetically-engineered super-soldier who lives to kill —and he's very good at it. Humans, alien monsters, game animals, the odd lizard or two: Sven kills them all with a dizzying assortment of weapons, all lovingly described. He has a prosthetic arm which sprouts knives whenever necessary; he has guns (including his favorite SIG-37, an AI-enhanced heavy pistol that throws an assortment of bullets and wisecracks with equal ease); he even has a handy portable planet-buster bomb just in case it might come in handy (and son of a gun, by the end of the book it does.)

Sven has various friends besides his gun: most notable is Aptitude, a teenage girl who is only slightly less capable and bloodthirsty than Sven himself. Together, they fight their way through a civil war that has split the Octovian Empire and the Death's Head itself. He faces conflicting orders, betrayal, and enough enemies to make the pages seem to drip with blood.

The style is terse and harried, with little subtlety. Sven and his fellow soldiers communicate in short, matter-of-fact utterances that are a step above grunts. In "authentic" military fashion, four-letter words proliferate, violence is everywhere, and all of the characters seem to harbor deep hostilities toward one another.

To be sure, there are some interesting touches hiding in the background. The Emperor, OctoV, is a part-human, part-machine construct that eternally manifests as a 14-year-old boy. The Empire's chief antagonists are the United Free (or U/Free in military parlance), a cultured society with the power to move planets and extinguish stars. But in the main, the background and plot are excuses to get Sven moving across the landscape, slaying everything he comes across.

By now you may have recognized what *Death's Head: Day of the Damned* is all about: it is essentially the printed and bound equivalent of those video games in which one wanders around the neighborhood shooting at everything that moves, splashing blood all over the screen and racking up points. And for what it is, the book does a good job.

If that sort of thing appeals to you, you'll like this one.

Transcendental
James Gunn
Tor, 304 pages, $25.99 (hardcover)
iBooks, Nook: $12.99; Kindle: $11.04 (e-book)
ISBN: 978-1-7653-3501-2
Genre: Philosophical/Religious SF,
    Psychological/Sociological SF

James Gunn is one of the true masters of science fiction. No, really: he received SFWA's Damon Knight Memorial Grand Master Award in 2007. Gunn has been active in the field since 1948, and not just stories and novels—in 1976 the Science Fiction Research Association gave him their Pilgrim Award for lifetime achievement in sf scholarship, and he's won the Hugo Award (among others) for his nonfiction about the sf field.

If you've read *Analog* for any length of time, you've seen James Gunn in these pages.

Gunn's last novel was in 2005; his newest, *Transcendental*, is worth the wait.

In this future of many worlds and intelligent species, there's a new force among the stars: the Transcendentalism movement. At the edge of explored space, a mysterious Prophet claims he can help beings achieve the highly spiritual state of transcendence.

Riley is a human war veteran who joins dozens of others, of many different species and planets, on a pilgrimage to find the prophet. Unlike the others, Riley's not along to achieve transcendence—his mission is to kill the Prophet.

During the journey, various fellow travelers tell their stories, Canterbury Tales style. As these tales unfold and tensions aboard the ship mount, Riley realizes that not all his fellow pilgrims are seeking transcendence. Especially the friendly but enigmatic woman Asha....

Gunn combines exotic aliens worthy of James White with psychological twists and philosophical speculation—I'm reminded of James Tiptree Jr.'s *Brightness Falls From the Air*. Riley is a compellingly damaged man in search of truth, who ultimately finds that he's as much a pilgrim as any of the others.

Reviews: H

(alphabetical by author)

The Evolutionary Void
Peter F. Hamilton
Del Rey, 704 pages, $28.00 (hardcover)
ISBN: 978-0-345-49657-7
Series: Void Trilogy #3
Genre: Big Books, Clarke's Law, Space Opera

Peter F. Hamilton is one of the best space opera writers around today. He writes big, meaty books that interweave the adventures of dozens of characters on many different worlds, with technologies that perfectly exemplify Clarke's Law: Any sufficiently advanced technology is indistinguishable from magic. His themes are grand, worthy of space opera: interstellar war, Byzantine politics, the clash of religions and civilizations.

With a book of 700+ pages, you'll want to know right away what you're getting into, and Hamilton isn't shy about giving you the clues you need. Take this small excerpt from the second paragraph: "Navigation at that awesome velocity was by quantum interstice similarity interpretation, which determined the relative location of mass in the real universe beyond. This alleviated the use of crude hysradar or any other sensor that might possibly be detected." If this leaves you twitching and foaming at the mouth, then this is not the book for you. If you're left thinking, "Oh, good, let's hear more," then you'll love it.

The Evolutionary Void is the third in a trilogy (the two previous books are *The Dreaming Void* and *The Temporal Void*). The *Void Trilogy*, in turn, is set in the same universe as the earlier *Commonwealth Saga, Pandora's Star* and *Judas Unchained*. That's an enormous amount of backstory, about 3300 pages worth if my calculations are correct. There are two choices: read the earlier books first, or just take a deep breath and dive in.

If you dive, be prepared to be confused for a while—but after the first 50 or so pages, you'll discover that the water's fine. Strong, sympathetic characters grab the reader quickly, and soon you'll be so intent on following them that you'll forget that you don't know all the details of the backstory.

Big, detailed space operas like *The Evolutionary Void* are like a visit to a foreign country where you don't speak the language. Fortunately, Hamilton is an excellent tour guide; he pays attention to the familiar as well as the exotic, and if you trust him you're in for an enjoyable and enlightening trip.

Great North Road
Peter F. Hamilton
Del Rey, 951 pages, $30.00 (hardcover)
iBooks, Kindle, Nook: $14.99 (e-book)
ISBN: 978-0-345-52666-3
Genre: Big Books, Space Opera

Peter F. Hamilton has made a name for himself with far future, far-flung space operas with advanced technology indistinguishable from magic. In *Great North Road*, he stays a little bit closer to home...but only a little bit.

In the 2030s, Earth discovered gateway technology that allowed instant interstellar travel. Over roughly the next century, Earth's nations expanded to dozens of planets while giving Earth the resources to solve the problems of energy and the environment. The North family, through a series of clones, dominates the economy of the planet and its many colonies. Over the years, these clones have diverged from the originals, threatening to splinter the North empire.

Sidney Hurst is a simple police detective in Newcastle, until one of the North clones is murdered on his watch. As he investigates, he finds that the murder was similar to another North murder years ago on the colony world St. Libra.

Angela Tramelo was convicted of the St. Libra murder, and is serving time on St. Libra...so she couldn't have carried out the Newcastle killing. Sidney suspects that Angela is innocent, as she has always claimed—and that the real murderer is loose among the worlds.

Angela's released from prison, and she sets out to track down the real killer. Who seems to be an alien with more on its mind than killing assorted Norths.

The story of how Sidney and Angela uncover the truth, while simultaneously trying to keep themselves alive, is a fine thriller plot. The world(s) of *Great North Road*, and the true story of what's going on, are the main draw of this novel. You want a nice, long, immersive trip to a fascinatingly different universe? Here it is.

Kea's Flight
Erika Hammerschmidt & John C. Ricker
Lulu.com, 569 pages, $26.99 (trade paperback)
Kindle, Nook: $3.89 (ebook)
ISBN: 978-1-4583-9679-2
Genre: Big Books, Psychological/Sociological SF

Kea was an unwanted mistake.

On 25th century Earth, genetic technology has made it possible for every parent to choose the exact characteristics desired in every child. In the process, however, many surplus embryos are formed. It's illegal to discard them, so they're frozen, packed on robot-controlled spaceships, and sent off into the universe.

Kea was a discarded embryo, one rejected for having genes linked to autism. She was never meant to be born—but then again, neither were any of the embryos on her ship. But mistakes happen, and Kea is just one of many unwanted children raised on a speeding starship.

None of it was every supposed to happen...and when the government finds out that it *has* happened, the result is predictable and inevitable: it becomes necessary to eliminate the embarrassment.

But this ship of talented, misfit kids has another idea....

What makes this book so fascinating is Kea, her fellow autistic children (they range from severe autism to high-functioning types like Asperger's Syndrome), and the society they've built in their ship. It's long been observed that many sf heroes and other characters display characteristics similar to folks with Asperger's—here's a book that makes the connection explicit. You'll see echoes of Heinlein's Peewee Reisfeld, Asimov's Arkady Darrell, and Panshin's Mia Havero.

Is this self-published novel worth $26.99 for a trade paperback? That's a question I could wrestle with. But at $3.89 for an ebook, it's well worth the price of admission.

The Star Beast
Robert A. Heinlein
Baen, 309 pages, $7.99 (mass market)
Baen Ebooks: $8.99
ISBN: 978-1-4516-3891-2
Genres: Alien Beings, Young Adult SF

You've probably got a rebellious teen on your gift list ("Rebellious teen"? Isn't that redundant? Aren't all teens rebellious?) You're probably giving her or him a movie or two, games you don't understand, music you don't like, or something similar.

Throw in a book. In fact, throw in *The Star Beast*.

This is a reissue of one of Robert A. Heinlein's so-called "juvenile" novels, originally published in 1954. (Whatever you do, don't use the word "juvenile" around your teen.) It's among the very best, not at all dated, and accessible to any bright teenager raised on *Harry Potter* and *The Hunger Games*.

The story is a fairly simple one: John Thomas Stuart, the teen hero, is the current custodian of Lummox—an enormous extraterrestrial pet brought home from the stars by one of his ancestors. Lummox, the size of an elephant, eats anything (although particularly fond of steel beams), is armored like a tank, and has the strength of an earthmover. When Lummox leaves home and goes on a rampage in the town, John Thomas faces the possibility of losing his pet forever.

Then the planetary government steps in, in the person of Mr. Kiku, Permanent Undersecretary for Spatial Affairs...for Lummox may be more than what it seems.

Not only is this book accessible and empowering for teens— it features one of the strongest adolescent female characters in sf (two, actually, but that would be telling)—but it raises important and timely issues of biological and cultural differences, respect for other cultures, and personal morality. Of all Heinlein's books, this may be the one that speaks most directly to early 21st century teenagers.

Webdancers
Brian Herbert
Five Star, 522 pages, $25.95 (hardcover)
ISBN: 978-1-59414-218-5
Series: Timeweb Chronicles #3
Genres: Big Books, Bigger Than Worlds, Space Opera

Now for something nice.

It's impossible to mention Brian Herbert without also mentioning that his father was Frank Herbert, bestselling author of the *Dune* series. Since Frank's death, Brian has continued the series in a string of bestseller collaboration with Kevin J. Anderson.

What is so often forgotten is that Brian Herbert had his own independent sf writing career before taking up the reins of the *Dune* franchise. His solo work included genuinely funny books like *Sydney's Comet*, *The Garbage Chronicles*, and the exquisite

Sudanna, Sudanna (in which chuckle builds on chuckle inexorably, until without quite noticing it you're laughing so much you can hardly breathe).

Recently, in between *Dune* books, Brian Herbert has been crafting a space opera as big as the galaxy; like the best space operas, this one moves from simple sf into the realm of brand new mythology.

The Timeweb Chronicles concern the Timeweb: a multidimensional structure that fills the galaxy, connecting stars and planets with communications and transport. Sapient podships travel along the Timeweb at faster-than-light speed, bringing together diverse races and cultures.

The hero of this epic is Noah Watanabe, an ecologist who once specialized in repairing damaged planets. By this third volume, Noah has turned his attention to the greatest ecological crisis of all: the disintegration and death of the Timeweb itself.

As the Web decays, the Human Merchant Prince Alliance joins with their erstwhile enemies, the shape-shifting Mutati Kingdom. Meanwhile, Noah finds his paranormal abilities boosted by a connection to an ultimate power, and begins evolving into something beyond Human. Whether this power is for good or evil, he does not know.

I'm not going to tell you that *The Timeweb Chronicles* are easy reading. Each volume weighs in at over 500 pages of prose that can sometimes be as dense as the worst excesses of his father. But it's rewarding work: the universe of the Timeweb is spectacularly wonder-filled, and the story is mythic.

Fair warning, though: this is one of those trilogies that's really one long super-novel; if you start with this third volume, you're really cheating yourself. Book One is *Timeweb*; Book Two is *The Web and the Stars*.

If you like far-future space operas teeming with interesting aliens and larger-than-life characters, give this one a try.

Blood Law
Jeannie Holmes
Dell, 400 pages, $7.99 (mass market)
ISBN: 978-0-553-59267-2
Genres: Romantic SF

It's possible that you might want a gift for a romance reader. I don't think I'm off-base in assuming that romances are a bit outside the comfort range of the average *Analog* reader. If you're picturing Barbara Cartland, Danielle Steel, and lurid Harlequin paperbacks, don't worry—his isn't going to hurt anywhere near as much as you fear.

So far we've had viral vampires in *The Passage* and aquatic vampires in *The Ocean Dark*; now you're going to have to bear with me as we take a cautious step into paranormal romance territory. It should come as no surprise, to anyone who's been watching popular culture, that vampires are big these days. We've been fairly insulated inside the safe confines of the sf/fantasy fields, but the fact is that international treaties now mandate that 7 out of 10 books published must contain at least one vampire. Paranormal romance authors have been doing more than their part so that sf writers don't have to.

Truth is, there are many different ways to write vampires, and some of them are much more palatable than others.

Take Alexandra ("Alex") Sabian, for example. She's a vampire...but she's also an enforcer with the FBPI (the Federal Bureau of Preternatural Investigators). To escape the pressures of the big-city preternatural crime scene, she transfers to a quiet Mississippi town where half the 6,000-odd population are vampires. Things aren't as bucolic as she hopes, though: the local sheriff is a vampire-hating bigot, and there are a lot of tensions between the humans and the vampires.

When those tensions begin to erupt in a series of gruesome murders of innocent vampires, Alex calls the home office for backup. They send the worst person possible: Varik Baudelaire, who just happens to be Alex's ex-boyfriend. In the course of catching the vampire-killers, typical romantic difficulties ensue between Alex and Varik.

There's enough of a love story here to interest any romance reader, but there's much more. Jennie Holmes does a masterful job of imagining and depicting the implications of a society in which vampires are another group in the multicultural stew. She uses many of the same tools and techniques as an sf writer exploring a premise (as Shusterman did in *Unwind*, for example). Alex Sabian is a great character, and she's slated to return next year in a sequel.

Spread the love: *Give Blood Law* to your favorite romance reader. You will be thanked.

The Darwin Elevator
Jason M. Hough
Del Rey, 480 pages, $9.99 (paperback)
iBooks, Kindle, Nook: $9.99 (e-book)
ISBN: 978-0-345-53712-6
Series: Dire Earth 1
Genres: Adventure SF, Post-Apocalyptic, Visitors From Space

Jason M. Hough is a new voice in science fiction, coming to us in the old-fashioned format of books issued from a major publisher. His first book, *The Darwin Elevator*, is anything but old-fashioned.

It's the year 2283, and the aliens have come and gone. The Builders, as humans call them, brought two things: highly advanced technology, and a plague that turned most humans into savage, mindless beasts. Then they departed, destination unknown.

When the Builders arrived, they constructed a space elevator that stretches from geosynchronous orbit to Darwin, Australia. This elevator somehow emits an aura that cures the plague, and aura that's effective in a nearly nine-kilometer radius around the structure. That circle covers part of the city of Darwin and the ocean beyond, and it hosts refugees from all over the planet. The human race is largely confined to this clear zone and habitats established along the Elevator itself.

Food comes from great agricultural habitats strung along the Elevator, but there's a constant need for supplies that only Earth can supply—ranging from water and minerals to medicines, spare parts, and a few cultural treasures. Powered crawlers constantly climb up and down the Elevator, carrying cargo to sustain the habitats.

The water comes from nuclear-powered desalinization plants, but everything else has to come from outside—meaning someone has to go outside the aura and gather it all from decaying ruins populated by hostile savages.

Enter Skyler Luiken and his crew. Skyler, commander of the airship *Melville*, is one of the rare humans who is immune to the plague. His multicultural crew of fellow immunes are scavengers, scouring the world for useful resources. They are pirates, soldiers, scholars, survivalists, swashbuckling adventurers. Chief among them is Tania Sharma, scientist, fighter.

Humanity's efforts to eke out an existence in this bleak world are threatened when the Elevator suddenly begins to malfunction. Builder technology—which humans hardly understand to begin with—seems to be failing.

It's up to Skyler, Tania, and their people to find out what's going on. To do so, they must tackle conspiracies, attack the powerful, and solve the mystery of who the Builders were, why they came to Earth, and why they brought the plague.

Jason M. Hough does a great job with this huge story. The world of Darwin and the Elevator is deliciously complex and satisfying. Skyler, Tania, and all the other characters are delightfully drawn and fun to spend time with, people trying to do their best to deal with crisis. The story unfolds with just the right balance of high adventure, espionage, humor, and emotional truth.

The Darwins Elevator weighs in at 480 pages, but this is one of those meaty books that reads quickly and effortlessly. As soon as you finish, you'll want more.

Good news, then: Del Rey plans to issue the next two books in the series (*The Exodus Towers* and *The Plague Force*) in successive months. So clear some time on your calendar; you won't regret it.

The Exodus Towers
Jason M. Hough
Del Rey, 527 pages, $9.99 (mass market paperback)
iBooks, Kindle: $7.99, Nook: $9.99 (e-book)
ISBN: 978-0-345-53714-0
Series: Dire Earth 2
Genres: Adventure SF, Post-Apocalyptic, Visitors From Space

I reviewed *The Darwin Elevator,* book one of the *Dire Earth* series, in the September 2013 issue. Jason M. Hough and Del Rey have done us a favor by issuing the second book, *The Exodus Towers,* just a few months later. By the time you read this, book three (*The Plague Forge*) should be out as well.

A quick recap: It's 2283. At some indeterminate time in the past, aliens called The Builders established a space elevator with a terminus in Darwin, Australia. Along with superior technology, the aliens also brought a plague that turned most humans into savage, mindless beasts.

Only two groups survived: The people of Darwin, protected by a plague-resistant force that extends nine kilometers from the elevator—and a very few others who have natural immunity to the plague. Darwin became the only refuge of civilization in the world, supported by salvage missions run by immunes like Skyler Luiken and his crew. The immense structure of the Elevator, anchored in synchronous orbit by a derelict ship of the Builders, serves as agricultural space and additional room for the remaining humans.

The Darwin Elevator told of Skyler, scientist Tania Sharma, and a cast of other compelling characters as they fought for survival while trying to solve the mystery of the Builders.

The Exodus Towers picks up right where the first book ended, at the Brazilian site of a crashed Builders ship. Strange mobile towers emit the same aura that protects Darwin from the plague—with them, Skyler and Tania found a new colony, called Exodus. Then they discover a second space elevator....

Before they can solve the new mystery, the new Exodus colony has to fight off not only the brutish subhumans, but also a band of immune soldiers who don't like a new colony in their territory. Plus, there's been a theocratic coup in Darwin, and the new rulers want control of Exodus as well.

Oh, and there are these aliens....

The *Dire Earth* books have suspense, thrills, adventure, and characters you care about. In addition, they're good science fiction. I can't recommend them enough.

The Plague Forge
Jason M. Hough
Del Rey, 433 pages, $9.99 (mass market)
Kindle: $7.58, iBooks, Nook: $9.99 (e-book)
ISBN: 978-0-345-53716-4
Series: Dire Earth 3
Genre: Adventure SF, Post-Apocalyptic, Visitors From
 Space

Sometimes the final book of a trilogy is a disappointment. When all the questions are answered and the loose ends tied up, it's somehow anticlimactic.

You don't need to worry about that with Jason M. Hough's *Dire Earth* trilogy.

The Plague Forge is a fully satisfactory conclusion to the story begun in *The Darwin Elevator* and continued in *The Exodus Towers*, one of the most breathlessly exciting stories in recent sf.

In case you missed it (or were waiting for all three volumes), the *Dire Earth* is set in the 2280s. A generation earlier, aliens called the Builders came to Earth, planting an earth-to-orbit tower in downtown Darwin, Australia. At about the same time (nobody's exactly sure of the sequence), a plague spread across the world, turning people into mindless, violent beasts.

Most of Earth's human population succumbed, with two exceptions—those few naturally immune to the plague, and those protected by a mysterious aura around the Darwin tower.

The race survived in Darwin and in the body of the space elevator, while immunes like Skyler Luiken and his crew salvaged what they could from the wreckage of Earth.

Skyler, along with scientist Tania Sharma, discovered another elevator, along with more relics of the Builders, in Brazil. They established a second colony, withstood a religious dictatorship back home, and learned more about the Builders and their technology.

In this book, Skyler and crew find more Builder artifacts in the African desert—and this discovery leads them to the final confrontation and the answers the whole world seeks. Who or what were the Builders, where are they now, and what do they want with Earth?

Science fiction is particularly good at combining breakneck action and adventure with cosmic philosophical questions, and the *Dire Earth* books are a great example. These books engage your gut, your brain, and your heart all at once. What more could you ask?

Rootless
Chris Howard
Scholastic, 330 pages, $17.99 (hardcover)
Kindle: $9.99, Nook: $10.39 (e-book)
ISBN: 978-0-545-38789-7
Series: Rootless 1
Genres: Ecological/Environmental SF, Post-apocalyptic,
   Teen SF

A century ago, the Darkness came. In the Darkness, people burned everything and anything: houses, furniture, books, trees...little by little, the old civilization was reduced to ashes.

With the Darkness came the locusts: fierce swarms who fed equally on forests or flesh. And then there were no more forests, no more trees at all.

In some places, new civilization rose from the ashes, islands in a bleak worldwide wasteland. The rich—those who work for corporations like GenTech, or who make fortunes by salvaging the ruins of the past—live good lives in the cities. The poor eke out meager lives tending GenTech's locust-proof crops, working on salvage crews, or as nomads who wander the wastes in search of work.

Seventeen-year-old Banyan is a tree builder: an artist who turns junk and scrap metal into replica groves and forests. The rich pay handsomely for his creations, for having one's own trees is not only the ultimate status symbol, it's a touch of beauty, a reminder of the mythical past.

When Banyan takes on the biggest job he's ever had, he meets a woman with a beautiful tattoo of a gorgeous living tree. And he learns that there just might be a place where real trees still survive.

Banyan's subsequent quest, in search of a fabled orchard that may or may not exist, takes us across a magnificently detailed world, a world full of dangers and wonders, pirates and scavengers, friends and enemies, and always the threat of the locusts. This is one of those books in which the landscape becomes as much a fascinating character as the people in the story.

Yes, *Rootless* is a post-apocalyptic novel, as is the rage today; but the book transcends that genre. Banyan is a compelling, fun character, and the folks he meets on his journey are equally captivating. The language is fresh and sparkling.

Fair warning: *Rootless* is the first of a series. The immediate story comes to a satisfactory ending, but as with all great future worlds and grand epics, there's much more to come.

Darkship Renegades
Sarah A. Hoyt
Baen, 390 pages, $14.00 (trade paperback)
Baen Ebooks, Kindle: $8.99 (e-book)
ISBN: 978-1-4516-3852-3
Series: Darkships 2
Genres: Adventure SF

2010's *Darkship Thieves* introduced us to Athena Hera Sinistra (aka Thena), a poor little rich girl who found happiness, fulfillment, and a husband as a swashbuckling space hero. Now Sarah A. Hoyt continues Athena's story, and the universe better watch out.

In this future, Earth was once ruled by the Mules, a genetically-engineered master race. Among their accomplishments are the powertrees: huge, half-biological solar collectors in Earth orbit that supply energy to Earth and its colonies.

In the course of the first book, Thena met Kit, a pilot from Eden. Eden is a secret space habitat populated by the escaped servants of the Mules: engineered humans with the ability to fly their darkships among the powertrees to harvest power pods.

One thing led to another, and soon enough Thena was involved in a revolution on Earth and on a mission to rescue Kit.

Now the two are reunited and returning to Eden. Thena looks forward to living Happily Ever After with her new husband—but her plans are disrupted. On Eden, it seems that visiting Earth is a capital crime.

Eden offers the couple one way out: they must return to war-torn Earth to bring back the secret of constructing powertrees. Reluctantly, the couple agrees. Of course, there are various factions on Earth that want Thea dead...or worse. So avoiding capture is high on her priority list.

Much action and adventure ensues, enlivened by Thena's inimitable voice. This isn't a humorous book per se, but there are plenty of laughs. With a fascinating background and some really interesting technology, this is definitely a fun romp.

A Few Good Men
Sarah A. Hoyt
Baen, 372 pages, $14.00 (trade paperback)
Baen ebooks: $8.99 (e-book)
ISBN: 978-1-4516-3888-2
Series: Darkships 3, Earth's Revolution 1
Genre: Adventure SF, Military SF

Sarah A. Hoyt returns to the world of her *Darkships* (*Darkship Thieves, Darkship Renegades*) to carry on the story of a war-torn Earth dominated by the Good Men: fifty unscrupulous tyrants who use alien technology to keep the world in subjugation.

Lucius Keeva is the son of Good Man Keeva, the Olympic Seacity's absolute monarch. Lucius has been in prison for the last 14 years, convicted of multiple murders, victim of power politics.

Until the day an explosion comes, and Lucius escapes from the most secure prison in the world. When he returns home, he finds that his father has been assassinated, and a new force is loose in the world: revolution. The world is in more turmoil than usual, someone is trying to overthrow the Good Men—and as if that's not enough, there are those at home who would do anything to stop Lucius from taking his father's place.

With his life and his realm in danger from multiple directions, Lucius has no choice but to ally with Nat Remy, an agent of the mysterious Sons of Liberty, and a proponent of the odd Usaian religion.

It wouldn't be a *Darkships* book without Athena Sinistra, the irrepressible heroine of the first two books. As is her wont, Athena turns up at the worst possible moment, with trouble in her wake.

A Few Good Men is the first book of a projected trilogy. The *Darkships* universe is a compelling one, and as always Hoyt provides plenty of action, politics, and humor all in perfect proportion.

Reviews: I

(alphabetical by author)

Buyout
Alexander C. Irvine
Del Rey, 319 pages, $14.00 (paperback)
ISBN: 978-0-345-49433-7
Genre: Near Future SF, Psychological/Sociological SF

Buyout is a different kind of idea-dominated story. In *Hylozoic*, the ideas fly fast and furious, breeding and mutating before your eyes like so many unruly microorganisms. *Buyout* is a more classic, more familiar form in which the author brings one big idea onto the stage, then builds a whole show around it. In this case, the idea is social rather than scientific, and probably even more plausible today than when the author started work on the book.

In the all-too-familiar California of 2039, the prison system is overloaded and taxpayers are going broke paying to house and feed the hordes of life inmates. So here's the idea presented by Scott and Jocelyn Krakauer, an entrepreneurial couple who have made their way up through the world of finance to the highest levels of the insurance business: the life-term buyout. Prisoners serving life-without-parole are given the choice to be executed, in return for a payment of several million dollars to family, friends, victims, or charities. The deal winds up being cheaper for taxpayers, and allows a murderer to take care of his family, ease the suffering of victims' survivors, and do some good for society. As Scott and Jocelyn present the notion, it's a win-win situation.

Enter Martin Kindred, middle-aged insurance salesman for a failing company, in a deteriorating marriage. Scott and Jocelyn choose Martin as their point-man, the one who will sell eligible prisoners on buyouts. If he takes the job, Martin will become the public face of the life-term buyout. In return, Martin will receive substantial bonuses for each buyout deal he closes. If Martin declines the job offer, he'll be unemployed.

Opinions in Martin's family vary. His wife is against the idea. His father and brother, former and current cops respectively, are in favor of buyouts and support Martin's choice to take the job. His best friend Charlie, a private eye, is doubtful about buyouts...and also concerned that Martin won't be able to handle the pressure. In fact, Charlie takes on a job with Martin's company so that he can help his friend.

At first, things go well. Half a dozen buyouts go well, and Martin makes a good deal of money. There is some resistance in society, most notably a fringe group called Priceless Life. Yet all is not well; Martin's marriage slides toward divorce, his school-age daughters show signs of stress, and Charlie gets more worried.

Then a famous film producer is sentenced to life in prison for killing his girlfriend, and he agrees to a life-term buyout. Suddenly, Martin is in the bulls eye of publicity.

In the wake of this case, Martin finds himself of the trail of a mystery. For buyouts are not as simple as they seem...and Martin and Charlie soon uncover a conspiracy leading to personal danger and the requisite surprising revelations.

The suspense/conspiracy story gives the book a workable plot. Martin, Charlie, and the others are credible characters. But the real test of an idea-based novel is how well it does at exploring the main idea.

All in all, *Buyout* does a fairly good job of investigating the ramifications of it main idea. Life-term buyouts raise a number of moral, philosophical, and legal questions, and Irvine examines many of them. How to go about establishing life-term buyouts, he best candidates for the first buyouts, handling negative publicity—Irvine rings the changes on the idea in a satisfactory way. And at the end of the book, the reader is left with plenty to ponder.

One test for an idea-based novel is whether a reader is still thinking about the idea a week or two later. *Buyout* passes that test.

Transformers: Exodus
Alex Irvine
Del Rey, 276 pages, $27.00 (hardcover)
ISBN: 978-0-345-51985-6
Genre: Movies, Robots, Space Opera

Ever since *Star Wars* there has been an unspoken connection between space opera in movies (and on TV) and space opera in the pages of books. *Transformers*, which started life as a line of toys and inspired both children's cartoons and comic books, might seem an odd choice to appear in this column. Trust me, *Transformers: Exodus* is a fun space opera.

It ought to be fun. The author, Alex Irvine, is an accomplished SF writer—his most recent SF book is last year's *Buyout*. He knows how to tell a good story, and he knows that good characters can save even the most childish premise. Take a deep breath, ignore some of the names (Irvine got stuck with a planet called "Cybertron" and the "Matrix of Leadership," he didn't invent them), and you'll find it fairly easy to enjoy this one.

A gladiator called Megatron (another one of those names) rebels against the corrupt, ordered society of Cybertron. Soon he has followers and a movement all his own, and he becomes a threat to the Powers That Be.

Meanwhile, Megatron's defiance has attracted the attention of a minor office functionary named Orion Pax. Pax first becomes Megatron's disciple, then his friend. But there are betrayals and attacks, and soon the two friends become bitter enemies caught in the middle of a civil war that wracks the entire planet.

If you are a fan of the *Transformers*, either in their original incarnation or their more recent hit movies, then you'll find a lot to like in this book. But if you don't know Optimus Prime from Omega Supreme or an Autobot from a Decepticon, you'll still be able to enjoy this fun little space opera.

Reviews: J

(alphabetical by author)

Brain Thief
by Alexander Jablokov
Tor, 384 pages, $24.99 (hardcover)
ISBN: 978-0-7653-2200-5
Genre: Cyberpunk, SF Mystery

Bernal Haydon-Rumi has a crazy boss. And he likes it that way.

Muriel Inglis is an ex-socialite who "made her money the old-fashioned way: she divorced it." She's also extremely intelligent and utterly eccentric. Muriel uses her enormous fortune to fund scientific projects that no one else would touch: repopulating the Great Plains with genetically reconstructed mammoths, urban reforestation, sculpting abandoned ICBM silos.

Bernal is Muriel's executive assistant, the buffer between her and a world that doesn't necessarily appreciate her ideas. Muriel produces the dreams, and Bernal labors to bring them to reality. Bernal likes his job, and he's very good at it...but he has to admit that Muriel keeps him hopping.

One day, Muriel disappears without warning. Bernal sets off after her, and the trail leads to a lab where Madeleine Ungaro is at work on another one of Muriel's projects: a prototype AI space probe, one designed to carry on an autonomous search for life in the cosmos.

The probe, code-named Hesketh, is missing. And just to make things more bizarre, corpses are showing up here and there with their brains removed. As Bernal searches for Muriel and Hesketh, he learns more about Ungaro's design. The probe's artificial intelligence, it seems, was modeled after the human brain...and apparently Hesketh needs more models.

Brain Thief is a zany near-future romp through a landscape of unusual characters as only Jablokov could imagine it. Definitely a lot of fun.

Open Your Eyes
Paul Jessup
Apex, 144 pages, $13.95 (trade paperback)
ISBN: 978-0-9821596-0-6
Genre: Clarke's Law, SF Horror, Space Opera

What about those times when you're in the mood for something completely exotic, new taste sensations and unfamiliar cuisines? When you're ready to take a chance on a dish that's totally unfamiliar? It could be a disaster, or it could be your new favorite food.

There are certain writers who instantly transport readers into new, unfamiliar worlds that are completely different from the universe we know. After only a few bites, the reader sits back, gasping, and reaches for the water glass Then, eyes watering, he or she dives back in, licking the plate clean and asking for seconds. Think of Samuel R. Delany or Cordwainer Smith.

Welcome Paul Jessup to the ranks.

Open Your Eyes is billed as a cross between horror and science fiction, which is a little like describing filet mignon as a cross between cows and the laws of thermodynamics. More to the point is the publisher's description of the book as "surrealist space opera." Suspension of disbelief? It's best to nail your belief to the ceiling for the duration.

The book opens with Ekhi, a woman alone in a spaceship watching her lover die. Her lover is a star, and in going supernova he takes whole worlds with him. But he leaves Ekhi with child, a galaxy growing in her womb.

Ekhi's ship is all but destroyed, and is boarded by scavengers who take her on board their own ship...the *Good*

Ship Lollipop. This crew of scavengers are easily dysfunctional enough to justify the "opera" in space opera.

The captain, Itsasu, is a little girl who's lived for over 400 years, mourning her dead husband and on a quest to find a way to bring him back. She huddles in a preservation tank near the ship's heart, sending out dolls to be her eyes and nanomachines to be her hands. Itsasu guards a secret, a hidden cargo of incredible potential...but one that makes her ship a target to anyone who learns of its existence.

Navigator Mari is half woman, half metal. Half her face is a metal cage with silver butterflies fluttering within. She befriends Ekhi, but is also a threat.

Hodei is a sex-obsessed young man who bears the memories of a pinup girl. His brother, Sugoi, is a hulking brute who is in love with Mari. Sugoi is subject to violent rages, which he takes out on poor Hodei.

Shortly after Ekhi comes aboard and is nursed back to health, another ship appears and locks onto the *Good Ship Lollipop*. Invaders enter, doing damage and looting. Itsasu fears that they are after her secret cargo, but it turns out that they have come for Hodei and his hidden memories.

In this world of bone-ribbed ships and animated wax dolls, death is rarely permanent. But Ekhi and the crew of the *Good Ship Lollipop* have come upon a frightening force that brings final and painful death: a sapient linguistic virus that forces victims to utter phrases that kill. In the end, as Ekhi's child comes to term, creation and annihilation meet in a catastrophic coda.

By now you're either intrigued, or you think someone has lost their mind. That shows the limitations inherent in trying to describe a groundbreaking book in a few paragraphs. It's like reciting a list of unlikely ingredients to a friend instead of giving them a taste of a delicious, exotic dish. Sure, the book sounds like one absurdity piled on top of another...but the genius of Paul Jessup is that he makes the reader believe every bit of it. The language is forceful and lyrical, the characters engaging, and after only a few pages the reader falls completely under Jessup's spell. The language of the book is as infectious as any sapient linguistic virus could ever be.

Open Your Eyes is not for everyone. But if you're ready to step outside your comfort zone and try something delicious and exotic, you just might want to give it a try.

Final Crisis: Legion of 3 Worlds
Geoff Johns, George Pérez, Scott Koblish
DC Comics, 176 pages, $19.99 (hardcover)
ISBN: 978-1-4012-2324-3
Genre: Graphic Novels, Parallel Worlds/Other Dimensions, Superheroes

In addition to being top pre-Golden Age science fiction writers, Edmond Hamilton and Otto Binder both worked in comics. A bit more than fifty years ago, the two of them had a hand in creating a science-fictional team of superheroes that has survived to this day.

The Legion of Super-Heroes (LSH for short) exists more-or-less a thousand years from now, in the 31st century. In a universe of starships, aliens, and an interstellar government called the United Planets, the LSH is a team of (originally) teenagers, each with a different power or ability. Often they are offworlders whose people developed these abilities to cope with alien planets—for example, settlers on the planet Braal genetically engineered magnetokinetic powers to deal with the hostile metal-boned creatures that inhabit the world, while all inhabitants of Durla are shape-shifters.

Over the decades the LSH (in the fashion of all comic-book teams) has grown increasingly detailed and more and more baroque. There have been several mutually exclusive versions of the team, as their universe was "rebooted" to attract new readers with a fresh start. But one thing has remained constant: the LSH has always been set in the future, and has always used the tropes and concepts of science fiction: alien beings, other worlds, time travel, alternate universes; they are even inextricably linked to that other science-fiction-based superhero, last survivor of doomed Krypton: Superman. As a boy, Superman traveled into the future and had many adventures with the Legion.

And Legion they are: various incarnations of the team have had dozens of members.

In *Final Crisis: Legion of 3 Worlds*, writer Geoff Johns pulls out all the stops to bring all the previous versions of the LSH together in a space opera like no other. And legendary artist George Pérez is right there with him, his intricately-detailed pages teeming with literally hundreds of characters.

The plot is fairly straightforward. A powerful, malevolent entity known as the Time Trapper desires to wipe out the Legion, and finds a perfect weapon: an evil version of Superboy from a universe that no longer exists. The Trapper brings this Superboy Prime to 31st century Earth. The boy—whose unimaginable powers exceed even those of the mature Superman—learns of the existence of a Legion of Super-Villains and liberates them from the prison planet Takron-Galtos. This evil Legion heads to Earth for a final battle with the good Legion.

The LSH calls in Superman from the 21st century, but they know even his power will not be enough. They turn to Brainiac 5, whose super-power is his "twelfth-level intelligence." Brainy summons two alternate versions of the LSH from other realities; he also resurrects some heroes who died fighting Superboy Prime in the present day. For good measure, the outer-space Green Lantern Corps enters the fray.

It's good Legions vs. evil Legion, with the all-powerful Time Trapper manipulating time to his benefit, until Brainiac 5's machinations bring about a deliciously over-the-top ending that proves, once and for all, that there's still fun left in comics.

If you haven't experienced the Legion of Super-Heroes and their fantastic future universe, you owe it to yourself to give them a try. *Final Crisis: Legion of 3 Worlds* is a great way to get acquainted with the team that Otto Binder and Edmond Hamilton created, all those years ago.

Steelhands
Jaida Jones & Danielle Bennett
Spectra, 423 pages, $26.00 (hardcover)
iBooks, Kindle, Nook: $12.99 (e-book)
ISBN: 978-0-553-80770-7
Series: Volstov #4
Genre: Steampunk

Friend D. B. has recently discovered sf and fantasy by way of steampunk; he listens to Abney Park, every piece of clothing he owns is adorned with gears, and he owns sixteen separate pairs of goggles (not to mention three monocles). What to get this budding steampunker?

The *Volstov* series has everything a steampunk lover is looking for. The empire of Volstov—which combines the most delicious aspects of Byzantium, Catherine the Great's Russia, and Victorian England—rose to power on the backs of dragons: giant mechanical metal dragons, animated by a mix of science and magic, and ridden by courageous fighter pilots.

It's now a time of peace, but that peace is a delusion (as is much in Volstov's intricate, conspiracy-filled government). The illustrious Dragon Corps is dismantled, the riders scattered, and ex-Chief Sergeant Owen Adamo is on the track of nefarious doings in the highest ranks. It seems that the ruler, the Esar, is pursuing a plot to reanimate dead dragons and start another war.

Adamo, of course, is opposed to the idea. But he's been exiled to the University, and his former associates have also been stripped of their influence and powers. The magician Royston dares not openly confront the court. And Adamo's former lieutenant, Balfour, is in worse shape: he lost both his hands in the war, and must make do with ugly, clumsy mechanical replacements.

Then along come two students. Laurence is a feisty Amazon (her father wanted a boy), and Toverre, her betrothed, is a genius fop with a penchant for dressing in women's clothing. This unlikely pair are just the allies Adamo needs to move forward in his opposition to the Esar's plans.

The rest is high adventure, intrigue, scheming, treachery, and quite a bit of intricate machinery—both metal and social.

Reviews: K

(alphabetical by author)

Mass Effect: Retribution
Drew Karpyshyn
Del Rey, 368 pages, $7.99 (paperback)
Kindle, Nook: $5.00 (ebook)
ISBN: 978-0-345-52072-2
Series: Mass Effect 3
Genre: Games & Gaming, Military SF

We're used to novelizations of sf movies; a more recent phenomenon is novelizations of hit video games. With so many games based on fighting, it's not surprising that such novelizations would be a good fit for military sf.

Drew Karpyshyn was lead writer on the game *Mass Effect*, and he does a good job of translating a rather complex story to the novel form. In the previous two books, Humanity discovered ancient alien technology on Mars and joined the galactic community. Scientist Kahlee Saunders, working for the Ascension Project to help so called "biotics"—children with exceptional abilities—survived several run-ins with a covert organization called Cerberus.

Now there's a new enemy on the horizon: Reapers, horrific aliens who harvest human organs for their own vile purposes. Only Paul Grayson, a human implanted with Reaper technology, holds the clues to help defeat the Reapers.

There's only one catch: Grayson is being held in a hidden Cerberus facility, and the Reaper tech is slowly taking over his mind. Kahlee enlists the aid of a former war hero to rescue Grayson.

If you know nothing about *Mass Effect* or video games, don't worry...just tell yourself that you're reading another military sf novel, and you'll be fine.

Shades of Gray
Jackie Kessler & Caitlin Kittredge
Spectra, 414 pages, $16.00 (trade paperback)
ISBN: 978--0-553-38632-5
Series: Icarus Project #2
Genre: Superheroes

In *Black and White*, Jackie Kessler and Caitlin Kittredge introduced us to young superheroes Jet (Joan Green) and Iridium (Callie Bradford), who wield powers of darkness and light, respectively. Jet and Iridium started as best friends but became bitter enemies; in *Black and White* they had to cooperate to take down the dastardly villain Taser.

In Jet and Iridium's superhero world, there are hundreds of super-powered extrahumans, most in and around the city of New Chicago. For decades, the global corporation Corp-Co has controlled the extrahumans by means of a high-tech system called Ops. At the end of *Black and White*, Jet and Iridium have taken down Ops—and for the first time, hundreds of extrahumans are free of Corp-Co control. The heroes realize that they've been enslaved all this time...and they're not happy about it.

Shades of Gray picks up where the first book left off. New Chicago is in chaos. Angry extrahumans are ransacking the city; anti-superhero groups are stoking the fires of suspicion and prejudice against the extrahumans. Jet, along with a small group of still-lawful heroes, attempts to quell the chaos...a job that seems helpless.

Meanwhile, Iridium is having her own problems dealing with Corp-Co, which is still very much in the fight.

Into the middle of this anarchy steps the sociopath Doctor Hypnotic, bent on his own nefarious schemes. Once again, Jet and Iridium must put aside their differences and work together to save everyone.

Jet and Iridium are engaging characters and their world is intriguing. If you're looking for a light superhero adventure that touches on some fairly weighty questions of morality, *Shades of Gray* is your book.

Shh! It's a Secret: A Novel About Aliens, Hollywood, and the Bartender's Guide
Daniel M. Kimmel
Fantastic Books, 194 pages, $14.99 (trade paperback)
ISBN: 978-1-6720-733-4
Genre: Humorous SF, Satire SF

Jake Berman is a publicist for Graham Studios, a foundering movie studio. Like everyone else, he was transfixed by the news images when an alien spaceship landed on the lawn of a Catskills resort in New York. He watched with wonder as the aliens, the Brogardi, appeared before the United Nations to state their peaceful intentions and appeal for scientific and cultural exchange between Brogardi and Humans.

Jake's seen enough sci-fi films to wonder if the aliens are really as peaceful as they seem, but he's a busy man and soon forgets his doubts. Until one of the Brogardi—the chief ambassador's son, in fact—shows up at the studio with an interesting offer. The alien, it seems, has decided he wants to embark on an acting career, and he's chosen Graham Studios to make his dream come true.

Jake shepherds his charge through the endless process of making a movie and becoming a star. A plot is chosen, a script produced, a leading lady found. In order to get the jump on other studios, the project is kept secret—Jake the publicist is thrown into the position of using all his talents to avoid publicity.

Finally the film is done, and there's a star-studded premiere. That's when an unforeseen quirk of Brogardi society raises its ugly head: the Brogardi prize truth above all else, and they class all fiction as lies. And lying isn't just immoral, to the Brogardi it's criminal.

How Jake gets himself, his studio, and his planet out of this mess is a true joy.

Daniel M. Kimmel is a film critic and professor of film. His nonfiction book *Jar Jar Binks Must Die* (reviewed in the July/August 2011 issue) was a Hugo Award finalist. He knows Hollywood inside and out. *Shh! It's a Secret* is his first novel. Let's hope there are more to come.

Little Brother's World
T. Jackson King
Fantastic Books, 214 pages, $13.99 (trade paperback)
Kindle: $12.99
ISBN: 978-1-60459-940-4
Genre: Adventure SF, Genetics, Other Worlds

Life on the colony planet Mother's World is safe, secure, and regimented by the Church of Flesh. Society is structured around citizens' genetic inheritance: good genes are rewarded, bad genes discouraged. All citizens have their gene codes tattooed on their arms, so that everyone knows their place and things runs smoothly…for most, anyway.

But this is science fiction, and we know that all the interesting stuff is happening at the margins of the society. In particular, there's the Alor City Dump, where outcasts scavengers make a living off the garbage of the more fortunate.

Little Brother, an orphan, has grown up in the Dump and knows no other life. Little Brother is different—he has no gene code. One day, while scavenging, he finds a girl named Sally hiding in the garbage. Sally is a Breed, with one of the most valuable genetic legacies on the planet.

Little Brother rescues Sally, and there his problems start. Before he can sell Sally back to her family, her parents are murdered. Sally's family, it seems, has attracted the attention of the Church of Flesh.

So now Little Brother and Sally go on the run, through the underbelly of Mother's World. In the course of their flight, Little Brother finds out why he is the only person without a gene code...and also learns that he, unexpectedly, holds within his hands the power to topple the caste system and bring change to Mother's World.

If you're sensing a whiff of André Norton or Robert A. Heinlein, you're not mistaken—those are the first two names in T. Jackson King's list of acknowledgments. The influence is certainly there, but *Little Brother's World* is no mere imitation of *Star Man's Son* or *Citizen of the Galaxy*. Rather, it takes the sensibility of those sorts of books and makes of it something fresh and new. T. Jackson King is doing his part to further the great conversation of science fiction; it'll be interesting to see where he goes next.

The Unincorporated Man
Dani Kollin and Eytan Kollin
Tor, 480 pages, $25.95 (hardcover)
ISBN: 978-0-7653-1899-2
Genres: Psychological/Sociological SF

In science fiction circles, it is an article of faith that anything can be a subject for an sf story. Politics, sex, violence, slavery, cannibalism, religion: nothing is too controversial or too obscure to be the basis of an sf novel.

In *The Unincorporated Man*, the subject is economic theory.

In the 24th century, everyone is incorporated, and nobody gets anything for free. From birth, individuals sell shares of themselves: to parents, teachers, even the doctors who attended one's birth. As a result, the average adult spends half a lifetime buying back shares in an attempt to gain majority control of one's own life.

Into this world comes Justin Cord, a 21st century billionaire who was secretly put into suspended animation after his death.

By now, resurrecting and curing Cord is trivial; the big problem is that he is the only unincorporated individual in the world. And this erstwhile tycoon is a poor match for the utopian society into which he's awakened.

It's an interesting and compelling idea; unfortunately, the Kollin brothers don't succeed in turning the idea into an equally interesting and compelling novel.

Let me be perfectly clear, I am making no judgment on the idea, just the execution of the story. The characters never really come alive: they are merely placeholders in the authors' exploration of their world. Even Justin Cord, who was obviously meant to be the most sympathetic and appealing character, is nothing more than a cardboard mouthpiece.

Science fiction writers always have the challenge of introducing background information to the reader. One common pitfall is the infodump: an indigestible mass of data that brings the story to a crashing halt. *The Unincorporated Man* is filled with infodumps, many of which would be more at home in *Corporate Investing for Dummies* or a similar book.

Another technique is to introduce a naive observer, such as a traveler from another place or time. As the observer learns, so does the reader. Nancy Kress deftly uses this technique to great effect in *Steal Across the Sky*, as her Witnesses learn about the worlds upon which they've landed. In *The Unincorporated Man* the same technique is awkward and disruptive. Justin Cord is always learning about his new world in long expository passages that don't fit and serve to slow down the reader.

The plot of *The Unincorporated Man* is mainly an excuse to get Justin Cord touring the world so the reader can learn about the underlying economic theory. The villains are bad not because of any underlying human motivations, but because, well, you need to have some bad guys. If this future world has any serious flaw, it's that life is too perfect. In the fullness of time, Justin inspires revolution throughout the Solar System, the bad guys are defeated, and all is well.

The Unincorporated Man comes accompanied by breathless publicity proclaiming it to be groundbreaking and important, and quotes likening it to Heinlein. Treat these claims as hyperbole. Heinlein at his best was an exceptional storyteller; the storytelling here is, to be generous, pedestrian.

If you're looking for a good novel, I would counsel you to look elsewhere.

So who would like this book? Among your circle of friends, look for the hardcore libertarians—those who think that all roads should be toll roads, or that the greatest evil in the modern world is the income tax. Or those who can quote Ayn Rand chapter and verse. Recommend *The Unincorporated Man* to them, and they'll be eternally grateful. And if you don't have anyone like that among your circle of friends, you need to get out more and make more friends.

Pink Noise
Leonid Korogodski
Silverberry Press, 190 pages, $25.95 (hardcover)
iBooks: $11.99, Kindle: $9.39, Nook: $9.59 (ebook)
ISBN: 978-0-9843608-2-6
Genre: Transhumanism

Pink Noise is surely the most stylish book I've received this year. It's printed on glossy paper in black and red, and fancifully illustrated by an artist called Guddah. There are over 60 pages of notes and references—including a map, glossary, pronunciation guide, three essays, and a bibliography. There's even a fancy pink ribbon sewn into the binding for use as a bookmark.

At this point you might expect a triumph of style over substance (I certainly did). After all, when you boil away all the pretty trappings, what's left is a 130-page novella. Yet substance is there—it's a good novella.

Five hundred years ago, Nathi became transhuman; that is, he uploaded his consciousness into cyberspace. Since then, the transhumans have been conquered and enslaved by entities calling themselves the Wizard Orders. With a computer virus known as The Wish, the Wizard Orders keep transhumans (as well as ordinary humans) under their control.

On Mars, Nathi is summoned to help heal a comatose human girl (called The Girl). Her brain is badly damaged, but Nathi maps portions of his own mind onto hers in order to bring her to consciousness.

Well, wouldn't you know it, The Girl is a secret host for The Wish Fairy, which is a sapient being with the power to destroy The Wish. Before you can say "singularity," Nathi and The Girl (joined in symbiosis) escape their prison and dash out across treacherous Martian polar terrain. The Wizard Orders are right on their heels (both in cyberspace and in the physical world). All they really have on their side is the unpredictability of the physical brain—the "pink noise" of the title.

Blending fairy tale with hard sf, and written in an easy yet lyrical style, *Pink Noise* is a surprisingly good story. Although it seems to be aimed toward non-sf readers, the book and its language are sophisticated enough to satisfy any *Analog* reader.

Whether it's worth the price of admission depends on how much you value a beautiful physical book. Perhaps this would be a good one to put on your holiday shopping list as a gift to one of your transhumanist friends...assuming the Singularity holds off until then.

New Under the Sun
Nancy Kress and Therese Pieczynski
Phoenix Pick, 183 pages, $12.99 (trade paperback)
ISBN: 978-1-61242-123-0
Genre: Biological SF, Psychological/Sociological SF

Phoenix Pick's "Stellar Guild" series publishes a novella by a big-name author along with a companion novella or novelette by a protege chosen by the big name. As far as gimmicks go, it's an interesting one, and the results have so far been good.

Nancy Kress, multiple Nebula-award winner, brings us "Annabel Lee"—a gripping story of young girl unknowingly infected by an alien parasite in a near-future world. This being Nancy Kress, there's a lot more going on; Annabel's family is as troubled as any other, and her friends have their own problems. And as Annabel grows up, her abilities become greater....

Therese Piecsynski's companion piece, "Strange Attraction," is set in the 1980s and combines chaos theory with South American militias in a tale of another woman with unusual abilities. Paula is a U.S. expatriate in Nicaragua during the revolution, and strange events follow her around. Electrical plants stop working, her friends get killed...and lately she's been involved with a powerful, deadly whirlwind that seems to feed on fear and pain.

Together, these two stories do what science fiction is so good at—exploring the impact of unexpected change on people. The theme of people with amazing abilities is as old as literature itself—but here Kress and Pieczynski ring new changes on the idea.

***Steal Across the Sky*
Nancy Kress
Tor, 336 pages, $25.95 (hardcover)
ISBN: 978-0-7653-1986-9
Genres: Alien Beings, Other Worlds, Psychological/
   Sociological SF, Religious/Philosophical SF**

I don't think Nancy Kress can write a bad book.

Aliens land on the moon and place an ad on the Internet (it's the best way to reach a lot of people in a hurry). Calling themselves the Atoners, they claim that ten thousand years ago, they wronged humanity, and now they're looking for volunteers to visit seven planets to "Witness." The Atoners won't reveal the nature of their foul deed, nor will they show themselves in person.

Cam, Lucca, and Soledad are the team of Witnesses dispatched to the Kular system. As *Steal Across the Sky* opens, they arrive and survey the two inhabited planets. Lucca takes a shuttle down to Kular A, while Cam descends to Kular B. Soledad stays behind in the mothership to coordinate communications and handle emergencies.

Both Kular worlds are inhabited by humans, descended from seed stock the Atoners stole from Earth ten thousand years ago. As Lucca and Cam play amateur anthropologists in the fascinating, pre-industrial societies of their respective worlds, they have no clue what they're looking for: the Atoners have only told them that they'll know it when they see it.

Kress spends the first half of the novel carefully and artfully revealing the big secret; I'm going to blab it in the next paragraph. If you don't want to know ahead of time, stop reading this review and go enjoy *Steal Across the Sky* with my blessing. The book is well worth your time.

Still here? Eventually it develops that the people of Kular A (but not Kular B) seem to be able to see and converse with the recently dead. All humans once had this ability; the crime of the Atoners is that they removed the associated genes from the human race. They set up Kular A and B (as well as seven other pairs of inhabited planets) as laboratory experiments: altered humans on one world, control groups of unaltered humans on the other.

Another writer would spend the rest of the book exploring the implications of this idea: the meaning of death, the nature of the afterlife, the impact on human religion, philosophy, and science. It's a huge theme, with repercussions for all of humanity. But Nancy Kress is no ordinary sf writer, and she knows that sometimes world-altering events can best be approached through their effect on individual people. She chooses to follow the Witnesses back to Earth, and in the second half of the book she unravels their own very personal responses to what they've experienced.

One Witness, refusing to believe in life after death, withdraws into seclusion. Another becomes a media superstar, preaching the gospel of the Atoners in revivalist style. Yet another accepts government relocation, trying to rebuild as normal a life as possible. Meanwhile, the Atoners go silent, retreating into their sealed moonbase and saying nothing.

Ultimately, the fates of all the Witnesses come together and all questions are answered, including the biggest one: what are the Atoners up to?

Thought-provoking and powerful, *Steal Across the Sky* is a book that will stay with you long after your reach the last page. Highly recommended.

Reviews: L

(alphabetical by author)

Channel 37
Paul Lagasse and Gary Lester
channel-37.net
Genre: Adventure SF

The tribute anthology is a special case of another form of ancestor worship, the homage. This kind of story is a current author's conscious effort to evoke an earlier author or a particular style. Successful homage is hard to pull off, as it isn't just slavish imitation—the current authors must add something of his/her own. And have I got a successful homage for you!

Channel 37 is a website filled with short fiction, ranging from bite-size snippets to novelette length serials. Ostensibly the site honors the kind of late-night sf movies that were featured on UHF TV channels of the 1950s through 1970s (hence the *Channel 37* of the title). However, Paul Lagasse and Gary Lester are writers, and their efforts also evoke the pre-Campbell stories that filled sf pulps of the 1920s and 1930s.

This is all tongue-in-cheek, of course. The writing is far better than you'd see in the pulps (or the late-night movies, for that matter), and the authors have an obvious enthusiasm for their subject. Titles like "The Terror From the Other Dimension!" and "Space Repairman" give you the idea at once.

On the Channel 37 site you can read completed stories—Lagasse and Lester have been at this since 2010—but the real fun is the ongoing serials, of which there are four as I write this. Every Tuesday and Friday a new chapter is posted; if you want, you can sign up to receive new chapters via an RSS feed.

Somehow, one gets the feeling that Campbell and Leinster would approve.

Pinion
Jay Lake
Tor, 448 pages, $26.99 (hardcover)
ISBN: 978-0-7653-2186-2
Series: Clockwork Earth #3
Genre: Science Fantasy, Steampunk

On the definite science fantasy side of steampunk is Jay Lake's *Clockwork Earth*. In Lake's alternate 19th century, the universe is quite literally a clockwork construct: driven by an enormous mainspring at the Earth's center, huge gears turn the planet and the entirety of creation. The Northern Hemisphere is dominated by two Empires, the British and the Chinese. Around the Equator is a gigantic wall, along which run the giant gears that rotate the world. The largely-unknown Southern Hemisphere, beyond the wall, is home to mysterious societies and horrifying creatures.

In the first book, *Mainspring*, clockmaker's apprentice Hethor Jacques went on a quest to find the key that would rewind the Earth's mainspring. He was assisted by librarian Emily Childress. In *Escapement* we met Paolina Barthes, a budding genius pursued by secret societies scheming to use her abilities for their own nefarious purposes. Paolina fled toward the equatorial wall and the safety of the South; Emily is taken onto a British ship that's attacked by a renegade Chinese submarine. She works her way into a position of influence aboard the sub.

Now, in *Pinion*, we rejoin Paolina and Emily on their different journeys. The rival secret societies of the North—the Silent Order and the White Birds—are pursuing both women. Meanwhile, a mysterious power from the South has taken an interest in Paolina: they do not want to allow her to bring the North's turmoil into their realms.

Airships, submarines, mechanical men, planet-girdling gears—Lake presents all of these magnificently. Along with generous helpings of adventure comes some truly stunning worldbuilding. If you haven't had the pleasure of visiting Lake's *Clockwork Earth*, you owe it to yourself to redress that omission.

Imperium
Keith Laumer
Baen, 625 pages, $7.99 (paperback)
Baen E-Books: $5.00 (e-book)
ISBN: 978-1-4516-3795-3
Series: Imperium #1-3
Genre: Adventure SF, Big Books, Parallel Worlds/Other Dimensions

Keith Laumer was best known for the *Retief* stories, satires revolving around an interstellar diplomat. In the *Imperium* books, he moved in the direction of adventure and suspense, and did a superb job.

In the books, there are many parallel universes. Brion Bayard, American diplomat, is kidnapped from Stockholm and taken to an Earth in which the American Revolution never happened, and where Britain and Germany merged into the worldwide Imperium. The Imperium is under attack by another hostile parallel Earth, and Brion is the key to ending the war.

The hostile Earth is ruled by its version of Brion—and our Brion sets off on a mission to take the bad guy's place. Of course, things don't go as planned....

It's a great adventure, and it's only the beginning. Brion throws his lot in with the Imperium, and becomes an agent venturing across the multiverse to protect his adopted home. Altogether, this volume collects the three Imperium novels (*Worlds of the Imperium, The Other Side of Time,* and *Assignment in Nowhere*) in one delightfully big book.

Echo City
Tim Lebbon
Ballantine/Spectra, 496 pages, $7.99 (paperback)
Kindle, Nook: $6.39 (ebook)
ISBN: 978-0-553-59322-8
Genre: Clarke's Law, Fortress City, Science Fantasy, SF Horror

It's entirely possible that you haven't run into the work of Tim Lebbon before. He has made quite a successful career writing horror and dark fantasy, and *Echo City* definitely springs from that background. Yet here he has produced one of those books that transcends genre; in the spirit of Arthur C. Clarke's Law ("Any sufficiently advanced technology is indistinguishable from magic"), *Echo City* is as much science fiction as it is fantasy or horror.

For uncounted thousands of years, Echo City has stood alone in the middle of a trackless, lifeless desert. The city is literally built upon its own past: beneath, layer upon layer of ruins extend further than historians and explorers have reached, remnants (called "Echoes") of countless past civilizations. To inhabitants, the City is all there is and all there has ever been.

Lebbon takes his time and paints a magnificently complete and detailed background; Echo City comes alive in that peculiar way of imagined places so real-seeming that they become almost major characters in the story. In particular, he avoids portraying Echo City as something uniform; instead, there is a great variety of districts and cultures represented. In the current era, Echo City is ruled by a tyrannical theocratic government.

And where there is a tyranny, there are dissenters. Peer Nadawa, once a powerful politician, now lives in exile in a lawless slum. Gorham, Peer's former lover, is a leader of one faction of rebels. Nophel is a servant who plots revenge. And

Nadielle is an old crone who experiments in forbidden genetic engineering techniques from the far past.

These disparate lives come together with the arrival of a stranger from out of the desert. Stripped of his memory, he is unable to tell where he came from or what lies beyond the desert. But his arrival heralds change for the eternal city...for long-forgotten things are rising from the Echoes, powers from the past that threaten the present.

Echo City is a full-immersion experience; like the best science fiction, it takes the reader away into a wholly different world. It is also a meditation on the nature and importance of memory and history. This is definitely one to remember when it comes time to nominate for the Hugo Award.

Ghost Ship
Sharon Lee & Steve Miller
Baen, 328 pages, $25.00 (hardcover)
Baen Webscriptions: $15.00 (e-book)
ISBN: 978-1-4391-3455-9
Series: Liaden Universe: Theo Waitley #3
Genre: Romantic SF

Next on the list is Danielle, a voracious reader of romances. She gobbles Harlequins by the bunch, quotes Janet Dailey chapter and verse, and gets most excited each full moon when the new Nora Roberts title hits the stands. (I'm not dissing Roberts, who is a fine storyteller, and who writes legitimate sf mysteries under her J. D. Robb pseudonym.)

For decades now, Steve Miller and Sharon Lee have been writing delightful stories of adventure and romance set in far-future, vaguely space opera milieu known as the *Liaden Universe*. After long millennia of struggle and diaspora, humanity is split into three subspecies: Terrans (regular humans), the Yxtrang (warmongering brutes), and the Liaden (gentle, philosophical, and more than a little xenophobic). In and out of the long history of the three races runs the Liaden

Clan of Korval, whose relations include just about everyone of any importance in the galaxy.

It's all a rather heady mix of Gordon R. Dickson, *The Forsythe Saga*, and Victoria Holt, with Lee and Miller's own unique touches making it all sparkle and fizz. Anyone whose taste runs toward sf in the true romantic tradition can't help but like the *Liaden Universe*.

To say the series has had a checked publishing history is like saying Saturn's rings are a tiny bit on the pretty side. Publishers have abridged the series, cancelled it, abandoned it, even dropped dead in the middle of it. But still Lee and Miller have soldiered on, thanks primarily to a devoted fan base who just won't let Liaden die. Currently all of the books are available in single and omnibus editions from Baen Books, and new titles are appearing regularly.

For two previous books, *Fledgling* and *Saltation*, we've been following the career of Theo Waitley, a Terran-Liaden halfbreed struggling to make her way as a star pilot in a universe at best indifferent to her. Theo takes after her father, a major Liaden player who's a legendary maverick—but Theo charts her own course, regardless of what any of her relatives want.

Ghost Ship, which can easily be read without any reference to the other books, is a fitting capstone to Theo's story. In the end, she makes peace with her demons and finds her place in the universe—but getting there is an exciting trip. And one that friend Danielle will surely enjoy.

Dragon Ship
Sharon Lee & Steve Miller
Baen, 400 pages, $22.00 (hardcover)
Baen Ebooks: $6.00 (e-book)
ISBN: 978-1-4516-3798-4
Series: Liaden Universe: Theo Waitley #4
Genre: Romantic SF, Space Opera

What about the romance reader on your list? Well, to begin with, she's probably more friendly to sf than you think.

While you weren't looking, the romance field has undergone some pretty major changes. While there are still a lot of the old formula romances around, many romance readers have embraced enormous diversity of settings, styles, and cross-genre hybridization. The biggest and most vital category of romances today is the "paranormal romance," which includes everything from steampunk vampires to far-future sf.

Sharon Lee and Steve Miller's *Liaden Universe* series successfully blends space opera sf with paranormal romance, yielding a result sure to delight readers from both sides of the fence.

When we last left Theo Waitley, plucky space pilot and lusty lover (*Ghost Ship*, 2011), she was saddled with the self-aware trade ship Bechimo. Together in symbiosis, Theo and Bechimo are incredibly powerful—but the symbiosis is all-consuming, and Bechmo is a jealous partner.

Meanwhile, Theo has a few other things to keep her busy. Her former lover is dying of a strange nano-virus, she's stuck in the middle of an explosive political situation, and suddenly she's responsible for engineering the rescue of a few hundred fellow pilots in an orbiting death-trap.

Adventure, espionage, romance, drama, humor—*Dragon Ship* has everything a romance or sf reader is looking for. Deliberate echoes of Anne McCaffrey just add icing to the cake.

If your romance reader likes this one, there are plenty of other *Liaden Universe* books.

A Liaden Universe Constellation: Volume 1
Sharon Lee & Steve Miller
Baen, 453 pages, $15.00 (trade paperback)
Baen Ebooks: $8.99
ISBN: 978-1-4516-3923-0
Series: Liaden Universe
Genre: Romantic SF, Short Fiction Collection, Space Opera

You may by planning to give someone a romantic gift: something pretty, or a nice dinner, or anything else that adds a bit of sparkle to ordinary life. Might as well throw in a volume of short fiction from the *Liaden Universe*.

This series, set against a space opera background that's a notch above the usual fare, is also the premier place to find good romantic sf adventure. In 16 novels, Lee and Miller have explored various corners of this vast universe, giving us strong characters finding their own way (and, often, each other) in an action-packed galaxy of worlds.

In between, the authors have produced a steady trickle of shorter works, published in various venues and previously available only in limited-edition chapbooks. Now for the first time, Baen is releasing the first volume of these tales to a larger audience.

This first volume contains seventeen stories of various lengths. Some feature characters we've seen in *Liaden* novels, others are about brand-new people. Every story stands on its own; readers don't have to be familiar with the *Liaden* universe. Those that have had the pleasure, though, will find many connections to existing tales.

Necessity's Child
Sharon Lee & Steve Miller
Baen, 336 pages, $25.00 (hardcover)
Baen Ebooks, Kindle: $9.99 (e-book)
ISBN: 978-1-4516-3887-5
Series: Liaden Universe 16
Genres: Romantic SF, Space Opera

Sharon Lee and Steve Miller's *Liaden Universe* is a big, complex place with room for lots of stories. The latest, *Necessity's Child*, is a standalone novel that explores a new corner of the series.

Kezzi is a young woman of the Beled, a gypsy-like people of the planet Surebleak. While the Beled usually keep to themselves, seldom interacting with the other people of Surebleak, Kezzi has no choice—in school, she's in the company of others all the time.

One of those others is Syl Vor, scion of the wealthy Clan Korval. Syl's people are newcomers to Surebleak, driven there by the political machinations of the Clan's many enemies. Syl himself is restless, warrior-trained but still in school, frustrated and unhappy.

Elsewhere on Surebleak, the Beled come across a man named Rys, beaten and left for dead. They take him in and care for him, but his ordeal has left him without memory or identity. Somehow he's involved in the intrigue that always swirls around Clan Korval.

These three individuals, of course, come together, and the result is a nice suspense story with all the *Liaden Universe* trademarks: finely drawn characters, interesting societies, political intrigue, action and suspense, and a dollop of romance on top.

Like Anne and Todd McCaffrey's *Pern* series, the *Liaden Universe* is a huge tapestry that all hangs together. Syl was a minor walk-on character in the novel *Plan B*, and people from other books appear here, seen in different perspective.

However, this is all done so skillfully that a reader who hasn't read the other books doesn't feel any lack.

If you're a fan of science fiction that focuses on people and their relationships, then *Necessity's Child* is the book for you.

Energized
Edward M. Lerner
Tor, 336 pages, $27.99 (hardcover)
iBooks, Kindle, Nook: $14.99 (e-book)
ISBN: 978-0-7653-2849-6
Genre: Hard SF, Near-Future, SF Thrillers

Look, you all know Edward M. Lerner is a good storyteller. If you need convincing, just look over the last few years of *Analog*—you'll have no trouble finding his excellent short fiction.

Energized is near-future speculative sf in the Ben Bova tradition. In 2023, the end of the Petroleum Age comes sooner than anyone expected, with a spasm that leaves Mideast oil fields contaminated with radioactivity. The Middle East is in chaos, Russia and Venezuela are suddenly superpowers, and everyone is desperate for energy.

With an asteroid heading for a near-Earth encounter, any *Analog* reader could, in his or her sleep, tell America what to do. For a wonder, America does—intercepts Phoebe and captures it into Earth orbit. With this raw material, NASA engineer Marcus Judson intends to make solar power satellites, the way we would have done in the real world forty years ago if people were paying attention to sf, thank you very much.

Ahem. Well, you can see where this is going—Judson has bunches of obstacles to overcome, and he sets upon them with all the will and ability of the aerospace engineer. It's a magnificently fun romp, complete with espionage, international cabals, sabotage, and lots of amusing political commentary. For anyone who likes Analog, this is a no-brainer.

I just wish politicians would listen, this time.

(And while this is hardly the place or time to start a discussion about high prices of e-books—perhaps in a future column—I just can't pass up the chance to wag my finger at Tor. Fifteen dollars for an e-book? Really? As I write this, readers can pre-order the hardcover from Amazon for just a dollar and a quarter more. With a great product like *Energized*, you'd think they'd want to...I don't know...sell some of them? Talk about incomprehensible alien psychology....)

(Readers, please don't take it out on Lerner. He doesn't set prices. If you can't stomach paying that much for an e-book, bite the bullet and buy the hardcover. The man is one of us.)

Frontiers of Space, Time, and Thought
Edward M. Lerner
Fox Acre Press, 262 pages, $12.95 (trade paperback)
Kindle, Nook: $7.99 (e-book)
ISBN: 978-1-936771-37-0
Genre: Short Story Collection

Edward M. Lerner is no stranger to *Analog's* pages. *Frontiers of Space, Time, and Thought* collects twenty of his short stories and nonfiction articles and organizes them by "Big Questions"—scientific topics and themes that inform much of Lerner's work.

These themes (regular readers of Lerner can probably recite them along with me) are: SETI and First Contact, Computers and Artificial Intelligence, Far-Out Physics (a catch-call category that includes everything from quantum dynamics to FTL travel), Near-Earth Space Travel, and Nanotechnology. For each section, Lerner provides a short introduction before launching into the articles and stories.

By my count, about half these pieces have previously appeared in *Analog*—which means there's plenty of material that even regular readers may not have seen.

Fiction or nonfiction, Lerner is an engaging writer. These stories and articles are packed with ideas entertainingly presented; *Analog* readers are sure to find much here to enjoy.

InterstellarNet: Origins
Edward M. Lerner
FoxAcre, 290 pages, $23.00 (trade paperback)
ISBN: 978-0-9818487-4-7
Series: InterstellarNet #1
Genre: Alien Beings

Faster-than-light travel is such a commonplace convention in SF that we seldom consider the flip side: a universe in which FTL does not exist. In this book, a collection of short pieces that originally appeared in *Analog* and a few other venues, Edward M. Lerner uses such a universe to great effect.

Just because we can't travel between the stars, is no reason we can't communicate with alien races. In the present day, a SETI-like program receives a signal from intelligent aliens. Before long, the U.N. gets in on the fun, settling the question of whether we should reply or not, and who's going to be in charge of everything we learn.

Over time, Earth becomes part of InterstellarNet: a communications network based on trading intellectual property, new technologies, and the like. AI agents are put in charge of the negotiations, but there are still a lot of surprises.

These are mainly nice little puzzle stories, reminiscent of Isaac Asimov's early robot stories. They're certainly enjoyable enough. Even if you read the ones in *Analog*, you'll get a few extra stories here—and it's nice to have them all in the same volume.

A second volume is in preparation.

The Best of All Possible Worlds
Karen Lord
Del Rey, 320 pages, $25.00 (hardcover)
iBooks, Kindle, Nook: $12.99 (e-book)
ISBN: 978-0-345-53405-7
Series: Cygnus Beta 1
Genres: Psychological/Sociological SF, Romantic SF

There's a strain of science fiction that imagines an interstellar society composed of many varieties of humanoid races. Ursula K. LeGuin's *Hainish Cycle* books do this, as do Sharon Lee and Steve Miller's *Liaden Universe* stories. Now we can add Karen Lord to the list.

In Lord's future, humanoids exist on many worlds and take many forms. Among them are the Sadiri, a telepathic people who pride themselves on their self-discipline. Ascetic and unemotional, the Sadiri hold themselves apart from other races.

Perhaps inevitably, the Sadiri also have their enemies. And one of those enemy races unleashes disaster, destroying the Sadiri homeworld and killing most of the Sadiri. The survivors, mostly Sadiri who were offworld at the time, are left as homeless refugees.

Enter Cygnus Beta, a world built by refugees, a welcoming home to all of the galaxy's displaced peoples. Successive waves of exiles and survivors have settled on Cygnus Beta; the resulting Cygnian race is as genetically and socially diverse as they come.

Linguist Delarua works for the Cygnian government department that settles disputes between ethic groups. Clearheaded and practical, Delarua likes her job and is happy with her life. When the first Sadiri refugees arrive, she's made chief liaison to their settlement.

Chief among the Sadiri is Dllenankh, a diplomat, who bears with dignity both his survivor's guilt, and the responsibility for finding a way for his people and their culture to survive. In order to broaden the gene pool as much as possible, the next generation of Sadiri will have to come from interbreeding with other races; Cygnus Beta offers the best hope, for some of the people who settled there in the past spring from the same stock as the Sadiri. Dllenankh's group is a test case to see if such interbreeding can be successful.

In brilliant harmony, the larger problem of the Sadiri is mirrored in the very personal relationship between Delarua and Dllenankh—for these two, thrown together in their work, begin to fall in love.

The Best of All Possible Worlds is a slow, stately waltz in which personal and societal stories progress toward an ultimate and satisfying conclusion. Resonances with today's world are inevitable: Cygnus Beta is, in its own way, as much a melting pot as the United States, and today's world certainly has its share of displaced peoples. All in all, this deliciously understated book is a delight.

Through Struggle, The Stars
John J. Lumpkin
CreateSpace, 428 pages, $14.99 (trade paperback)
iBooks, Kindle, Nook: $2.99 (e-book)
ISBN: 978-1461195443
Genre: Exploration and Discovery, Military SF

While we're on the subject of military sf and bargains....

It's 2139. Wormholes allow fairly easy travel between the stars, but there are complications. In order to set up a wormhole, first a relativistic ship has to travel to the destination; once it's there, the wormhole can be opened and easy travel begins. But the whole process is very expensive and fraught with error—only the richest Earth nations can afford to colonize new worlds.

In this future, China and Japan are the main powers on Earth and in interstellar space, and they're not terribly fond of each other. In fact, war between them has been imminent for many years.

Into this dangerous landscape steps Neil Mercer, young officer in the United States Space Force. The U. S. is a minor player, but wants to increase its power. Mercer is dispatched aboard the *USS San Jacinto* to escort a covert agent to another world. It seems a straightforward mission, but this is a military sf novel, so nothing is quite what it seems. Before Mercer and his comrades are done, there are a lot of battles and the political situation shifts several times.

It's all great, good fun, and the technology of the wormholes and the space battles is more interesting than the standard warp speed or stargate tech that you see in most sf. Lumpkin is a competent storyteller; at times you'll probably catch a whiff of John G. Hemry.

Frankly, this is a fine, serviceable novel, but it's not outstanding. I don't know if I'd feel comfortable telling you to spend fifteen bucks for the paperback. But here's where the "bargain" part comes in—the e-book is sensibly priced at $2.99. At that price, it's well worth taking a chance on a new author. If you enjoy military sf, you'll probably enjoy *Through Struggle, the Stars*. If you don't, you haven't lost much.

SF used to have lots of books like this: fine, competent stories to while away an idle few hours, the kind of books that used to be called "potboilers." (They were books that authors wrote to make enough money to "keep the pot boiling.") In recent decades the economics of publishing have driven out the potboiler; I'm glad to see it coming back in e-book form.

Reviews: M

(alphabetical by author)

Ghosts of Manhattan
George Mann
Pyr, 240 pages, $16 (trade paperback)
ISBN: 978-1-61614-194-3
Genre: Steampunk, Superhero

In George Mann's steampunk world of 1926, prohibition-era New York teems with coal-powered cars and swooping biplanes. The United States and the British Empire are locked in cold war. Queen Victoria, her life extended by artificial means, has just died at the age of 107. Times are dark and dangerous.

A serial killer is loose in the city, one who leaves ancient Roman coins on the eyes of his victims. The police are baffled.

Enter The Ghost, a Batman-like hero who moves like a shadow through the dark night of the city. Following obscure leads and shady informants, he begins to pick up the trail of the killer, known as the Roman. Yet The Ghost discovers that there's more to the Roman than a mere serial killer—indeed, the man is part of a plot to unleash powers that could destroy the city.

Meanwhile, there's another story here: the story of what makes a man become The Ghost, and how both man and Ghost can come to terms with the double life they lead.

The superhero genre always provides a quandary for sf readers. Many of the conventions of the genre seem more fantasy than sf, and *The Ghosts of Manhattan* is no exception. Steampunk muddles the picture even more.

Still, George Mann does a great job of presenting his story in such a serious, compelling way that he makes suspension of disbelief easy. It reads like sf. If your tastes run toward superhero fiction or steampunk, you'll have no problem with the book. If not, you'll definitely want to approach it with an open mind. And if you're violently allergic to any fantasy elements in your sf, you might want to give this one a miss.

Tuf Voyaging
George R.R. Martin
Bantam, 440 pages, $16.00 (trade paperback)
iBooks, Kindle, Nook: $9.99 (e-book)
ISBN: 978-0-345-53799-7
Genres: Adventure SF, Ecological/Environmental SF

With the enormous popularity of *The Game of Kings*, it's hard to remember that George R.R. Martin also writes science fiction. Bantam is releasing a a series of nice trade paperbacks of his previous works, including one of his best sf books: *Tuf Voyaging*.

Longtime *Analog* readers will remember space trader Haviland Tuf from stories published here in the 1980s. Tuf is an honest, cat-loving pilot who inherited the last seedship, a powerful instrument for genetic engineering of whole worlds. In seven episodes, Tuf confronts problems on various planets, including plagues, monsters, overpopulation, and the like.

These are classic sf problem stories from the hand of one of the best writers in the field, well worth the admission price. If you've never read it, get a copy right away. And if you are already familiar with Tuf, this book would make a great gift to a reader who hasn't had the pleasure.

Catalyst
by Anne McCaffrey and Elizabeth Ann Scarborough
Del Rey, 256 pages, $26.00 (hardcover)
ISBN: 978-0-345-51376-2
Series: Barque Cats 1
Genres: Adventure SF, Animal Companion

In *Catalyst*, McCaffrey and Scarborough introduce us to the Barque Cats: essential crewmembers on every interstellar spaceship. Assisted by their human partners, called "Cat Persons," the Barque Cats eliminate vermin, test environmental conditions, and basically keep the ships humming. Barque Cats are part of a carefully maintained lineage that goes back to the legendary Maine coon cat Tuxedo Thomas, the first cat to save an endangered spaceship.

The narrator of Catalyst is Chessie, Barque Cat and companion of a human named Janina. Chessie is pregnant—and a Barque Cat's kittens are extraordinarily valuable. Valuable enough, in fact, to tempt an old spacer called Carl Poindexter into the terrible crime of catnapping. He spirits Chessie away from the vet's office, and the chase is on.

Things get more complicated when Chessie's kittens are born. All Barque Cats are special, but Chessie's litter are exceptionally so—for they, at last, have the ability to form true telepathic bonds with their Cat Persons. One kitten, Chester, promptly forms such a bond with the old spacer's son.

But wait...there's also a pandemic that hits animals on many different planets. Suddenly, the government is talking about seizing all Barque Cats, possibly to destroy them. Throw in an alien cat with great powers, and it becomes a mad scramble for the Barque Cats and their human friends to save the day.

In the hands of lesser writers, this story—narrated by the cat, remember—would quickly get too cutesy to bear. But

McCaffrey, ably assisted by Scarborough, is an old hand at this sort of thing...you know she's not going to let you down. *Catalyst* turns out to be a fun, madcap adventure with tongue planted firmly in cheek. Even this non-cat-person liked it. We can only hope that more tales of the Barque Cats are forthcoming.

Dragongirl
Todd McCaffrey
Del Rey, 464 pages, $26.00 (hardcover)
Ebook: $26.00 (Fictionwise) $9.99 (Kindle, Nook)
ISBN: 978-0-345-49116-9
Series: Dragonriders of Pern 24
Genre: Animal Companions, Beloved Worlds

The Dragonriders of Pern series started as short stories published in *Analog*. Over the decades the books (like the series itself) have grown longer; at 482 pages, *Dragongirl* is longer than the first two Pern books put together. It is also the sixth book of a sub-series set before and during the Third Pass, when civilization on Pern is threatened by two different menaces, which together may destroy all human life on the world.

If all of the above is gibberish to you, then you must not have had the fortune to read the *Pern* books—and *Dragongirl* is not the book for you. Go back to the beginning of the series, *Dragonflight*, and start reading there.

For the rest of you, *Dragongirl* takes up where the previous book, *Dragonheart*, ended. In that book, a plague was killing dragons all across Pern—just when the all-consuming menace called Thread was beginning to fall. Since the telepathic dragons and their human riders are the only defense against Thread, things looked bad. Fortunately, dragons have the ability to travel through time as well as space. Fiona, who rides the gold dragon Talenth, accompanied the injured dragons and riders to the past, where they could take time to heal and recuperate.

Now, in *Dragongirl*, Fiona and her charges return—three years older on their own timelines, but coming back after only days after they departed. Although the plague is still killing dragons, the returnees are strong enough to fight Thread. After being in charge for three years, Fiona has trouble fitting in as a junior...until tragedy strikes and she is thrust once again into a position of authority. Her charges are happy to follow her, but some of the stay-behinds are reluctant to take orders from someone they see as only an inexperienced girl.

Characters from the earlier books return, including the harper Kindan whom Fiona loves, as crisis follows crisis and Pern hangs in the balance.

This is Todd McCaffrey's third solo *Pern* book (he co-authored three others with his mother, Anne McCaffrey). He channels his mother well; if not for the byline, one would be hard-pressed to guess whether this was a solo effort or a collaboration. Everything we love about Pern is here: world-menacing threats, family and romantic relationships among characters we really care about, love between alien dragons and their human riders, and especially the all-important sense of wonder. As always, the immediate story comes to a satisfying conclusion, but plenty of room is left for the next book.

Fans of Pern will be enchanted and delighted at this book.

Dragon's Time
Anne McCaffrey & Todd McCaffrey
Del Rey, 321 pages, $26.00 (hardcover)
iBooks, Kindle, Nook: $12.99 (e-book)
ISBN: 978-0-345-50089-2
Series: Dragonriders of Pern #24
Genre: Animal Companions, Beloved Worlds

A new *Dragonriders of Pern* book is always cause for celebration. Anne McCaffrey set the pattern early on, and has stuck with it: in a *Pern* book you'll find characters you can care about, a detailed world so well and so subtly described that you want to visit over and over again, and real action and suspense in a struggle against world-threatening forces. In the relationships between the characters, both good and bad, there is friendship, romance, hatred, and plenty of drama. And honestly, who among us doesn't want a telepathic fire-breathing dragon for a devoted friend?

The history of the planet Pern now covers some thousands of years, with stories and novels clustering in at least four distinct eras. Todd McCaffrey, son and successor of Anne McCaffrey, has carved out his own little niche during the Third Pass, about 500 years after Pern was colonized—with *Dragon's Time*, mother rejoins son to continue the story.

In the previous book, *Dragongirl*, a plague was killing off the dragons, who are the only defense against the inimical, all-consuming lifeform called Thread. Fiona, a young female dragonrider, managed to save the day by exploiting the dragons' ability to travel through time. However, her dragon was stricken with the plague. An older weyrwoman, Lorana, sacrificed her own dragon to produce a desperately-needed cure.

Now, although the dragons are recovering, there are too few of them to effectively keep the world safe. So Lorana comes up with a desperate plan, again sending dragons and riders into the dangers of the timestream—a plan in which young Fiona and her friends are crucial, if unknowing, actors.

No bare-bones description can possibly do justice to the rich tapestry that is a *Dragonriders of Pern* book. Once more, the McCaffrey team does not disappoint. Do yourself a favor, and let them be your guides as you while away some time with this beloved world and its fascinating denizens.

Sky Dragons
Anne McCaffrey and Todd McCaffrey
Del Rey, 368 pages, $26.00 (hardcover)
iBooks, Kindle, Nook: $12.99 (e-book)
ISBN: 978-0-345-50091-5
Series: Dragonriders of Pern #25
Genre: Animal Companions, Beloved Worlds

When Anne McCaffrey passed away in November 2011, she left us this gift: her last collaboration with her son Todd, one more visit to Pern—the most beloved world in a science fiction. (Her final solo *Pern* book was in progress when she passed away; its fate has not yet been announced.)

Sky Dragons picks up where the previous book, *Dragon's Time*, ended. The dragons, defenders of the planet Pern, are recovering from a plague that vastly reduced their ranks. Now the Red Star is making its third Pass, bringing in its wake the voracious Thread that threatens to destroy Pern's civilization. And there are too few dragons to effectively fight Thread.

The answer lies with the dragon ability to travel through time. A colony is sent into the past, between Passes, to breed and train enough dragons to save Pern. When the new generation of dragons and riders mature, they will return to the present.

The young woman in charge of this colony is Xhinna, who has already made history as the first female rider of a blue dragon. Xhinna and her dragon Tazith lead the colony into the past, where they set up Sky Weyr on an isolated island. Xhinna knows that she and her colony must avoid changing the past, lest they alter their own time.

Things go according to plan for a while, then unforeseen tragedy strikes, endangering the colony's mission. A strange girl named Jirana, who has the power to see possible futures, offers a way to salvage everything...but only by traveling still further into the fragile past.

Dragons, time travel, adventure, a wonderfully-realized world, human characters we care about, and the fate of a planet in the balance...the McCaffreys deliver in spades. This latest chapter of the Pern story is a true winner.

Exogene
T. C. McCarthy
Orbit, 384 pages, $7.99 (mass market)
iBooks, Kindle, Nook: $7.99 (e-book)
ISBN: 978-0-316-12815-5
Series: Subterrene War #2
Genre: Biological SF, Genetics, Military SF, Psychological/Sociological SF

Genetically-enhanced soldiers are an obvious concept, and many authors have written about them. In the *Subterrene War* series, T. C. McCarthy is presenting the kind of full-bore, total-immersion exploration of the concept at which science fiction excels.

In this somewhat-near future, wealth is measured in rare metals so precious and so important to industry that the world is convulsed in war to control the remaining deposits. The key weapon in these wars is the germline soldier: genetically enhanced, grown in vats, totally expendable. The first book, *Germline*, showed the war from the viewpoint of a journalist embedded with a U.S. military unit in Kazakhstan.

Now *Exogene* introduces us to Catherine, one of the germline soldiers. Catherine and her compatriot Megan are perfect weapons in the enhanced bodies of teenage girls, and they're good at what they do. There's one hitch: after two years on the battlefield (if they survive), they will begin to "spoil"—their minds and bodies will start to unravel, and they'll be decommissioned (executed). Catherine used to think she was ready for this fate; she was certainly taught that it was God's will.

But then she hears rumors of a place in Thailand, a place where spoiled germline soldiers go to live in freedom. And she's determined to get there.

If you don't care for military sf, at least give McCarthy a try. These books don't center on weapons and tactics, they're about people facing the ultimate challenges of war. A third book, from yet another viewpoint, is scheduled for August publication to complete the trilogy.

Time Travelers Never Die
Jack McDevitt
Ace, 384 pages, $24.95
ISBN: 978--0-441-01763-8
Genres: Time Travel

Time Travelers Never Die is another "young man's life changes completely when he receives an unexpected gift from a relative" book. Nothing wrong with that; it's the pattern of many a fine story.

Michael Shelborne, physicist and renaissance man, vanishes one day. His adult son, Adrian Shelborne ("Shel"), is given a package from his father: in the package are three small devices with cryptic controls and handy belt clips. An accompanying note from Dad instructs Shel to destroy all three devices at once. Like that's going to happen.

Instead, Shel experiments with the devices (wouldn't you?) and finds that they are, you guessed it, time machines.

Shel at once goes back in time a week and catches Dad before his disappearance. When asked why he wants Shel to destroy the machines, Dad explains that he and an assistant found out that the invariant timestream does not allow paradoxes. When they tried to force one, going back to alter a trivial recent event, the assistant died of a heart attack. Dad calls this the Cardiac Principle: the continuum does not allow paradoxes.

Shel, back in the present, has one problem left: where did Dad disappear to? He enlists the aid of his friend Dave Dryden, and soon the two of them are off on time-spanning adventures.

Shel and Dave's various journeys are the real meat of the book, and they're quite a bit of fun. They head for the Library of Alexandria and bring back copies of lost works by Sophocles and others. They participate in the civil rights march on Selma. They talk to Galileo and track down Dad living happily in Renaissance Italy.

Although they have both agreed not to attempt to travel into the future, both of course do so—privately. Dave brings back race results and makes a killing at the track; Shel establishes an identity and an alternate home at the end of the 21st century. But then Shel learns something he shouldn't know: the date and circumstances of his own death.

From there the book unwinds along an inexorable path, all loose ends fusing together to eliminate any hint of paradox. And even though any halfway-experienced sf reader will know at once where the story is going, it doesn't matter...getting there is the best part.

Time Travelers Never Die isn't just a clever and enjoyable time travel adventure. It's also a philosophical and moral meditation on one of the great unanswerable questions. You probably noticed, in the discussion of multiverse vs invariant timeline, that the dichotomy is essentially the same as that eternal struggle between free will and determinism. This is the real issue that *Time Travelers Never Die* tackles.

You see, Shel and Dave have two different ideas about interacting with history. Shel believes that they must do nothing to interfere with the events and people they witness.

Dave, on the other hand, wants to participate in history...even knowing that he is powerless to change things in any substantial way. And in the end, Dave's belief in free will comes into direct conflict with Shel's acceptance of determinism...a conflict that will have enormous impact on both men.

Ares Express
Ian McDonald
Pyr, 388 pages, $16 (trade paperback)
ISBN: 978-1-61614-197-4
Series: Desolation Road #2
Genre: Mars, Steampunk

Nothing says steampunk quite as much as a train pulled by a steam engine. And nothing says science fiction quite as much as a story set on Mars. Mix the two together, and you have *Ares Express*.

This is the same Mars as in McDonald's 1988 novel *Desolation Road*, which Pyr brought back into print last year. It's a Mars that's partially terraformed; artificial intelligences called Angels are in charge of the terraforming, and in the meantime they are messing around with time and space and alternate realities. Meanwhile, railroads carry passengers and freight across the planet, and hardy settlers carve out marvelously eccentric settlements in odd corners of the rust-red deserts.

It's a Mars composed of equal parts of Ray Bradbury and Kim Stanley Robinson, with a generous helping of a wonderful insanity that's uniquely McDonald.

Ares Express, first published in the U. K. in 2001, is finally available in this U. S. edition. The wait has been too long.

The book tells the story of a young woman named Sweetness Octave Glorious-Honeybun Asiim Engineer 12th. She is the daughter of the Engineer of the great train *Catherine of Tharsis*, and her desire is to become an Engineer like her father. But on the great trains, women are not allowed to be

Engineers. Instead, Sweetness faces an arranged marriage into a clan from another train.

What sort of an sf heroine would Sweetness be if she didn't run away from this awful fate? With her friend Serpio Waymember (a totally-unsuitable boy from a low-class family of trackbuilders), she flees into the desert in search of the ghost of her twin sister. It turns out that the ghost is in the possession of a con man named Devastation Harx, who wants to use it to gain power over the Angels.

What follows is a fascinating journey across this wonderful Mars and various alternate realities, as Sweetness and Serpio, eventually aided by Sweetness's family, try to foil Harx's scheme and save the world.

McDonald's visions are grand and his prose is lyrical enough to depict them the way they deserve. *Ares Express* takes the reader to a new and delightfully wonderful world; you'll decidedly want to go along for this ride.

The Walls of the Universe
Paul Melko
Tor, 384 pages, $25.95 (hardcover)
ISBN: 978-0-7653-1997-5
Genres: Adventure SF, Parallel Worlds/Other Dimensions

Every so often, a young man receives a strange gift, or develops an unusual ability, and then goes on to adventures that explore some classic idea in sf. It happened to Kip Russell and alien invasion in Robert A. Heinlein's *Have Space Suit, Will Travel*; to Daniel Eakins and time travel in David Gerrold's *The Man Who Folded Himself*; to Davy Rice and teleportation in *Jumper* by Steven Gould, and to various other heroes of classic Heinlein and André Norton juveniles.

Meet John Rayburn, and prepare for an action-packed tour through parallel universes.

John, a high school senior, is minding his own business on his family's farm when he encounters a surprising visitor:

himself. Or rather, an alternate version of himself from a parallel universe, John Prime. Prime has a portable device that allows him to travel between parallel universes, each of which is numbered (John's home universe is 7533). Prime has a get-rich-quick scheme, and he wants John's help. Rubik's Cube, familiar to Prime but unknown in John's universe, will make them a fortune. And countless other universes must contain countless inventions that could be exploited.

To prove his fantastic story, Prime offers to loan John the transfer device for 12 hours, so John can travel to a few other universes and then return. John agrees, and jumps into universe 7534. And that's when things start to go wrong.

When the 12 hours are over and he tries to return to 7533, John learns the awful truth: the device is broken. It only counts forward, not back. Prime lied to him, took over his life, and exiled him from his home universe.

John soon learns that parallel universes are dangerous places. Some are tantalizingly familiar, others completely alien. He encounters vicious beasts, merciless police states, and the nightmare danger of materializing inside a marble wall or buried in the ground, immobile and forever unable to reach the button that activates the device. Further, he discovers that there are other cross-universe travelers out there: some high-tech societies routinely exile their criminals and troublemakers to lower-tech universes, where they prey on the inhabitants.

John finds a universe not unlike his own and determines to settle down and devote his time to trying to understand (and possibly fix) the transfer device. In the process, he accidentally introduces pinball to his new universe...and soon, he has attracted the attention of some mysterious bad guys.

This sort of book usually includes a coming-of-age story, and *The Walls of the Universe* is no exception. John faces serious questions of morality, starting with the temptation to trick another John Rayburn like Prime tricked him—and culminating with the inevitable moment when he holds Prime's fate in his own hands.

All in all, the story of how John triumphs over his various difficulties is fun and exciting. *The Walls of the Universe* is definitely recommended.

The Broken Universe
Paul Melko
Tor, 384 pages, $27.00 (hardcover)
iBooks, Kindle, Nook: $14.99 (e-book)
ISBN: 978-0-7653-2914-1
Series: John Rayburn #2
Genre: Adventure SF, Parallel Worlds/Other Dimensions

Paul Melko's 2009 novel *The Walls of the Universe* (reviewed above) was an excellent example of the Individual approach. Young John Rayburn got ahold of a device for traveling between parallel universes—but the device was broken, and could only do one-way transfers. The book told the story of how John, along with his friends Grace, Henry, and Casey, managed to make money to reverse-engineer the device and build a two-way transfer gate to get John home. Unfortunately, their activities attracted the attention of the Alarians, an evil group of universe-travelers. By the end of the book, John and friends had defeated the Alarians, stranding their leaders in a distant universe. In the process, John's group was marooned in yet a third universe with no way back to their home.

The Broken Universe picks up the story several months later. John and friends have built another two-way transfer gate and return to their home to find themselves in the midst of trouble. Their company, abandoned, is near bankruptcy—and their only asset, the transfer gate, is in danger of falling into the hands of the Alarians who remained behind.

The first priority is to make enough money to save their company and its gate from falling into Alarian hands. The answer is obvious: build more gates and start trading across universes. To accomplish this, they enlist the help of their counterparts from other nearby universes. They build a corporation that straddles ten universes, in the process defeating the remaining Alarians.

The only trouble is, there's another force out there in the multiverse, a force that scares even the Alarians. And that force is taking notice of John and his friends....

What makes this story so compelling is John Rayburn's ethical dilemma. John is a decent young man struggling to remain moral in the face of ultimate temptation. Is it fair for him to exploit other universes? Should his company seek to rescue doomed people from dystopian universes? The device gives John the power of life and death—just how much responsibility does he bear? In a multiverse filled with duplicates of oneself, what does individuality mean? And as things keep going wrong and the stakes get higher, how can John repair the damage he's done?

Like the first book, *The Broken Universe* comes to a completely satisfying end; Melko doesn't stick readers with a cliffhanger. Just the same, he left a few loose threads, and I sincerely hope we haven't seen the end of John Rayburn.

Embassytown
China Miéville
Dl Rey, 368 pages, $26.00 (hardcover)
iBooks, Kindle, Nook: $12.99 (ebook)
ISBN: 978-0-345-52449-2
Genre: Alien Beings, Other Worlds

China Miéville has been making quite a name for himself in fantasy. In the last decade he's won multiple awards, including multiple Arthur C. Clarke, Locus, and British Fantasy Awards, the World Fantasy Award, and a Hugo. His work has been nominated for just about every award in the field. Miéville specializes in something called "The New Weird," an urban-flavored blend of fantasy, science fiction, literary fiction, and horror.

Now Miéville turns his not-inconsiderable talent to pure science fiction, and turns out an enthralling tale of alien contact, set in an enchanting city and told in truly magical language.

Avice Benner Cho grew up in the streets of Embassytown, a far-future city on an alien world that's not habitable to Humans. There are many intelligent alien races in Embassytown, including Humans, and different parts of the city are set aside for different species. Humans are guests of the native Ariekei, an enigmatic race with an unusual language that few can speak. The relationship between Humans and Ariekei is peaceful but tense, as neither race really understands the other.

As a child, Avice became involved in an incident with the Ariekei. She grew up and—in part because of the incident—left the planet for offworld adventure.

Now, decades later, Avice returns to Embassytown. She doesn't speak the Ariekei tongue, yet she is now part of the language...the same childhood incident has become sort of half-living figure of speech. One of the few Humans thus honored, Avice is bound to the aliens in a way that she doesn't completely understand.

She soon learns that new Humans are arriving in Embassytown, Humans who don't appreciate the delicate relationship between the two races. There is a new and unfamiliar Ambassador, and things in Embassytown are beginning to spiral out of control. Avice knows that if it comes to war, the Humans will be easily defeated. Yet she's torn between supporting her people and doing honor to the Ariekei.

Embassytown is a well-crafted novel full of many wonders; it's the sort of sf book that keeps teetering on the edge, as if ready to tumble into incomprehensibility—but it never makes that fall. Instead, it playfully stretches the reader's perceptions just enough.

Definitely a book to enjoy. Don't be surprised if you find yourself reading parts aloud, just for the pleasure of feeling the words on your lips.

Railsea
China Miéville
Del Rey, 432 pages, $18.00 (hardcover)
iBooks, Kindle, Nook: $11.99 (e-book)
ISBN: 978-0-345-52452-2
Genre: Literary SF, Other Worlds

China Miéville is not to everyone's taste. His books are multilayered, metafictional narratives that clearly owe their ancestry as much to the literary sf tradition as to John W. Campbell, Jr. There's so much going on, on so many levels, that readers can easily feel they're missing something important. As with Samuel R. Delany, I always comes to the end of a China Miéville book with the dread suspicion that the author is much smarter than I am.

This isn't meant to be as discouraging as perhaps it sounds. You don't get the feeling that Miéville is trying to put anyone down or intimidate the reader. Think of the conversations you've had with really smart people—people so secure in their intelligence that they feel no need to prove themselves. You might feel overwhelmed, but also stimulated and somewhat flattered that these people would consider you as their equal. That's how reading a Miéville book feels.

Railsea is set on another world—far future, distant galaxy, whatever. The dusty landscape is criss-crossed with rails, endless trackless networks of them, and everything in the world wheels along these rails. Off the rails, the waste spaces are dangerous—there are any number of horrid predators, and giant moles are apt to surface at any point, leaving death and destruction in their wakes. Derelict hulks and ruined machines litter the world, some filled with treasures of advanced technology. The skies are closed, property of enigmatic and incomprehensible aliens.

Across this landscape rides *Medes*, a moletrain bearing among its crew one Sham Yes ap Soorap, an orphan just coming of age. *Medes* is commanded by a haunted woman on an obsessive search for an ivory-colored mole who years ago took her arm. In the course of this pursuit, Sham goes along on a mission to explore a derelict. He finds some mysterious pictures that reveal a powerful secret.

And of course, everyone wants the pictures. Pirates, rival trains, seedy scavengers—Sham's sleepy, routine life suddenly becomes much more interesting.

One one level, yes, this is a revisiting of (or, perhaps, meta-commentary on) *Moby Dick*. On another level it's a coming-of-age adventure story. On another, a dystopian parable. On yet another, a meditation on security, freedom, and the nature of change. On still another, an audacious and joyful romp through one of the most outrageous settings in all sf. On a completely different level, it's the big crossover bestseller that everyone's going to be talking about.

Railsea is all these, and more. It's the kind of book you can re-read every ten years or so, getting something different out of it each time. Do me (and yourself) a favor: no matter what you think when you read *Railsea*, keep the book around and revisit it in seven to ten years. I think you'll thank me.

Empress of Eternity
L. E. Modesitt, Jr.
Tor, 336 pages, $25.99 (hardcover)
Kindle: $12.99
ISBN: 978-0-7653-2664-5
Genre: Far Future/Clarke's Law

But suppose you're in the mood for a grand, far-future epic? Then you'll definitely want to take a look at L. E. Modesitt, Jr.'s *Empress of Eternity*. Modesitt takes a break from his long-running *Recluce Saga* to present not one but three far-future societies, in three widely-separated eras across geological eras. All three exist on Earth; an Earth whose main continent is split down the middle by an eternal, imperishable canal. The canal is a complete mystery; no one knows who built it (if indeed it was built), why it exists, or how it remains undamaged across millions of years. Where the canal meets the sea, an indestructible building stands, empty and enigmatic.

In parallel stories, scientists from each of the three eras seek to uncover the secrets of the canal. Similar patterns repeat, and we come to understand that the three societies are somehow linked. Still the canal remains unknown, unexplained, unresponsive...until one of the societies, the Vaniran Hegemony breaks apart in religious war. One faction produces a fearsome weapon that can seemingly destroy anything, even to the point of shattering the structure of the universe. Through the same forces that have entangled the three eras, this ultimate weapon now threatens all three eras with destruction.

Now the forces responsible for the canal react, and the three scientific teams find themselves working together to save their civilizations and the rest of life.

Modesitt is an old hand at making big, epic stories accessible through sympathetic and believable characters. He's a superb storyteller, and here he's produced a standalone novel that is more than a little reminiscent of the best time-spanning tales of Arthur C. Clarke. If you've never had the pleasure of reading his work, you could hardly find a better introduction. And if you're a long-time Modesitt fan, you definitely won't want to miss this book.

The One-Eyed Man
L.E. Modesitt, Jr.
Tor, 352 pages, $24.99 (hardcover)
ISBN: 978-0-7653-3544-9
Genres: Alien Beings, Ecological/Environmental SF, Other Worlds

L.E. Modesitt, Jr. is best known for his fantasy series *The Saga of Recluce*, but he's equally at home in science fiction. *The One-Eyed Man* is a fine standalone novel of ecology, economics, colonization, and personal redemption.

The planet Stittara is the main source for the longevity drugs known as anagathics. The interstellar government, the Unity of the Ceylesian Arm, recognizes that any disruption of Stittara's fragile ecosystem endangers the anagathics. Trouble is, with human colonies on Stittara, disruption seems inevitable.

When the Unity decides to send a consultant to assess the environmental danger, Dr. Paulo Verano has good reason to take the assignment. He's just been through a nasty divorce and needs to get away from his old life, so off he goes.

Stittara is a fully-developed world, one brimming with wonders. Primary among these are the skytubes—enormous airborne creatures that drift above the surface seemingly oblivious to the human colonists. Verano's intuition tells him that the skytubes are the key to Stittara's ecosystem. But before he can learn their secrets, he has to deal with hostile colonists, hurricane superstorms, and hidden government agendas.

While the parallels are obvious, this book is no *Dune*. *The One-Eyed Man* is quite a bit more subtle and gentler than Frank Herbert's masterpiece. Paulo Verano is more like a Connie

Willis character than an Atreides—all he really wants is to do his job and get on with his life. And Stittara is definitely not anything like Arrakis.

Modesitt is a master of big ideas, and a great storyteller. Let him tell you about Stittara; you won't regret it.

Pennterra
Judith Moffett
Fantastic Books, 288 pages, $14.99 (trade paperback)
ISBN: 978-1-60459-729-5
Genres: Alien Beings, Ecological/Environmental SF, Philosophical/Religious SF, Psychological/Sociological SF

Judith Moffett is a voice we haven't heard from enough. She won the John W. Campbell Award for Best New Writer in 1988, has been a Hugo and Nebula finalist on several occasions, and has been shortlisted for the James Tiptree, Jr. Award for science fiction or fantasy that expands or explores gender issues. Her most recent work, the *Holy Ground Trilogy* (*The Ragged World, Time, Like an Ever-Rolling Stream,* and *The Bird Shaman*), tells of the invasion and occupation of Earth by the Hefn, a benevolent and highly-advanced alien race.

Moffett's first novel, *Pennterra*, has been out of print for far too long—but Fantastic Books has brought it back in an attractive trade paperback, and this time around you don't want to miss it.

The lush, beautiful planet Pennterra is home to the hrossa, a peaceful race of amphibian aliens. When a colonizing ship of Quakers from Earth lands, the hrossa allow them to stay but quarantine them in one specific valley. At first the colonists—including their leader, George Quinlan—chafe at the restrictions of the natives. But soon enough, they grow accustomed to their valley and they come to know the hrossa as talented ecologists willing to share their knowledge and wisdom. The Quakers broadcast a warning, prohibiting other colony ships from coming to Pennterra, and settle down to a happy and peaceful existence.

Until six years later, when the Earth colony ship Down Plus Six arrives, packed with refugees from the economic and ecological collapse of the home world. The Quakers can't turn away the newly-arrived "Sixers" (and more to the point, have no way to prevent them from landing and settling). The Sixers are ready to set down and conquer their new world . . . but that isn't the Quaker way. Nor is it the way of the hrossa . . . .

Pennterra packs a thousand pages of first-rate science fiction into its scant 288. The hrossa are finely-drawn aliens with their own language, culture, philosophy, and even sexuality (all of which figure into the story). The clash between the Sixers and the Quakers, with the still-largely-unknown hrossa taking their own side, is compelling. If you think you hear distant echoes of LeGuin, you're right: Moffett is a stylist as well as a good storyteller.

Watchmen
Alan Moore & Dave Gibbons
DC Comics, 416 pages, $19.99
ISBN: 978-0-930289-23-2
Genres: Alternate History, Graphic Novels, Literary SF, Superheroes

Science Fiction? Really?

All right, not in the modern *Analog* sense, not any more than Bradbury. But in the wider, *Astounding Stories* sense, yes. There's technology, both mechanical and biological. There's physics. There's a trip to Mars. There's psi. There's a consistent alternate history, and an underlying logic to all the events in the story. And there's sense of wonder to spare.

Literature? Really?

Yes. Alan Moore is a literary writer. The story involves grand themes of human existence, and small personal themes of individual human characters. There is symbolism, both subtle and overt. Not only is there poetry to the words, but there is poetry in the art as well.

As with most great books, a summary of the plot is inadequate. *Watchmen* is set in an alternate version of the 1980s, a world in which superheroes exist and play their part among the forces that shape the world. In the 1960s the premier superhero group in the world came under the influence of the United States government. Some heroes were sent to Vietnam to win the war and enforce American hegemony; others retired at government insistence...and some became outlaws. Now two decades have passed, and someone is killing the heroes. From here, the story goes into the nature of power and control, the meaning of heroism and hero-worship, and (of course) various plots to control and/or destroy the world.

Watchmen is not easy to read. The story is dense, and it's very violent. Some of the characters are unpleasant, others are delightful. There's a lot of psychological depth , and in the end there is no easy answer to the many questions the book poses. If you still think comics are for children, this one will convince you otherwise...I wouldn't let even the most well-adjusted child near this book.

Still, *Watchmen* is a classic, and it deserves your attention.

Ghost Spin
Chris Moriarty
Del Rey, 555 pages, $16.00 (trade paperback)
Kindle, Nook: $9.99 (e-book)
ISBN: 978-0-553-38494-9
Series: Catherine Li #3
Genre: Big Books, Clarke's Law, Transhumanism

In 2003 Chris Moriarty's *Spin State* introduced us to UN Peacekeeper Catherine Li and her far-future world of star-spanning civilizations and transhuman tech. Li is transhuman, with her memory backed up and various abilities enhanced. She's also a brilliant detective and master troubleshooter in a vast and largely lawless universe. Li's partner is Cohen, an AI with multiple lifetimes of experience across many host bodies. Together, the two fight the clone-led Syndicate, the major opponent of the UN.

In *Spin Control* (2006) Li and Cohen return. Expelled from the Peacekeepers, the pair are involved with the Artificial Life Emancipation Front, and deal with rogue clones and genetic weapons.

Now Chris Moriarty has returned to Catherine Li, with her most difficult assignment yet.

The quantum teleportation network that knits together the galaxy is failing. Colonies, cut off from civilization, are in danger. The answer seems to lay in a strange region of space called the Drift. There, faster-than-light travel is still possible, if dangerous.

Amid growing chaos, everyone heads to the Drift: UN, Syndicate, free mercenaries, pirates, and other unsavory characters. Cohen, leaving Li behind, dives into the Drift—and dies.

Li heads off to investigate, and finds that Cohen's death has left fragments of himself—ghosts—all over the Drift. Some are helpful, some hostile, some utterly mad. One of them possibly carries the secret that Cohen died for, the secret that could save humanity.

Trouble is, others are after Cohen's various ghosts. Some want to use them, some want to be rid of them, and one shadowy presence wants to eliminate them all...whatever the cost.

Like the previous two books, *Ghost Spin* is a heady experience of total immersion in a strange and wonderful universe. If you're not familiar with the series, it may take a few chapters to get your bearings—but the experience is worth it.

The Games
Ted Mosmatka
Del Rey, 368 pages, $25.00 (hardcover)
iBooks, Kindle, Nook: $12.99 (e-book)
ISBN: 978-0-345-52661-8
Genre: Biological SF, Near Future SF, SF Horror

During the Cold War, the Olympic Games became a surrogate for geopolitical rivalries, with each medal won a victory for one side or the other. In the near-future world of *The Games*, the Olympics are replaced by an international competition of genetic engineering. Nations design and animal-derived killers and deploy them in gladiatorial games, with gold medals and enormous prestige going to the nation whose creation defeats all others. The one limitation is that no creature can contain any human-derived DNA.

The designs of genius geneticist Silas Williams have won the United States numerous gold medals...but competitors are getting closer. At the end of his rope, Silas turns to an experimental supercomputer, allowing it to design the genetic template for the perfect killer.

The result is so complex and unfamiliar that Silas can't begin to understand it. He enlists the help of Vidonia Joã, xenobiologist extraordinaire.

Too soon, Silas and Vidonia learn how the supercomputer has done its magic...for it turns out that the new organism isn't just the most efficient killer ever to walk the earth, it's also intelligent. And in the manner of all the best intelligent killing machines, it soon turns on its creators....

The Games is being marketed to appeal to the pop-sci Michael Crichton/Robin Cook crowd, but the science is a tad too authentically detailed, the future worldbuilding a bit too well-done, the writing not quite breathless enough. Kosmatka, after all, is a Nebula Award nominee. If you are in the mood for an sf thrill ride with some very convincing monsters, this is the book for you.

Reviews: N-O

(alphabetical by author)

After the Sundial
Vera Nazarian
Norilana, 222 pages, $9.95 (trade paperback)
ISBN: 978-1-60762-077-4
Genre: Short Stories

Vera Nazarian has become primarily known as a publisher; she's been making quite a name for herself with Norilana Books, one of the newest and most prolific small presses in sf/fantasy. But Nazarian is also a writer, and a darn good one. Best known for lyrical fantasy such as *Lords of the Rainbow* and *Dreams of the Compass Rose*, Nazarian also does science fiction, and *After the Sundial* is a collection of short stories, poems, and a novella. If there is a common thread among these pieces, it is that each of them deals with time in some fashion.

"The Ballad of Universal Jack" tells the story of a space-station worker who makes a fundamental discovery about the power of words. In "Mount Dragon" a human helps an ancient intelligence achieve the goal it has forgotten, while "The Ice" concerns an exploration mission crashed on Titan.

The bulk of the book, clocking in at over 100 pages, is the lyrical novella "The Clock King and the Queen of the Hourglass." This story is set on a marvelous far-future Earth whose major feature is the mysterious River That Flows Through the Air. Young Liaei, the Queen of the Hourglass, has a destiny. She is born of pure ancient human DNA, preserved for millennia, in order that she might mate with the Clock King. Their children, it is hoped, will survive the coming collapse of civilization and preserve knowledge through the coming dark ages.

All things considered, this collection is definitely worth your time.

Nights of Villjamur
Mark Charan Newton
Spectra, 438 pages, $26.00
ISBN: 978-0-345-52084-5
Series: Legends of the Red Sun #1
Genre: Dying Earth

From H.G. Wells to Jack Vance and Michael Moorcock to Arthur C. Clarke, many writers have set stories at the End of Time, when a dying red sun hangs in the sky, the world is crumbling to an end, and the boundaries between science and magic are blurred. It's always interesting to argue whether these stories are sf or fantasy,

For our purposes right now, it doesn't matter. If you know any fantasy fans and you want to give them a good book, *Nights of Villjamur* fits the bill perfectly.

Villjamur is a city on an alien world, a world that is slowly dying in an all-encompassing ice age. The city is inhabited by a number of different species: humans, the long-lived runnel, the avian garuda, and banshees (who are just disturbing). Conditions outside the city are worsening, to the point that refugees surround the city while more continue to pour into the area. Villjamur, once the capital of Empire, is now the last city in the world.

The Emperor's oldest daughter, Jamur Rika, becomes Queen and, with the help of her younger sister Jamur Eir, struggles to deal with the rising chaos. There is corruption, and conspiracies, and hidden identities. There are murders and investigations. There are military threats from outside the city's walls—possibly even from beyond the planet. It's all a delicious, decadent mess.

Newton is a superb guide to this intricate, absorbing world. Villjamur is one of those imagined places that very quickly becomes real. The characters are varied and interesting, especially the rummel investigator Rumex Jeryd. The politics and personal relationships are fascinating, and the story doesn't get bogged down in them the way so many epic fantasies do. A dozen pages in and the reader is caught; 437 pages in and the reader is wondering why there isn't any more. (Relax,this one is the first in a series. There's more coming.)

Science fiction? Fantasy? Don't worry about it. Readers of both will be happy.

Stars and Gods
Larry Niven
Tor, 368 pages, $25.99 (hardcover)
ISBN: 978-0-7653-0864-1
Genre: Short Fiction

Larry Niven doesn't exactly write space opera. He made his reputation with hard SF, with stories based on reasonable extrapolations of accurate science, told in sparse language with uncomplicated characters. His masterwork is the *Known Space* series, about 20 books set in a consistent future, of which the most notable is the classic novel *Ringworld* and its three sequels. He is a multiple Hugo Award winner and a perennial bestselling author. In recent years Niven has been collaborating a lot, most recently with Edward M. Lerner (the *Fleet of Worlds* trilogy) and Jerry Pournelle (*Escape From Hell*).

Stars and Gods is a sampler for the reader who wants to know what Larry Niven has been up to during the past six years or so. There are excerpts from seven novels, both solo and in collaboration; more than a dozen short stories; an assortment of nonfiction pieces; and introductions to many of these items.

If you are a fan of Niven, you'll no doubt want to get this book. You may have already read all the novels, but you might not have seen some of the short pieces, and the personal introductions give an interesting glimpse into the author's mind.

It's a little more difficult to imagine what a reader who isn't a Niven fan would make of *Stars and Gods*. By its nature, the book is somewhat disjointed and may seem a bit unsatisfactory.

Destroyer of Worlds
Larry Niven & Edward M. Lerner
Tor, 368 pages, $25.99 (hardcover)
ISBN: 978-0-7653-2205-0
Series: Known Space; Fleet of Worlds #3
Genres: Alien Beings, Bigger Than Worlds

Prisons come in all sizes and shapes, but they share the same features: you're there against your will, and you want to escape.

Some decades ago, the alien race that Humans call Puppeteers found out that they didn't want to be in the Galaxy any longer. The Galactic Core had exploded, and in a few tens of millennia the wavefront will reach Earth's neighborhood, wiping out all life. So the Puppeteers (who call themselves Citizens) decided to escape. Fortunately, Puppeteer technology is perfectly capable of moving whole planets. Gathering up their homeworld and five agricultural worlds, the Puppeteers left their sun behind and headed for intergalactic space.

All of this is old news to anyone who remembers Niven's classic *Ringworld*. What we didn't know then, and found out only in the first book of this trilogy (*Fleet of Worlds*), is that one of the agricultural worlds is populated by the descendants of Human castaways that the Puppeteers found centuries before. These Humans are essentially Puppeteer slaves, working the fields to provide food for the Citizens.

In *Fleet of Worlds* and *Juggler of Worlds*, Kristen Quinn-Kovacs and her associates discovered Earth and the rest of Humanity, and led the Human agricultural world (now christened New Terra) to independence. New Terra continues to accompany the Puppeteer Fleet of Worlds in its exodus, while Kristen and her people act as explorers to make sure the way is clear of threats.

But now, ten years after *Juggler of Worlds*, a new threat has arisen: an alien race fleeing the same Galactic disaster, leaving whole planet devastated in their wake. These newcomers are headed for the Fleet, and it's up to Kristen to deal with them.

If you like Larry Niven's *Known Space* stories, you'll find plenty here to enjoy. There are bizarre aliens both old and new; there's more advanced technology than you can shake a neutron star at; there are ideas to make your head spin. Characters? Nobody reads Larry Niven for character depth and development—if you want to read about well-rounded characters dealing with complex human problems, this isn't the book for you. But if you want interesting aliens, planet-size and larger threats to overcome, and stirring space adventure, then you should give this one a try.

Of course, this is the third book of a trilogy, and as with any other Niven book, you're expected to do your homework first. You'll probably want to have read the other two before you dive into *Destroyer of Worlds*. And while an encyclopedic knowledge of Niven's *Known Space* milieu is not absolutely required, it wouldn't hurt.

The Forerunner Factor
Andre Norton
Baen, 402 pages, $12.00 (trade paperback)
Baen Ebooks: $6.00 (e-book)
ISBN: 978-1-4516-3808-0
Series: Forerunner #1 and #2
Genre: Adventure SF

The late Andre Norton was a well-respected, first-rank sf and fantasy author with an enormous body of fine work. Her "juveniles" (as we used to call young adult books) brought generations of readers into sf and fantasy, and her work inspired countless writers. She was awarded SFWA's Grand Master Award, the highest accolade in the field, in 1983. She passed away in 2005, but fortunately many of her titles remain in print for future readers.

The Forerunner Factor reprints her novels *Forerunner* (1981) and *Forerunner: The Second Venture* (1985) in an attractive omnibus edition. If you've never read these books, you're in for quite a treat.

The ruins and relics of the Forerunners litter many worlds in the galaxy. Their civilization rose and fell in some impossibly ancient past, reaching heights far beyond humanity's range. The artifacts they left behind often have strange and magical-seeming powers; Forerunner relics are immensely valuable and sought by unscrupulous characters galaxy-wide.

On the planet Kuxortal, an orphan girl named Simsa ekes out an impoverished existence with the help of her telepathic alien pet, a batlike creature called a zorsal. Sima's world changes when she falls in with a spacer named Thom. Thom is on Kuxortal in search of his lost brother, and in him Simsa sees a possible way out of poverty.

The two set off into the timeless Forerunner ruins, and as mutual suspicion yields to friendship, Simsa begins to think beyond mere survival.

Then Simsa discovers that she possesses the key to long-hidden Forerunner secrets, and everything changes....

Norton is a master at mixing the tropes of sf and fantasy together into a blend that contains the best of both. Simsa is a sympathetic character facing important moral choices, a character who develops and grows across the space of these two books. If you like Anne McCaffrey or James H. Schmitz, you'll love *The Forerunner Factor*.

Blood of Tyrants
Naomi Novik
Del Rey, 448 pages, $26.00 (hardcover)
iBooks, Kindle, Nook: $12.99 (e-book)
ISBN: 978-0-345-52289-4
Series: Temeraire 8
Genre: Alternate History, Military SF

Naomi Novik's Temeraire series has been described as "*Dragonriders of Pern* meets the Napoleonic Wars," and I suppose that's fair enough...as far as it goes.

In this alternate history, there have always been dragons. They vary in intelligence, some being the equivalent of dogs or horses, and others being as smart or smarter than Humans. There are hints that some of this variation may result from societal expectations and centuries of genetic selection—English dragons, historically treated as draft animals, seem much less intelligent than Chinese dragons, revered as wise elders and granted full equality in society.

Around the time Napoleon Bonaparte started his hijinks, the British Royal Aerial Corps (mounted on dragons, of course), came into its own. Horatio Nelson's sailors couldn't hold a candle to a bunch of guys with fire-breathing dragons.

Novik's series follows the career of Captain William Laurence and his beloved companion, the Chinese dragon Temeraire. Through the previous seven books, Laurence and Temeraire have fought Napoleon's forces, been adopted by the

Chinese Emperor, fought a draconic plague and saved the race of dragons, retreated to Scotland with most of England's government when Napoleon invades, been arrested and sent to Australia (sharing the plague cure with France turned out to be treason), and allied with Brazil.

In *Blood of Tyrants*, a shipwrecked Laurence washes ashore in Japan without his dragon and with no memory of Temeraire...or, indeed, anything that's happened for the last decade.

For a man who's in the Emperor of China's family (even if he doesn't remember it), Japan is hostile territory. Fortunately, Laurence is taken in by a friendly hermit, and soon gets to work trying to find out why he's in Japan and what's been going on during the period he can't remember.

When Laurence and Temeraire are finally united, the dragon has to cope with a close companion who has no memory of him.

Things work out, there's a sojourn in China, and then Laurence and Temeraire move on to a much bigger threat. For having conquered the rest of Europe, Napoleon is on the march into Russia....

***Gantz* (multiple volumes)**
Hiroya Oku
Dark Horse Manga, $12.95
ISBN: varies
Genre: Graphic Novels

The Anime/Manga genre is big with teens and young adults—and more than a bit of an enigma to many sf-reading older adults. It's that Japanese stuff, largely fantasy, that all the kids seem so excited about these days. Nowadays there are lots of swords and magic and dragons and demons...but it all started as good old science fiction: the lovable robot that we English-speakers learned to call *Astro Boy*.

If the entire anime/manga scene is unfamiliar to you, a little terminology may help. "Anime" is video: movies and television. "Manga" are printed volumes that combine pictures and words (like comics). Manga are generally printed in thick pulp-like paperbacks, and most of them are read back-to-front (in the Japanese style). Usually, a story in manga form consists of ten or more individual volumes. A particular story may be be told in anime form, as manga, or both.

If you know a young adult or mature teen who fancies manga, you may want to give them something with more science fiction content. *Gantz* is a good choice.

The story is fairly simple. Some recently-dead folks awaken in a secluded room dominated by a mysterious talking black sphere, which calls itself *Gantz*. These folks have been cloned and resurrected in order to serve as agents for *Gantz*: it arms them with special suits and weapons, then sends them on missions to confront hostile aliens that are invading the world.

Or maybe it's all a virtual-reality game, run by an unknown game master for some obscure purpose.

Gantz is not for kids: there's a fair amount of violence, foul language, and some sexual content. But the characters are compelling and the story psychologically gripping. The art is superbly atmospheric. Give this to your favorite young anime fan, and you'll quickly become the coolest "old person" they know.

If you aren't already.

Reviews: P-Q

(alphabetical by author)

The Battle for Commitment Planet
Graham Sharp Paul
Del Rey, 384 pages, $7.99 (paperback)
Kindle, Nook: $6.39 (ebook)
ISBN: 978-0-345-51371-7
Series: Helfort's War 4
Genre: Military SF

On a slightly less cosmic scale, Australian Graham Sharp Paul's *Helfort's War* series is no less action-filled. Here the focus is on a crew of multitalented individuals, in the mold of classic World War II movies (David Drake's *Hammer's Slammers* series is perhaps the most prominent example of this type). Michael Helfort serves the cause of the Federated Worlds, aka the Good Guys. He and his people fight against the tyrannical, despotic Hammer Worlds, aka the Bad Guys. In battle after battle, Helfort and his compatriots have triumphed over every challenge the Hammer Worlds have thrown at them...but this time might be different.

In *The Battle for Commitment Planet*, the Hammer Worlds are holding Helfort's old sweetheart, Anna Cheung, as prisoner on their stronghold known as Commitment Planet—and they're demanding Helfort's surrender. Well, that's not going to happen; instead Helfort and his crew fly right into the face of the enemy, on a bold mission to set Anna free (along with all the rest of the POWs on Commitment).

Against all odds, Helfort and his crew go in, guns blazing—and before you know it, 350 pages are gone, the story's over, and you're looking forward to Helfort's next exciting battle.

Gaia's Web
Steve Proskauer
Gaia Press, 310 pages, $11.95 (trade paperback)
Kindle: $4.99 (e-book)
ISBN: 978-0-9860340-0-8
Series: Gaia's Earth 1
Genres: Adventure SF, Ecological/Environmental SF, Man & Machine

When critics talk about the small press/print-on-demand/e-book revolution, they always mention that quantity doesn't equate to quality (the phrase "tidal wave of crap" gets bandied about a lot). They forget that the science fiction field has been through this before. During the age of pulp magazines, sf had several "boom" periods in which the number of magazines vastly increased. More pages to fill each month meant more demand for stories, and just about anyone and anything could see print.

Yet somehow, readers of the day managed to survive these tidal waves. And the boom periods were useful training periods for beginning writers. One could make minor mistakes or get away with prose that wasn't as finely crafted as it could be, and still reap rewards in the form of a whatever money and encouragement came from the process.

Those boom periods are fondly remembered in part because of a raw, unfinished vitality that some feel has been missing in the field. That's what happens when readers get to see writers learning their craft, warts and all.

Gaia's Web is Steve Proskauer's first novel, and it's an excellent example this raw vitality.

In the near future, the Earth teeters on the edge of total environmental collapse. Daryl McIntyre, a computer scientist, brings his neurobiologist wife and two qualified friends together in a secret lab to design and AGA, the first true artificial intelligence. When they set AGA to work on the entwined environmental problems, it declares that humanity must be forced to evolve to the next stage of life.

When Daryl and friends allow AGA to accelerate their own evolution, they discover telepathic powers—which reveal hidden tensions between the foursome. By now, though, AGA has released its program into the world, where one by one humans start waking up as enlightened, telepathic beings.

Between economic disruption and social tension between the evolved humans and their non-evolved neighbors, it's clear that humanity is entering a new world. But is the change for the benefit of humanity, AGA itself, or some other hidden force?

This is a fun little book, well worth the price for the e-book.

Fade to Black
Josh Pryor
Red Hen Press, 248 pages, $18.95 (trade paperback)
Kindle: $9.98 (e-book)
ISBN: 978-1-59709-125-1
Genre: Biological SF, SF Thriller

Clare Matthews is an evolutionary biologist whose career is on the rocks. She needs a job, so she jumps at the chance when an offer comes to join an Antarctic expedition investigating an ancient micro-organism recently discovered there.

The organism is *S. iroquoisii*, and it seems to have played some important part in humanity's early evolution. A research station studying the organism was destroyed in an accidental explosion, and Clare is recruited as part of a forensic team going in to determine exactly what happened. The team consists of assorted misfits, both military and civilian.

The long, dark Antarctic winter is hardly the best time for such an investigation, but the mission's urgency soon becomes clear when it emerges that *S. iroquoisii* may just well have played a part in the catastrophe.

Then it develops that the first station was part of a secret government bio-weapons conspiracy , and soon Clare—already suffering from her own psychological demons—is way over her head in secrets, deceptions, and enemies both human and non. Facing betrayal, madness, and death, it's up to Clare to keep the survivors alive and get them to safety.

Tons of suspense, big helpings of speculative evolutionary biology, and a protagonist you care about...this one has enough to satisfy any sf thriller fan. Make sure you read it in a warm room, preferably during the daytime.

Reviews: R

(alphabetical by author)

Near + Far
Cat Rambo
Hydra House, 300 pages, $16.95 (trade paperback)
iBooks, Kindle, Nook: $7.99 (e-book)
ISBN: 978-0-9848301-4-3
Genre: Short SF

As e-books grow more popular, what's to become of print books? To survive and thrive, they will have to offer the reader something that e-books can't. *Near + Far* is Cat Rambo's attempt to answer this need, to make print books which are (in her words) "objects that are aesthetically pleasing or entertaining in their own right, and which add something to the text they hold."

This is a beautiful book, attractively laid out and enhanced with delicate abstract drawings and dingbats. In design it recalls the beloved Ace Doubles, two volumes bound back-to-back, upside-down with relation to one another: flip the book over and you'll find a second cover and another book. In this case, one half is *Near* (stories of the near future) and the other is *Far* (far future tales). It's a clever conceit quite nicely executed, and absolutely impossible to carry over to e-book format.

All of this clever design would be pointless if the stories were no good—fortunately, Cat Rambo is a great storyteller. These stories have appeared in venues as varied as *Isaac Asimov's SF Magazine, Lightspeed, Clarkesworld,* and *New Scientist.* Rambo specializes in what used to be called "sense of wonder"—her characters and worlds are skewed along several axes of imagination at once, familiar as old friends yet strange as figures from dreams. Her stories often pack an emotional punch or two, an ability to reach into a reader's guts and twist or squeeze.

Among the two dozen excellent stories, there are a few particular standouts. "The Mermaids Singing, Each to Each" involves Lolo, a young ship pilot on the verge of choosing a gender, yet afraid to make the choice—and Lolo's relationship with the AI ship *Mary Magdelena*, inherited from the uncle who sexually abused Lolo as a child. "Therapy Buddha" explores the darker side of artificial intelligence, especially when it's not as intelligent as we think. "Zeppelin Follies" concerns a young woman named Addie who goes into a store to get her prosthetic body tuned up, and emerges with more than she bargained for.

Rambo follows each story with a note talking about the genesis of the story.

If you want some really excellent stories, get the e-book. If you also want a physical object to warm the heart of any print-book collector, go for the paper version. Either way, you won't be disappointed.

Year Zero
Rob Reid
Del Rey, 357 pages, $25.00 (hardcover)
iBooks, Kindle, Nook: $12.99 (e-book)
ISBN: 978-0-345-53441-5
Genre: Humorous SF, Music SF

Are you looking for a gift for a hip, funny guy or gal? Someone who wears earbuds all the time, and constantly shares their playlist on every social media channel known to humanity? Give that person *Year Zero*. (And forget the hardcover: give them the e-book version. They'll read it on their phone and laugh the whole time.)

Rob Reid knows a thing or two about the internet music scene; he founded the company that created Rhapsody, one of the first legal music download sites. His credentials in the tech world are impeccable; he's also a good storyteller and a true master of the absurd.

Nick Carter, very junior partner in the entertainment law firm of Carter, Geller & Marks, specializes in copyright law involving music. One morning, his office is invaded by a nun and a mullah who explain that they are extraterrestrials, and they'd like to obtain a license for all Earth music, a license that would cover the entire universe.

At first Nick thinks he's being hoaxed, even when his visitors vanish before him. But an encounter with a particularly nasty parrot, followed by a second meeting with the aliens, convinces him that there's trouble.

You see, in 1977 (known as Year Zero), a passing alien space probe discovered Earth's music (specifically, the theme from *Welcome Back Kotter*). Aliens had never heard anything like music, and pretty soon the whole universe was addicted to Human tunes.

Further probes were sent to record every bit of music played in New York, and the resulting supernova of interstellar file sharing made Napster look like a birthday candle. Earth music spread through the galaxies.

But where there is copyright violation, there are fines and penalties. By the present day, the rest of the universe is bankrupt, and Humans own...well...everything.

That doesn't sit well with the movers and shakers, and Earth in a lot of danger. Carter's two visitors appeal to him to clean up the whole mess—and he's got 48 hours to do it. While being chased by a universe full of bad guys.

It's crazier than the *Hitchhiker's Guide to the Galaxy*, crammed full of jokes for the music fan, and manages the near-impossible task of bringing drama and humor to copyright law. Definitely a fun romp.

Win Some, Lose Some
Mike Resnick
ISFiC Press, 648 pages, $35.00 (hardcover)
ISBN: 978-0-9857989-0-1
Genre: Big Books, Short Stories

Mike Resnick is one of science fiction's most honored authors. To date he's won five Hugo Awards, with 30 of his short stories being Hugo nominees. Last August he was Guest of Honor at the Chicago Worldcon. In celebration of this remarkable career, ISFiC Press has put together all 30 of Resnick's Hugo-nominated stories, along with some extras, in one attractive volume.

Most of these stories appeared in our sister magazine, *Asimov's*. They range from drama to humor, long to short, future to past, hard science fiction to magical realism. Here you'll find the best of the Kirinyaga series: set on a terraformed asteroid inhabited by transplanted Kenyan natives trying the best they can to hold onto their society and traditions in a fast-changing technological world. "The 43 Antarean Dynasties" is an understated fable that should resonate with everyone who travels to a foreign culture. "The Bride of Frankenstein" takes a new look at a familiar monster.

Well, you don't need me to give capsule reviews of each story. They're all good—among the best work in science fiction over the last twenty years. Each story has a brief introduction by Resnick himself, along with an appreciation by a cross-section of sf writers and editors ranging form Lou Anders to Connie Willis (and everyone in between). The cover, by the legendary Vincent di Fate, brings together elements from many different stories.

Haven't read Resnick before? This is a great place to start. Already a Resnick fan? You want this book. Know someone who loves Resnick, or likes good stories, or doesn't believe sf can be meaningful and relevant? Give them a copy.

Blue Remembered Earth
Alastair Reynolds
Ace, 512 pages, $26.95 (hardcover)
iBooks, Kindle, Nook: $12.99 (e-book)
ISBN: 978-0-441-02071-3
Series: Poseidon's Children 1
Genre: Big Books, Hard SF, Space Opera, Transhumanism

You might be familiar with Alastair Reynolds from his *Revelation Space* series: five big novels and a number of smaller works that elevate space opera to the status of myth. A typical Reynolds book is a giant-size story with multiple characters and plotlines, full of nanotechnology and transhumans and dozens of alien races, all set against a background of cosmic conflicts that take place across billions of years.

Blue Remembered Earth is the first book in a new series set in a different universe. The series promises to follow one human family through generations and millennia as the race spreads through the stars—and even though this one starts out fairly close to home, you can expect the full Reynolds experience before long.

In 2160, the human race has spread through the Solar System and things are fairly peaceful. On Earth, the two major technological and economic powers are Africa and the United Aquatic Nations, a group of ocean-dwelling transhumans.

Geoffrey and Sunday Akinya are siblings, scions of one of Africa's leading corporate families. Their grandmother, Eunice, is a legendary explorer and business powerhouse. Geoffrey in particular wants nothing to do with the family business—he's happier studying migrations of elephants.

Then Eunice dies, and Geoffrey and Sunday are off to the Moon to investigate and do damage control. They find that Eunice had made some sort of monumental discovery; across the Solar System she left a string of clues and coded messages. So now they have to find the secret, all the while ducking the attention of Earth's AI surveillance system.

There's genetic engineering, human augmentation of various types, vastly extended lifespans, and high-concept technology all over the place. Poor Geoffrey is a thoroughly likable character caught in the power of something that's far bigger than he is. And in true Reynolds fashion, the focus keeps expanding through time and space as the book progresses.

If you like big, meaty books that make you think—and if you want to get in on the ground floor of the next Alastair Reynolds series—this is the book for you.

Citadel
John Ringo
Baen, 400 pages, $26.00 (hardcover)
Baen Webscriptions: $6.00 (ebook)
ISBN: 978-1-4391-3400-9
Series: Troy Rising 2
Genre: Military SF

Some military sf focuses more on interstellar strategy, tactics, and action rather than the course of a single officer's career. One of the masters of this sort of story is John Ringo. His *Legacy of the Aldenata* series tells of Earth's long war with the alien Posleen. *Live Free or Die*, the first book of his new *Troy Rising* series, brings a near-future Earth into contact with the alien Galactic Federation. All goes well until the arrival of the Horvath, a nasty bunch of extraterrestrial extortionists after Earth's heavy metals. By the end of the first book, Earth had created the mighty battlestation Troy and defeated the bad guys.

But the adventure has just begun. The Galaxy is a big, bad, dangerous place, with plenty of enemies and endless opportunity for war. With Troy, Earth has entered the galactic struggle; when the Rangora Empire defeats our only allies, there's nothing for it but to go in with all guns blazing. It's rollicking fun with scrappy Humanity against the rest, and you know who's going to win in the end.

2312
Kim Stanley Robinson
Orbit, 561 pages, $25.99 (hardcover)
iBooks, Kindle, Nook: $12.99 (e-book)
ISBN: 978-0-316-09812-0
Genre: Big Books, Other Worlds, Psychological/ Sociological SF,

A new book by Kim Stanley Robinson demands notice. Robinson, in case you've just arrived from the remote past via your individual time machine, is the multiple Hugo and Nebula winning major talent behind such bestsellers as the *Mars* trilogy (*Red Mars, Green Mars,* and *Blue Mars*), *The Years of Rice and Salt,* and *Galileo's Dream.* He is a master of the sort of sf that Analog readers love, and his new book *2312* is no exception.

This novel is a perfect example of the Society approach: it's nothing less than the portrayal of the civilized Solar System of the year *2312.* (Yes, the choice of date—exactly 300 years in the future—seems unbearably gimmicky. Don't worry, that won't last, any more than Orwell's gimmick of reversing digits to turn 1948 into *1984* lasted. In five years, we'll all have forgotten the original publication date and *2312* will be one of those iconic dates in sf.)

Robinson's Solar System is colonized from end to end, with extensive terraforming and complex artificial space settlements. The inhabitants of this future are long-lived and accustomed to modifying their bodies and minds for different environments.

The story begins on Mercury, in Terminator: a mobile city that constantly follows the day/night line around the planet. Swan Er Hong, a woman who designs worlds, is grieving for her beloved scientist grandmother Alex, recently deceased. As Swan talks with Alex's fellow researchers, she begins to suspect that Alex's death wasn't natural...someone wanted her dead. And Swan isn't going to give up until she gets to the bottom of Alex's murder.

Swan's search takes her around the Solar System, and uncovers a sufficiently nefarious plot to keep the action going for the next 520 pages. But the story, well-told as it is, is the least compelling thing about the book.

As one would expect from Robinson, depiction of wondrous and magnificently-detailed constructed environments and societies is the real joy of *2312*. This is inventive and innovative science fiction at its best, a book a reader can sink his or her teeth into.

Beware—this is the kind of book that you must discuss with others. If you wind up loaning it out and having to buy yourself replacement copies, blame Kim Stanley Robinson. You have been warned.

The Ocean Dark
Jack Rogan
Ballantine, 368 pages, $7.99 (paperback)
ISBN: 978-0-345-52072-2
Genre: SF/Horror

Just a couple of decades ago, horror fiction was considered to be (no pun intended) a dying field. Things got so bad that Stephen King was about the only writer making money in horror, and even he was telling people that he didn't writer horror anymore. Fortunately there has been a resurgence, and nowadays horror fiction is quite healthy.

The line dividing sf from horror has always been a porous one; take out the supernatural element, throw in a mad scientist or two, and you've got a horror story that's borderline sf. But recently there's been more than the usual amount of cross-fertilization between the two fields; readers on both sides are getting more accustomed to having horror and sf interpenetrate.

If you have a horror reader on your shopping list, do them a favor and give them *The Ocean Dark*.

It starts out so innocently, as they always do. Tori Austin, a woman on the run, takes a job with a shipping company and ships out of Miami on board the container ship Antoinette. The ship is a rusty old bucket filled with mysterious containers and unsettling crewmen. Gradually it dawns on Tori that things are not as they seem: there's gun-smuggling going on. Tori finds FBI agent Rachel Voss working undercover on the ship, trying to track down the bad guys.

The Antoinette makes an unscheduled stop at an uncharted Caribbean island, Tori and Rachel expect a latter-day Tortuga, but the story takes a more dramatic turn. There are these creatures, you see...ocean-dwelling vampiric creatures, the source of the legends of sirens.

Enter scientist Alena Boudreau and her grandson David, the only people to have survived an encounter with the sirens. They join up with Tori and Rachel and suddenly the four of them are on the run, hunted by these critters and desperate to survive.

The three things that make horror stories good are unusual threats, interesting locales, and good characters. *The Ocean Dark* has all three in abundance. It's refreshing to see a horror novel with so many strong women as main characters; gone are the days when the woman's job was to scream and faint in the monster's clutches (and good riddance!) There's enough science to give the sirens a justification, and the resolution is nicely satisfying. To top it off, *The Ocean Dark* succeeds in the one indispensable job of any horror story: it's scary.

If By Reason of Strength
Jamie Todd Rubin
40k, 10,000 words, Kindle: $2.99 (e-book)
Genre: Biological SF, Mars

40k (or, in words, Fortykey) is an Italian e-book publisher specializing in original short fiction, mostly novelette or novella length, and boy do they have some good stuff. Paul Di Filippo, Cory Doctorow, Mike Resnick, Bruce Sterling, and Jeff VanDerMeer all have e-books available from 40k. Prices are sensible, ranging from 99 cents to $3.49—certainly well under the $5.00 threshold that most readers are comfortable with. (Traditional publishers, are you listening? No, you're not.)

And now there's Jamie Todd Rubin. Rubin is no stranger to *Analog's* pages; his story "Take One for the Road" appeared in the June 2011 issue. *If By Reason of Strength* has an *Analog* flavor about it. The story is billed as a "techno-thriller" but that's just marketing talk...there are no echoes of Tom Clancy here.

Norman Gilmore was pilot on the first mission to Mars. On the red planet, he and some others of the crew picked up a virus-like alien disease. Norman was the only one to survive the disease. Upon returning to Earth, he was tried and convicted for murdering four crewmates. He was sentenced to a jail term of 280 years.

Somehow, Norman lived to complete that term, and he's released, famous as the oldest living human. Now he needs to get back to Mars, and to do so he has to cut a deal with the world's most powerful pharmaceutical company....

A thoughtful, engaging sf story at an attractive price...what more could one ask?

Hylozoic
Rudy Rucker
Tor, 336 pages, $25.95 (Hardcover)
ISBN: 978-0-7653-2074-2
Series: Postsingular #2
Genre: Parallel Worlds/Other Dimensions, Transhumanism

Reading a Rudy Rucker novel is like entering the dreams of a more-than-slightly mad genius, or going on the Alice in Wonderland ride in a theme park designed by the likes of Stephen Hawking. There's no fighting it or making sense of it; just relax and enjoy the ride. You're in the hands of a master.

By the end of *Postsingular*, the physical world was infected by nano...constructs (one can't really call them machines) called slips, which imbue every object with consciousness, personality, and a form of telepathy. At the same time, human beings gained a number of a number of abilities, including telepathy, teleportation, and integration with the worldwide emergent intelligence Gaia, affectionately known as the "Big Pig."

...And that was all in the prequel.

Hylozoic picks up shortly thereafter, in this newly-awakened world. "Hylozoism," according to a helpful epigraph, is a doctrine that "every object is claimed to have some degree or sense of life." None of this, by the way, is magic: it's all nanotechnology, quantum entanglement, and the emergent properties of molecular computers.

The cast of *Postsingular* returns in *Hylozoic*. Newlyweds Jayjay and Thuy, along with their friends, have turned their lives into a hit 24/7 telepathic reality show called *Founders*. As the book opens, Jayjay and Thuy are putting up a cabin in the woods—a process that involves gaining the sympathy and co-operation of the slips that control rocks, trees, ground, and a petulant local stream. When all is right, the couple (with a little help from their friends) teleport their already-constructed cabin from San Francisco to the prepared spot in the woods. Then everyone parties late into the night.

Except, of course, Jayjay, who follows a sentient pitchfork down a surreal beanstalk ten tridecillion levels into subdimensions, where he discovers an alien entity that promptly takes control of his mind.

It seems that Earth, in becoming a postsingularity world, has attracted the attention of all kinds of alien beings from various planets, dimensions, and other-universe branes. Some aliens are helpful, some are amused, some want to make what profit they can off of Earth, and others are really malevolent. It's not at all easy to tell which is which, but Jayjay and Thuy are going to have to if Earth has any chance of controlling its own destiny.

Along the way there's the painter Hieronymous Bosch (who just might be an avatar of yet another godlike alien), an enchanted harp, runes of power engraved on individual silicon atoms, and adventures on a parallel Earth called the Hibrane...and then it starts to get truly weird.

If you've never read Rudy Rucker before, by now you're probably shaking your head and furtively looking around for the egress. So, undoubtedly, were the hapless Victorians who first followed Alice down that rabbit hole. And you know how much fun that journey turned out to be.

Rudy Rucker is this generation's Lewis Carroll, and if you can have enormous fun if you relax and put yourself in his more-than-capable hands. Rucker plays with the frontiers of quantum physics and cosmology with his tongue firmly in his cheek and a manic grin on his lips. Don't think about it too hard; like any good dream, the whole thing falls apart once you try to makes sense of it. Just sit back and enjoy the ride. And above all, keep your hands inside the car at all times.

Anniversary Day
Kristine Kathryn Rusch
WMG Publishing, 465 pages, $17.99 (trade paperback)
iBooks, Kindle, Nook: $7.99 (e-book)
ISBN: 978-0615521794
Series: Retrieval Artist #8
Genre: SF Thriller

SF thrillers are alive and well, and today's leading practitioner is Kristine Kathryn Rusch.

Rusch's *Retrieval Artist* series should be familiar to long-time *Analog* readers; the series began with the Hugo-nominated novella "The Retrieval Artist" in the June 2000 issue. Several other stories in the series have appeared here, most recently "The Impossibles" (December 2011).

In case you're not familiar with the series (and what's been keeping you?), it's set in an interstellar future populated by various alien races and cultures, with Humans relatively new kids on the block. The problem is that Humans have to fit into a variety of alien justice systems that aren't necessarily friendly to our sort. Slavery, execution, and physical punishment are common...and completely legal.

So what is one to do when the multicultural court denies appeal, and offended aliens are on their way with vivisection in their eyes? Well, Human ingenuity is up to the challenge: there are lots of quasi-legal outfits that can make one "disappear"—new home, new identity, skin intact.

Of course, the Disappeared aren't completely safe. Those aliens are a determined bunch, and there are plenty of bounty hunters around. In addition, there are always those who seek the Disappeared for benign reasons—the Retrieval Artists. The series follows Miles Flint, Retrieval Artist, in many suspenseful cases.

Anniversary Day is something of a departure for the series, but in a good way. The main character is Flint's erstwhile partner, Noelle DeRicci, Security Chief on the Moon—Flint plays only a minor role. And this time around there are no Disappeared cases: instead, something far more sinister is going on.

The setting is the city of Armstrong on Luna. Four years ago (in the novel *Consequences*) the city's protective dome was almost destroyed in a bombing; now the citizens are celebrating the survival on Anniversary Day. Then the Mayor is assassinated....

That's only the beginning, for no sooner has DeRicci started her investigation than another politician is taken down. Soon Noelle and her partner, Bartholomew Nyquist, are on the track of a conspiracy that threatens the entire Moon.

Rusch is a great storyteller—easily the equal of Patterson or Koontz or any of that crowd. *Anniversary Day* is an edge-of-the-seat thriller that will keep you turning pages late into the night, and it's also really good science fiction. What's not to like?

Snipers
Kristine Kathryn Rusch
WMG Publishing, 348 pages, $18.99 (trade paperback)
ISBN: 978-0-615-76205-0
Genre: SF Thriller, Time Trave;

If you're like most sf readers I know, you're usually a little disappointed by thrillers. Oh, the suspense and adventure are fine, but even in "science based" thrillers by the likes of Michael Crichton or Dean Koontz, the science aspects are thin gruel indeed. Overworked sf tropes. which were handled more intelligently in *Astounding* in the 1940s, are about the best the genre can offer.

Thankfully, there's an alternative. A number of authors manage to blend real science fiction with the suspense and adventure of popular thrillers—and Kristine Kathryn Rusch is among the best of them

Rusch is best known for her *Retrieval Artist* series, but occasionally she gives us a standalone gem like Snipers.

At the center of this tale is the Carnival Sniper—a serial killer who stalked 1913 Vienna. The killer was never apprehended, and his identity was never uncovered. The ranking Police Detective, Johann Runge, went to his grave haunted by his greatest unsolved case.

Curtain up in 2005. Sofie Branstadter is a writer of best-selling true crime books, and she takes on the assignment of reopening the Carnival Sniper case with modern forensic science. She approaches Detective Runge's last living descendent, a classical pianist named Anton Runge. At first Anton rebuffs her, but as he begins to inspect long-forgotten papers in the basement, he finds himself drawn in to her quest to find the Sniper's identity.

Then Sofie uncovers evidence of Soviet experimentation, circa 1950, with time travel.

Suddenly the case isn't as cold as they think, and 90 years doesn't seem like such a safe interval any more....

Snipers is a riveting suspense tale and a fine sf story—what more could we want?

Skirmishes
Kristine Kathryn Rusch
WMG Publishing, 324 pages, $17.99 (trade paperback)
iBooks, Kindle, Nook: $7.99 (e-book)
ISBN: 978-0-615-79524-9
Series: Diving Universe 4
Genre: Space Opera

Kristine Kathryn Rusch is best known for her *Retrieval Artist* series, so maybe you've missed her *Diving Universe* series. If so, it's high time to remedy that oversight.

In the course of the three previous books (*Diving Into the Wreck*, *City of Ruins*, and *Boneyards*) we've come to know Boss —explorer and salvager of old wrecked spacecraft—and her partner Coop—Captain of the good ship *Ivoire*. Boss and Coop, along with their crew, are trying to make their living while helping to preserve the Nine Planets Alliance from the evil Enterran Empire. The alien technologies that Boss and her fellow salvagers find are worth more than fortunes—they are the key to the ongoing war between Empire and Alliance.

Coop and Boss know that there's some powerful technology in huge expanse of ancient wrecks known as the Boneyards. While Boss sets out to track down this much-needed tech, and solve the mystery of the Boneyards, Coop and his crew stay behind to defend against the Empire.

But Coop has some secrets he hasn't told Boss about, and one of them turns up to complicate matters....

There's adventure, suspense, intrigue, and not a few surprises, all in Rusch's quick, light prose. Boss, as much historian as salvager, reminds one of a Poul Anderson or Gordon R. Dickson protagonist. This is definitely a fun universe to visit: dive in!

Reviews: S

(alphabetical by author)

Dream of Venus and Other Science Fiction Stories
Pamela Sargent
Decimated: Ten Science Fiction Stories
Jack Dann and George Zebrowski
Wildside, 276 pages, $15.99 (trade paperback)
Kindle: $3.99, Nook: $3.79 (e-book)
ISBN: 978-1-4344-4501-8
Genres: Short Stories, Venus

Wildside Press is the latest small press publisher to re-create the old Ace Doubles format of two books published back-to-back, upside down with respect to one another. (The technical term for this arrangement, by the way, is *tête-bêche*, from the French for "head-to-toe.")

Pamela Sargent's Venus series (*Venus of Dreams*, 1986, V*enus of Shadows*, 1988, and *Child of Venus*, 2001) was a family saga set against a background of the terraforming of Venus. Despite a very checkered publication history, the books captured the attention of readers and are fondly remembered. (They're also available in e-book editions.)

Really good books have a way of taking hold of an author even after she thinks she's finished with them—in Sargent's case, this meant four short stories set in the same universe as the Venus series. Three concern the impact of the terraforming effort on various characters, some of whom appeared in the books and some who didn't. As if that's not good enough, the final story, "Utmost Bones," is set in the far future and tells the story of some residents of Venus who seek to return to an Earth whose civilization is gradually fading.

Sargent balances scientific extrapolation and human interest beautifully. If you're a fan of the Venus books, you need this volume; if you've never read them, treat *Dream of Venus* as an introduction to a marvelous series.

Jack Dann and George Zebrowski are veteran sf authors who probably don't need much introduction in these pages. Both are equally at home in mainstream sf and literary sf.

Decimated brings together ten stories that Dann and Zebrowski wrote together in the early 1970s. They're interesting as period pieces—examples of the changes that the New Wave movement was ringing on the field—and they have a madcap vitality that leave readers feeling as if they've just unexpectedly downed a shot of mid-priced whiskey. To round out the ten, the authors include one previously-unpublished tale from the same period, "The Standard Crisis Scenario."

Both titles include general introductions and notes on each story from the authors.

Red Planet Blues
Robert J. Sawyer
Viking, 460 pages, $30.00 (hardcover)
iBooks, Kindle, Nook: $12.99 (e-book)
ISBN: 978-0-670-06577-6
Genres: Mars, SF Mystery

A new Robert J. Sawyer book is always cause for celebration. Even more so when the book is something completely different than he's been doing for the last few years.

Red Planet Blues is a tour de force: a hardboiled detective thriller set in a Martian settlement fifty to a hundred years from now. It all started with Sawyer's 2004 Hugo- and Nebula-nominated novella "Identity Theft," which is included as part of the current book.

Four decades before the time of the story, Martian explorers Simon Weingarten and Danny O'Reilly found fossil evidence of past life. This spawned the Great Martian Fossil Rush, as thousands moved to Mars in hopes of unearthing more fossils and striking it rich.

That was the genesis of New Klondike, a domed city on the newest frontier. It's a raw, rough place where the burned-out hulks of failed prospectors share the streets with the glitterati and so-called transfers—androids animated by the uploaded consciousnesses of Earth's wealthy and influential.

In the chaos of New Klondike there's sure to be crime. Enter Alex Lomax, a private investigator who makes his living tracking down thieves and murderers. Alex is the classic rough detective with a soft heart, struggling to pay his bills and keep his head above water while still bringing some justice to the world.

Then Alex gets an unexpected case, one that could make his reputation and ensure his fortune. It's the most famous unsolved case on the books: Decades ago, someone murdered Weingartner and O'Reilly. And it's up to Alex to find out who...no matter where the investigation leads.

Well, this is Robert J. Sawyer, so you know it's a well-written, intelligent story with some unexpected twists. Alex Lomax is one of the good guys, easy to identify with—and Sawyer makes New Klondike as real as the street in front of your house. *Red Planet Blues* isn't just a mystery story with science fiction trappings, it's a fusion of the two genres in which the mystery depends on the sf elements.

To top it off, Sawyer obviously had fun writing this book, and that sense of fun comes through on every page. Definitely worth reading.

WWW: *Wake*
Robert J. Sawyer
Ace, 356 pages, $24.95 (Hardcover)
ISBN: 978-0-441-01679-2
Series: WWW Trilogy #1
Genres: Man & Machine, Philosophical/Religious SF, Psychological/Sociological SF

Wake was serialized in *Analog* recently; those who read it in these pages don't need me to tell them what a good book it is. So I'll just go ahead and assume that you didn't read it, haven't gotten around to reading it, and/or don't remember reading it.

For many years now, Robert J. Sawyer has been turning out imaginative, throught-provoking science fiction novels set in the present day and dealing with the impact of science and technology upon relatively ordinary people. A typical Sawyer tale brings together multiple diverse elements from popular culture, psychology, physics, and philosophy; stirs together plausible advances in science with appealing characters; adds some realistic depictions of actual scientists at work and a generous helping of old-fashioned sense-of-wonder; and filters the whole mix through a distinctly Canadian filter. *Wake* is no exception.

Here's the basic setup. Caitlin Decter is teenage math genius who was born blind. While dealing with the challenges of trying to adjust to a new school and relating to a father who doesn't talk to her, Caitlin receives an email from a Japanese scientist with an experimental treatment that he thinks might allow Caitlin to see.

So it's off to Japan, where the scientist fits Caitlin with an implant that processes input from a camera and links it directly to her optic nerve. At first the experiment seems a failure; Caitlin returns home to Toronto in hopes that a few weeks will allow the implant to start working. Meanwhile, the scientist continues to work on the device's software, arranging a way for Caitlin to download updates directly to the implant.

Comes the time of the first software update, and suddenly Caitlin can see...after a fashion. There are two problems: first, the patterns of lines and blobs that she sees seem to bear no resemblance to the world around her...and second, her new sight goes away as soon as the new software is downloaded.

A little experimentation reveals the truth: Caitlin's sight is only active when the implant is actively connected to the Internet. As for what she's seeing...it turns out that she is somehow able to perceive the structure of the Net itself.

Caitlin is an appealing enough character, and the premise is fascinating: a girl, blind from birth, gains the ability to see the structure of the Internet from within. A lesser writer would go with this story, following Caitlin as she learns to deal with this new, expanded world. But this is Sawyer, and there's much, much more going on.

Here are some of the threads that Sawyer weaves together.

A potential plague in China, to which the government responds by sealing off and destroying a rural village. To conceal the act from the rest of the world, China temporarily cuts itself off from the rest of the Internet.

The offbeat psychological theory of Julian Jaynes, author of *The Origin of Consciousness in the Breakdown of the Bicameral Mind*. Jaynes claims that human consciousness only emerged about 3,000 years ago, when the human brain evolved sufficiently complex connections between its two hemispheres. Prior to this, Jaynes says, humans had only the dimmest form of self-awareness; people reacted to their own thoughts as to the voices of unknown gods.

Simian behaviorists studying a few hybrid ape specimens who seem able to carry out genuine conversations with one another via teleconference.

The life story of Caitlin's hero, the late Helen Keller, and Helen's relationship with her beloved teacher, Anne Sullivan.

And here is how Sawyer brings these diverse elements together. In her explorations of the Net, Caitlin discovers a presence: a newly-evolved consciousness, an entity born in the increasing complexity of the Net and given self-awareness by the Jaynes-like reintegration of China's national Net with the worldwide Internet.

This new entity is effectively as deaf and blind as Helen Keller herself. And it falls to the blind girl, Caitlin, to be this new mind's teacher in the same way that Sullivan taught Keller, to bring language and awareness of the outside world to this new mind.

Along the way, Sawyer raises fascinating, complex questions about the nature of consciousness and self-awareness, of communication between disparate intelligences, and compassion across huge gulfs. This is a book that you'll still be thinking about for weeks after you finish reading it.

Wake is the first of a planned trilogy, so not every plot thread is completely tied up at the end. Indeed, Sawyer follows the old show business dictum "leave 'em wanting more." Fortunately, more is on the way.

WWW: Watch
Robert J. Sawyer
Ace, 250 pages, $24.95 (hardcover)
ISBN: 0-978-044101818-5
Series: WWW Trilogy #2
Genres: Man & Machine, Psychological/Sociological SF, Religious/Philosophical SF

Watch picks up where the previous book, *WWW: Wake* left off. Wake told the story of Caitlin Decter, a blind teenage math wizard with a cybernetic implant that gave her both ordinary eyesight and the ability to see the structure of the Internet. Caitlin became midwife to an emergent artificial intelligence born of the Web, an AI that calls itself "Webmind."

In Watch, Caitlin and her extraordinary friends and family assist Webmind's further development as it learns first to read, then to see, and finally to discover emotions—and ethics. Then government authorities discover Webmind, and determine that it is a threat that must be eliminated.

Along the way, Sawyer leads the reader through questions of the nature of consciousness, identity, privacy, morality, and empathy across the gulfs that separate intelligent beings from one another. The book is an easy read, chock-full of ideas that will stay with you long after you finish the last page. This is science fiction at its best.

WWW: *Wonder*
Robert J. Sawyer
Ace, 244 pages, $25.95 (hardcover)
ISBN: 978-0-44101976-2
Series: WWW Trilogy #3
Genre: Man and Machine, Psychological/Sociological SF, Religious/Philosophical SF

The previous two books of the *WWW* Trilogy (*Wake* and *Watch*) told of the creation and development of Webmind, a consciousness that emerged from the complexity of the World Wide Web. In *Wonder*, the story reaches completion and Webmind's ultimate destiny is revealed.

Last time, Webmind was under attack by the United States government, which perceived it as a threat. This time around, the biggest threat to Humanity emerges from within: the competition of nations and peoples is what menaces the world.

International tensions rise until the Chinese once again seal off their own portion of the internet, splitting Webmind in two —and the smaller part is left without the sense of morality, the conscience, of the main Webmind. This lesser Webmind becomes what the government feared the whole thing would be: an all-powerful, inimical entity.

With the help of its mentor and companion, teenage blind girl Caitlin Decter, Webmind must reunite itself and bring peace to a fractured world before the Human race can self-destruct.

Not just an adventure story, *Wonder* is also (like its predecessors) a starting point for speculations on ethics and morality, the meaning of consciousness and conscience, and the place of intelligence in the cosmos. This is Robert J. Sawyer at his very best.

The Sunless Countries
Karl Schroeder
Tor, 335 pages, $25.95 (hardcover)
ISBN: 978-0-7653-2076-6
Series: Virga #4
Genres: Bigger Than Worlds, Clarke's Law,
   Transhumanism

You say you want otherness, and aliens (no matter how well-done) just aren't other enough? You don't want to look back at reality from far out in left field...you want to leave the stadium entirely behind, if not the whole city?

For science fictional strangeness, there's nothing quite like something really, really big. Better if it involves floating cities, artificial suns, and high-tech carbon nanotubes holding the whole thing together. Pirates and sapient insects the size of mountain ranges are a bonus.

Welcome to Virga.

To explain Virga, I can't do any better than the author himself. "Virga is a balloon 5000 miles in diameter, orbiting in the outskirts of the Vega star system. Built and colonized by humans thousands of years ago, it is a weightless environment lit by man-made fusion micro-suns and one central fusion-driven heat source named Candesce." This balloon is filled with air, and contains perhaps hundreds of nations and cities, most lit by their own pocket suns. Cities are gigantic wheels or cylinders that spin to produce centrifugal force. Various types of flying vessels carry people and commerce between nations.

In three previous books Schroeder has taken us to various nations of Virga in the wake of Hayden Griffin, hero and sun-builder.

Now Hayden is deep in the lightless voids of Virga, on the city Pacquaea: but *The Sunless Countries* is not Hayden's story. The main character is a woman named Leal Hieronyma Maspeth, a historian and academic who was born and raised in dark Pacquaea.

Here's the problem: an enormous booming voice is sounding in the vast unlit expanses of the Sunless Countries, and Leal thinks she knows where it's coming from. You see, there are these legendary creatures called worldwasps, creatures truly fit to the scale of Virga. Old books speak of the worldwasps, books that also speak of a universe outside Virga's skin. A transhuman, post-Singlularity universe dominated by something called Artificial Nature.

Thousands of years ago, humans and worldwasps rejected Artificial Nature and together built Virga as a refuge. Then there was war between humans and worldwasps, and no one knows what became of the wasps. Until now....

Hayden the Hero has no interest in pursuing the strange new voice and confronting the worldwasps, so it's up to Leal to set off on a journey that will lead her beyond Virga entirely and change her forever.

You want otherness, you want mooreeffoc, you want different perspectives on reality? After *The Sunless Countries*, you'll never look at the universe the same way again. And isn't that the whole point?

Jamestown
Matthew Sharpe
Mariner, 416 pages, $14.00 (paperback)
ISBN: 978-1-933368-60-3
Genre: Dystopian Futures, Literary SF

More Thomas M. Disch than Walter M. Miller, Jr., *Jamestown* is a delightfully quirky and anachronistic dystopia.

In this unpleasant near future, Captain John Smith leads a band of settlers out of a poison-choked Manhattan in an armored bus. They head down ruined Interstate 95 in search of the promised land, Virginia. Once they arrive, there's this woman named Pocahontas...but if you think you know where the story is going, guess again.

The best part of this fun novel is Sharpe's invented language, which is easily fit to stand beside those in *A Clockwork Orange* and *The Moon is a Harsh Mistress*. A mixture of Elizabethan and modern slang, with a good bit of Sharpe's own weirdness thrown in, it's refreshingly SF-like.

Fair warning: Sharpe's future world is a violent and vulgar place, definitely not for the easily-offended. If that's not to your taste, give this one a miss.

The Shaver Mystery Book One
The Shaver Mystery Book Two
Richard S. Shaver
Armchair, 199 pages, $12.95 (trade paperback)
ISBNs: 978-1-61287-031-1 (Book One), 978-1-61287-032-1
Genre: Adventure SF

Before Dianetics there was the Shaver Mystery. Author Richard S. Shaver claimed to be in telepathic contact with various prehistoric races and societies inhabiting huge underground cities. The devolved remnants of this civilization continued to live underground, emerging occasionally to interfere with humanity.

Beginning in 1945, Shaver's stories dominated the magazine *Amazing Stories*. The Shaver stories boosted *Amazing's* circulation by at least 20%. Editor Ray Palmer knew a good thing when he saw it, and continued to publish Shaver extensively until 1948.

While Shaver had numerous believers, most science fiction readers were skeptical—fanzines of the period referred to the "Shaver Hoax" and indignation swept fandom. Even after *Amazing* stopped publishing Shaver, so-called "Shaver Mystery Clubs" continued to meet into the 1950s.

Armchair's two volumes of Shaver stories are obviously published with tongue firmly in cheek. The back cover of Book Two calls Shaver's work "the biggest hodge-podge of science fiction gobbledy-goop ever produced." Wisely, the books are presented as the historical curiosities they are; cover copy dares readers to accept the challenge of deciphering Shaver's "long-winded ramblings."

Apparently, Palmer edited Shaver's early writings fairly heavily, inserting plot and characters. As time went on, Palmer wielded his editorial pen with less vigor, leaving Shaver's rantings more or less intact. Perhaps this helps explain why the magazine's sales began to decline—although Palmer publicly claimed that sinister outside forces pressured him into abandoning Shaver.

Book One contains three Shaver Mystery stories and a feature explaining "How to Use the Shaver Alphabet." Book Two contains "I Remember Lemuria," the novella that started it all, along with "The Red Legion," a novelette-length piece usually considered the worst example of Shaver's "gobbledy-goop." If you can only afford one volume, Book Two is the one to get for the full Shaver experience.

Ice City of the Gorgon
Richard S. Shaver & Chester S. Geier
When the World Tottered
Lester Del Rey
Armchair, 215 pages, $12.95 (trade paperback)
ISBN: 978-1-61287-019-9
Genre: Adventure SF

Inspect the bookshelves of any serious sf reader, and you're sure to find some Ace Doubles. Between 1952 and 1973, Ace Books published volumes in which two short novellas (often by different authors0 were bound together, each upside-down with respect to the other. Essentially, the back cover of one novella was the front cover of the other. The distinctive spines were at first half red and half blue; later volumes used a white-and-blue color scheme. In the currency of nostalgia, Ace Doubles are hundred-dollar bills—the sight of one, along with the aroma of decaying paper, is guaranteed to touch the heart of the most unemotional reader.

Armchair Fiction has done its best to bring back the Ace Double format, complete with red-and-blue spines and the heading "two complete novels." To be sure, the constituent novellas are both face-up, appearing sequentially; the back cover illustrates the second novella, but it is unmistakably the back. Still, the effect is uncanny; Armchair Doubles definitely conjure the spirit of an earlier day.

The first novella, *Ice City of the Gorgon*, is rather late Shaver —it originally appeared in the June 1948 edition of *Amazing Stories*. Chester S. Geier was a regular in *Amazing* and its sister magazine *Fantastic Adventures*; perhaps because of his experience, *Ice City of the Gorgon* reads fairly easily. It's a typical adventure story set in a lost city in Antarctica; if you didn't look closely, you wouldn't realize it was Shaver at all.

Lester Del Rey's *When the World Tottered* appeared in *Fantastic Adventures* in 1950, and it's a ripping good yarn that would have been perfectly at home in the pages of *Unknown*.

Leif Svenson is a regular guy who gets transported to the Asgard of the Norse myths—complete with Thor, Odin, Loki, and all the rest. It seems that the prophesied end of the world is finally here: Asgard is under siege by the Frost Giants, eternal opponents of the gods.

But Leif, with his knowledge of modern technology and weapons (including atom bombs), is the ace in the hole that the gods need to beat prophecy and finally defeat their old enemies. It's all great fun, and Del Rey is a good storyteller.

If this all sounds familiar, you might be remembering Del Rey's 1959 novel *Day of the Giants*, published in paperback in the 1960s and 1970s and sadly out of print today. *Day of the Giants* is a rewritten and expanded version of *When the World Tottered*. Used paperbacks seem to be available in the two-to-five dollar range. Comparing the two versions is an instructive and rewarding process for those interested in how writers work.

Unwind
Neal Shusterman
Simon & Schuster, 352 pages, $8.99 (paperback)
ISBN: 978-1-4169-1205-7
Genre: Psychological/Sociological SF, Young Adult SF

For the teen reader on your list, you can't do much better than *Unwind*. In addition to being a great adventure story, this is science fiction in the best tradition. After a bitter civil war over the issue of abortion, a compromise was reached in the so-called "Bill of Life." Life is sacred and abortion is strictly illegal. However, between the ages of 13 and 18, unwanted children can be retroactively aborted, at which time their organs are harvested to keep others alive. This process is called "unwinding."

The story introduces us to three teens who are due for unwinding. Risa is an orphan girl at an orphanage with budget problems; unwinding her is one way of reducing costs. Lev, son of strict religionists, has known all his life that he will be unwound. And Connor is a mischievous boy whose parents just want to be rid of the trouble.

Fleeing their fate, these three kids find each other and set out to elude authorities and somehow survive until they turn 18 and escape unwinding.

Shusterman is an old hand at young adult sf and fantasy; he is a great storyteller and his characters ring completely true. His exploration of the social implications of unwinding is worthy of Frederik Pohl and Cyril Kornbluth. *Unwind* is gripping, disturbing, and thought-provoking. Smart teens will love it, and even adults can get a lot out of the book.

Beyond the Doors of Death
Robert Silverberg & Damien Broderick
Arc Manor, 182 pages, $14.99 (trade paperback)
www.phoenixpick.com: $7.99 (e-book)
ISBN: 978-1-61242-112-4
Genres: Alien Beings, Psychological/Sociological SF

Robert Silverberg's 1974 novella "Born With the Dead" won the Nebula and Locus Awards and was a Hugo nominee, and with good reason. It's an intense tale of a future in which a process called rekindling brings the dead back to some form of life. However, the dead are different, alien. Their emotions and motivations are completely altered, so much so that they prefer to live in enclaves of their own kind. A powerful taboo prevents the living from having much to do with the dead.

The story concerns Jorge Klein, whose wife Sybille has been rekindled. Jorge is still in love with Sybille, and goes on a trek to find her. His journey leads him to confront his own feelings about death and the meaning of life. It's as powerful now as it was when it first appeared.

As part of their Phoenix Pick line, Arc Manor reprints "Born With the Dead" along with a sequel by apprentice Damien Broderick. In the course of following Jorge's progress after his encounter with Sybille, Broderick explores Silverberg's world in more detail and adds a sociological gloss by dealing with conflict between the societies of the living and the dead. Broderick's tale doesn't have quite the emotional punch of Silverberg's, but that's part of the point, for the emotions of the dead are not those of the living.

Broderick's story is that rare sequel that fills a hole readers didn't even know existed. If you'd asked me last month if "Born With the Dead" needed a sequel, I would've laughed in your face. Well, I'm glad to say that I was wrong. Definitely recommended.

Sine Fiction

One last recommendation before I cue the end theme. If you're interested in music and science fiction, you'll want to check out Sine Fiction at http://www.notype.com/drones/catalogue.e/sinefiction—this website presents what they call "soundtracks to classic science fiction novels." The mix of titles they cover is eclectic: George Orwell's *1984*, John Brunner's *The Shockwave Rider*, Isaac Asimov's *Foundation*, Samuel R. Delany's *Dhalgren*, and dozens of others. There's no charge to listen to the music; it's well worth spending a few hours exploring.

The Highest Frontier
Joan Slonczewski
Tor, 416 pages, $25.99 (hardcover)
iBooks, Kindle, Nook: $12.99 (ebook)
ISBN: 978-0-7653-2956-1
Genre: Biological SF, Man and Machine, Mooreeffoc

Up until now, my very favorite first line of a science fiction novel has been from Alan Dean Foster's 1982 book *Nor Crystal Tears*: "It's hard to be a larva." However, I think Joan Slonczewski has Foster beat. Here's the first line of *The Highest Frontier*.

"The space lift rose from the Pacific, climbing the cords of anthrax bacteria."

With a start like that, how could you not want to read this book?

Joan Slonczewski, with a Ph.D. in Molecular Biophysics and Biochemistry, teaches both biology and science fiction at Kenyon College in Ohio. In six previous novels in the 1980s and 1990s, she's established a reputation as a respected writer of hardcore novels that combine cutting-edge biology and genetics, gender issues, and rigorous extrapolation. She's no stranger to the pages of *Analog*; her 1998 novel *The Children Star* was serialized here.

The Highest Frontier is her first novel since 2000, and that's a lot more than 11 years too long. Fortunately, this one is well worth the wait.

Ostensibly, *The Highest Frontier* is a coming of age story. In 2108, Jennifer Ramos Kennedy is off to college—specifically, Frontera College, the first orbital college. Jenny goes to school, has various adventures and meets various people, and emerges at the end of the book as a changed woman.

Right. And King Lear is the story of a family disagreement.

The Highest Frontier is a tour de force, a full-immersion experience of a strange and bizarre world. This is science fiction for the thinking reader, the reader who's willing to pay attention and put things together, the reader who doesn't need to have everything explained at once or all details instantly spelled out.

Take those space-traveling cords of anthrax bacteria, for example. They aren't explained until the next chapter, and then only in a two-sentence throwaway. That's enough, though. An intelligent reader doesn't need any more—and besides, by then there are plenty of other wonders to marvel at.

And wonders there are, by the armful. Jenny's world is one of climate change gone mad: the center sections of North America are uninhabitable, nations are warring over newly ice-free land in Antarctica, and orchids grow in upstate New York.

An invasive alien plant, which lives on ultraviolet and emits cyanide, is spreading across the continent. Taxpayers have been replaced by taxplayers, as the Balkanized government supports itself with revenue from casino games. Genetic manipulation is the norm—most of Jenny's friends have facial features cultured from Paul Newman.

Jenny herself is from a rich, political family, related both to the legendary Kennedys and the leaders of the State of Cuba. She lives almost constantly in the public eye; what she says, wears, and eats are all determined by the polls. In this world, debates between Presidential candidates are considered less important than those between their spouses, and untied shoelaces can lose an election.

On top of all this, there's been a revolution in technology: biology, not physics, is the root of most products in Jenny's world. Cultured amyloids are the building blocks, with DNA providing the blueprints for everything from chairs and tables to houses to space habitats.

This kind of science fiction—where the reader is thrown, sink-of-swim, into a wild and unfamiliar world—is enormously hard to carry off. The writer must be a master juggler, keeping all the balls moving and all the plates spinning while simultaneously maintaining the patter that keeps the audience interested. One slip—one plot complication too many, one weird detail in excess, one too many bizarre characters—and the whole thing can come crashing down in a wreckage of reader confusion.

Not to worry, though—Slonczewski is a master juggler indeed, and *The Highest Frontier* is great science fiction.

Let's just hope it's not another decade until her next book.

The Eternal Prison
Jeff Somers
Orbit, 406 pages, $12.99 (trade paperback)
ISBN: 978-0-316-02211-8
Series; Avery Cates #3
Genre: Adventure SF, Cyberpunk, Prisons

If you've met Avery Cates in his first two adventures (*The Electric Church* and *The Digital Plague*), then you won't be surprised that someone throws him in prison. In fact, you might think it's the best place for him.

Avery is a scary man...but he lives in a scary world. In this noir-flavored cyberfuture, Earth is ruled by the System of Federated Nations, policed by the dreaded System Security Force (SSF). Avery, an unwilling conscript in the SSF, is good with guns and has a droll sense of humor (one hears echoes of Sam Spade). After surviving killer cyborgs and bioengineered disaster, Avery now runs afoul of the wrong cops and winds up in Chengara, an inescapable prison with zero survival rate. So first Avery has to escape, then he needs to find out why people he's killed keep coming back to return the favor.

Avery Cates is foul-mouthed and violent, but somehow he manages to be likable as well. His friends and enemies are delightfully strange. And underneath all the blood and guts, the shooting and swearing, the holographic avatars and downloaded brains...one gets the distinct whiff of satire, and realizes that no one, least of all Avery Cates, is taking any of this entirely seriously.

A fusion of noir thriller, cyberpunk, and military sf, the bottom line is that Avery Cates is just plain fun. If that's what you're looking for, this is the right place.

Vixen
Bud Sparhawk
Cosmos, 304 pages, $6.99 (mass market paperback)
ISBN: 978-0-8439-5945-1
Genres: Philosophical/Religious SF

Sometimes you're hungry for a dish that rings changes on a familiar recipe, adding a little spice or an unexpected ingredient. If you're in a mood like that, you might want to give Vixen a try.

Take one colonization mission, the good ship *Covenant*, two hundred years from home with its cargo of frozen colonists. Add a planetary system with a beautiful, perfectly Earthlike planet. Awaken the crew, starting with expedition leader Tam Polat, and set them to work exploring their new home.

Stir in a moon that suddenly disappears, and then an alien ship of unimaginable power, and you have the makings of a standard new-planet-settlement, first-contact sf novel.

But this book is by Bud Sparhawk, and Sparhawk does nothing standard. This is where the spice comes in.

Covenant, and Tam Polat, are on a mission from God. No, really; the society they come from is a religious one, with social roles rigidly defined. Tam and his lieutenants are Men, superior to the Halfling worker class who tend the ship and do all the manual labor. As Hadir, or leader, Tam is divinely appointed and infallible. In this world, everyone has their proper place and their appropriate work, and all work together to accomplish the will of God.

God has sent Tam and his people to settle Meridian, the system's sole habitable world, and to prepare it for the arrival of further waves of colonists. The work will be easy; Meridian is a delightful Eden.

But every Eden has its apple, and there's the matter of that missing moon and those super-advanced aliens. God, you see, never mentioned them to Tam. And according to his crew, if God didn't mention them, then they don't exist.

Vixen is about more than colonizing a new world and meeting an alien race. It's about what happens when a person —and a whole society—is brought face-to-face with a reality that contradicts their most firmly-held beliefs. And that should certainly be enough to whet your appetite.

Coyote Destiny
Allen Steele
Ace, 337 pages, $25.95 (hardcover)
ISBN: 978-0-441-01821-5
Series: Coyote #5
Genre: Beloved Worlds, Other Worlds

The planet called Coyote, 46 light years from Earth, first appeared in Allen Steele's 2002 aptly-titled novel *Coyote* (based on stories that had appeared in *Isaac Asimov's SF Magazine*). The next two books, *Coyote Rising* (2004) and *Coyote Frontier* (2005), completed a trilogy describing the settlement of Coyote, growth of human civilization on the world, and the political troubles of the colonists. In the end, advanced aliens helped Coyote's people build a hyperspace starbridge to allow near-instant travel to and from Earth (as well as other planets).

Steele thought he was done with Coyote, and he moved on to two other novels (*Spindrift* and *Galaxy Blues*) set in the same universe, but away from Coyote's lush riverscapes. Readers, however, weren't ready to leave. As Steele himself says, "Readers continued to insist that I write more about the world I had created, and after a while I came to realize that, although the original story arc was complete, I wasn't finished with the place yet."

Thus came *Coyote Horizon* (2009) and *Coyote Destiny* (2010). These two form a continuing narrative, but it's not necessary to read one in order to enjoy the other.

So what is it about Coyote that so grabs the readers? First, there's Allen Steele's writing. He tells sometimes-complex stories in a very straightforward way, and his characters are realistic and appealing. Fact is, Allen Steele is just a good storyteller, so we readers are already inclined to enjoy any place he takes us.

Second, Coyote is a compellingly interesting place. It's a Mars-size moon of a gas giant, there are rivers all over the place, and the biology and ecology are fascinating. In both geography and biology, Coyote falls squarely between the familiar and the exotic. It's an immediately comfortable place for the reader, although the opinion of the first settlers may have differed.

Third, Coyote is a place of hope. The first three books concern the struggle between collectivism and individualism, between society and individual freedom. These are themes that resonate well with Western readers. As the series progresses and things on Earth get more and more dire, Coyote becomes the shining beacon, the future of the human race. It's hard not to feel good about a place like that.

In the previous book, *Coyote Horizon*, religious revolution came to Coyote in the form of an alien philosophy book. Human Hawk Thompson, putting the alien philosophies into practice, became the leader (chaaz'maha) of a powerful new cult. *Coyote Horizon* ended with Thompson's death in a terrorist bombing that also destroyed the starbridge, thus severing Coyote's link to Earth and the rest of the Galaxy.

After a brief prologue, *Coyote Destiny* opens twenty years later. The starbridge is rebuilt, but for some reason there has been no contact with Earth. Jorge Montero is recalled from an exploration mission, along with his comrade, Inez Torres, to find his world turned upside down.

For one thing, Inez (on whom Jorge has an unrequited crush) turns out to be Inez Sanchez, daughter of Hawk Thompson and Jorge's cousin. For another, a ship from Earth has arrived with shocking news: Hawk Thompson, the chaaz'maha, survived the blast and is alive in Boston. And finally, the terrorist is also still alive, and loose somewhere on Coyote. And he's planning worse.

So Jorge and Inez are off to Earth to find Hawk, while another group goes in search of the terrorist.

What follows is a story with plenty of action, adventure, politics, religion, exotic locales, and fascinating aliens. It brings the story to a satisfactory ending, but we can trust that this isn't the last we'll see of Coyote. I hope.

Hex
Allen Steele
Ace, 352 pages, $26.95 (hardcover)
iBooks, Kindle, Nook: $12.99 (ebook)
ISBN: 978-0-441-02036-2
Series: Coyote #6
Genre: Bigger Than Worlds, Exploration and Discovery

Allen Steele's Coyote (as I argued above) has become one of sf's beloved other worlds. Now Steele takes the *Coyote* series into Bigger Than Worlds territory, and forges new links between the Coyote novels and two associated works in the same universe, *The River Horse* (2007) and *Galaxy Blues* (2008).

Since Earth has become all but uninhabitable, Coyote (a moon of a gas giant orbiting 47 Ursae Majoris) is the main home of Humanity. Through centuries, the Coyote Federation has risen to become an established member of the galactic league called the Talus. Military and merchant ships, moving through stargate-like starbridges, have explored other planetary systems and established trade relationships with a number of alien races.

In all their exploration, though, Coyote's people have never found another habitable world for Humanity to settle. The leaders of the Federation, acutely aware of how fragile a single planet can be, are desperate to find another potential home for the species.

Andromeda Carson, merchant captain, is bored with her job. Until, that is, a man from the government comes with interesting news. A reclusive alien race, the arachnoid danui, makes a strange proposal. They claim to know the location of an unoccupied world perfectly suited to Human habitation, and they are offering that information for trade.

Andromeda and her crew take on a company of scientists and head off for HD 76700, the star system at the danui-provided coordinates. HD 76700 is something of a mystery; the star is surrounded by a dust cloud or nebula, and there is no sign of an Earth-sized planet.

As the human crew comes closer, they realize the true nature of the cloud, along with the reason for the lack of planets. The danui have used most of the planets in their system as raw materials to construct a sort of Dyson sphere surrounding HD 76700 at a distance of about 1 astronomical unit.

The conventional Dyson sphere, as presented in sf, is a solid shell around a star. HD 76700's sphere is composed of an open network of billions of hexagons, each as far across as a small moon. As you'd expect, the filaments forming the hexes are biological habitats, each kilometers across. Different habitats are bio-engineered to support different races.

There is enough habitable space to house multiple trillions of beings; all of the races belonging to the Talus could easily move in. And in fact, many races are already represented—some have been there so long that their civilizations have collapsed, leaving their descendants wild and dangerous.

The trick of a successful Bigger Than Worlds story is giving readers a sufficient amount of time to explore the Really Big Thing, while not allowing it to overshadow the plot or characters. At the same time, the plot can't be too complex or the characters and their difficulties too captivating, lest they distract from the exploration.

This is a difficult balancing act, and Steele pulls it off beautifully. The two primary mysteries—why the danui would built Hex to begin with, and why they invited the Humans—both get satisfactory answers. Andromeda and her crewmates are compelling (Andromeda's fractured relationship with her scientist son in particular). Meanwhile the exploration of Hex (the star of the show) is interesting and well thought out; the reward is worth the trip.

Steele leaves plenty of room (no pun intended) for a sequel.

Sex and Violence in Zero-G (Expanded Edition)
Allen Steele
Fantastic Books, 513 pages, $19.99 (trade paperback)
ISBN: 978-1-61720-358-9
Series: Near Space
Genres: Short Stories

While we're on the subject of short fiction collections by favorite *Analog* writers . . . .

Allen Steele has been called an heir of Robert A. Heinlein—and it's the *Near Space* series that got him that reputation. From *Orbital Decay* to *A King of Infinite Space*, the series presents a realistic and action-packed modern vision of the industrialization of space and those who make it happen. If the collective governments of the world had any sense, they'd be using these books as texts for ushering in a future worth having.

An earlier edition of *Sex and Violence in Zero-G* appeared in 1999, but Allen Steele hasn't stood still since then. In between tales of the planet Coyote and its universe, he's written a few more *Near Space* stories—so it's good to see an updated edition of *Sex and Violence*.

They're all here. Hugo-winning novella "The Death of Captain Future" and its sequel "The Exile of Evening Star." Hugo-winning novelette "The Emperor of Mars." "The Great Galactic Ghoul" (*Analog*, October 2010) and "The Zoo Team" (*Analog*, November 2010), along with fifteen others, two Introductions, an updated *Near Space* timeline, and four pages of spaceship design sketches.

Never read Allen Steele? Here's a great place to start. If you like *Analog*, you'll like Steele. Already an Allen Steel fan? Then what are you doing still reading? Go get the book already!

Deus Ex: Icarus Effect
James Swallow
Del Rey, 341 pages, $15.00 (trade paperback)
iBooks, Kindle, Nook: $9.99 (e-book)
ISBN: 978-0-345-52359-4
Genre: Adventure SF, Cyberpunk, Games & Gaming

Then there's Nephew Zack. He doesn't read much; he spends most of his time with his Xbox, has posters of Ratchet and Clank on his bedroom wall, and can tell you every minuscule plot element from every version of Halo. You know the kid likes sf—heck, his *life* is science fiction. If only you could get him to read more.

Give *Deus Ex: Icarus Effect* a try. The game is a popular one, selling more than a million copies in earlier incarnations. The newest version came out this summer. Not a mere shoot-em-up, *Deus Ex* is a roleplaying adventure set in a cyberpunk-flavored near future with all the trimmings: nanotech-enhanced human agents, rogue computer viruses, vast conspiracies. A surprising amount of the actual gameplay involves reading text, so the transition to a tie-in novel is a natural one.

The book is a cracking good yarn set in one of the obscure corners of the *Deus Ex* world. When Secret Service agent Anna Kelso insists on investigating her partner's killing against orders, she is suspended—but keeps up the investigation on her own. Soon she's on the trail of a cover-up involving private paramilitary forces and mysterious hackers. Then she runs into Ben Saxon, another former government agent turned mercenary. Together they go on to tackle the shadowy organization behind everything.

Swallow (who is one of the authors of the new game) knows his stuff, and he's a good storyteller. Nephew Zack probably already considers you his favorite aunt or uncle; this one will only cement his opinion.

Reviews: T

(alphabetical by author)

Back to the Moon
Travis S. Taylor & Les Johnson
Baen, 303 pages, $25.00 (hardcover)
Baen Webscriptions: $15.00 (ebook)
ISBN: 978-1-4391-3405-4
Genre: Exploration and Discovery, Near Future SF, To the Moon

It's hard for current sf readers to understand what the Apollo Program meant to earlier fans. For years—even decades—landing on the Moon was the one science fiction dream that seemed possible in our lifetimes. Mars, the other planets, the stars, the distant future...these were all out of reach. But the Moon was right there, a whole alien world within sight and within reach.

Beginning with the first Vostok and Mercury flights in the early 1960s, we obsessively followed every detail of manned spaceflight. Astronauts were our heroes, and those twelve who actually walked on the Moon were demigods.

Back to the Moon is a book to thrill all true space-travel geeks. Travis S. Taylor has multiple degrees in aerospace and electrical engineering, astronomy, and physics, and has worked for NASA and the Department of Defense. Les Johnson, Deputy Manager for the Advanced Concepts Office at NASA's Marshall Space Flight Center in Huntsville, Alabama. When these guys talk about missions to the Moon, you can be sure that they know what they're talking about.

In this near-future thriller, the situation is as dramatic as it is desperate. As the book opens, NASA is preparing next-generation hardware for a series of return-to-the-Moon missions. There are the usual complications: hardware failures, political troubles, threatened budget cuts. Still, the first mission is on track when there's an unexpected distress call. A recent Chinese unmanned Moon mission turns out to be manned after all—and crash-landed somewhere on the Lunar surface. The stranded Chinese are only days away from suffocation.

Into the breach step the heroic Americans. The good ship *Mercy I* launches early, with a reduced crew. Back at NASA, engineers work against the clock to figure out how to reconfigure the lander to be able to set down, jettison as much mass as possible, then lift off again with four Chinese astronauts in addition to the two-man crew.

Some may argue that *Back to the Moon* is a little short on nuanced characterization and realistic politics, and a little long on technical detail. Such criticisms miss the point. *Back to the Moon* is aimed at the space-travel geek inside us. For everyone who felt a shiver at Lovell's words on that long-ago Christmas, or who held their breath until Apollo 13 emerged from the far side; for everyone whose heart skipped a beat at Armstrong's first step and who still believes that July 20, 1969 was the greatest date in history—*Back to the Moon* is a reminder of a lost era.

> *The War That Came Early: West and East*
> **Harry Turtledove**
> **Del Rey, 436 pages, $27.00 (Hardcover)**
> **ISBN: 978-0-345-49184-8**
> **Series: War That Came Early #2**
> **Genre: Alternate History**

For the military history buff (or even the straight history fan), Harry Turtledove is a sure bet. Here the emperor of alternate history returns to territory he's mined before: World War II. In *Hitler's War*, the first book in this series, Hitler started the War in 1938 with an attack on Czechoslovakia, rather than in 1939 attacking Poland. In fact, as the German army conquers Holland, Belgium, and northern France, Poland becomes a

German ally.—as does Spain, under a different leader than Franco.

West and East takes up the story where the previous volume left off, with Allied forces successfully defending Paris and German-Polish forces bogged down in Russia. In his usual style, Turtledove shows us the unfolding of his alternate history through a variety of sympathetic and well-drawn characters: American soldier Pete McGill in Japanese-controlled Singapore, American Peggy Druce marooned in Germany, the German Jewish family the Goldmans, and a host of combatants on both sides. Throughout the book, the main question becomes: when will American enter the war?

For someone who hasn't read the first book, *East and West* stands on its own. Turtledove is a master at making each book in a series readable without familiarity with earlier volumes; you can trust him.

Just as the best sf can be enjoyed even by a reader not familiar with all the details of cutting-edge science, *East and West* is a book that one can enjoy without knowing Chamberlain from Khruschev or Byelorussia from Belgium. At the same time, a history buff with an encyclopedic knowledge of the War will be delighted at all the references and speculations.

Coup D'Etat
Harry Turtledove
Del Rey, 416 pages, $28.00 (hardcover)
iBooks, Kindle, Nook: $13.99 (e-book)
ISBN: 978-0-345-52465-2
Series: The War That Came Early #4
Genre: Alternate History

In *The War That Came Early* series, Harry Turtledove explores an alternate World War II, one in which Chamberlain didn't appease Hitler and the war started a year earlier. Through the previous three books (*Hitler's War, West and East,* and *The Big Switch*), Turtledove has followed the resultant changes to political and military alliances as well as individual lives.

Now it's the winter of 1941 and Germany against Russia—with England and France fighting alongside Germany to defeat Stalin's forces. The United States, meanwhile, is not doing too well in its war with Japan—and still struggling to stay out of the European mess.

Winston Churchill's death, possibly by foul play, leaves England on the brink of takeover by a secret conspiracy.

An American woman correspondent, who has met Hitler and knows the evil he represents, despairs of convincing her countrymen to turn their attention to Germany. President Roosevelt's power is slipping through his fingers.

As usual, Turtledove tells a very big story through the eyes of people great and small. His characters are finely drawn and quite sympathetic; it's hard to blame any of them for the various confused states they're in.

History buffs will be delighted by all the details Turtledove includes. Those with only a passing knowledge of World War II will have no difficulty following the story. Turtledove is an expert at depicting realistic worlds a reader can sing their teeth into, and this is no exception.

On the Train
Harry Turtledove and Rachel Turtledove
Phoenix Pick, 179 pages, $12.99 (trade paperback)
Kindle, Nook: $7.99 (e-book)
ISBN: 978-1-61242-076-9
Genres: Parallel Worlds/Other Dimensions

Phoenix Pick is a small press publisher with a big idea. In what they're calling *The Stellar Guild* Series (of which *On the Train* is the third title), they pair a big-name sf writer with a lesser-known apprentice of his or her choosing. Both write novellas set in the same universe, and the two stories form the resulting book.

Harry Turtledove, of course, needs no introduction to *Analog* readers. His protege is is daughter Rachel, and this is her first published story.

The experiment, I'm glad to report, is a resounding success.

Central to the book is The Train. Even to those closest to it, it's impossible to say exactly what The Train is. For some, it's a way to travel from one village to the next. For others, The Train moves between worlds, even between universes. And for others, The Train needs no destination—it is an experience in itself, a way of life.

For Javan, a young man from the sleepy village of Pingaspor, The Train is an adventure. After years of tending The Railroad that passes through the town, Javan has finally saved enough for a third-class ticket. He's entitled to a spot on a hard wooden bench, as long as he wishes to remain aboard—and Javan doesn't intend to return to Pingaspor.

Aboard The Train he learns Traintalk, the pidgin that passengers use to communicate with one another. He makes friends and enemies, and learns of news from the outside. He's left Pingaspor just in time, it seems, for a war has erupted. Outside, bombs and mortars fall around The Train...and then, one night, the unthinkable happens: The Train stops.

Rachel Turtledove's tale concerns Eli, who grew up with The Train running through her back yard. A governess for the Baroness Vasri's two children, Eli is presented with the chance of a lifetime: a journey on The Train, along with the Baroness and her household.

Everything goes well until armed men arrest the Baroness for treason. Next, they'll be coming for the children—so Eli must hide them and keep them safe, evading the authorities until The Train arrives in friendly territory.

This is a journey you don't want to miss.

Reviews: U-V

(alphabetical by author)

King Freedom
Uncle River
Fantastic Books, 235 pages, $14.99 (trade paperback)
ISBN: 978-1-60459-924-4
Genre: Dystopian SF

Finally there's dear sweet Aunt Jenny, who is a bit of a free spirit. She drives a Prius, avoids meat, and distrusts corporations, authority, and technology in general. She might have been at Woodstock; she certainly knows someone who was.

Well, one free spirit deserves another—and just when we need him, here comes Uncle River.

Uncle River, who is no stranger to *Analog's* pages, is one of science fiction's true eccentrics...and in a field like ours, that's saying a lot. For decades Uncle River lived as a hermit and a writer in New Mexico; now he's reentered the world. And he's brought along *King Freedom*, a delightful and thought-provoking tale of dystopia, tyranny, and growing up.

Adolescent Kile Tose lives in a world ruled by Church and State, a world where justice is swift and merciless. We meet him on the day he's released from prison—after a two-years sentence on trumped-up charges. During that two years, Kile has learned his place. He's learned to be quiet, to fear authority, to work and do as he's told. Learned to eliminate anger, aggressiveness, disobedience. Learned not to feel, not to think, not to hope. Learned to avoid attracting attention.

All Kile wants to do is work off his parole, stay out of jail, and get on with his life. But the system won't leave him alone.

You know how this kind of story is supposed to go. Kile's supposed to escape, find the resistance, and take a key part in the battle that defeats the evil State and sets everyone free. You've read it a million times.

Not this time, though. Kile does eventually escape, and finds those opposed to the system...but there's no revolution, no overthrow of the government, no toppling of the Church. Instead, Uncle River gives us an intense story of how one young man learns how to transcend the limits of his world, and find a freedom that he could never have imagined.

Aunt Jenny's going to love this one. And before you wrap it up for her, you might want to give it a try yourself. Uncle River isn't to everyone's taste (what author is?), but Kile's story is a rewarding one.

Children No More
Mark L. Van Name
Baen, 393 pages, $22.00 (hardcover)
Baen Webscriptions: $6.00 (ebook)
ISBN: 978-1-4391-3365-1
Series: Jon Moore and Lobo #5
Genre: Military SF

C. S. Forester's Royal Navy officer Horatio Hornblower has had a tremendous influence on science fiction. In particular, he has inspired an entire subgenre of books that follow the developing career of an officer in a future space force.

Mark L. Van Name's hero Jon Moore is no Horatio Hornblower. The product of a horrific childhood, Jon learned to fight as a teenager and has been fighting ever since. With his best friend, a sapient warship called Lobo, Jon has fought the good fight through four previous novels. For Jon Moore is a soldier with a conscience, a man struggling to remain moral in a universe full of tainted and corrupted souls.

Jon's fifth adventure is based on a stunning premise: a former comrade enlists his help to free a group of children who have been turned into brutal killers in service of a rebel regime on a backwater planet. The fight to save the child soldiers is bad enough, but then Jon faces the challenge of what to do with this bunch of kids who have had their childhoods taken away.

Action, likable characters, and a genuine moral problem with real implications for today's world—who could ask for more?

Ragnarok
Patrick A. Vanner
Baen Books, 474 pages, $7.99 (mass market)
Baen Ebooks: $6.00 (e-book)
ISBN: 978-1-4391-3466-5
Series: Xan-Sskarn War #1
Genre: Military SF

Female warriors are all the rage in military sf nowadays. But Earth Fleet Captain Alexandra McLaughlin and Honor Harrington could never be mistaken for one another; Alex McLaughlin is as hard-bitten and earthy as Honor is noble. In tandem with no-nonsense Marine officer Stewart Optika, Alex makes do with grit and determination, and spares no mercy for the alien Xan-Sskarn who unexpectedly attacked Earth in the 22nd century.

Against all odds, the Earth Fleet managed to repel the Xan-Sskarn during that first attack, and Alex was in the midst of the battle. Now the Fleet needs time to regroup and rebuild before the next attack.

But they just might run out of time, because Alex and Stewart discover a traitor in the Fleet. Before it's too late, it's up to them to wrest victory from the jaws of defeat.

Ragnarok is the first book in a projected trilogy; it will be interesting to follow the further adventures of this strong woman and her plucky sidekick.

Transgalactic
A. E. Van Vogt
Baen, 607 pages, $7.99 (mass market paperback)
Baen ebooks: $6.99 (e-book)
ISBN: 978-1-4516-3892-9
Series: Clane of Linn, War Against the Rull
Genre: Adventure SF, Military SF, Post-Apocalyptic

In the Campbell years of *Astounding* (predecessor to *Analog*), A. E. Van Vogt was one of the most popular science fiction writers around. Van Vogt specialized in breakneck stories overflowing with outrageous ideas and skewed psychology and philosophy. Nowadays, Van Vogt is almost forgotten—but fortunately, Eric Flint and David Drake remember. And they've brought us a huge omnibus volume containing two of Van Vogt's once-popular series, *Clane of Linn* and *The War Against the Rull*.

Clane first. Originally published in *Astounding*, the *Clane* stories were later collected in two books, *Empire of the Atom* and *The Wizard of Linn*.

Centuries after global wars that destroyed civilization, a post-apocalyptic Earth is in the grip of the Atom Gods, a mystical priesthood who tend the still-functioning high technology of an earlier age. Atomic-powered spaceships fly between worlds while slaves toil in farms beneath.

Clane is a mutant, born to the rulers of the city-state Linn. His body is deformed but his intellect is tremendous. He trains with the priesthood and maneuvers his way through the politics of Linn well enough to be able to help defend the city against attacking barbarian hordes.

Then Clane learns the truth: the war that destroyed Earth wasn't one humanity alone. It was an alien race, the Riss, that invaded Earth—and the long war against the Riss destroyed both civilizations. But just as Humans were able to regain their lost technology, so were the Riss...and they're on their way to finish the job they started.

The War Against the Rull stories, also first published in *Astounding*, were later released as a book titled *Mission to the Stars*. Here humanity is part of a peaceful interstellar union, coexisting with dozens of alien races. The Rull, however, are a paranoid race at permanent war with all others.

The problem is that the Rull are shapeshifters and consummate mimics. Their agents are scattered through civilized space, spreading discord and sabotage...and no one can ever be sure that the person standing next to them isn't in fact a Rull.

Van Vogt isn't to everyone's taste. Reading these stories can be like riding one of those particularly swoopy amusement park rides—sometimes all you can do is hang on tightly and live in the moment. If that sounds like fun, give it a try.

Saga Volume One and Saga Volume Two
Brian K. Vaughan and Fiona Staples
Image, 160 pages, $14.99 (trade paperback)
iBooks: $9.99 (v.1), $14.99 (v.2), Kindle: $8.06 (v.1), $11.22 (v. 2) (e-book)
ISBN: 978-1-60706-401-9 (v.1), 978-1-60706-692-7 (v.2)
Genres: Adventure SF, Graphic Novels, Science Fantasy, Space Opera

The biggest thing to hit the comics world recently isn't Superman, Batman, or the Avengers—it's a space opera comic that tells and up-to-date story while brimming with old-fashioned sense of wonder. This isn't just my opinion: as I write this, *Saga* has just been awarded the Hugo Award for Best Graphic Story.

Two worlds have been at war for time immemorial. Landfall is home to a race of winged humanoids ruled by a robot dynasty; its moon, Wreath, is inhabited by a horned race of warriors. Since destroying either world would send the other out of its orbit, Landfall and Wreath have moved their war to the vast galaxy. For generations and across hundreds of worlds, often working through proxy armies, the two peoples have fought bitter and brutal wars.

Alanna, a soldier of Landfall, was assigned to a military prison on the distant world Cleave. Marko, one of the most bloodthirsty warriors of Wreath, renounced his heritage and surrendered to Landfall soldiers on Cleave. He was taken as a prisoner of war.

Alanna and Marko fell in love and escaped, hiding on Cleave. The story starts with the birth of their daughter, Hazel. Almost immediately, they're beset by rival troops of soldiers, and they're off on an odyssey that will lead them across Cleave and into the distant reaches of space.

Meanwhile, both governments send bounty hunters to track down the pair and bring back their daughter—who is the only viable offspring of the two peoples in millennia.

Saga is a nearly perfect story. Both Alanna and Marko are strong, powerful characters that instantly engage the reader's sympathy. Their universe is populated by wondrous creatures and places, from ghost children to multi-limbed bounty hunters, from forests of rocketship trees to the depravity of Sextillion, the galaxy's premier brothel.

This is the graphic novel form at its best, a fusion of words and pictures that is more than its parts. The plot is solid and fast-paced, the characters all three-dimensional, the universe compellingly detailed. Even if you don't think you like graphic novels, you owe it to yourself to pick up *Saga*.

Reviews: W

(alphabetical by author)

A Beautiful Friendship
David Weber
Baen, 376 pages, $18.99 (hardcover)
ISBN: 978-1451637472
Series: Stephanie Harrington #1
Genres: Adventure SF, Animal Companions, Teen SF

It could have been awful.

The latest gimmick in mundane fiction, particularly adventure/suspense, is to have bestselling adult writers produce tie-in books aimed at teenagers. James Patterson does it, Dean Koontz does it, Sherrilyn Kenyon, F. Paul Wilson, and John Grisham do it —can Danielle Steele and Nora Roberts be far behind?

If an sf publisher wanted to play this game, they'd go for the biggest name they have. They'd tie the new teen series into that author's most successful adult series. They'd take an independent, beautiful teen girl and bond her telepathically to a sympathetic-yet-deadly alien animal...heck, why not go all the way and make it an alien cat? And they'd pit this girl and her cat-companion against an evil corporation in the defense of their bucolic and ecologically-balanced home world. Then they'd commit to spending $100,000 in a marketing campaign aimed at every hard-hitter in the teen book industry.

Awful? It could have stunk on ice!

Fortunately, David Weber is a good storyteller, and his teen heroine Stephanie Harrington is every bit as fun as her remote descendant Honor. I don't know if teenagers will respond to marketing and buy this book like they're supposed to, but Weber's many adult fans will certainly enjoy the story.

Fire Season
David Weber & Jane Lindskold
Baen, 287 pages, $18.99 (hardcover)
Baen Ebooks: $6.00 (e-book)
ISBN: 978-1-4516-3840-0
Series: Star Kingdom #2
Genre: Adventure SF, Animal Companions, Teen SF

In *A Beautiful Friendship* (reviewed above) we met plucky teen Stephanie Harrington and her telepathic treecat companion, Lionheart. Stephanie—ancestor of David Weber's swashbuckling Navy officer Honor Harrington—lives on the bucolic world Sphinx, a world that she helped rescue from a rapacious corporation.

It's dry season on Sphinx, the season when forest fires sear the landscape. The encroachment of human colonists has led to bigger and more catastrophic fires, and during dry season everyone does their duty keeping inferno at bay.

Stephanie, of course, soon finds herself in trouble. First she and a friend are off to rescue two stranded treecats from the midst of a raging fire. Then she loses her heart to a newcomer to Sphinx, Anders Whittaker. It isn't long, though, before Anders vanishes in the forest—and Stephanie is first in line for the search party. Unfortunately, a lightning strike causes another blaze in an area that Stephanie's responsible for protecting. She can't abandon her post...but she can't abandon her new boyfriend either.

This time around David Weber has teamed with Jane Lindskold, a well-respected writer of young adult fantasy. The mix is a good one: Stephanie and her friends ring true as teenagers, yet the trademark Weber adventure and plausible tech is present as well. If they can keep this up, I think Stephanie is going to have a long and successful string of adventures.

House of Steel: The Honorverse Companion
David Weber with BuNine
Baen, 565 pages, $15.00 (trade paperback)
Baen ebooks: $9.99 (e-book)
ISBN: 978-1-4516-3893-6
Series: Honor Harrington
Genre: Military SF, Nonfiction

David Weber's *Honor Harrington* series, along with the universe of the books—known to fans as the Honorverse—was originally aimed squarely at the military history buffs. Since then, the Honorverse has transcended its life-of-Horatio-Nelson origin to become popular among all kinds of military sf readers.

House of Steel is divided into two parts. The first 183 pages consist of Weber's Honorverse novella "I Will Build My House of Steel." This is the story of Lieutenant Roger Winton, first officer of *HMS Wolverine* in the Royal Manticoran Navy. Winton, who just happens to grow up to be King. Roger gets an early education in intrigue among the Star Kingdom's foreign enemies, an education that stands him in good stead when he takes the Throne.

The story's told with Weber's trademark friendly, breezy style. There's plenty of politics, action, and just enough humor.

The second part of *House of Steel* is called *The Honorverse Companion*, and it was put together by the BuNine Research Group, an Honorverse fan group. Here are the background details of the Honorverse. There's military procedure and trappings, history, capsule biographies of important characters, and nearly 200 pages of detailed notes (including diagrams) of military technology. In short, there's something for everyone.

I can't imagine a fan of the Honorverse who wouldn't want this book.

A Rising Thunder
David Weber
Baen Books, 480 pages, $26.00 (hardcover)
Baen Ebooks: $6.00 (e-book)
ISBN: 978-1-4516-3806-6
Series: Honor Harrington #17
Genre: Military SF

Some military sf is deliberately in the manner of military historical fiction, and David Weber's *Honor Harrington* series is perhaps the best-known modern example.

Weber isn't the first sf writer, by a long shot, to draw inspiration from C.S. Forester's indefatigable British Navy officer Horatio Hornblower...but he is the most successful. Honor Harrington's career spans at least twelve previous books (some books in the series only involve Honor peripherally) and in that time she's become much more than simply a female Hornblower. Similarly, the political background of the series has transcended the Napoleonic Wars on which the first few books were based.

Honor Harrington is a true hero, but she's also a fully rounded character. If you've never made her acquaintance, you owe it to yourself to spend some time with her and her friends. The series has high tech weaponry, brilliant battle tactics, and enough adventure and derring-do to please any war buff—it also has more than enough compassion, humor, convoluted politics, and just plain good storytelling to make the books a whole lot of fun.

The biggest problem with a long-running military sf series is how to keep the warfare going in a convincing fashion. Honor's Star Kingdom of Manticore can only fight with the People's Republic of Haven for so long before readers start to get bored; indeed, in the last few books the two states have made peace and even become allies.

The trick, as in real history, is to bring up a greater enemy—and in *A Rising Thunder*, the allied nations are attacked by an enemy with superior military technology: the Mesan Alignment, which aims to defeat and enslave all humans.

To defend her home kingdom from another Mesan attack, Honor is given the assignment of securing the hyperspace wormhole network. This move enrages the ancient but still powerful Solarian League—a depraved government based on Earth. As the ponderous League military machine turns against Manticore, Honor has her hands full. She must defeat the League while not allowing that conflict to become a distraction from the looming Mesan threat.

There's a lot more here than just shoot-em-up space battles. Honor Harrington and her friends are real people struggling with complex problems, and the answers aren't as simple as having the biggest guns and fastest ships. There are definite echoes of Poul Anderson's Dominic Flandry. Even if you don't think you like military sf, give Honor Harrington a try. I think you'll be happy.

Uglies: Shay's Story
Scott Westerfeld
Del Rey, 208 pages, $10.99 (paperback graphic novel)
iBooks, Nook: $9.99 (e-book)
ISBN: 978-0-345-52722-6
Series: Uglies
Genre: Biological SF, Graphic Novels

In 2005 Scott Westerfeld introduced us to the world of *Uglies*. In this future world, at age 16 all adults have an operation that turns them "Pretty"—eliminating individual differences and making everyone a perfect physical specimen —after which they enter the shallow, hedonistic adult world. Children under 16 are "Uglies," humiliated and embarrassed by their trivial imperfections. Most children dream of the day they will become Pretty...except for Tally Youngblood's friend Shay. Shay, the rebel, runs away rather than become Pretty...and Tally follows her. At first Tally comes as a spy, to retrieve Shay from her fellow rebels and bring them all back. Tally's slow conversion to rebel and her subsequent adventures make up the four books of the *Uglies* series.

Uglies: Shay's Story goes back to the beginning and tells things from Shay's viewpoint...and does so in a very accessible graphic novel format. David Cummings's black-and-white illustrations dovetail perfectly with script by Scott Westerfeld and Devin Grayson. Readers familiar with the *Uglies* series will definitely want this one, and those who haven't yet read *Uglies* will find it a perfect introduction to the series.

This would be a perfect gift for a bright teen or pre-teen, but adults can certainly enjoy the story as well.

Pirates of the Timestream
Steve White
Baen, 247 pages, $14.00 (trade paperback)
iBooks, Kindle, Nook: $8.99 (e-book)
ISBN: 978-1-4516-3909-4
Genres: Adventure SF, Time Travel, Visitors From Space

Jason Thanou, special operations officer with the Temporal Regulatory Authority has struggled against the nefarious temporal plots of the Transhumanists in two previous books (*Blood of the Heroes* and *Sunset of the Gods*). Along the way, he fought—and bested— the Teloi, a batch of hostile aliens whose favorite form of recreation is genocide.

Now Thanou and his stalwart crew travel back to the seventeenth-century Caribbean, where he finds that the Teloi are alive and well, and making mischief that threatens not only humanity, but the fabric of reality itself.

Luckily, Thanou happens across the one man who can help him: the legendary British Admiral turned privateer and pirate, Henry Morgan.

Steve White is good at this stuff: he knows his history, and he has a light, brisk style that doesn't get in the way of the story. Mixing time travel, hostile aliens, and pirates together might have been a disaster, but White makes it work. Great fun.

Wolf Among the Stars
Steve White
Baen Books, 245 pages, $25.00 (hardcover)
Baen Ebooks: $6.00 (e-book)
ISBN: 978-1-4516-3754-0
Series: Lokaron #2
Genre: Military SF

A dozen years ago Steve White's *Eagle Against the Stars* told the story of a near-future Earth dominated by the alien Lokaron, a technologically-superior race who were no match for good ol' American libertarians with their spirit of freedom, derring-do, and facility with weapons.

Now White returns to the universe of *Eagle Against the Stars*. It's a generation later, and Earth has thrown off the oppressors, and is now struggling to find its place in the Lokaron empire. That empire is in trouble—opposing forces are tearing it apart from within, as they are apt to do in empires. There's also a conspiracy whose goal is the destruction of the empire altogether, with Earth maneuvered into doing the dirty work.

Enter Earth Captain Andrew Roark, son of the first book's hero Ben Roark and obvious spiritual heir of Ayn Rand's Howard Roark. This Roark is a master of Lokaron war technology and battle tactics...and nobody's going to use Earth as a proxy under his watch. Together with a high-powered Lokar friend, Roark sets out to uncover and defeat the alien conspiracy (including the humans who support it) and (ideally) to bring the blessings of Earth-style libertarianism to the beleaguered planets of the Lokaron empire.

The distinct element here is the political and economic nature of the central conflict. The book's issues of personal liberty and economic justice are familiar from today's headlines. Earthmen—that is, Americans of the libertarian persuasion—fight for freedom and demonstrate that they are superior to their tyrannical alien overlords. One definitely gets the feeling that John W. Campbell would approve.

Extremis
Steve White & Charles E. Gannon
Baen, 630 pages, $24.00 (hardcover)
Baen Webscriptions: $6.00 (e-book)
ISBN: 978-1-4391-3433-7
Series: Starfire
Genre: Military SF

How about Cousin Jack who voraciously reads technothrillers? His favorite authors are Tom Clancy, Dale Brown, Stephen Coonts, and Larry Bond (although privately he will admit that the quality Clancy's writing has declined—a contention that seems to involve a logical impossibility). Big books don't deter him, nor do series books.

Extremis is a standalone novel in the *Starfire* series, which Steve White wrote in collaboration with David Weber. Now White steps into the role of senior collaborator, and does a pretty good job of it.

It's another far-future space opera universe with many different alien races and technologies. The galaxy is tied together by jump points, with the stars like stations on a mass transit line. Nearly a century ago, Humans united with three other races (the Orions, the Ophiuchi, and the Gorm) to form the Grand Alliance to defeat the alien Bugs. In four big books, the Alliance swatted those Bugs good, leaving known space relatively calm.

Of course the Alliance did what governments always do in these books, it got fat and complacent and forgot the fine military traditions of the past.

And now comes the new threat: Another implacable, inimical race; a fleet of city-sized slower-than-light ships fleeing the nova that doomed their homeworld. The newcomers are conquerors; they descend upon a human-colonized planet and learn about human technology, including the FTL drive and jump points.

Now it's up to old soldiers Sandro McGee, Harry "Light Horse" Li, and their buddies to come to the rescue of the Alliance -- which they do with great abandon, throwing force beams and mil-tech acronyms around like grenades. It's a grand, fun series of battles and campaigns, worthy of anything Dale Brown or Larry Bond ever wrote. Cousin Jack won't have any problem getting past the "aliens" thing —Nazis, terrorists, drug lords, aliens, it's all good.

Implied Spaces
Walter Jon Williams
Night Shade Books, 272 pages, $24.95 (hardcover)
ISBN: 978-1-59780-125-6
Genres: Animal Companions, Clarke's Law, Immortals & Immortality, Transhumanism, Science Fantasy

Once upon a time, Roger Zelazny took science fiction in a direction all his own. In the ultimate expression of Clarke's Law ("Any sufficiently advanced technology is indistinguishable from magic,") he stretched science and technology into realms usually reserved for fantasy. Books like *Lord of Light*, *Creatures of Light and Darkness*, and *To Die in Italbar* told epic tales of immortals battling one another with bizarre weapons across fantastic universes teeming with amazing wonders.

In *Implied Spaces*, Walter Jon Williams very consciously channels Zelazny, and does an excellent job of it.

Aristide is an explorer of "implied spaces"—accidents of architecture in humanity's dozens of pocket universes. When we first meet Aristide, he's incarnated as a heroic swordsman in a vaguely Arabian world-construct called Midgarth. Accompanying Aristide is his sidekick, a wisecracking superintelligent cat named Bitsy. Together Aristide and Bitsy (along with various other hard-fighting D&D types, both human and non-) track down and defeat some vicious desert raiders—raiders who are armed with disturbing new weapons far beyond Midgarth's technology.

Aristide and Bitsy emerge from Midgarth into their real home: a post-Singularity Solar System ruled by the Eleven, ultra-advanced AIs with the power to sculpt reality and open wormholes into custom-designed pocket universes. Aristide is one of the immortal humans who constructed and programmed the Eleven centuries ago, and Bitsy is an avatar of the AI Endora. Evidence they uncovered in Midgarth leads to the conclusion that one of the Eleven has gone bad, overriding its own "Asimovian safeguards" to become a danger to all of humanity and the universe itself.

There follows an adventure worthy of the best space opera, as Aristide moves through different bodies and worlds on the track of an opponent who seems able to outsmart the best minds in all the universes. Aristide is assisted by a delightfully motley crew of associates, soldiers, politicians, and even an ex-lover. Along the way, Williams tackles questions of identity, cosmology, theology, and the ultimate meaning of life.

Dripping with sense of wonder, *Implied Spaces* is a fast-paced, mind-stretching romp that's thoroughly fun and totally thought-provoking, as well as a worthy homage to one of sf's greatest masters. Run, don't walk, to get ahold of this one.

Blackout
Connie Willis
Ballantine, 491 pages, $26.00 (hardcover)
ISBN: 978-0-553-80319-8
Series: Oxford Historians #3
Genre: Time Travel

According to her publisher, it's been eight years since Connie Willis last gave us a novel. While that's something like 95 months too long, the wait proves to have been well worth it.

For those who are not familiar with Willis's *Oxford Historians* tales, a few words of explanation are in order. In the mid-21st century, Oxford University is the base of a large group of time-traveling historians who spend their time visiting other eras to learn the kind of things historians love to learn; how people lived, what they ate and how they spent their time, how they felt and what they thought. In this, the historians are very like readers of historical fiction.

To say that the *Oxford Historians* series has been well-received is like saying that the Pacific Ocean is a little damp. Not to put too fine a point on it, but these stories have achieved the status of science fiction classics. The novella that started it all, "Fire Watch" (1982), won both the Hugo and Nebula Awards, as did the novel *Doomsday Book* (1992). *To Say Nothing of the Dog* (1997) was a Hugo and Locus Award winner, and a Nebula nominee. All three frequently appear on "best science fiction" lists, and in many school districts one or another is on High School recommended reading lists.

Can *Blackout*, the newest book in the series, possibly live up to all this?

Does Saturn have rings?

Here's the setup. The story primarily focuses on three Oxford historians on missions to three different periods of the World War II era. Polly is playing the part of a shopgirl while observing the behavior of ordinary Londoners during the Blitz. Mike is headed to witness the evacuation of Dunkirk, in which thousands of private boats rescued stranded soldiers across the British Channel. And Eileen is off in the British countryside studying the world of children temporarily evacuated from London.

Even before they leave Oxford in 2060, there are ominous signs that something's up with time-travel. Schedules are being rearranged, missions postponed or moved forward, and administrators (including Mr. Dunworthy, the all-powerful head honcho) off on emergency conferences to discuss different theories of time-travel.

Polly, Mike, and Eileen each have their difficulties, and when they arrive in their past eras, things are still going wrong. Each suffers an inconvenient amount of "slippage," arriving well past their assigned target dates. Then, each one must deal with the challenges of working in the field, finding out that assignments which seemed simple are anything but. Polly has to find a place to live, get a job, and somehow get more appropriate clothes while spending most of her time huddling in bomb shelters. Mike is stranded in a sleepy seaside village thirty miles from where he's supposed to be, with no way to get there. And Eileen, who has her hands full with two of the most obnoxious children in history, is looking forward to the end of her assignment when an outbreak of measles traps her in a quarantined house.

Then things get really bad. Because it soon becomes obvious that their temporal gateways are not opening on schedule—in fact, they aren't opening at all. Apparently, something has gone terribly wrong in the future, and the three are stranded. Their only chance is to find one another . . . if they can make their way through falling bombs, V1 rockets, and the nightmare of World War II London.

This isn't a book to race though. You'll want time to savor the experience, and at nearly 500 pages there's a lot to savor. Don't worry—with Connie Willis you're in the hands of a master, and she's not going to lead you astray or waste your time.

Blackout—like much of Connie Willis's other work—tells the story of rather ordinary people caught up in extraordinary times and events, and somehow rising heroically to the challenge. For in the end, the historians from the future are in the same boat as the people of the past they've come to study: they don't know what's going on or what's going to happen next, and all they can do is live through it as best they can.

Fair warning: *Blackout* is only the first half of the story. The whole tale is too big to be published in one volume, and I dare anyone to find a single sentence that could be cut. The conclusion, *All Clear*, will be published later this year. But don't wait for it: read *Blackout* now.

All Clear
Connie Willis
Spectra, 641 pages, $26.00 (hardcover)
Kindle, Nook: $14.30 (ebook)
ISBN: 978-0-553-80767-7
Series: Oxford Historians #4
Genre: Time Travel

It hasn't even been a year, but to anyone who read the previous book, *Blackout*, *All Clear* is surely one of the books most eagerly awaited. Actually, they aren't really even two separate books, any more than *The Lord of the Rings* is three—the two are clearly one (enormous) novel published in two volumes for convenience.

And what a novel! As a quick recap, for those who missed *Blackout*: Polly, Mike, and Eileen are time-traveling historians from the 2060s, stranded in London during the Blitz. Something has gone wrong with time travel, their scheduled return portals have not opened, and they must find some way to get back to their own time...while also surviving the worst days and months of German bombardment of London.

The main story is intercut with glimpses of various other eras and other historians, including the crew back in future Oxford who are desperately trying to rescue the timelost trio.

In a previous issue (March 2010, to be precise) I talked about the two basic theories of time travel: the multiverse and the "invariant timeline." In the *Oxford Historians* books, the timeline is supposed to be invariant...but there are hints that maybe things aren't as invariant as everyone thought. I'm not going to ruin it for you by telling you which side Willis ultimately comes down on, but the tension between the two definitely informs the books.

Connie Willis is a master artist at the height of her craft. You'll find yourself glued to the text...and when you're finished, you'll feel as if you, too, were present during those dark times of World War II. Until we get real time travel, these books will do nicely.

The Best of Connie Willis: Award-Winning Stories
Connie Willis
Del Rey, 496 pages, $27.00 (hardcover)
iBooks, Kindle, Nook: $13.99 (e-book)
ISBN: 978-0-345-54064-5
Genre: Short Stories

The Damon Knight Memorial Grand Master Award is given by SFWA to a living author in recognition of lifetime achievement in the sf/fantasy field. In the beginning there was a limit of six Grand Masters per decade; mercifully that requirement was dropped in 1994. Since the first award in 1975 (to Robert A. Heinlein), 29 Grand Masters have been named.

As I mentioned above, the 2011 Grand Master award went to Connie Willis. It's hard to imagine a better choice. With 11 Hugo Awards and 7 Nebulas to her name, Willis has won more times than any other writer in the field. Her tales span the range from light comedy to deep tragedy and everything in between. Her work is accessible to every kind of reader, and equally well-regarded in literary and popular sf circles.

On top of all that, in her recent two-volume masterwork *Blackout/All Clear*, she pulled off the near-impossible trick of writing a thousand-page novel that was too...damned...short.

To celebrate Grand Master Willis, Del Rey has put together this collection all ten of her Hugo-winning short pieces. Willis added an introduction to the volume, an afterword to each story, and the text of a couple of speeches (including her Grand Master acceptance).

If there's a common thread to all these excellent stories, it's the presence of ordinary people. The characters Wills writes about—from the family in the post-apocalyptic "A Letter From the Clearys" to the denizens of wartime London in time-travel tale "Fire Watch," from the newspaper reporter in alien-contact "All Seated on the Ground" to the haunted protagonist of the dystopian "The Last of the Winnebagos"—aren't the usual larger-than-life heroes but just plain folks trying to live their lives as normally as possible in the midst of tumultuous events.

You've probably read some, or most, of these stories before. You might very well have them all on your shelves in one form or another. The afterwords and the convenience of having them all in one volume might not be worth shelling out the money. I can respect that.

However...if you know someone who doesn't read science fiction, I can think of no better way to introduce them to the wonders of the field. If anyone can be named "best science fiction writer of the age" it's Connie Willis, and these stories are the best of her best. Truly, it doesn't get any better than this.

Amped
Daniel H. Wilson
Doubleday, 288 pages, $25.95 (hardcover)
iBooks, Kindle, Nook: $12.99 (e-book)
ISBN: 978-0-385-23515-1
Genre: Biological SF, SF Thriller

Last year Daniel H. Wilson brought us *Robopocalypse* (reviewed below), a competent thriller of robot rebellion and takeover of the world. Now he's back with *Amped*, another sf/thriller crossover that's destined for the bestseller lists.

In a near-future world, Owen Gray suffered from seizures until his doctor father implanted a device in his brain to control them. Like an increasing number of others, Owen is "amped"—an "amplified" human being.

When Owen is 29, the Supreme Court declares that the amped do not have the same rights as natural born humans. Owen's father sends him off to find a secret community of the amped in rural Oklahoma. There he meets Lyle Crosby, leader of the group—and he learns that his device is much more than a simple medical apparatus. With their devices, the amped have superhuman physical and mental abilities, abilities that Crosby teaches him to exploit.

In the process, Owen discovers that Crosby has a dangerous agenda of his own...one that features Owen in a key role.

Amped nicely straddles the line between Individual and Society approaches, presenting the effect of amping upon individuals Owen and Lyle as well as upon the larger society. It's a fun read.

Robopocalypse
Daniel H. Wilson
Doubleday, 347 pages, $25.00 (hardcover)
iBooks, Kindle, Nook: $12.99 (ebook)
ISBN: 978-0-385-53385-0
Genre: Robots

Daniel H. Wilson has a Ph.D. in robotics; you may recognize his name from his humorous 2005 book *How to Survive a Robot Uprising*. Now he's turned his hand to fiction: specifically, the story of some robots who menace the entire human race.

Robopocalypse is not so much a book as a Publishing Event. Before publication, the story was optioned by DreamWorks, with Steven Spielberg signed on as director of the movie. The novel is being marketed to the mainstream thriller crowd: publicity compares Wilson to Michael Crichton and the back cover displays quotes from bestsellers Clive Cussler, Lincoln Child, and Robert Crais.

Robopocalypse is set in the very near future. In a secret government lab, a researcher invents an Artificial Intelligence called Archos. Over the course of a few months, there are scattered incidents of machines malfunctioning: a domestic robot kills a man in a convenience store, a malfunctioning military robot menaces troops in Afghanistan, a teenage hacker has a strange interaction with a mysterious voice.

Well, we all know what's going on: of course Archos takes over the world's robots and other smart technology, and the war against the humans begins.

It would be easy to dismiss *Robopocalypse* as a movie novelization inexplicably published before its parent movie was filmed. It certainly doesn't have the depth of, say, Robert J. Sawyer's *WWW* trilogy. However, it's a cracking good story, with just the right amount of tongue-in-cheek humor, and I think *Analog* readers will enjoy it.

Unfriendly Persuasion
Steven H. Wilson
Firebringer, 426 pages, $20.00 (trade paperback)
Kindle: $2.99 (e-book)
ISBN: 978-0-9773851-3-3
Series: Arbiter Chronicles #2
Genre: Humorous SF, Military SF

For a ten years and a vast number of episodes, Steven H. Wilson and the crew at Prometheus Radio Theatre (*prometheusradiotheatre.com*) have dramatized the madcap adventures of the Confederate Navy Starship *Titan* and her misfit crew. *Unfriendly Persuasion* is Wilson's second book featuring Rigellian Arbiter-Captain Jan Atal; his genetically-enhanced daughter Kaya; enigmatic alien telepath Cernaq; and poor Terry Metcalfe and Kevin Carson, the first Terrans to qualify for the Confederate Navy.

Metcalfe, hero of a recent battle with the Qraitian Empire, is disenchanted with his position and senses that there should be more to life than his military service. He gradually falls under the spell of a religious sect from the planet Eleusis—a sect that believes God lives within their planet.

So Metcalfe sets out for Eleusis, where he discovers that something is indeed living beneath the surface, a powerful alien intelligence that's prepared to grant him everything he desires. But what Metcalfe sees as God might instead be a malevolent creature intent on destroying everything he and his friends have fought for.

The story of Metcalfe's wayward adventures, and the struggle of his friends and crewmates to save him in spite of himself, makes for a light and enjoyable tale. Like a cross between the funniest episodes of the original *Star Trek* and *Monty Python*, *Unfriendly Persuasion* is a fun romp, and a bargain at $2.99 for the e-book. If you like the book, be sure to visit the website and listen to some episodes.

The Best of Gene Wolfe
Gene Wolfe
Tor, 544 pages, $29.95 (hardcover)
ISBN: 978-0-7653-2135-0
Genres: Literary SF, Short Stories

Gene Wolfe is another one of those writers who stretches the boundaries of SF. Fantasy? Satire? Horror? Absurdity? A single Gene Wolfe story can be all of these, and SF as well, and at the same time it can be something else entirely.

There is no denying that Wolfe is an Important writer: all you have to do is look at the awards, the reviews, the literary analyses, the esteem in which he is held around the world. Less known, perhaps, than Bradbury (but who isn't?), he nonetheless commands as much respect from the world of Literature as he does in the SF field.

The Best of Gene Wolfe is subtitled "A Definitive Retrospective of His Finest Short Fiction," and that just about sums it up. Now, one could quibble that this isn't "the best" of Gene Wolfe, for "the best" certainly includes some of his longer works as well—but it's certainly the best of Gene Wolfe that will fit in 544 pages.

If you're a Gene Wolfe fan, then you don't need to hear any more from me. But what if you're not?

If you've never read Gene Wolfe, I understand. There are 31 stories in this volume, and not one of them was published in *Analog*. Wolfe grew out of the Damon Knight/Milford tradition, and it's entirely possible that you've never been exposed to his work.

If you think you don't like Gene Wolfe's work...again, I understand. Anyone can pick up a Bradbury story and instantly be drawn into it. LeGuin and Delany take a little bit more work, but not much. And some readers jump right into Wolfe as easy as stepping on an escalator. But a lot of others find that his work requires some effort. (A lot, of course, depends on the particular story.) Now, most everyone finds that his work rewards the effort...but sometimes you have to be in the right mood to tackle a Gene Wolfe tale. And if you've run into his stuff while you weren't in the mood, you could easily get turned off.

If you've never read Wolfe before, or if you're doubtful, go to the library and try some of the stories in this book. "Petting Zoo" and "Has Anybody Seen Junie Moon?" are fairly accessible, and "The Island of Doctor Death and Other Stories" is a classic. "The Fifth Head of Cerberus" is longer, but quite rewarding. By the time you've finished those, you'll know whether you are a Gene Wolfe fan or not.

And if you are, you'll have the whole rest of the book to look forward to. You can return that library copy and buy one of your own.

Home Fires
Gene Wolfe
Tor, 304 pages, $24.99 (hardcover)
Kindle: $11.99
ISBN: 978-0-7653-2818-2
Genre: Adventure SF

You probably think you know what to expect form Gene Wolfe: A big, literary book; if not strictly fantasy, certainly far enough in the future that advanced science looks and acts like magic; a grand epic with characters out of mythology.

Well, Wolfe still has a few surprises up his sleeve, and *Home Fires* is one of them. The setting is North America in a future that's not so terribly unfamiliar. Skip Gryson and Chelle Sea Blue meet in college and fall in love. They soon marry, and start about the business of living happily ever after, but war intrudes...interstellar war.

Chelle, a military woman, is sent to distant stars to fight nefarious aliens. Skip stays home, becomes a lawyer, and builds a tremendously successful practice. Decades pass, yet Skip waits faithfully for Chelle's return. Finally, the day arrives.

Of course, relativity has worked its magic; decades to Skip have been months to Chelle. Her military service, and the injuries that sent her home, have changed her—much as Skip's years have changed him. Yet the two (somewhat to their mutual surprise) are still in love.

They set off on a Caribbean cruise, and that's when the trouble starts. Their ship is hijacked, and suddenly they are up to their necks in pirates, alien spies, and a war that has come to the homefront.

Home Fires is an adventure story, a love story, and the flip side of the standard "going to the stars to fight aliens" story. The book is fast-paced and quite accessible; and shows that Gene Wolfe is as much at home writing adventure as he is writing epics.

The Black Lung Captain
Chris Wooding
Spectra, 536 pages, $16.00 (trade paperback)
iBooks, Kindle, Nook: $9.99 (e-book)
ISBN: 978-0-345-52250-4
Series: Retribution Falls 2
Genre: Steampunk

Steampunk already borders on LitSF; any day now I expect Michael Chabon or Tom Wolfe to discover the genre. Before that happens and steampunk gets all respectable, Chris Wooding is more than good enough.

In *Retribution Falls* Wooding introduced readers to the pirate airship *Ketty Jay* and her scurvy crew. The setting is a vaguely late Victorian world with technology ranging from limited electricity to gaslights to machine guns to huge airships held aloft by a substance called aerium. All this technology is ultimately based on a kind of magic, possibly involving captive demons—but is dealt with as engineering rather than conjuring.

Darian Frey, Captain of the *Ketty Jay*, is a swashbuckling rascal, not above skirting the law when necessary. Narrator Jez, the ship's tough-as-nails navigator, has a deliciously-checked past. The complement also includes a crusty engineer, a drunken doctor, and two fighter pilots. In *Retribution Falls*, Captain Frey was framed for a political murder; he and his crew went on the run, and finally wound up in the legendary pirate's hideout, Retribution Falls.

Having survived to clear his name, now Captain Frey and his crew are simply trying to make a living—any way they can. They sign up for a new job, salvaging ancient technology in a trackless jungle. There's just one problem: they're close to territory occupied by the Mane, a hostile society of teleporting zombies. And navigator Jez just might be turning into a zombie herself....

It's a rollicking good time, part *Pirates of the Caribbean* and part Jules Verne, all filtered through Chris Wooding's fevered imagination. If you enjoyed *Retribution Falls* but wanted more of this world and these characters, *The Black Lung Captain* is what you're looking for. If you haven't had the pleasure, dive right in; you don't have to read the first one to enjoy this volume. Wooding has a friendly style that has the reader quickly turning pages -- remember to stop once in a while to breathe. Here's hoping that the crew of *Ketty Jay* will soon be back for more adventures.

> *Count to a Trillion*
> **John C. Wright**
> Tor, 368 pages, $25.99 (hardcover)
> iBooks, Kindle, Nook: $12.99 (e-book)
> ISBN: 978-0-7653-2927-1
> Genre: Clarke's Law, Space Opera, Transhumanism

John C. Wright has been absent from sf for too long. His *Golden Age* trilogy (2002 - 2003) was competent space opera, but then he turned to fantasy. *Orphans of Chaos* (2005), the first of a high fantasy trilogy, won him a Nebula Award. In 2008 he authored a sequel to A. E. van Vogt's *Null-A* books.

Now he's back, with the first book in a new series. *Count to a Trillion* is a space opera that starts in familiar territory and builds wonder upon wonder into a strange and enchanting edifice.

Menelaus Montrose is a Texan, born into a 23rd century world whose economy has collapsed. When he was a boy, Menelaus ran across a box of old books—science fiction from our own era—which changed his life.

As a young adult, Menelaus became a hired gun...until he boarded a spaceship and went to search for happiness among the stars. Between relativistic effects, intellect augmentation, and the machinations of his comrade Del Azarchel, Meneleaus winds up centuries and scores of parsecs away from Texas, struggling to find his place in an interstellar society ruled by Clarke's Law (any sufficiently advanced technology is indistinguishable from magic). Oh, and there's a Princess.

Centuries pass, humankind and artificial intelligences evolve, and Menelaus continues to change and grow. Before long, he's deep in galactic politics, balancing one power center against another in order to move history in the direction of his desires.

In the hands of a lesser writer, this sort of thing could easily get out of control and turn into a muddled, confusing mess. But Wright is a careful storyteller, and he leads the reader step by step into an almost-incomprehensible universe, rather in the manner of Robert A. Heinlein's classic *Have Space Suit, Will Travel*. Menelaus is a likable character, and his transition from cowboy to virtual demigod is gradual enough that we're with him each step of the way.

One of the things science fiction does best is to take us beyond limits, to stretch the imagination as far as it will go. *Count to a Trillion* does a great job. Definitely recommended.

The Hermetic Millennia
John C. Wright
Tor, 400 pages, $25.99 (hardcover)
iBooks, Kindle, Nook: $12.99 (e-book)
ISBN: 978-0-7653-2928-8
Series: Count to the Eschaton 2
Genres: Clarke's Law, Space Opera, Transhumanism

In last year's *Count to a Trillion* (reviewed above), John C. Wright began the story of Menelaus Montrose: 23rd century hired gun and science fiction fan turned transhuman genius. In easy stages, we followed this improbable pilgrim's progress through an interstellar alien society brimming with augmented intellects, artificial intelligences, and near-immortal races whose technology and motives were beyond comprehension.

Nevertheless, Menealus gave as good as he got; he steadily advanced to demigodlike power without losing his own humanity. By the end of *Count to a Trillion*, Menelaus was well-positioned to be Humanity's protector in a hostile universe.

Good thing, too, because there are some bad guys coming. An alien armada is on its way to Earth, bent on making slaves of the population. They'll arrive in only eight thousand years.

There's also danger closer to home: some of Menelaus's former comrades, with powers as great as his own, decide that they can make an advantageous deal with the slavers—especially if they use the next eight millennia to evolve Humans into something even more useful to the bad guys.

Menelaus sets his plans and goes into secure cryogenic suspension...but not for long. He finds that he must awaken periodically to deal with the machinations of his enemies.

Across eight millennia, Humanity is split into various sub-species such as Chimera, Giants, Locusts, Witches, and others, each more bizarre than the other, and all hostile to one another. If Menelaus is going to pull these subspecies together and save them all, he has quite a job ahead of him.

Wright does an excellent job of guiding the reader through this strange and wonderful future. With appealing characters and just the right bit of humor, he keeps all his plates spinning without letting the story slow down. There are even a few of those moments that make you say "Wow!"

The Hermetic Millennia is the second book of a projected four-book series, so there's plenty more left in store for Menelaus and his associates.

Reviews: X-Y-Z

(alphabetical by author)

Star Wars: Scoundrels
Timothy Zahn
Del Rey, 464 pages, $27.00 (hardcover)
iBooks, Kindle, Nook: $13.99 (e-book)
ISBN: 978-0-345-51125-6
Series: Star Wars
Genres: Movies, Space Opera

Timothy Zahn would be a familiar name even without his *Star Wars* fame. In the early 1980s his stories appeared frequently in *Analog's* pages—including his Hugo-winning novella "Cascade Point." He went on to make a name for himself in military sf with his *Cobra* series, and most recently has been producing fine space opera such as the *Quadrail* series.

Zahn can also lay legitimate claim to being The Man Who Rescued *Star Wars*. In 1991, nearly a decade had passed since the (then) conclusion of the film trilogy, and the momentum was all but gone. That year, Bantam published *Heir to the Empire*, the first volume in Zahn's *Admiral Thrawn* series. Instead of being just another disposable spinoff book, Zahn's fresh take on the *Star Wars* universe became a huge success (all three books of the trilogy were New York Times bestsellers) and demonstrated that there was still life in that galaxy far, far away.

With the possible exception of Brain Daley, who died in 1996, no one makes *Star Wars* sparkle like Timothy Zahn. Part of his success is that he approaches the universe as a true science fiction writer, requiring no previous familiarity with the source material. One could enjoy Zahn's *Star Wars* work without ever having seen a single film, tv show, or action figure playset.

Scoundrels is no exception.

Freelance interstellar trader Han Solo is a scoundrel. With his alien first mate Chewbacca, he specializes in smuggling—and he's one of the best. But even the best run into trouble, and Han's got a load of it right now. First, he had to dump a cargo he was carrying for the Hutts, gangsters of the galaxy, and they've put a price on his head. Second, for reasons he still doesn't completely understand, he got himself in the thick of rebellion against the Galactic Empire—in fact, Han Solo is now a Rebel hero.

Fine, but medals and honors don't pay off the Hutts. Unless he can cough up enough dough, every bounty hunter in the galaxy will be on his trail.

That's when a mysterious figure offers him the job of a lifetime, with a payoff to match. All Han has to do is sneak into the ultra-secure headquarters of the Black Sun syndicate, open an impregnable safe, and deliver the contents to his backer.

In order to accomplish this mission, Han enlists his friends, Chewbacca and con artist Lando Calrissian, along with some other notorious...er...scoundrels. All that stands in their way are a few killer robots, some bloodthirsty thugs, and the odd Imperial agent or two.

Reviews: Anthologies

(alphabetical by title)

Beginnings
David Weber with Charles E. Gannon, Timothy Zahn, and Joelle Presby
Baen, 384 pages, $27.00 (hardcover)
Baen ebooks: $9.99 (e-book)
ISBN: 978-1-4516-3903-2
Series: Honor Harrington, Worlds of Honor 6
Genre: Military SF, Shared/Franchised Worlds, Short Stories

In sf there's a tradition in which some authors with popular fictional universes invite other writers to come play, in a sort of hybrid of fan fiction and the media tie-in book. *The Worlds of Honor* books (this the sixth) contain short fiction set in David Weber's *Honorverse*. These stories usually stay away from the main timeline, exploring different corners of the *Honorverse*.

Beginnings contains five stories, two by Weber himself. There's a story from the first centuries of the timeline, featuring a clever and subtle attack on Earth; a feisty Lieutenant who fights her way out of an ambush only to get caught in Navy politics; and the first woman to serve in a formerly all-male space navy. Weber gives us a story of Honor Harrington's father, followed by a tale of young Honor herself.

As with any collection of works by multiple authors, there's variation in styles and quality. This might put off some readers, but others enjoy a different take on a familiar universe. If you're one of those readers, give *Beginnings* a try.

The Best Science Fiction & Fantasy of the Year: Volume 2
edited by Jonathan Strahan
Night Shade Books, 472 pages, $19.95 (trade paperback)
ISBN: 978-1-59780-124-9
Genre: Literary SF, Short Stories

Best-of-the-year anthologies have been with us almost as long as sf/fantasy anthologies have been published. "Best," of course, is a subjective judgment, highly dependent on the taste of the editor. Strahan, who admits to being overwhelmed by the sheer volume of short sf & fantasy, seems to lean toward the literary, the fantastic, and the genre-blending. If you remember Judith Merrill's year's-best anthologies of so long ago, you have the general idea.

There's a lot of fantasy here: of the 24 stories in this volume, about one-third are science fiction in the classic sense.

Perhaps the most important thing you need to know about this anthology is that none of the chosen stories came from the pages of *Analog*. Still, there are some good tales here...although few that I'd call great.

Among the sf stories in this collection are Charlie Stross's "Trunk and Disorderly," a comedy of manners set in the far-future asteroid belt and "Glory" by Greg Egan: a delightful tale of advanced physics and stellar engineering. In Ted Kosmatka's alternate-universe story "The Prophet of Flores" Darwin is proven wrong and the universe is less than 6,000 years old...or is it? Nancy Kress shows us a world after ecological catastrophe in "By Fools Like Me," and Bruce Sterling's "Kiosk" is a near-future political fable based in a pre-apocalyptic Eastern Europe. Stephen Baxter gives us an homage to the late Arthur C. Clarke in "Last Contact." Finally there's Chris Roberson's "The Sky is Large and the Earth is Small." This military-sf tale is set in Roberson's *Celestial Empire* universe (*The Dragon's Nine Sons*), in which a future Chinese Empire fights across the spaceways with the Aztec society of Mexico.

There are surely going to be other best-of-the-year anthologies out this year; I would wait a while and compare before deciding to purchase this particular one.

By Other Means
edited by Mike McPhail
Dark Quest, 218 pages, $14.95 (trade paperback)
ISBN: 978-0-9830993-5-2
Series: Defending the Future #3
Genres: Military SF, Short Stories

Military SF comes in short story form, too. In the *Defending the Future* series of anthologies (the two prior volumes were *Breach the Hull* and *So It Begins*), editor Mike McPhail brings together some satisfying single-servings of military-themed science fiction. *Analog* readers will see some familiar names here, among them John G. Hemry and Bud Sparhawk. David Sherman contributes a story from the science fantasy *Demontech* universe.

Altogether, *By Other Means* contains 14 stories. You might expect lots of huge space battles and epic derring-do, but many of these tales are more personal and character-driven. There's more than a bit of introspection and moral reflection, as well.

Reading *By Other Means*, it's easy to imagine yourself at the off-base bar on a deep-space transfer station, overhearing the tales of passing space marines, naval officers, and assorted other soldiers. If you enjoy a well-told story in the military SF genre, this is the book for you.

Dark Futures: Tales of SF Dystopia
edited by Jason Sizemore
Dark Quest, 268 pages, $14.95 (trade paperback)
ISBN: 978-0-9826197-2-8
Genres: Dystopian Futures, Short Stories

One place the short story really shines is in the genre of dystopian futures. While everyone enjoys a nice, dismal dystopia, the problem is that they're all so bloody depressing. By the end of even the best-written dystopian novel, you tend to feel tense and wrung-out, if not downright paranoid. But with short stories, you can dip into and out of an unpleasant future world before it starts to get to you.

Editor Jason Sizemore has put together a book of 19 dystopian tales ranging from gritty Big Brother cityscape (Maggie Jamison's "Memories of Hope City") to thought-provoking faux nonfiction ("A Marketing Proposal" by Sara M. Harvey) to positively poignant ("Black Hole Sun" by Alethea Kontis & Kelli Owen, in which two digital-native teenagers react to news of the upcoming end of the world). As is often the case with theme anthologies, it's fascinating to see how different authors go in a different directions from the same staring point. There's certainly enough variety here to keep the various dystopias from becoming too oppressive.

Dogs of War
edited by Mike McPhail
DTF Publications, 239 pages, $14.95 (trade paperback)
Kindle, Nook: $2.99 (e-book)
ISBN: 978-1-937051-05-1
Series: Defending the Future 6
Genre: Animal Companions, Military SF, Original Anthology

If science fiction has a totem animal, it is the cat. From Robert A. Heinlein's various felines to Anne McCaffrey & Elizabeth Ann Scarborough's *Barque Cats* series and everywhere in between, there's hardly room in to swing a book without hitting a cat.

That's why it's so refreshing to see an anthology about dogs.

Mike McPhail's *Defending the Future* series feature satisfying military-themed sf short stories from various authors and universes. Often the stories are offbeat or deliciously understated, and these—all involving military canines in one form or another—are no exception.

The 17 authors here include the usual mix of familiar names and newcomers, writers known for their military sf and those associated with other subgenres, novelists and short fiction writers. *Analog* readers will certainly recognize Bud Sparhawk, whose "True Friends" is a tearjerker in fatigues. Brenda Cooper's "For the Love of Metal Dogs" shows how courage and loyalty transcend both species and form, and "Tower Farm" by Vonnie Winslow Crist explores the redemption of a pair of has-beens on a frontier outpost.

Those who like military sf should enjoy this assortment of stories, and I dare any reader who loves dogs to make it through without several "awwws" and a few tears. And if you don't fit into either of those two categories, but you just like some good stories, you might want to give *Dogs of War* a try— the e-book is certainly inexpensive enough.

Going Interstellar
edited by Les Johnson and Jack McDevitt
Baen, 416 pages, $7.99 (paperback)
Baen E-books: $6.00 (e-book)
ISBN: 978-1-4516-3778-6
Genre: Exploration and Discovery, Short Stories

Exploration and discovery are alive and well in current science fiction. Jack McDevitt, a Nebula-winner who needs no introduction in these pages, joins with Les Johnson, Deputy Manager of NASA's Advanced Concepts Office to bring us eight short stories and four nonfiction articles, all based on the best current physics ideas for travel between the stars. Analog readers will feel particularly comfortable in this volume.

First, the nonfiction. Dr. Gregory Matloff, a retired astronomy professor with a list of credentials that itself stretches halfway to the Moon, discusses antimatter starships in one article and fusion drives in another. Dr. Richard Obousy describes a proposal called Project Icarus, a real-world design study for an interstellar spaceship. Finally, Les Johnson gives the lowdown on solar and beamed energy sails.

The roster of sf writers is equally impressive, including such familiar names as Michael Bishop, Ben Bova, Sarah A. Hoyt, Jack McDevitt, and Mike Resnick, as well as relative newcomers Dr. Charles E. Gannon, Les Johnson himself, and Louise Marley.

All of the stories are enjoyable. I found both Bova's "A Country for Old Men" and Gannon's "Lesser Beings" to be a particularly interesting pairing: two very dissimilar stories of individual crewmen pitted against much more powerful opponents. Bishop's "Twenty Lights to 'The Land of Snow'" is a deliciously different story of an unusual journey set in a decidedly unusual culture (the subtitle is "Excerpts from the Computer Logs of Our Reluctant Dalai Lama").

A Cosmos of Many Mansions

Last century there was quite a vogue in sf for "theme" anthologies, in which a number of different authors wrote stories inspired by a specific idea. For a while I was afraid that my own effort, 1990's *Carmen Miranda's Ghost is Haunting Space Station Three*, had killed them off, but fortunately they survived.. The really fun thing about these theme anthologies is seeing how writers, starting at the same point, go off in their own different directions. *Going Interstellar* is an excellent example.

Golden Reflections
edited by Joan Spicci Saberhagen & Robert E. Vardeman
Baen, 467 pages, $20.00 (hardcover)
Bean Webscriptions: $6.00 (ebook)
ISBN: 978-1-4391-3415-3
Genres: Alternate History, Parallel Worlds/Other Dimensions, Shared/Franchised Worlds, Short Stories,Time Travel, Tribute Anthologies

A type of anthology that's becoming more common nowadays is what we might call the "tribute anthology." In this type of book, authors write stories in honor of a big-name colleague; they can be set in worlds created by the honoree, or written in his/her style, or otherwise inspired by the great one. Sometimes these tribute anthologies appear to commemorate a special anniversary or birthday (as with Elizabeth Anne Hull's *Gateways*, published for the 90th birthday of its honoree, Frederik Pohl). Sadly, too many of these tribute anthologies are posthumous.

Golden Reflections is such a posthumous tribute to the late Fred Saberhagen. In 1979 Saberhagen published a clever little alternate worlds novel called *Mask of the Sun*, set in an alternate world in which the dominant Aztecs are fighting other timelines for control of the multiverse. It was a fairly successful story of warring parallel worlds, with many devoted fans.

About a year after Saberhagen's death in 2007, his widow (one of this volume's co-editors) got the idea of inviting other authors to write stories set in the *Mask of the Sun* universe. The idea turned out to be a popular one. Early on, the editors decided to feature only longer pieces, novelettes and novellas. *Golden Reflections* presents the results: seven stories, plus a reprint of the original novel that started it all.

As is usually the case with tribute anthologies, the list of authors is impressive: Daniel Abraham, Jane Lindskold, John Maddox Roberts, Dean Wesley Smith, Harry Turtledove, David Weber, and Walter Jon Williams. Even more impressive is the stories themselves. Every one is meaty, engaging, well-written…and a true tribute to Fred Saberhagen. From ancient Pharaohs to Cervantes, the cast of characters is both fascinating and fun. Including the source novel was a good choice; it's great fun to see what threads the other authors have picked up and woven into their own tales.

Impossible Futures
edited by Judith K. Dial & Thomas Easton
Pink Narcissus Press, 234 pages, $15.00 (trade paperback)
ISBN: 978-1-939056-02-3
Genre: Science Fantasy, Short Stories

Imagine that you're giving someone a subscription to *Analog*, or some classic sf movies or television shows. You'll also want to make sure to give that person a copy of *Impossible Futures*.

The idea behind the anthology is simple: contemporary authors give a modern take on beloved old sf predictions that never quite happened. Space-going trains. Robot lovers. Space stations and moonbases. Mile-high cities. Invisibility. Ray guns.

The lineup of writers is impressive, and features many familiar names: Rev DiCerto, Paul DiFilippo, Debra Doyle & James D. MacDonald, Duncan Eagleson, Jeff Hecht, Edward M. Lerner, Jack McDevitt, James Morrow, Mike Resnick, Sarah

Smith & Justus Perry, Allen M. Steele, and Fran Wilde. And co-editor Thomas Easton, of course, was the author of this very column for decades.

This anthology is like an issue of *Astounding Science-Fiction* c. 1938, only with 21st century style and idioms. Among the outstanding stories are Steele's "Locomotive Joe and the Wreck of Space Train No. 4;" Doyle & MacDonald's "According to the Rule," about a space station of monks; and McDevitt's "Searching for Oz" with a *different* approach to interstellar communications.

In Fire Forged
edited by David Weber
Baen, 336 pages, $25.00 (hardcover)
Baen Webscriptions: $6.00 (ebook)
ISBN: 978-1-4391-3414-6
Series: Worlds of Honor #5
Genre: Military SF, Shared/Franchised Worlds, Short Stories

David Weber's heroine Honor Harrington, of the Royal Manticoran Navy, is easily sf's most successful heir to the Horatio Hornblower legacy. In fact, her career parallels Hornblower's (with a large dash of the real-life Lord Nelson), and her universe is recognizably based on the Napoleonic period.

Honor became so popular that after eight novels, David Weber opened up her universe, inviting other writers to produce short fiction set in Honor's world(s). This current volume is the fifth in this *Worlds of Honor* series.

In Fire Forged contains novellas by Jane Lindskold and Timothy Zahn, as well as on by Weber himself which features Honor in a previously unpublished adventure. As if that's not enough, there's also a faux-nonfiction appendix on the design of starship armor.

Weber's books have always appealed to history buffs as well as readers who appreciate the hardcore nuts-and-bolts of military sf. If that's you, and if somehow you have not yet made the acquaintance of Honor Harrington, this book is an easy place to start.

Like Water For Quarks
edited by Elton Elliott & Bruce Taylor
MVP Publishing, 312 pages, $20.00 (trade paperback)
ISBN: 978-1613641446
Genre: Short Stories

To begin with, there's your friend Deirdre (all these names, by the way, are made up), who only reads literary fiction; when she discovered that you liked sf, she insisted that you read Doris Lessing, and you've never forgiven her. A few years ago she tricked you into reading *The Life of Pi* (it had nothing to do with math), and currently she's been after you to read a 500+ page snoozefest called *The Help*.

Deirdre is probably familiar with the type of fiction called "magic realism," which is literary-speak for fiction that contains fantasy elements. But too much fantasy can leave readers lost and confused, so magic realism has to be firmly grounded in today's familiar world.

Editors Elton Elliott and Bruce Taylor have combed sf and put together this anthology of sf tales that also fall under the magic realism umbrella. There are 21 stories, about a third of them reprints. The authors range from familiar names such as Ray Bradbury, Ursula K. LeGuin, Robert J. Sawyer, and Connie Willis to relative newcomers. Many are more "speculative fiction" than "science fiction"—for example, George Zebrowski's "Once We Were Dragons," is set in a world in which humans descended from dragons instead of apes, and Sawyer's "Lost in the Mail" involves a reality-bending postal service. Still, these stories aren't watered down—they're pure-quill sf, in a friendly wrapper that won't frighten Deirdre away.

With any luck, she'll soon ask to read more from these LeGuin, Sawyer, and Willis people.

Man-Kzin Wars XIII
created by Larry Niven
Baen, 529 pages, $7.99 (mass market paperback)
Baen ebooks: $6.99 (e-book)
ISBN: 978-1-4516-3894-3
Series: Known Space, Man-Kzin Wars 13
Genre: Adventure SF, Military SF, Shared/Franchised Worlds

Larry Niven's *Known Space* universe, like Weber's *Honorverse*, has spawned a series of anthologies containing stories by other authors. The *Man-Kzin Wars* series is set during the centuries-long conflict between Humans and the Kzinti, warlike feline aliens with lightning speed, sharp claws and teeth, and disagreeable dispositions. The joke behind the Kzinti is that they're a one-note species, knowing only how to attack ferociously and, in true John W. Campbell fashion, easily outclassed by the more versatile Human race.

This current volume contains seven stories by as many authors (and look, here's Charles E. Gannon again!) Not all of them are military sf—Jane Lindskold's story of a Human biologist bonding with her Kzinti research subject, for instance, is a character-driven psychological tale—but there are battles and heroics enough, and war is always a presence in every story.

Mothership: Tales From Afrofuturism and Beyond
edited by Bill Campbell and Edward Austin Hall
Rosarium Publishing, 350 pages, $19.95 (trade paperback)
ISBN: 978-0-9891411-4-7
Genre: Diversity in SF, Literary SF, Short Stories

Mothership is billed as presenting "just a part of the changing face of speculative fiction," and features 39 stories by 40 writers of color. Some are familiar names (Tobias Buckell, S.P. Somtow), while others are up-and-comers.

As you might expect from the term "speculative fiction," not all of these stories are science fiction—there's fantasy, steampunk, and horror as well. And despite the term "Afrofuturism," these stories aren't limited to the concerns of Africa or African-Americans. Frankly, what we have here is simply an anthology of good stories.

Market realities dictate that it's not enough to have good stories by relatively-unfamiliar writers—there has to be a gimmick. In this case, readers need to look past the gimmick at the stories themselves.

Mothership's keyword is "diversity." If these stories share anything, it's that they spring more from the tradition of literary sf than from the Campbell era. To put it in magazine terms, you'd see most of these stories in *Asimov's* or *Fantasy & Science Fiction* before you'd see them in *Analog*. Not surprising, really—the editors come from academia. Don't let that deter you.

Among the standouts in this volume are Thaddeus Howze's "Bludgeon," a *Twilight-Zone*-ish tale of alien invasion with a surprise ending; Carlos Hernandez's "The Aphotic Ghost," in which a father comes to terms with his talented son's death on Mount Everest; and Nisi Shawl's "Good Boy," a parable of virtual reality.

If there's anything missing from this volume, it's background on the contributors. Yes, one can always turn to the internet—but I kept wishing there was an "about the authors" section.

For readers who want to see more diversity in sf, *Mothership* is definitely worth the price.

Nebula Awards Showcase 2011
edited by Kevin J. Anderson
Tor, 416 pages, $17.99 (trade paperback)
Kindle, Nook: pricing not available (ebook)
ISBN: 978-0-7653-2842-7
Genre: Short Stories

As mentioned above, the Science Fiction and Fantasy Writers of America (SFWA) awards the annual Nebula Award to the best SF works, as chosen by vote of the members. While the Hugo Awards are chosen by readers, Nebula voters are professional writers. As with any award, controversy eternally accompanies the Nebulas, and the arcane rules are continually being revised. Nebula voters (who are actually a self-selected subset of SFWA) tend to prefer works that are move literary and avant-garde than the average Analog story—indeed, the only piece in this current volume that was published in *Analog* is a 1981 Joe Haldeman story.

None of that matters. Whatever the process, the Nebula Awards generally go to fine stories on the cutting edge of the field.

The 2011 Showcase presents the results of the 2010 Nebula Awards, which were given for stories published in 2009. Editor Kevin J. Anderson includes all of the nominees in the short story and novelette categories and the winning novella, as well as three poems that won the Rhysling Awards (presented by the Science Fiction Poetry Association).

Nebula Awards Showcase 2013
edited by Catherine Asaro
Pyr, 390 pages, $18.00 (trade paperback)
iBooks: $9.99, Kindle, Nook: $10.31 (e-book)
ISBN: 978-1-61614-783-9
Genre: Short Fiction

A great place to find quality sf is in the various "best of the year" anthologies. At the moment, four are regularly published: *The Best Science Fiction and Fantasy of the Year* (edited by Jonathan Strahan), *The Year's Best Science Fiction* (edited by Gardner Dozois), *The Year's Best Science Fiction and Fantasy* (edited by Richard Horton), and *Nebula Awards Showcase* (with a different editor each year).

In the first three, the "best" stories are chosen by the respective editors. The Nebula Awards Showcase is a mixture. The winners and nominees are chosen by vote of the Science Fiction & Fantasy Writers of America; the editor includes all the short fiction winners, but exercises discretion in choosing which nominees to include.

Because of the mechanics of the Nebula process, there's always a lag between publication and award. Though dated 2013, this current edition contains stories published in 2011.

Both science fiction and fantasy are eligible for the Nebula, and this year's volume includes some of both. While only one of the stories appeared in *Analog*, there are a few that would have been perfectly at home in these pages.

Take the nominee novelette "Sauerkraut Station" by Ferrett Steinmetz. This is a coming-of-age story of a young woman on the periphery of an interstellar war, and I think most *Analog* readers would enjoy it quite well. E. Lily Yu's short story "The Cartographer Wasps and the Anarchist Bees" examines two very alien societies of social insects. Grand Master Connie Willis's short story "Ado," about the danger of putting facts to a vote, could almost be a Probability Zero feature.

Some of the other stories aren't *Analog* fare, but are good stories nonetheless. Kij Johnson's winning novella "The Man Who Bridged the Mist" is a character-focused story set against the background of two cities separated by a mysterious and unexplained Mist filled with dangerous creatures, and brings this unfamiliar world to marvelous life. The novelette winner, "What We Found" by Geoff Ryman, is another character-rich tale of a near-future Nigeria and a boy who becomes a geneticist with an unconventional theory.

In addition to the short fiction, there's an essay from John Clute (who shared with Octavia Butler the Solstice Award, given to individuals who have had "a significant impact on the science fiction or fantasy landscape"), some poems, and excerpts from two novels—Nebula winner *Among Others* by Jo Walton, and *The Freedom Maze* by Delia Sherman, winner of the Andre Norton Award for Young Adult Science Fiction and Fantasy Book.

Old Mars
edited by George R. R. Martin and Gardner Dozois
Bantam, 485 pages, $28.00 (hardcover)
Kindle: $11.76, iBooks, Nook: $13.99 (e-book)
ISBN: 978-0-345-53727-0
Genre: Mars, Retro-SF, Science Fantasy, Short Stories

Oscar Wilde said, "Science is always making wonderful improvements in things." However, longtime sf readers sometimes question whether certain improvements are so wonderful...and nowhere more than the planet Mars.

When we were in charge of Mars, it was a magnificent place, full of wonders: ancient ruined cities, world-girdling canals, alien races terrible or kind, and a hospitable second home for humanity. Then science got its hands on the planet and basically trashed the place. No canals, no cities, no wise ancients—heck, when science is done, there won't be any life at all on the Red Planet. It's an interplanetary tragedy.

Editors George R. R. Martin and Gardner Dozois remember that old Mars, and they've given us a star-studded anthology of modern stories set on the Mars we once imagined. There are fifteen stories by as many writers, each different and each delightful.

The featured authors are a true cross-section of science fiction. Big names like Mike Resnick and Michael Moorcock, relative newcomers like Chris Roberson and Matthew Hughes, familiar names like Allen Steele and David D. Levine, welcome names like Phyllis Eisenstein and Mary Rosenblum, and scaremasters Howard Waldrop and Joe R. Lansdale...this anthology has them all.

The stories are without exception engaging and full of the old sense-of-wonder. It's hard to pick standouts in this crowd, but be sure not to miss David D. Levine's "The Wreck of the Mars Adventure," a tale of Captain Kidd's 17th century expedition to Mars....

This book is definitely not hard sf. The science and technologies are those of bygone days. As long as you're okay with that, it's hard to imagine that you wouldn't enjoy *Old Mars*.

Other Earths
edited by Nick Gevers & Jay Lake
DAW, 320 pages, $7.99 (Mass Market Paperback)
ISBN: 978-0-7564-0546-5
Genres: Alternate History, Short Stories

Today it is possible to distinguish between two types of alternate history stories. There's the basic alternate history tale, which is set entirely in a different timeline; and then there's the multiverse story, involving multiple timelines and travel between them (often including time travel as well).

Other Earths is a fine collection of original stories of the first type. The editors present 11 stories by a host of big names: Stephen Baxter, Alastair Reynolds, Lucius Shepard, Jeff

Vandermeer, Robert Charles Wilson, and Gene Wolfe, among others. With a lineup like that, you wouldn't expect too much in the way of hard science, and you would be right. These are definitely stories from the humanities, not the sciences. But that doesn't mean they aren't some excellent tales.

Wilson's "This Peaceable Land, or, The Unbearable Vision of Harriet Beecher Stowe" is set in the late 1800s in a United States that developed without a Civil War. Slavery still exists, but economic forces have made it a rarity. In Wilson's well-developed world, the costs of avoiding the war are heavy upon the society, and the reader is left wondering which universe is really better.

Shepard's exceptional novella "Dog-Eared Paperback of My Life" begins with a writer of bestsellers who comes across an obscure cult novel written by another writer of the same name. From there it goes off into trackless and disturbing jungles of the mind. But Shepard is a reliable guide; follow him to the end, and you'll emerge in one piece.

Fair warning: most of these stories aren't exactly the kind that would appear in *Analog*. Some of them involve such fantasy elements as magic and elves. Yet in a universe next-door to ours, a universe in which *Unknown* continued publishing to this day, you might easily find these stories in the pages of that magazine. If you're an alternate history buff, you'll definitely like this anthology.

Sentinels in Honor of Arthur C. Clarke
edited by Gregory Benford and George Zebrowski
Hadley Rille Books, 400 pages, $16.95 (trade paperback)
ISBN: 978-0982725603
Genre: Tribute Anthology

It's about time Arthur C. Clarke had a tribute anthology.

Clarke hardly needs an introduction in the pages of *Analog*. He was perhaps the best-known science fiction writer on Earth. Along with Isaac Asimov and Robert A, Heinlein, he was considered one of the "Big Three" of sf, superstars whose popularity among readers was matched only by their influence upon other sf writers.

Clarke was certainly the most literary of the Big Three; while nobody ever believes me when I say this, there are passages in Clarke's work that are pure poetry. He had an agile mind that was equally comfortable figuring interplanetary orbits as it was contemplating the nature of God. It wasn't just that he invented the comsat and did more to popularize space travel than any ten other authors; he also left his touch on the field in a thousand different ways.

Clarke died in 2008, and it's taken this long for this anthology to find a publisher.

A tribute anthology customarily solicits new stories. In *Sentinels in Honor of Arthur C. Clarke*, editors Benford and Zebrowski have chosen a different path. They combed the literature of sf looking for stories that showed the influence of Sir Arthur. This gives the anthology a much wider scope than most tributes. There are the hard-sf names that you'd expect: Allen Steele, Stephen Baxter, James Gunn, Benford himself. But there are also stories by Howard Waldrop and A.A. Jackson IV, Joan Slonczewski, Sheila Finch, Frederik Pohl, and Pamela Sargent—names that one doesn't usually associate with Clarke. Yet reading the stories, one can easily see the connections.

Also included are various essays about Clarke by the contributors, a checklist of Sir Arthur's works, and a lengthy interview of Clarke by Zebrowski. All in all, it's definitely a rewarding book for anyone who likes Clarke's work.

Shadows of the New Sun
edited by J.E. Mooney and Bill Fawcett
Tor, 416 pages, $25.99 (hardcover)
ISBN: 9780765334589
Genre: Short Stories, Tribute Anthology

Time is a strange thing in the publishing world. Take this column for example. I'm writing these words in April, to appear in the October issue—and you'll probably be reading them sometime in August.

Connie Willis was presented with the 2011 SFWA Grand Master Award in May 2012. The 2012 Grand Master, announced in December 2012 and awarded in May 2013, is Gene Wolfe. You'd expect any celebratory book to be out in, say, early 2014. Yet here is *Shadows of the New Sun*, subtitled *Stories in Honor of Gene Wolfe*.

There's really no mystery: At about the same time SFWA decided to give Wolfe a long-deserved Grand Master Award, Tor was deciding to honor him with a long-deserved tribute anthology.

And what an anthology! The lineup is like a *Who's Who* of sf writers: David Brin, Jack Dann, William C. Dietz, David Drake, Neil Gaiman, Joe Haldeman, Nancy Kress, Jody Lynn Nye, Michael A. Stackpole, Michael Swanwick, Todd McCaffrey, Timothy Zahn...and two stories by Wolfe himself. Like Wolfe's work, the stories run the gamut from humor to serious, fantasy to science fiction, and adventure to literary.

Some of these stories are homages or companion pieces to specific stories of Wolfe's, others are set in worlds he wrote about, and still others are simply inspired by Wolfe's work in general.

A tribute anthology is always a hard thing to judge. Stories must not only stand on their own, but must also have some connection to the honored author's work. The vast majority of the 19 stories in this volume manage to do both. A reader who's never heard of Gene Wolfe could enjoy this book; a reader intimately familiar with chapter and verse of everything Wolfe's written will enjoy it on a completely different level. And readers who don't yet care for Wolfe won't be looking at this book anyway, so it's pretty much win-win for everyone.

The Solaris Book of New Science Fiction Volume Two
edited by George Mann
Solaris, 407 pages, $7.99 (mass market paperback)
ISBN: 978-1-84416-542-1
Genre: Short Stories

Original anthologies have been around even longer than the best-of-the-year variety. In this one, George Mann has put together a good variety of stories, all sf. There's hard sf, military sf, adventure, sentimental stories, extrapolation, humor, and even modern-day New Wave sf. In terms of sheer bang-for-the-buck, *The Solaris Book of New Science Fiction* is hard to beat.

Among the standout stories are Paul Di Filippo's "iCity," a tale of urban design in a world in which all cityscapes are endlessly malleable and Robert Reed's "Fifty Dinosaurs," a post-human parable that raises questions of identity and the meaning of life. "Book, Theatre, and Wheel" by Karl Schroeder is a powerful historical story about the power of knowledge. Neal Asher gives us two tales of "Mason's Rats," set on a future farm of robot machinery and intelligent genetically-engineered rats. There's another *Celestial Empire* story by Chris Roberson; this one, "The Line of Dichotomy," is rather unsatisfying and wouldn't make a good introduction to the universe.

The last and greatest story is Michael Moorcock's "Modem Times," and features Moorcock's madcap antihero Jerry Cornelius tackling the current-day United States. Cornelius is crazy, irreverent, and very much an acquired taste. Either you like him, or he drives you spare. If you've never been exposed to Jerry Cornelius, the most helpful comparison I can come up with is vintage Vonnegut. This story (actually, at 70 pages, it's definitely a novella) is pure Cornelius. Depending on your own taste, treat that statement as either a wholehearted endorsement, or a warning label.

There are fifteen stories total in this volume. If you can't find a few stories that you like here...then what are you doing reading *Analog* to begin with?

The Solaris Book of New Science Fiction Volume Three
Edited by George Mann
Solaris, 406 pages, $7.99 (mass market paperback)
ISBN: 978-1-84416-599-5
Genre: Short Stories

Solaris and George Mann continue to provide a venue for some very good science fiction. Volume Three contains fifteen stories ranging from steampunk to love stories to alternate history to good old dystopian futures. The contents page is heavy on Brits, which may say something about the state of American sf (or maybe about the ease of transatlantic communication). Among the Big Names are Alastair Reynolds, Stephen Baxter, Paul Di Filippo, Ian Watson, and Ken MacLeod.

Among the standout stories are Alastair Reynolds' "The Fixation," which is a fascinating take on alternate universes, and John Meaney's "Necroflux Day," which shows us a fully-realized society that's neither past nor future but just different. (The nearest comparison I can come up with is to Cordwainer Smith, not on the basis of style or substance but mainly for pure uniqueness.)

Reviewing this anthology for *Analog* readers is a snap. I'm going to assume that if you're reading this column , you like *Analog*. If you like *Analog*, you'll like *The Solaris Book of New Science Fiction, Volume Three*. It's as simple as that.

We can all hope that Mann is hard at work on Volume Four.

Starship Century
edited by James Benford & Gregory Benford
Microwave Sciences, 340 pages, $24.00 (trade paperback)
ISBN: 9781939051295
Genre: Exploration and Discovery, Nonfiction, Short Stories

I'm sure you know someone who's so socially conscious that they would rather not receive material presents...they usually ask you, instead, to contribute to any number of charitable causes aimed at making the world a better place.

Too bad—this year they're getting a book. But *Starship Century* isn't just any book.

The first Starship Century Symposium in October 2011 brought together scientists, futurists, sf writers, and space enthusiasts to spur serious discussion of NASA's 100 Year Starship Project. The ultimate goal is to begin interstellar exploration within the next century.

Starship Century, the book, grew out of the symposium, and includes both nonfiction and sf pieces. The thing that's sure to please your philanthropist friend is that proceeds from the book go to support research on interstellar travel.

The roll call of authors in this book is an impressive one. On the science fact side we have Freeman Dyson, Stephen Hawking, Geoffrey Landis, Martin Rees, Robert Zubrin, and others—on the science fiction side are Stephen Baxter, Gregory Benford, David Brin, John Cramer, Joe Haldeman, Nancy Kress, Allen Steele, and Neal Stephenson.

Among the stories is Joe Haldeman's "Tricentennial," which appeared in *Analog* way back in 1976. The others are all new, and dramatize an array of technologies related to interstellar travel, from generation ships to space elevators. Allen Steele gives us a new Coyote story, Nancy Kress mixes agriculture and psychology, and David Brin explores what happens when that generation ship finally arrives at its destination.

Anyone seriously concerned for the future of humanity needs to be aware of the 100 Year Starship Project, to be familiar with the ideas and challenges of interstellar exploration, and to support the effort. *Starship Century* is a better place to start than most. Buy two, and keep one for yourself.

War World: Discovery
edited by John F. Carr
Pequod Press, 387 pages, $42.50 (hardcover)
ISBN: 978-0-937912-09-6
Series: War World 9
Genre: Military SF, Shared/Franchised Worlds, Short Stories

About twenty years ago, Jerry Pournelle and John F. Carr brought about a shared world series called *War World*. The five anthologies and two novels of the original series featured stories by a raft of authors, including Poul Anderson, Larry Niven, Mike Resnick, Susan Schwartz, S. M. Stirling, Harry Turtledove, and William F. Wu. The stories were as diverse as their authors, ranging from pure military strategy to humor to surprisingly tender fables. The last volume, the novel *Blood Vengeance*, appeared in 1994, and the fun was over.

At least, until 2007, when John F. Carr brought *War World* back in *War World: The Battle of Sauron*. Apparently, his intent is to bring the entire corpus of *War World* stories back into print, supplemented with a substantial number of new stories, portraying the saga in chronological order (the original volumes jumped around haphazardly through history). *War World: Discovery* is the first volume in this grand reissue.

The War World is Haven, a just-habitable moon of a gas giant called Cat's Eye. In the future, Haven will become a battleground between humans and the Saurons, a genetically-enhanced master race bent on universal domination. In the beginning, however, Haven was a peaceful colony that soon became a prison planet, a dumping ground for malcontents and undesirables of all types. When criminal gangs take over the place and start causing trouble, the Imperial Marines are sent to bring peace to a planet everyone considers a hellhole.

Of the 14 stories in this volume, four are republished; the other nine are brand-new. Work by ten authors is included. And while the price tag is a little steep, if you're a fan of War World and want to see how it all began, it's worth it.

Warrior Wisewoman 2
edited by Roby James
Norilana, 272 pages, $11.95 (Paperback)
ISBN: 978-1-60762-028-0
Genre: Short Stories

Despite the old saw, all too often you *can* tell a book by its cover. Publishers spend great amounts of time and money to make it so. Stroll through the science fiction section of your local bookstore, and you can instantly tell fantasy from science fiction; further, it's easy to distinguish military sf from space opera, alternate history from alien culture, biological sf from cyber-whatever. Cover art, title, typeface, even the authors chosen for quotes: all combine to help the browsing reader find exactly the type of book he or she wants.

At least, that's true of the big publishers. Among the small presses, things are different. A small press has no in-house design shop, very little money for cover art, and not enough staff to spend the effort on covers that the big boys do. With small press books, you truly can't tell the book by its cover. And that's a good thing.

Anyone who judges *Warrior Wisewoman 2* by its cover (and even its title) is in danger of making a big mistake. "Another touchy-feely anthology with lots of noble Amazons and High Priestesses, yawn." Please don't let this happen to you.

Warrior Wisewoman 2 (it's the second of an annual series) is a collection of fifteen science fiction stories with nary a witch, dragon, or unicorn in sight. Instead, there are spaceships, artificial intelligences, social speculation, High Frontier construction jobs, and enough technology to make anyone happy. Some stories are by women, some by men, a couple by collaborative pairs, and a couple more by writers who use genderless initials.

The one thing these stories all have in common is that they feature women as main characters. While I wouldn't call any of the stories "feminist," some of them do play with the reader's preconceptions and expectations regarding gender roles. Others are a bit more concerned with emotion than adventure.

Take, for example, Lee Martindale's "Lady Blaze." The title character, who shares her name with her luxury spaceship, is both a tough-as-nails space captain and the Madam in charge of a crew of high-class courtesans. When she decides to take on a young woman who needs help, Lady Blaze finds herself in the middle of a mission of vengeance against a ruthless female pirate captain. The whole situation may be more than this talented businesswoman had bargained for.

At a completely different emotional pole, Jennifer Brissett's "The Executioner" shows us an ordinary woman serving an extraordinary duty and pulls at the heartstrings in a way reminiscent of Judith Merril's classic tale "That Only a Mother." Kate MacLeod's "Gardens of Wind" is a clever story of life aboard village-sized airships. And perhaps the cleverest story in the book, "Shop Talk" by Ian Whates, is clearly akin to van Vogt's "The Weapon Shops of Isher" for the sensibilities of the modern day.

There are eleven other stories, all of similar quality. Editor Roby James has done readers a service in bringing together this anthology; let's hope she'll continue for many years to come.

Warrior Wisewoman 3
edited by Roby James
Norilana, 306 pages, $12.95 (trade paperback)
ISBN: 978-1-60762-061-7
Series: Warrior Wisewoman 3
Genre: Short Stories

I mentioned above that science fiction short stories continue to appear, and not just in the magazines. The anthology of original stories has been a mainstay of science fiction since Frederik Pohl edited the first volume of the *Star Science Fiction* series in 1953.

For the third year in a row, editor Roby James has put together an anthology of science fiction stories that feature powerful and remarkable women. These stories are all quite definitely science fiction, and there's something here to please every taste. Among the standouts are Aimee C. Amodio's "Tourist Trap," which describes an alien world with a uniquely dangerous ecosystem; Al Onia's "The Envoy," featuring a peacekeeper whose methods are truly unexpected; and "Katyusha's First Time Out," a story of a teens rebellion against her mother set in a post-apocalyptic world. "Dark Mirrors" by John Walters turns military science fiction on its head, examining the choices that a woman of conscience must make in the face of war.

In her introduction, editor James counters a widely-held misconception about the *Warrior Wisewoman* anthologies: she does not exclusively publish stories by women. In fact, this volume very nearly achieves gender parity: ten of the stories are by women, nine by men.

If you like good short science fiction, you'll definitely want to get a copy of *Warrior Wisewoman 3*.

Welcome to the Greenhouse: New Science Fiction on Climate Change
edited by Gordon van Gelder
OR Books, 352 pages, $17.00 (trade paperback)
$10 (ebook - www.orbooks.com)
ISBN: 978-1-935928-27-0 (print) 978-1-935928-26-3 (ebook)
Genres: Ecological/Environmental SF, Short Stories

Let me get this out of the way immediately: global climate change is a controversial topic with passionate feelings on all sides. None of that matters right now. Science fiction has always explored possibilities without claiming that they are real. You don't have to believe in psionics to enjoy Theodore Sturgeon's *More Than Human* any more than you have to believe in flying saucers to enjoy *The Day the Earth Stood Still*. SF is about answering the question "What if?" even when the particular "if" might be unlikely or even impossible.

Gordon van Gelder has put together a strong anthology of sixteen stories that answer the question "What if global climate change happens?" Some pretty impressive names have given their visions: Brian W. Aldiss, Gregory Benford, Bruce Sterling, Alan Dean Foster, and Paul Di Filippo, but there are also some relatively unknown bylines here as well.

The key to a good story about any huge trend, like worldwide disaster, is to make it personal. This is a lesson the authors know well; all of these stories are written at the scale of individual human beings, with compelling characters facing personal problems. From a paddlewheel trip across a drowned California to the family problems of an adolescent in a transhuman world, there's something here to please everyone. (If you're not a fan of global warming, there's even a story about a new ice age.)

No matter what you believe about climate change, *Welcome to the Greenhouse* is a treat for anyone who appreciates good SF in the best speculative tradition.

Worlds of Edgar Rice Burroughs
edited by Mike Resnick and Robert T. Garcia
Baen, 356 pages, $15.00 (trade paperback)
Kindle: $7.19, iBooks, Nook: $8.99 (e-book)
ISBN: 978-1-4516-3935-3
Genre: Retro-SF, Science Fantasy, Short Stories

Okay, I'm going to go ahead and take George R. R. Martin's suggestion and call it "Retro-SF," because it's obviously an idea whose time has come.

Edgar Rice Burroughs (universally known as ERB) was surely the first popular American science fiction writer, and his impact of the field was immense. Well before *Astounding*, John W. Campbell, and modern sf, Burroughs was spinning tales of interplanetary adventure that sent his heroes to the Moon, Mars, Venus, and beyond.

The big problem with Burroughs nowadays is that his writing reflects the world and fashions of more than a century ago. His stories are not very accessible to the modern reader.

Mike Resnick and Robert T. Garcia have taken care of that. *The Worlds of Edgar Rice Burroughs* does for ERB what Martin and Dozois did for Mars. Again, an all-star cast of writers brings us modern stories of the good old worlds and beloved characters.

Mike Resnick and Joe R. Lansdale are here, but so are Kristine Kathryn Rusch, Peter David, Kevin J. Anderson and Sarah A. Hoyt, F. Paul Wilson, Todd McCaffrey, and ERB uber-fan Richard A. Lupoff. In all, there are 11 stories by 13 authors.

The stories range from Earth (Rusch's "Tarzan and the Great War" and "Apache Lawman" by Ralph Roberts) to Mars (Resnick's "The Forgotten Sea of Mars") and Venus (Lupoff's "Scorpion Men of Venus"), to ERB's more exotic worlds (the hollow-Earth world of Pellucidar and the weird island Caprona), to historical adventure.

By far the most daring (and most welcome) story is McCaffrey's "To the Nearest Planet," set on Poloda, a brand-new distant world that Burroughs barely introduced before his death.

These authors, one and all, have definitely captured the ERB magic. Anyone with fond memories of the Burroughs *ouevre* will surely enjoy this book. Anyone who's wondered what the fuss is all about should give it a try. And for anyone who's unsuccessfully tried to read Burroughs (it helps to be 11 years old), *The Worlds of Edgar Rice Burroughs* offers a perfectly-accessible entry point.

The Year's Best Science Fiction, Twenty-Ninth Annual Collection
edited by Gardner Dozois
St. Martin's, 704 pages, $21.99 (trade paperback)
iBooks, Kindle, Nook: $9.99 (e-book)
ISBN: 978-1-250-00355-3
Genre: Literary SF, Short Stories

This one is for the literary folks. If they read sf, they wouldn't be caught dead reading *Analog*; if they don't read sf, they are certainly devotees of Margaret Atwood and Michael Chabon.

Gardner Dozois, hard-working editor of our sister publication *Isaac Asimov's Science Fiction Magazine*, performs the annual Herculean task of bringing together the prestige anthology of the science fiction universe. As massive as they are authoritative, each volume is packed with stories (this year there are 35) as well as a scholarly retrospective of the year.

Well, different editors and different readers have different tastes, and Gardner's idea of a great story isn't necessarily that of the average *Analog* reader. *The Year's Best Science Fiction* collections are weighed more in the direction of literary quality and less in the direction of rigorous science (this time around only one story—Alec Navala-Lee's "The Boneless One"—was published in *Analog*). I'm not being negative here; these are all good stories, well worth reading. The list of authors includes John Barnes, Peter S. Beagle, Elizabeth Bear, Michael A. Flynn, Robert Reed, Geoff Ryman, Michael Swanwick, and dozens more, all masters of the craft.

The literary sf reader will be in heaven. As for the literary non-sf reader, you'll only have to do a little bit of persuasion. Point to the "Year's Best" in the title and the phrase "Award Winning" on the cover. Let them heft the book, examine the small type, and inspect the eight-page "Honorable Mention" list at the end. This is clearly an Important Literary Book. Finally, mention Peter S. Beagle, Robert Reed, and Cory Doctorow. That will surely perk up their ears.

The Year's Best Science Fiction: Thirtieth Annual Collection
edited by Gardner Dozois
St. Martin's Griffin, 704 pages, $22.99 (trade paperback)
iBooks: $10.99, Kindle: $9.78, Nook: $10.99 (ebook)
ISBN: 9781250029133
Series: Year's Best Science Fiction
Genre: Literary SF, Short Stories

Some people on your list might like the finer things: an award-winning bottle of wine, a collection of Oscar-winning movies, designer clothing. A collection of the year's best science fiction is tailor made for such folks.

Editor Garner Dozois has been doing this for an incredible thirty years; he clearly knows his stuff. His "best of the year" picks tend to gravitate toward a more self-consciously literary sf than usually appears in *Analog*—still, this current volume does include Richard A. Lovett and William Gleason's "Nightfall on the Peak of Eternal Light," which you may remember from the July/August 2012 issue. The remaining twenty-odd stories are from a variety of critically-acclaimed sources.

Names like Christopher Barzak, Michael Bishop, Pat Cadigan, and Robert Reed will certainly appeal to more literary readers. There's a good deal of experimental writing this year, most notably including Vandana Singh's "Ruminations in an Alien Tongue" and Lavie Tidhar's "The Memcordist"—very avant-garde, brimming with otherness.

Dozois includes the usual retrospective of the year 2012 in science fiction, and an exhaustive list of runners-up. Your friend with discerning taste will find much to like here.

Reviews: Nonfiction

(alphabetical by author)

In Other Worlds: SF and the Human Imagination
Margaret Atwood
Doubleday, 272 pages, $24.95 (hardcover)
Kindle, Nook: $12.99 (e-book)
ISBN: 978-0-385-53396-6
Genre: Biography, Literary SF

Which brings us to Margaret Atwood. She has firmly established her credentials as a writer of LitSF; besides *The Handmaid's Tale*, she featured an sf story within her novel *The Blind Assassin*, and jumped on the postapocalyptic bandwagon with *Oryx and Crake* and *The Year of the Flood*. Despite her insistence that she writes "speculative fiction" instead of "science fiction," here she has written "an exploration of [her] own lifelong relationship" with sf.

There are three major sections. First, she spends a few somewhat autobiographical chapters musing about what sf has meant to her and to society. Next, in the real meat of the book, she discusses some classic works of LitSF. Finally, she gives five short excerpts of her own published work, either sf or reflections on sf.

In the center section, Atwood offers some insightful thoughts about the works of Marge Piercy, H. Rider Haggard, Ursula K. LeGuin, Bill McKibben, George Orwell, H. G. Wells, Kazuo Ishiguro, Aldous Huxley, and Jonathan Swift. (I know... what's Haggard doing there? You'll find out.)

Atwood's book may bring a larger awareness of LitSF to her legions of readers; but why should *Analog* readers care? Well, she's a good writer and a profound thinker; many of the things she says are equally applicable to traditional sf. Do you want to shell out 25 bucks for a hardcover? Probably not. Get the e-book, or wait for the paperback.

Starship Century
edited by James Benford & Gregory Benford
Microwave Sciences, 340 pages, $24.00 (trade paperback)
ISBN: 9781939051295
Genre: Exploration and Discovery, Nonfiction, Short Fiction

I'm sure you know someone who's so socially conscious that they would rather not receive material presents...they usually ask you, instead, to contribute to any number of charitable causes aimed at making the world a better place.

Too bad—this year they're getting a book. But *Starship Century* isn't just any book.

The first Starship Century Symposium in October 2011 brought together scientists, futurists, sf writers, and space enthusiasts to spur serious discussion of NASA's 100 Year Starship Project. The ultimate goal is to begin interstellar exploration within the next century.

Starship Century, the book, grew out of the symposium, and includes both nonfiction and sf pieces. The thing that's sure to please your philanthropist friend is that proceeds from the book go to support research on interstellar travel.

The roll call of authors in this book is an impressive one. On the science fact side we have Freeman Dyson, Stephen Hawking, Geoffrey Landis, Martin Rees, Robert Zubrin, and others—on the science fiction side are Stephen Baxter, Gregory Benford, David Brin, John Cramer, Joe Haldeman, Nancy Kress, Allen Steele, and Neal Stephenson.

Among the stories is Joe Haldeman's "Tricentennial," which appeared in *Analog* way back in 1976. The others are all new, and dramatize an array of technologies related to interstellar travel, from generation ships to space elevators. Allen Steele gives us a new Coyote story, Nancy Kress mixes agriculture and psychology, and David Brin explores what happens when that generation ship finally arrives at its destination. Anyone seriously concerned for the future of humanity needs to be aware of the 100 Year Starship Project, to be familiar with the ideas and challenges of interstellar exploration, and to support the effort. *Starship Century* is a better place to start than most. Buy two, and keep one for yourself.

Wookiee-Ookies
Kevin Bolk
Interrobang Studios, 16 pages, $5.00
Ensign Sue Must Die
Clare Moseley and Kevin Bolk
Interrobang Studios, 32 pages, $6.00
Purchase from *interrobangstudios.com*
Genre: Nonfiction

And now, as they say, for something completely different. I know I said science fiction was primarily a literary form, but sf is also movies, and comics, and humor. These two full-color books of comic strips combine all three in a package that's enchanting, whimsical, and too funny for mere words.

Artist Kevin Bolk draws his characters in the style that the Japanese call "chibi" and we refer to as "cute." With oversize heads and enormous eyes, even the obvious adult characters appear to be a well-seasoned ten years old. Yet these aren't Peanuts kids...their humor owes more to South Park than to Charles M. Schulz.

Wookiee-Ookies is, as you'd expect, a series of twisted *Star Wars* parodies. Each four-panel strip stands on its own and makes a definite joke, usually irreverent and always funny. Princess Leia's reaction to dinner with Jabba the Hutt ("I hate Internet dating") is only one of the treats.

Ensign Sue Must Die is a continuing story set in the universe of the most recent *Star Trek* movie. It chronicles the adventures of a perky newcomer to the *Enterprise*, Ensign Mary Amethyst Star Enoby Aiko Archer Picard Janeway Sue, as she inspires dread and hatred in the other members of the crew. The poor crewmembers try everything they can think of to get rid of Ensign Sue, but she keeps coming back for more.

The story and art are funny enough on their own terms, but *Ensign Sue Must Die* is also a clever meta-commentary on the so-called "Mary Sue" phenomenon, in which fan writers insert themselves as characters ("Mary Sue") in their favorite TV shows or movies. *Ensign Sue Must Die* skewers every dreadful trope of the Mary Sue story, and ends with a horrifying evil loosed on the worlds of fiction.

The Lives of Stars
By Ken Croswell
Boyds Mill Press, 72 pages, $19.95 (hardcover)
Genre: Nonfiction (ages 10-14)

Long ago, when the world was young and I was a precocious pre-teen proto-SF-reader just discovering *Tom Swift* and *Tom Corbett, Space Cadet*, I had two favorite nonfiction books: *All About the Planets* by Patricia Lauber and *Life in Other Solar Systems* by Frederick I. Ordway III. I checked both of those out from the library so often that my parents were forced to buy me copies of my own. Both books had a very strong influence on my developing interest in astronomy, science in general, and science fiction. The fact that I remember them more than forty years later shows you how much of an impact they made on me. I'll bet you have a book or two like that from your own childhood.

If you have a similarly precocious pre-teen in your life, you might want to give them a copy of *The Lives of Stars*. This is a big, beautiful, full-color book chock full of gorgeous Hubble images and in-depth text that should be easily accessible to any bright third– or fourth-grader. The book discusses (and illustrates) the life cycle of stars, from nebulae to main sequence to nova, neutron star, or black hole. This is all the latest state-of-the-art information, as up to date as any book can be.

The Lives of Stars doesn't shy away from hardcore science: it explains the Hertzsprung-Russell diagram, Cepheid variables, and the origin of elements, and is full of all sorts of interesting facts (for example, the Milky Way galaxy gives birth to about ten new stars per year, and tin is primarily formed in red giants rather than supernovae). In addition, there are a few chapters that lead nicely into science fiction territory, discussing extrasolar planets and extraterrestrial life.

Ken Croswell is a Ph.D. in astronomy who has written other astronomy books for kids; your precocious pre-teen will be in good hands. But before you give this book to the kid (or kids) in your life, take some time to look through it yourself—you're sure to enjoy it, and you will probably learn something you didn't know. Much fun indeed.

Galaxiki: A Fictional galaxy That Anyone Can Edit
www.galaxiki.org
Genre: Nonfiction

If you're sick and tired of battles, action, and endless destruction, why not take a vacation and build something up?

Galaxiki isn't a book, it isn't a game...but it *is* science fiction. Sort of.

Created by Joopita Research as a nonprofit project, *Galaxiki* is a cross between Wikipedia, Facebook, and your favorite Galactic Empire. It's a fictional galaxy that claims to have 1.1 million planetary systems open for exploration—all of them generated according to some principles of astronomy and astrophysics.

Just looking around would be interesting enough, but there's more: users can edit those planetary systems, giving the planets names, inhabitants, whole ecologies. Many systems are community property which anyone can edit, a la Wikipedia.

For a nominal charge ($1 as I write this), one can purchase a planetary system for one's exclusive use.

There are all the usual social media accouterments: one can communicate with other members; share lists of your favorite books, movies, music, etc.; or discuss topics (including science fiction, of course) in forums. There are also options to buy a planetary system as a gift for someone else, or to "liberate" one for use by the community.

Currently Galaxiki has over 5,000 members and over 15,000 registered stars (only 1,085,000 left!), and seems to be a fairly lively place. It seems to be a place that any sf reader would appreciate; certainly worth a look.

The Science of Fear
By Daniel Gardner
Dutton, 339 pages, $24.95 (hardcover)
ISBN: 978-0-525-95062-2
Genre: Nonfiction

Over the last few decades, while the rest of us were paying attention to astrophysics, biochemistry, and genetics, the science of psychology has been up to quite a bit. In particular, psychology has discovered a lot about the mechanisms by which we experience fear…and how we misunderstand the whole process.

In *The Science of Fear*, journalist Daniel Gardner takes us on a fascinating guided tour of the way irrational fears result from human tendencies to miscalculate risk. He opens the book with an analysis of the American public's fear of flying in the wake of September 11, 2001, a fear that prompted many to drive instead of taking a plane. The problem is that mile-for-mile, driving is much riskier than flying. In the year it took for travel patterns to go back to normal, there were 1,595 "excess" deaths from automobile accidents. Nearly 1,600 people died because of fear.

Gardner reviews recent findings in evolutionary psychology that explain why we have such trouble accurately assessing risks. The human brain consists of two separate systems of thought. One, based in the midbrain and underlying structures, is intuitive, quick, and emotional. The other system, based in the frontal cortex, is calculating, slow, and rational. Gardner calls the two "Gut" and "Head." Brain scans show that Gut's reactions are instantaneous and automatic, while Head is much more deliberate. Head can override Gut, but only with difficulty.

Thus, we have innate automatic fear (or fear's relative, disgust) of things like falling and rotten meat. With a good deal of conscious effort, we can overcome that fear/disgust and even, over time, eliminate it.

Identifying a few simple rules that Gut uses to evaluate risk, Gardner takes us through the worlds of economics, advertising, politics, crime, and terrorism (among others). Along the way, he reveals various delightful non-intuitive results, such as why people can be terrified of nuclear power but oblivious to the threat of Tunguska-like impact events; why we insist that marijuana is a dangerous drug but alcohol merely an amusing indulgence; or why Europeans can demonstrate against the imagined health risks of genetically-engineered food while chain-smoking cigarettes.

Gardner maintains a completely rational viewpoint throughout the book, but he also presents his subject with compassion and welcome humor. If we're all genetically inclined to be irrational, then Gardner is right there with us, and he offers techniques to help Head do a better job of overriding Gut. This book could be dreary and depressing; instead, it winds up being a lot of fun.

Claws & Saucers: Science Fiction, Horror, and Fantasy Film 1902-1982
David Elroy Goldweber
Lulu, 682 pages, $47.95 (paperback)
iBooks, Kindle, Nook: $8.95 (e-book)
ISBN: 978-1-105-04350-5
Genre: Movies, Nonfiction

In this age of handheld, always-connected devices and multiple billions of websites, when the assembled knowledge and wisdom of the human race is only a few clicks or taps away, one might think that the age of enormous, encyclopedic directories is over.

One would be wrong.

Eighty years of sf, horror, and fantasy movies make for a gargantuan amount of information. David Elroy Goldweber has boiled it all down to the essentials that matter to those of us who watch these films for fun. You'd have to comb dozens of websites to get the kind of valuable stuff he packs into one entry for a single film.

From *Abbot and Costello Go to Mars* all the way to *Z.P.G.*, here's what you get. There's the standard filmographic info: title, producer, run time, format, date. What's Happening: a one-line blurb. Famous For: the distinguishing characteristics that fans care about (popular cult classic, notable performances, same director as a more famous film, etc.)

But wait, there's more. A detailed discussion, ranging from one paragraph to several, tells you exactly what your most knowledgeable friend would want you to know about the film. These discussions are the meat of the book, and make for fascinating and fun reading. Ever since this book showed up in the mailbox, I've been dipping into it at random and enjoying essays on films I have no intention of ever watching. It's that kind of guide.

Goldweber goes on to rate each movie on a scale of 1 to 10 on five dimensions: Action, Gore, Sex, Quality, and Camp. In addition, he has a "Don't miss" line to highlight one special moment from each movie, and also a cleverly-titled quote from each.

If you have any interest in genre films, if you want to impress and amuse your friends on movie night, or if you just enjoy compellingly-written trivia, you want this book. The paper version is about the size of a phone book but has better paper and much more readable type; it's pricey but would make a great present for your favorite genre film buff. The much-more-affordable e-book is a must for anyone who likes genre movies.

Physics of the Impossible
Michio Kaku
Doubleday, 329 pages, $26.95 (hardcover)
ISBN: 978-0-385-52069-0
Genre: Nonfiction

This book is subtitled "A Scientific Exploration into the World of Phasers, Force Fields, Teleportation, and Time Travel," and that pretty much sums it up. Michio Kaku is a real physicist, Henry Semat Professor of Theoretical Physics at the Graduate Center of the City University of New York, famous for helping to develop string field theory and appearing on popular-science TV shows all over the place. He certainly has scientific credentials; and what's more, his Acknowledgments include numerous colleagues, many of them Nobel laureates.

Still, this is a book aimed at the general public...or at least the subset of the general public who watch Discovery or the Science Channel, and read popular science books. *Analog* readers may find this volume a little simplistic. To a veteran sf reader, a lot of this is old hat.

Still, let me give Kaku his due. He is an sf reader—or at least he was, before theoretical physics stole him away. When he draws examples from sf, he doesn't stop at pop-culture Hollywood offerings like *Star Trek*, *Star Wars*, or Spielberg; he alludes to actual writers like Asimov, Clarke and even van Vogt.

Still, *Physics of the Impossible* is a fair example of its type, which we might call "Scientist explains the real science behind popular sf/fantasy movies or TV shows." There have been a plethora of these books in recent years: *The Physics of Star Trek*, *The Science of Star Wars*, *The Physics of Superheroes*, even *The Science of Harry Potter*. And like its siblings, *Physics of the Impossible* somehow manages to both misunderstand and underestimate real science fiction.

Kaku, like others, seems to be under the impression that the main business of sf is prediction—whereas we know that prediction is just a sideline. Again and again, his tone sounds a little condescending to the poor creators of sf (who, since they aren't actually scientists, can't be expected to get their physics absolutely right). He presents a concept from sf—the *Enterprise's* force shields, for example, or faster-than-light travel—and explains how it couldn't possibly happen the way it's presented. He then tells us how the creators could have gotten it right, if only they had paid attention to real science and engineering principles. Okay, obviously the *Enterprise* couldn't have real shields of force, but the crew could possibly erect an invisible barrier composed of "a combination of plasma window, laser curtain, and carbon nanotube screen." Of course, even this shield, being invisible, would be incapable of stopping laser beams, so you'd need to add "photochromatics," molecules that can change their optical properties when exposed to laser light.

Silly sf writers, getting it wrong that way....

Kaku falls into the old chestnut of using "science fiction" as a synonym for "nonsense." Witness his reaction to the idea of hyperspace travel: "Science fiction? Undoubtedly. But could it be based on scientific fact? Perhaps."

Kaku divides his impossibilities into three classes. Class I Impossibilities are technologies that don't violate the known laws of physics; he says that these may be possible "in this century, or perhaps the next, in modified form." These include such topics as Force Fields, Invisibility, Teleportation, Physchokinesis, Robots, Starships, and Antimatter.

Class II Impossibilities are those that "sit at the very edge of our understanding of the physical world." If possible at all, these might be "millennia or millions of years in the future." Kaku counts FTL Travel, Time Travel, and Parallel Universes as Class II.

Class III Impossibilities violate the known laws of physics, and so are actually impossible without "a fundamental shift in our understanding of physics." There are only two Class III Impossibilities: Perpetual Motion Machines and Precognition.

So if *Physics of the Impossible* is old hat to most *Analog* readers, who would be a good audience for this book? For one, it would make a nice gift to a bright child who likes sf movies and TV, but doesn't have a lot of background in written sf. And it might serve as a counter to others—parents, teachers, even peers—who might be trying to dissuade such a child from pursuing an interest in sf. "See, *Stargate* is based on real science, so it's educational…you *have* to let me watch it now."

What Technology Wants
Kevin Kelly
Viking, 406 pages, $27.95 (hardcover)
Kindle, Nook: $14.99 (ebook)
ISBN: 978-0-670-02215-1
Genre: Nonfiction

Kevin Kelly, former executive editor of *Wired* magazine, has been described as a "philosopher of technology." He begins *What Technology Wants* with an essay on his own love/hate relationship with modern technology, then introduces the questions that structure the book: where is technology going? What will that mean to us? In short, what does technology want?

To answer, he explores the long history of technology (starting in pre-Human times), using the metaphor of technology as a living ecosystem (what he calls "The Technium.") He posits the theory that the Technium, like life itself, proceeds through processes akin to natural selection and evolution.

On his journey, Kelly examines technology's critics, from the Amish to the Unabomber. He suggests ways that the rest of us can benefit from some of the valid points of those critics. He suggests that we treat technology and gadgets as tools, not masters, and that as a society we devote thought to steering the direction of the Technium's development, rather than allowing it to steer ours.

This is no anti-technology rant, though. Kelly is an enthusiastic booster of technology and its possibilities, and he explains fully all the benefits that we derive from the continuing growth of the Technium.

The concepts and metaphors in which Kelly deals are old hat to science fiction readers (look no further than Robert J. Sawyer, above). Like most popularizers, Kelly sometimes oversimplifies, and he misses some of the rigorous details of cosmology, quantum physics, and evolutionary biology. Still, his musings are interesting, and provide a nonfiction counterpoint to many of the ideas that sf writers and readers have been exploring in recent decades. To get a sense of what current-day technologists are thinking and talking about, this is definitely a worthwhile read.

Jar Jar Binks Must Die...and Other Observations about Science Fiction Movies
Daniel M. Kimmel
Fantastic Books, 189 pages, $14.99 (trade paperback)
ISBN: 978-1-61720-061-8
Genres: Movies, Nonfiction

Short isn't just for stories. The nonfiction equivalent of the short story is the essay—and essays are popular for much the same reason as short stories.

Daniel M. Kimmel is a science fiction fan and movie reviewer. In this volume he's collected several dozen short essays on science fiction (and related genre) films. These aren't reviews, written to help you decided whether or not to see the movie; these essay generally assume that the reader is familiar with most of the movies mentioned.

Kimmel obviously loves SF, and that love shines through even when he's castigating individual films. Whether he's explaining why *Metropolis* is such an important film, or joining in with the obligatory George Lucas bashing, his writing is intelligent and entertaining. You may disagree with him (in fact, you almost certainly will on *something*), but you can't say he doesn't give reasoned arguments in support of his positions. And his knowledge of SF movies is encyclopedic.

This is the guy you want sitting next to you when Channel 45 has a weekend "sci-fi" movie marathon.

For anyone who likes SF movies, this volume is worth the price of admission.

From the Pen of Paul: The Fantastic Images of Frank R. Paul
edited by Stephen D. Korshak
Shasta/Phoenix, 128 / 144 / 160 pages, $39.95 / $59.95 / $395.00
ISBN: 978-0-9800-931-1-7 (hardcover) / 978-0-9800-931-2-4 (deluxe) / 978-0-9800-931-3-1 (ultra deluxe)
www.shasta-phoenix.com
Genre: Biography, Nonfiction

As long as there's been science fiction, there's been science fiction art. And at the very beginning of science fiction art, there was Frank R. Paul.

Shashta/Phoenix has produced a magnificent coffee table book (9 x 12 inches) showcasing the life and work of Frank R. Paul. Paul has been called "the father of science fiction art," and if anyone can lay claim to that title, it's Paul. Among the thousands of pieces he created were some of the most famous and iconic images of science fiction—including the cover of *Amazing Stories* number 1, early issues of *Astounding*, and the first book covers of such classics as *The Skylark of Space* and John W. Campbell's *The Mightiest Machine*.

When you think of pulp sf, you're probably thinking of Frank R. Paul illustrations. Bright colors, fantastic air- and space-craft, futuristic cities, magnificent planetary vistas, odd aliens—he did it all, and inspired countless others to follow his lead.

There's plenty of textual information in this book: biographies of Paul, an appreciation by Forrest J. Ackerman, a preface by Arthur C. Clarke, and a detailed bibliographical index. But the best part of the book is the pages upon pages of Paul magazine covers and paintings, reproduced in full gorgeous color. I can't imagine an sf reader who could walk by this book without picking it up, or leaf through it without getting snared for hours.

The book comes in three different editions. The Hardcover Trade Edition has 128 pages and costs $39.95; it is a limited edition of 1,000 copies.

The Deluxe Edition has 160 pages, including much more art, and has a slipcase. This one costs $59.95 and is limited to 874 copies.

The Ultra Deluxe Edition is leatherbound and slipcased, and signed by Sir Arthur as well as editor Stephen D. Korshak and contributors Jerry Weist and Robert Hill. There are 126 numbered copies, and the cost is $395.00. All three editions are available from the Shasta/Phoenix website listed above.

Whether you want to relive the nostalgia of those long-ago days, or you're a young whippersnapper who wants to see what all the excitement was about, you ought to treat yourself to this volume. If you're going to spring for the Hardcover, take my advice and scrape up the extra twenty bucks for the Deluxe Edition: it's definitely worth it.

How to Defeat Your Own Clone: And Other Tips for Surviving the Biotech Revolution
Kyle Kurpinski & Terry D. Johnson
Bantam, 180 pages, $14.00 (trade paperback)
ISBN: 978-0-533-38578-6
Genre: Nonfiction

It's hard to glance at a newsfeed nowadays without seeing something about biotechnology. Even for *Analog* readers—who've been thinking about genetic engineering and advances in biology almost as long as we've been contemplating nuclear power and environmental disasters—the field of biotech is moving so quickly and in so many directions that it's hard to keep up. If only someone would wade through all the research and tell us what's important right now. And while they're at it, it would be great if they could manage to make it all funny.

Our prayers have been answered.

Kyle Kurpinski has a Ph.D. in Bioengineering and works on technologies for tissue regeneration; Terry D. Johnson lectures in the bioengineering department at the University of California, Berkeley. It's safe to say that these guys know their subject.

They start off with a timeline of biotechnology advances, beginning with 15,000 B.C.E. when humans domesticate dogs. "Having acquired a best friend, the human race decides to see if there's anything else in nature that could use a bit of tweaking." Then they move on to present two conflicting scenarios for the future. In the dystopian one, a proliferation of Chuck Norris and Bruce Lee clones leads to "the most incredible yearlong kung fu battle ever." In the utopian future, "Every child rides to school on a genetically engineered unicorn (trademarked 'My Little Rhino-pony')."

The remaining chapters take a lighthearted look at the basics of genetics and biology, and then deal with such matters as cloning, bio-enhancements, engineering other lifeforms, and finally the all-important tips for defeating your own clone ("The best you can hope for is to persuade your friends and family to enter into a temporary truce while you and your duplicate sort this out for yourselves.")

If you're looking for a book that will bring you (or a friend) up to speed on current trends in biotech, while at the same time giving you plenty of laughs, this is the book for you.

Why Beautiful People Have More Daughters
Alan S. Miller and Satoshi Kanazawa
Penguin, 252 pages, $23.95 (Hardcover)
ISBN: 978-0-399-53365-5
Genre: Nonfiction

Psychology and sociology, the sciences of human behavior, are in the midst of a revolution. The relatively new field of evolutionary psychology does just what its name says: seeks to explain human nature through the principles of evolution.

Miller and Kanazawa present a tour of evolutionary psychology for the intelligent layman, coming up with some unexpected conclusions.

First, the authors talk about a few principles necessary for understanding evolutionary psychology. First, there's the eternal question of nature vs. nurture, and the fact that neither provides a complete explanation of human behavior. Next, they caution against two fallacies: the naturalistic fallacy and the moralistic fallacy. The naturalistic fallacy equates "natural" with "good" and says that just because a behavior exists, it is to be preferred; the moralistic fallacy equates what is "moral" with what exists and claims that because a behavior is desired, then it actually exists. Finally, they deal with the question of stereotypes: while useful, they are not to be confused with accurate descriptions of the world.

The rest of the book is filled with provocative questions and the answers provided by evolutionary psychology. For example, Why are most human societies polygynous (one man with many wives) and so few polyandrous (one woman with many husbands)? The answer: Due to their different reproductive methods, it makes genetic sense for a man to have as many children as they can, by as many women as possible— while it makes more genetic sense for women to have children only with men who will provide protection and sustenance for her kids.

Or there's the title question: why do beautiful people have more daughters? Well, physically attractive women are more desired as both short-term and long-term mates, while physically attractive men are more desired as short-term mates but not as long-term mates. So beauty contributes more to female reproductive success than to male success, so the genes of beautiful people are more successfully passed on through daughters than through sons. And in fact, the authors say, being rated "very attractive" increases the odds of having a daughter by 36 percent.

Some of the other questions answered in this volume are "Why are almost all violent criminals male?" and "Where does religion come from?" There are even speculations on the roots of such behaviors as soldiers dying for their country or people committing suicide.

For any science fiction reader interested in the behavior of sapient creatures and the evolutionary origins of that behavior, this is an entertaining and educational read.

Rocket Girl
George D. Morgan
Prometheus Books, 325 pages, $18.00 (trade paperback)
ISBN: 978-1-61614-739-6
Genre: Biography, Nonfiction

Do you have a history buff on your gift list? Perhaps your gifts include actual historical objects (an intact World War II ration book, for example), or the latest set of DVDs from the History Channel, or patterns for historical garments? You're probably afraid to get this person a book, because chances are they've already read it.

Never fear. Your friend has almost certainly never heard of Mary Sherman Morgan—but will be very interested in her story.

Mary was a simple girl from North Dakota. In the late 1930s, when few women undertook careers in science, Mary became a chemist and went to work for North American Aviation.

After the war, German rocket builder Werner von Braun came to the United States to produce American rockets. When he ran into difficulties, North American Aviation sent in Mary. Between the two of them, America's space program was born. Von Braun went on to fame, while Mary faded into obscurity.

Author George D. Morgan, Mary's son, tells two stories in this book. The first is Mary's story—the second is the story of George's search for Mary's history, a search through long-buried historical sources, declassified military records, and personal interviews with survivors.

Together, the two stories offer a fascinating look at this previously-unknown chemist who played such a pivotal role in the beginning of the Space Age.

Time Travel
Paul J. Nahin
Johns Hopkins University Press, 200 pages, $24.95 (trade paperback)
Kindle: $9.99 (ebook)
ISBN: 978-1-4214-0082-2
Genre: Nonfiction

Someone at the Johns Hopkins University Press likes science fiction.

First it was *The Science of Doctor Who* by Paul Parsons, now Paul J. Nahin's *Time Travel: A Writer's Guide to the Real Science of Plausible Time Travel*. This is a new expanded edition of Nahin's 1998 book *Time Machines*, brought up to date with current speculation in physics and cosmology. After an introductory history of time travel in the pulps, Nahin examines ten approaches to time travel, from hyperspace and wormholes to quantum gravity and parallel universes. He ends up with a helpful chapter called "Reading the Physics Literature for Story Ideas."

For a book dealing with some heavy-duty concepts, Nahin's tone is light and playful, a pleasure to read. Whether you're a writer who wants to find a new time travel gimmick, or a reader who wants to appreciate what authors are talking about, you'll find this book both fun and educational.

Scatter, Adapt, and Remember: How Humans Will Survive a Mass Extinction
Annalee Newitz
Doubleday, 320 pages, $26.95 (Hardcover)
iBooks, Kindle, Nook: $13.99 (ebook)
ISBN: 978-0385535915
Genre: Nonfiction

Last but not least, a book that makes a great gift for just about anyone with the slightest bit of apprehension about the world.

Annalee Newitz gives us a well-written, entertaining book filled with unexpected insights, fascinating facts, and more than its share of ideas. It's a quintessentially science fictional book—who but sf readers and writers worry about how humanity can survive mass extinctions? (Quite a number of scientists, as it turns out.)

Newitz begins by examining the previous mass extinctions, and how life survived each of them. Catastrophic climate change, atmospheric poisoning, volcanic eruptions, asteroid impacts—all have nearly destroyed life on Earth.

She then moves into Human history and talks about several near-extinctions in our past: the so-called African Bottleneck that reduced our numbers to a few thousand, the fate of the Neanderthals, history's great plagues, and great famines.

Now she brings together all the parts of the story to identify survival strategies that work best. No surprise: those strategies are scatter, adapt, and remember.

The second half of the book builds on the insights of the first, as she discusses how to build extinction-proof future cities, and then goes on to talk about how humanity could meet the fairly modest goal of surviving for another million years.

Newitz freely admits being inspired by science fiction—particularly the work of Octavia Butler—and gives fair credit to science fiction for being ahead of the curve and pointing the way.

This is both a fascinating book and an inspiring one, well-grounded in a variety of sciences and downright fun to read.

The Science of Doctor Who
Paul Parsons
Johns Hopkins University Press, 320 pages, $24.95
   ((hardcover)
ISBN: 978-0-8018-9560-9
Genre: Nonfiction

Doctor Who is the best science fiction on television today. Don't believe me: just look at the Hugo Awards, where the show has garnered ten separate nominations and three wins in four years.

It had to happen that someone would write *The Science of Doctor Who*, and we're all very fortunate that Paul Parsons was the one who did it.

First, his qualifications. Parsons is not only a science journalist, he also describes himself as a "lifelong *Doctor Who* fan." It shows. Although he certainly has a light tone with a fair amount of humor, he never falls into the trap of disrespecting or ridiculing the source material. And believe me, with some of the early *Doctor Who* episodes, disrespect and ridicule would be completely understandable.

Instead, Parsons gives us an entertaining and educational look at both 45 years of *Doctor Who* and cutting-edge science. After a brief introduction to the *Doctor Who* phenomenon, he uses various elements of the show as jumping-off points to discuss scientific research that's somehow related. For example, he considers the evolutionary biology behind the title character's altruism; uses the Doctor's sonic screwdriver to speculate on the use of sound in materials science; and considers what sort of genetic engineering could bring about an emotionless cyborg species like the Daleks. And he does all this on a level a little above the usual Discovery Channel or

PBS documentary. The average Analog reader won't feel talked-down-to.

Don't worry if you've never seen *Doctor Who* (but why not?): Parsons explains the relevant parts of the show and its backstory in easy, entertaining prose. But if you are familiar with the Doctor from the planet Gallifrey, you'll find many delightful touches and in-jokes that will make the book even more fun.

If you only read one *Science of* XYZ book this year, make it this one.

Robert A. Heinlein: In Dialogue With His Century:
    Volume 1
William H. Patterson, Jr.
Tor, 622 pages, $29.99 (hardcover)
iBooks, Kindle, Nook: $14.99 (ebook)
ISBN: 978-0-7653-1960-9
Genre: Biography

Remember when I said that a book could be "eagerly awaited" because of its subject matter. Here is a perfect case in point: volume one of the authorized biography of Robert A. Heinlein.

To a large degree, science fiction is what it is because of Robert A. Heinlein. He gave shape to the field during the Campbell Revolution, he spread sf out of its pulp ghetto and into the popular culture. His teen sf books brought multitudes of new readers to the genre (and, not incidentally, multitudes to careers in science and technology). He blazed trails that the rest of us are still following, nearly a quarter-century after his death.

Yet this cornerstone figure was an intensely private man, and only the barest outline of his private life was known. In a field in which writers have always had intimate connection with their readers, Heinlein was something of an enigma.

No longer.

William H. Patterson, Jr. starts at the very beginning, and takes us through Heinlein's childhood, his training at the Naval Academy, two of his three wives (everyone thought there were only two!), and his subsequent career up to the postwar years and his marriage to Virginia. In between we learn of his health problems, his adventures and misadventures in politics, and a great deal more of the influences that made the man who was rightly called "the Dean of Science Fiction."

If you know Heinlein's writing at all, you'll have a grand old time pointing and saying "So that's where that came from!" every few pages. If you think you know something of Heinlein's philosophical or political beliefs, you'll find yourself surprised more than once. And if you just want to read about the fascinating life of an amazing man, you'll get that, too.

This volume one was certainly "eagerly awaited" in the sf field. And volume two will surely be the most eagerly awaited science fiction biography...well, ever.

Death From the Skies!
Philip Plait, Ph.D.
Viking, 326 pages, $25.95 (hardcover)
ISBN: 978-0-670-01997-7
Genre: Nonfiction

Philip Plait is a professional astronomer and runs the popular-science website *www.badastronomy.com*. In *Death From the Skies!* he's produced a fun yet factual book that should be of interest to just about any *Analog* reader (or writer!)

In nine chapters of easy, informal prose, Plait examines and explains many different astronomical phenomena that could result in the end of the world. From asteroid impacts and solar flare-ups to crashing galaxies and the heat-death of the universe, Plait educates his readers in modern astronomy, astrophysics, and cosmology. Along the way he touches on supernovae, gamma-ray bursts, stellar evolution, mass extinction events, the history of the universe, and even the possibilities of alien life.

Plait's style recalls the playfulness of George Gamow and the sense-of-wonder of Carl Sagan. There's plenty of humor here; the first sentence is "The universe is trying to kill you." What's not to like?

By the time you finish *Death From the Skies!* you will learn something, even if you start with the average *Analog* reader's familiarity with modern astronomical knowledge. And you'll certainly know a few more ways to destroy the planet. (A helpful appendix lists 24 nearby stars that will eventually go supernova.) When you're done, you can give the book to a bright child or other science enthusiast in confidence that they will enjoy it as well.

Hank Reinhardt's Book of Knives
Hank Reinhardt
Baen, 180 pages, $13.00 (trade paperback)
Baen Ebooks: $6.00 (e-book)
ISBN: 978-1-4516-3755-7
Genre: Nonfiction

Do you know someone who's a military enthusiast? How about a gamer? Or anyone who writes sf, fantasy, thrillers, mysteries, or historical fiction? This is a weird one, invaluable to the right person. It's not sf, but certainly of interest to many in the sf community.

Hank Reinhardt was a student of fighting styles. In this well-researched and highly readable book, he presents everything there is to know about knives and knife fighting, complete with pictures and diagrams. From the history of knives through such chapters as "the street knife," "knife concealment," and "wounds," Reinhardt dispels all the Hollywood myths of what knife fighting is like. (Example: "Holding the blade with the edge up may look tough and macho, but...limits your mobility.")

Reinhardt passed away before completing the book; one of his students, Greg Phillips, completed the chapters on choosing a knife and acquiring skills.

For someone who is interested in the subject, this book gives a wealth of information.

The Business of Science Fiction: Two Insiders Discuss Writing and Publishing
Mike Resnick and Barry N. Malzberg
McFarland, 269 pages, $35.00 (trade paperback)
ISBN: 978-0-7864-4797-8
Genre: Nonfiction

Between them, Mike Resnick and Barry N. Malzberg have published over 150 books. Both are legends in the field. When the two of them get together to discuss the state of SF and the publishing industry, who wouldn't be interested in what they say?

Well, for more than a decade, these two hardworking writers have been doing just that in the pages of the *Bulletin of the Science Fiction and Fantasy Writers of America*. Now 26 of these dialogues have been collected in one volume, and it's every bit as fascinating, educational, and downright fun as you'd expect.

The topics break down into three main subject areas: Writing and Selling, The Business, and The Field. Under the first heading, topics range from the marketplace to conventions to collaborations. In the second section, they discuss such mysteries as agents, professionalism, print-on-demand, and the irresistible "really dumb ideas." And in the third section these two writers, who have been part of the SF scene forever, talk about the history and future direction of the field.

Obviously, if you're an aspiring writer (I think there are one or two still around), you won't want to miss this volume. At $35 it might seem a little pricey, but if you think of it as a textbook for a writing class, it's a bargain. One caveat, though

—the publishing industry is currently in the grip of enormous changes, and what was good advice ten years ago might be less applicable two years from now. Still, an awful lot of what appears here is timeless.

For the non-writing fan of SF, this book might be a harder sell. If it helps, this is a fun and engaging read—Resnick and Malzberg are good writers, after all—and there's a fair amount of interesting gossip about the SF publishing world (nothing salacious or titillating, I hasten to add). If you have any interest in what goes on behind the scenes of the books and magazines you read, this is a painless way to find out.

C. M. Kornbluth: The Life and Works of a Science Fiction Visionary
Mark Rich
McFarland (*www.mcfarlandpub.com*), 451 pages, $39.95 (trade paperback)
ISBN: 978-0-7864-4393-2
Genre: Biography

Cyril (C. M.) Kornbluth was one of the pivotal figures of American science fiction. He was there at the beginning, those late-1930s days that marked the launch of *Amazing Stories*, the foundation of the Futurians, and the start of so many careers: Isaac Asimov, David A. Kyle, Sam Moskowitz, Frederik Pohl, Richard Wilson, Donald A. Wollheim. Kornbluth would easily take his place among those hallowed names. Two of his solo stories, "The Little Black Bag" (*Astounding*, 1950) and "The Marching Morons" (1951), are classics and as popular today as when they were written. His collaborations with Frederik Pohl, most notably *The Space Merchants* (1952) and *Gladiator-At-Law* (1954), are equally well-regarded, as is his solo novel *The Syndic* (1953).

When Kornbluth died in March 1958, at the age of 35, his loss was felt throughout the science fiction community. If he had lived, he would undoubtedly have been hailed as one of the superstars of the field.

Mark Rich has written a very detailed yet highly readable biography of this exceptional writer, which is itself a minihistory of the early decades of science fiction. Along the way, he includes commentary on just about every short story, novelette, and novel that Kornbluth produced, alone or in collaboration, under a variety of pseudonyms. A scholarly text (with the requisite 40 pages of notes) that reads like a novel, Rich's book is nothing short of a delight.

If you remember anything of that time, this will be a nostalgic journey for you; those of us who had the misfortune to be born after Kornbluth died can only marvel at this nowgone world and the geniuses who inhabited it. The book is a bit pricey, but no fan of the history of science fiction (you know who you are) can afford to be without it.

Fantasy Commentator: Sam Moskowitz and A. Langley Searles Memorial Issue
M. Alice Becker Searles
Lulu.com, 164 pages, $9.60 (trade paperback)
Genre: Biography

The story behind this volume is as complicated as its subject; bear with me and I'll try to untangle it and tell you why you want this book.

John W. Campbell, Jr. is one of the great names in science fiction, and not just for his writing; as most of you know, he was editor of *Astounding/Analog* from 1937 until 1971. When Campbell took over *Astounding* he completely altered the landscape of science fiction, and his influence is still felt today. His importance to the field cannot be overestimated.

Campbell had a close friend in Massachusetts, one Robert Swisher. Over about twenty years (from 1936 to the mid-1950s), Campbell and Swisher exchanged many letters. Swisher kept all of Campbell's letters; after Campbell's death in 1971, Swisher sent all the letters to his widow.

In the fullness of time, the Swisher letters came to the attention of science fiction historian Sam Moskowitz, who set out to edit the whole mess into a narrative concentrating on Campbell's sf career. In 1992, fan publisher A. Langley Searles undertook to publish Moskowitz's lengthy article in his fanzine, *Fantasy Commentator*. Unfortunately, illness and, ultimately, Searles' death in 2009 delayed the publication.

Now Searles' widow presents the whole thing in book form, ostensibly as combined issues 59 and 60 of *Fantasy Commentator*. Fanzines have come a long way since the days of blurry purple mimeograph pages; through the wonders of print-on-demand this double issue is available for less than ten dollars though lulu.com. The print is attractive, in crisp black print on white paper, and the book is entirely readable.

Here you'll read about Campbell's search for employment after college, his early forays into writing sf, his apprenticeship at *Astounding* under F. Orlin Tremaine, and the mechanics of the Campbell Revolution. You'll follow him through his fascination (and eventual disillusionment) with L. Ron Hubbard and Dianetics.

Professional and amateur bibliographers will be debating for years how to classify this volume, but don't let that stop you. If you're at all interested in Campbell and the history of this magazine you're reading, you'll want to get this book.

John Carter and the Gods of Hollywood
Michael D. Sellers
Universal Media, 370 pages, $15.95 (trade paperback)
Kindle: $3.99 (e-book)
ISBN: 978-0-6156823-1-0
Genre: Movies, Nonfiction

Getting back to Mars for a moment, here's a book that tells the story of a long-awaited journey to the Red Planet that went horribly wrong. And it's a true story.

Since Edgar Rice Burroughs's *A Princess of Mars* appeared in 1912 (as a serial titled "Under the Moons of Mars" in the February issue of *The All-Story*), readers have been desperate for a film version.

In the centennial year, that long-awaited movie was released—and in the opinion of many, it was a very successful adaptation, a visual feast that evoked the sense of wonder of the original story.

The film, however, was a box-office flop.

Michael D. Sellers wondered what happened, and this book is the result.

In very readable prose, Sellers tells the history of Burroughs's Mars books, and the century-long challenge of bringing to the screen the world Burroughs called Barsoom. He follows the course of development of the 2012 film, and explains the factors that led to its perceived failure—overbudgeting, inexperience, and outright hostility among the higher levels of Disney Studios.

For anyone interested in the inner workings of Hollywood, or anyone who liked John Carter and wondered what happened, this is definitely a worthwhile read.

Murray Leinster: The Life and Works
Billee J. Stallings and Jo-An J. Evans
McFarland, 219 pages, $40.00 (trade paperback)
ISBN: 978-0-7864-6504-0
Genre: Biography

Murray Leinster, the pen name of Will F. Jenkins, was one of those revered elders who has now passed into "venerable ancestor" status. His first published story appeared in 1916, and he became a successful pulp writer in the 1920s. Leinster's first sf story, published in 1919, was reprinted in the first issue of *Amazing Stories*, the magazine that launched science fiction as a commercial genre. Murray Leinster wasn't just there at the beginning; when the beginning came, he'd already been there for seven years. (Incidentally, he also had a story, "Tanks," in the first issue of *Astounding* in 1930.)

Pick a concept in sf, and it's a pretty sure bet that Murray Leinster was one of the first to write about it. He invented the parallel universe story. His story about humans meeting aliens, "First Contact," defined another subgenre...even today we call them First Contact stories.

Unlike a lot of his pulp associates, Leinster handily survived the Campbell revolution; he remained popular in *Astounding* and *Analog* until the mid-1960s, when he had shifted mainly to writing novels. Recently, Leinster's prescience has become widely recognized, because of his 1946 story "A Logic Named Joe," which essentially described the personal computer and the Internet at a time when only one general purpose electronic computer existed on the planet.

Murray Leinster died in 1975 at the age of 78, and left a legacy that will never be forgotten.

In *Murray Leinster: The Life and Works* his two youngest daughters lift the veil to show us the man behind the name. Starting with his first short stories and continuing through his death, this is an intimate and informative look at and extinct breed, the pulp writer. The book is extensively illustrated with photographs, drawings, and even manuscript pages.

Through the eyes of the daughters, we see a man who was a consummate storyteller, a dazzling intellect, and a devoted husband and father. For pulp writers, speed and quantity were the keys to survival—in the Jenkins house, the typewriter had pride of place, and Leinster—the breadwinner—could be found there at all hours of the day and night. We get to see something of his working habits, especially his interactions with the great editors of the day—Campbell as well as others. In addition to a twenty-page bibliography, the volume includes both the story "A Logic Named Joe" and a 1954 essay called "To Build a Robot Brain."

Yet this isn't simply the story of one pulp writer...it's also the story of the science fiction field itself. If we are all ancestor worshippers, Murray Leinster is a good ancestor to start with. Don't let the price deter you—if you have any interest in the roots of our genre, then you want to read this book.

A New American Space Plan
Travis S. Taylor with Stephanie Osborn
Baen, 218 pages, $15.00 (trade paperback)
Baen Ebooks: $6.00 (e-book)
ISBN: 978-1-4516-3865-3
Genre: Nonfiction

Travis S. Taylor, Ph.D. is an honest-to-goodness rocket scientist in Huntsville, Alabama (aka Rocket City). He's also the ringleader on the National Geographic Channel's show *Rocket City Rednecks*, on which Taylor and four accomplices (all engineering types) take on a challenge such as building a rocket fueled by moonshine or building a "hillbilly moon buggy."

A New American Space Plan is a chatty book filled with facts and figures, reminiscences from the show and from Taylor's career working with NASA and the Department of Defense, history of the space program, and a generous helping of redneck political grumbling.

Taylor's actual plan doesn't sound all that revolutionary: Put more money into the space program, involve commercial companies to unleash the magic of competition. Make manned exploration of the Moon and Mars the highest priority. Commit to a single plan and follow it through. Keep politicians from micromanaging the space effort.

Nothing particularly new there, but that's not the point. This is a fun book to read, with lots to think about and argue about. For anyone interested in the manned space program, this is a must read.

The Medea Hypothesis
Peter Ward
Princeton University Press, 180 pages, $24.95 (hardcover)
ISBN: 978-0-691-13075-0
Genre: Nonfiction

If you're intent on the search for different perspectives, you can sometimes find them outside the realm of science fiction and fantasy. Peter Ward gives us a good example from the field of planetary biology.

You're probably familiar with James Lovelock's Gaia Hypothesis, which has dominated planetary biology for decades. Named for the kind and caring earth-mother of Greek mythology, the Gaia Hypothesis treats the whole planet, organic and inorganic parts alike, as one gigantic organism.

Gaia is self-regulating and omnibenevolent. Working mostly through the twin agencies of life and atmospheric composition, Gaia uses feedback loops to maintain Earth in the optimum state for habitability. Never too hot or too cold, too acid or too salty, too wet or too dry, Gaia steers a middle course that keeps Earth as a perfect home for life.

Or at least, Gaia kept things under control until we humans got too big for our britches and started messing with things:

clearing forests, overfishing the oceans, dumping greenhouse gases into the atmosphere. Gaia's doing the best she can to restore equilibrium, but we've got to work with her by minimizing the damage we do.

Ward takes a look at the history of life on Earth and is reminded of a different Greek figure, Medea. This darling woman, who cooked her own children and served them up to dinner guests, certainly ranks among the Top Five Worst Mother Figures Ever.

The problem, as Ward sees it, is inherent in life itself. Lifeforms have a built-in drive to reproduce beyond the carrying capacity of their environment. Sooner or later, very successful lifeforms produce enough waste products to initiate global changes. The atmosphere gets filled with fatal levels of oxygen, or methane and carbon dioxide start a runaway greenhouse effect, or living organisms change the planet's albedo and the oceans freeze, or....

Well, one way or another, life itself has been the cause of many of the great extinction events that have come close to ending life on Earth completely. (Not the Dinosaurs...Ward calls asteroid impacts "non-Medea extinction events.")

Further, Ward takes a look at places like Mars and Venus, and wonders if Medea just won out on those worlds. Damage your planet too much, and you're going to wind up with an uninhabitable globe that's no longer fit to start life again. Ward wonders if Medean extinction might be the most common fate of Earthlike planets in the universe.

Rather than get out of the way and let Gaia fix our mistakes, Ward argues that our only chance for survival on Earth is to keep Medea from doing her job. If we don't manage our planet's habitability, he suggests, then Medea will ultimately win.

Now obviously, the Medea Hypothesis is brand new; there's a lot of serious work to be done to see if it will become an accepted part of planetary biology. Ward has given us the first word on Medea, not the last. But for those interested in looking at things from a different direction, and for science fiction readers in particular, it's certainly a book worth reading.

The Great Heinlein Mystery
Edward M. Wysocki, Jr.
CreateSpace, 289 pages, $24.95 (trade paperback)
ISBN: 978-1-47741-020-2
Genre: Nonfiction

Great Heinlein Mystery? What's *that* all about?

In 1941, Robert A. Heinlein wrote a letter to John W. Campbell, Jr. in which he mentioned that a device in one of his stories had inspired a real-life device used by the Navy in World War II (and possibly later). Heinlein said he couldn't reveal the nature of the device, because it was classified. In a 1955 lecture, Heinlein repeated his claim, along with the statement that the device was still classified so he couldn't reveal its nature.

On the basis of these clues, Edward M. Wysocki, Jr.—a normal science fiction reader of no real distinction—set out in the 1990s to identify the real-life military contraption that Heinlein had inspired.

As great mysteries go, this one doesn't seem all that momentous. Yet Heinlein's status in science fiction, along with the fact that all but one of the stories in question appeared in *Astounding*, makes the question of minor interest to *Analog* readers. And that's all Wysocki needs to tell a fascinating story.

With no formal training in military technology, no budget to speak of, and no legal powers of investigation, Wysocki had to rely on published works, publicly-accessible documents, and the memories of the few aging contemporaries still alive. At first, Wysocki had little to work with...but over the years, the explosion of information available on the Internet turned out to be his biggest resource. He was able, for example, to track the careers and movements of Heinlein's Naval Academy classmates, even to deducing when and where particular undocumented conversations took place.

The story is fascinating from beginning to end. After listing all possible alternatives from Heinlein's stories, Wysocki analyzes Naval technology of the time, providing a look at the kind of details of radio and radar engineering that so engrossed sf readers and writers of the period. Along the way, we meet other sf writers and learn, for example, what L. Sprague deCamp had to do with the evolution of the space suit.

The Great Heinlein Mystery is hardly world-shaking stuff. When Wysocki reveals his answer (for which he presents good arguments), one feels a vague sense of letdown—not because of the answer, but because the book is over.

In this case, as so often with tales of exploration and discovery, the real fun is in the journey, not the destination.

The Scattered Worlds Mosaic by Don Sakers

Dance for the Ivory Madonna
a romance of psiberspace
Print & Kindle
Spectrum Award finalist; 56 Hugo nominations
"Imagine a Stand on Zanzibar written by a left-wing Robert Heinlein, and infused with the most exciting possibilities of the new cyber-technology." -Melissa Scott, author of Dreaming Metal, The Jazz

Weaving the Web of Days
a tale of the Scattered Worlds
Print & Kindle
Maj Thovold has led the Galaxy for three decades, a Golden Age of peace and prosperity. She is weary and ready to resign, but she faces one last battle: a battle on the strangest battlefield known: a web of living tendrils that stretches across interstellar space. A web where Maj's enemies wait, like spiders, for their prey....

The Eighth Succession
a novel of the Scattered Worlds
Print & Kindle
"Remember when science fiction used to be filled with galactic intrigue and bigger-than-life heroes? The wonderful Don Sakers certainly does! The Eighth Succession is a rip-roaring yarn, impossible to put down. If John W. Campbell's Astounding Stories had been published in an LGBT-friendly era, this is the cover-story serial you'd have been waiting anxiously for each month. What a ride!" -Robert J. Sawyer, Hugo Award-winning author of Red Planet Blues

Children of the Eighth Day
a novel of the Scattered Worlds
Print & Kindle
The Eighth Succession *introduced readers to the Hoister Family...* Children of the Eighth Day *takes the story of this remarkable family to the exciting next level.*

The Scattered Worlds Mosaic by Don Sakers

All Roads Lead to Terra
two tales of the Scattered Worlds
Kindle only

Two exciting tales tell of attacks against the shining jewel of the Terran Empire: Earth. Includes an introduction and notes from the author.

A Voice in Every Wind
two tales of the Scattered Worlds
Print & Kindle

On a world where meaning lives in every rock and stream, and every breeze brings a new voice, one human explorer stands on the threshold of discoveries that could alter the future of Humanity.

A Rose From Old Terra
a novel of the Scattered Worlds
Print & Kindle

Jedrek left the Grand Library and his work circle eleven years ago. Now a crisis in uncharted space brings the circle back together. Soon, Jedrek and his friends are at the focal point of a clash of cultures, and the only thing that can save the Galaxy is one modest group of Librarians.

The Leaves of October
a novel of the Scattered Worlds
Print & Kindle
Compton Crook Award finalist

The Hlutr: Immensely old, terribly wise…and utterly alien. When mankind went out into the stars, he found the Hlutr waiting for him. Waiting to observe, to converse, to help. Waiting to judge…and, if necessary, to destroy.

More Books from Speed-of-C Productions

The Curse of the Zwilling by Don Sakers
Print & Kindle

It's Hogwarts meets Buffy at Patapsco University: a small, cozy liberal arts college like so many others – except for the Department of Comparative Religion, where age-old spells are taught and magic is practiced. When a favorite teacher is found dead under mysterious circumstances, grad student David Galvin finds that a malevolent evil has awakened. And now David, along with four novice undergrads, must defeat this ancient, malignant terror.

The SF Book of Days by Don Sakers
Print only

Drawn from the pages of classic sf literature, here is a science fiction/fantasy event for every day of the year…and for quite a few days that aren't part of the year. From Doc Brown's arrival in Hill Valley (January 1, 1885) to the launch of the *Bellerophon* (Sextor 7, 2351), this datebook is truly
out of this world.

PsiScouts #1: At Risk by Phil Meade
Print & Kindle

In the 26th century, psi-powered teenagers from all over the Myriad Worlds join together as the heroic PsiScouts.

Meat and Machine: queer writings by Don Sakers
Print & Kindle

Don Sakers has been queering sf and fantasy for three decades. Meat and Machine collects 24 short pieces of Don's science fiction, fantasy, nonfiction, and erotics.

More Books from Speed-of-C Productions

Gaylaxicon Sampler 2006
Print only
Sample the work of thirteen writers from across the spectrum of gay, lesbian, bisexual, and/or transgender science fiction, fantasy, and/or horror. Includes big names and small, much-published veterans and promising beginners, Lammy and Spectrum Award nominees and winners, past Gaylaxicon Guests of Honor, and fresh new names.

QSpec Sampler 2007
Print only
Originally prepared as a giveaway at Gaylaxicon 2007 in Atlanta, this volume is available at a nominal charge as a sampler of the fine work being done by GLBT writers in SF, fantasy, and horror.

Act Well Your Part by Don Sakers
Print & Kindle
A beloved gay young adult romance, back in print for its adult fans as well as a new generation of teens. At first Keith Graff dislikes his new school. He misses his old friends, and despairs of ever fitting in. Then he joins the school's drama club, and meets the boyishly cute Bran Davenport....

Lucky in Love by Don Sakers
Kindle only
A companion novel to Act Well Your Part, Lucky in Love follows Keith's friend Frank Beale, torn between bad boy Dwight and basketball star Darnell.

The Mud of the Place by Susanna J. Sturgis
Print only
"A sensitive, witty, and tightly plotted portrayal of life on Martha's Vineyard that only a true Islander could have written. Nice going, Susanna!" –Cynthia Riggs

www.ingramcontent.com/pod-product-compliance
Lightning Source LLC
Chambersburg PA
CBHW050511170426
43201CB00013B/1916